A GLOBAL AGENDA

Issues Before
the 57th
General Assembly
of the
United Nations

*An annual publication of the
United Nations Association of the
United States of America*

Diana Ayton-Shenker, Editor

Rowman & Littlefield Publishers, Inc.
Lanham • Boulder • New York • Oxford

ROWMAN & LITTLEFIELD PUBLISHERS, INC.

Published in the United States of America
by Rowman & Littlefield Publishers, Inc.
A Member of the Rowman & Littlefield Publishing Group
4720 Boston Way, Lanham, Maryland 20706
www.rowmanlittlefield.com

PO Box 317
Oxford
OX2 9RU, UK

ISSN 1057-1213

ISBN 0-7425-2354-3 (cloth : alk. paper)
ISBN 0-7425-2355-1 (paper : alk. paper)

Cover design by Douglas Tait, Inc.

Printed in the United States of America

∞ ™ The paper used in this publication meets the minimum requirements of
American National Standard for Information Sciences—Permanence of Paper for
Printed Library Materials, ANSI/NISO Z39.48-1992.

A GLOBAL AGENDA

Issues Before the 57th General Assembly of the United Nations

Contents

Acknowledgments

As in previous years, the 2002–2003 edition of *A Global Agenda* is truly a collaborative effort, made possible by the hard work of many people.

First, I am indebted to this year's contributors. Each author brought professional expertise and intellectual vigor to meet the daunting challenge of analyzing the most urgent issues facing the United Nations. Ultimately, *A Global Agenda* reflects their trenchant insights and analysis. It has been my privilege and pleasure to work with such an outstanding roster of authors.

I am particularly grateful to John Calderone and Jennifer Knerr at Rowman & Littlefield Publishers, Inc., whose dedication to this project and uncompromising professionalism ensure that *A Global Agenda* is held accountable to the highest editorial standards.

I thank the terrific team of UNA-USA interns, who gave generously of their time and talent, providing essential research assistance, fact-checking, and proofreading. I appreciate and admire their commitment, enthusiasm, and drive while working on *A Global Agenda*. Special thanks to Elisabeth Tani Fukui, Olga Miroshnichenko, Mary Dailey Pattee, Iara Duarte Peng, Nicholas Rosen, Manav Sachdeva, William Schlickenmaier, V. Kate Somvongsiri, Khaita Sylla, and Eric Wiideman.

A Global Agenda would not be possible without the wonderful staff of the UNA-USA. I especially value the leadership and support of Ambassador William Luers, President and CEO, and I owe deepest gratitude to Elizabeth Chute, Executive Director of Communications and Marketing. Beth's guidance, warmth, and clear-headed perspective saw me through every step, making it an absolute delight to take on and complete this project.

Lastly, I am most thankful for those individuals whose personal support was invaluable to me in the preparation of *A Global Agenda*.

Diana Ayton-Shenker

New York, June 2002

Contributors

Diana Ayton-Shenker (Editor, Introduction, Latin America) is a writer and consultant working with academia, the United Nations, and international organizations to advance the cause of human rights and related issues. An honors graduate of the University of Pennsylvania, she received her LLM (master of laws) in international human rights law from the Law School of the University of Essex. Ms. Ayton-Shenker has taught at the American University of Paris and at Hunter College of the City University of New York, where she directed the Human Rights Program.

Nick Birnback (Asia), a former UNA-USA employee, has worked with U.N. Peacekeeping Operations since 1996, serving in Liberia (UNOMIL), Sierra Leone (UNOMSIL), Bosnia-Herzegovina (UNBIMH), East Timor (UNAMET), and Ethiopia/Eritrea (UNMEE). He is currently finishing a graduate degree at the Woodrow Wilson School of Public and International Affairs at Princeton University.

Roger A. Coate (Development) is Director of the Richard L. Walker Institute of International Studies and Professor of International Organization at the University of South Carolina. He is the author of numerous books and articles on the United Nations and international organizations, and he serves as director of the United Nations University's transnational research and professional development program, "Creating Effective Partnerships for Human Security."

Peter Danchin (Human Rights) teaches international law and human rights at the School of International and Public Affairs at Columbia University, where he is the Director of the Human Rights Program. He is editor of *Protecting the Human Rights of Religious Minorities in Eastern Europe* (Columbia University Press, 2002).

Ambassador Jonathan Dean (Security) joined the U.S. Foreign Service in 1949, after combat infantry service in Europe in World War II. He was a U.S. negotiator for the 1971 quadripartite agreement on Berlin, which ended three decades of East–West wrangling over the city. From 1973 to 1981, he was deputy U.S. Representative, and then U.S. Representative, to the NATO–Warsaw Pact force reduction negotiations in Vienna (MBFR talks). Since 1984, he has been advisor on arms control and international security issues to the Union of Concerned Scientists. The author of several books on European security and a coauthor of *The Nuclear Turning Point* (Brookings, 1999), he is the former president of the United Nations Association of the Washington, D.C., metropolitan region. A graduate of the National War College, Ambassador Dean has a Ph.D. in political science from George Washington University.

Dennis Dijkzeul (Humanitarian Assistance) is the Director of the Humanitarian Affairs Program at the School of International and Public Affairs at Columbia University. He has published widely on humanitarian assistance and management of international organizations. He is the author of *Reforming for Results in the UN System: A Study of UNOPS* (St Martin's and Macmillan Press) and coeditor, with Yves Beigbeder, of *Rethinking International Organizations: Pathology and Promise* (Berghahn Books).

Mark A. Drumbl (Law and Justice) is Assistant Professor at the School of Law, Washington & Lee University. He maintains teaching and research interests in public international law, international human rights, global environmental policy, and international criminal law.

Cristina Eguizábal (Latin America) is a program officer in the Human Rights and International Cooperation unit at the Ford Foundation in New York. Her portfolio includes grants on peace, security and regional cooperation in Latin America, the Caribbean, and the Western Hemisphere in general. She has held research and teaching positions at the University of Costa Rica, University of Bordeaux, University of Miami, Florida International University, and the Latin American Faculty of Social Sciences. Dr. Eguizábal holds a Ph.D. in Latin American Studies from the University of Paris-Sorbonne-Nouvelle.

Gordon Goldstein (Europe, Middle East) is a writer and former advisor to the U.N. Strategic Planning Unit and the Executive Office of the U.N. Secretary-General. His articles have appeared in the *New York Times*, *Washington Post*, *Newsweek*, and other publications.

Gail Karlsson (Environment) is a New York-based attorney specializing in international environmental law. She is currently working as a consultant to the U.N. Development Programme on sustainable energy policies.

David A. Lynch (Trade) is Assistant Professor of Political Science at Saint Mary's University of Minnesota. His research focuses on international political economy and American foreign policy, with a particular interest in the growing clash between trade, the environment, and labor. He received his Ph.D. from the University of California, Santa Barbara.

Anthony Mango (Finance and Administration) worked for the U.N. Secretariat from 1960 to 1987. Between 1970 and 1983, he headed the secretariat of the Advisory Committee on Administrative and Budgetary Questions and from 1983 to 1987 served as Secretary of the U.N. Pension Board. Since retirement, he has continued to work for the United Nations as a consultant.

Iara Duarte Peng (Children, Women), a UNA-USA intern, is currently completing a master's degree from the School of International and Public Affairs at Columbia University, with a concentration in advanced policy analysis. She was formerly vice-president of Doble Research Associates, Inc., a public interest consulting firm.

Christopher Reardon (Food and Population) writes about the arts and social policy for *The New York Times*, *The Boston Globe*, *The Christian Science Monitor*, and The Ford Foundation Report. He lives in Brooklyn, New York.

Nick Rosen (Drugs and Crime Prevention), a UNA-USA intern, is a recent graduate of Columbia University's School of International and Public Affairs. Mr. Rosen is a New York-based journalist who writes about international organizations, conflict in Colombia, and the global economy.

V. Kate Somvongsiri (Health), a UNA-USA intern, is a recent graduate of Columbia University's School of International and Public Affairs. She holds a master's degree in international affairs with a concentration in human rights; her particular focus is on the intersection of health and human rights, and her regional focus is on Southeast Asia. Prior to entering the program, she served as a Peace Corps volunteer in the health and community development sectors in Nepal.

Khaita Sylla (Women), a UNA-USA intern, is a graduate of the University of Senegal and Baruch College of the City University of New York.

Benjamin Weil (Africa) is a freelance writer who reports on international development and health. He has served as Program Adviser to the U.N. Development Programme's Regional Project on HIV and Development in sub-Saharan Africa, and as Program Adviser on HIV and other sexually transmitted diseases to the International Planned Parenthood Federation, Western Hemisphere Region.

Eric Wiideman (Ageing, Disabled Persons), a graduate of the Helsinki School of Economics and Business Administration, is a UNA-USA intern, currently completing graduate studies at the University of Antwerp's Institute of Global Policy and Management.

Introduction

By Diana Ayton-Shenker

1. A Global Agenda in the Age of Human Security

More than any singular event in recent history, the heinous September 11, 2001, terrorist attacks in New York and Washington, D.C., shook the global agenda of the United Nations and sent shockwaves through the international community. The reverberations of September 11 are still palpable today throughout the U.N. system and throughout the world.

The U.N. response was swift and decisive in an attempt to mobilize the international effort against terrorism. Within 24 hours, the Security Council declared the September 11 attacks a "threat to international peace and security," recognizing the right of individual and collective self-defense (thereby authorizing collective military action) in retaliation against terrorism [S/Res/1368 (2001)]. In recognizing this right, the Security Council broke a long-standing deadlock within the United Nations. In its landmark antiterrorism resolution 1373, the Security Council also called on member states to take immediate and concrete actions to suppress terrorism and established a Counter-Terrorism Committee to monitor implementation of the program [S/Res/1373 (2001)].

Meanwhile, world leaders, policy-makers, and individuals everywhere wrestled with large and fundamental questions. How could this happen and what does it mean? What really matters in our work and in our lives? How do we reshape a global agenda in the aftermath of these attacks? How can we create a secure world for our children? And in today's world, what does security mean?

As the international community moves forward in its struggle against terrorism, the concept of *human security* is emerging as the predominant lens through which international policy and practice is viewed. Indeed, September 11 appears to have catapulted the post-Cold War period into a new phase of the world's unfolding history: "the Age of Human Security."

The emergence of human security reflects a "humanization" of security in that it recognizes the centrality of basic human rights (such as nondiscrimination and fundamental freedoms from fear), human capabilities (such as education and health), and human development (in particular, alleviation of poverty and hunger). Human security focuses attention directly on human beings and their circumstances, rather than exclusively on national military security [Thomas Weiss et al., *The United Nations and Changing World Politics*, Third Edition (Boulder: Westview, 2001)]. The concept of human security has been described as the key idea in efforts to confront "the menaces that threaten the survival, daily life, and dignity of human beings" [Obuchi Keizo, "Opening Remarks," in *The Asian Crisis and Human Security*, 18–19 (1999)]. Underpinning human security is a focus on *individual human lives*, an appreciation of *the role of society and social arrangements* in making human lives more secure, and an emphasis on *basic human rights* [Amartya Sen, "Basic Education and Human Security," Background Paper, U.N. Commission on Human Security, January 4, 2002]. In this way, human security reflects the intertwining linkage between individual liberty and collective security.

In her annual report, U.N. High Commissioner for Human Rights Mary Robinson emphasized "human rights as a 'uniting framework' for states in the face of human insecurity created by international terrorism" [E/CN.4/2002/18, February 27, 2002]. While recognizing the need to stamp out terrorism, she cautioned against the threat of human rights violations posed by counterterrorism measures. In this light, she endorsed the idea of human security as it places "individuals and their universal rights at the centre of national and global security policies" and encourages a "comprehensive strategy to address the causes of insecurity, not only its consequences and manifestations" [ibid., paras. 27–28]. Furthermore, the High Commissioner added that there is now a "wide recognition that ensuring respect for human rights and dignity throughout the world is the best long-term guarantor of security" [ibid., para. 59].

This notion of human security represents a dramatic shift "from an exclusive stress on national security to a much greater stress on people's security, from security through armaments to security through human development, from territorial security to food, employment, and environmental security" [UNDP, *Human Development Report 1993*]. Accordingly, people's social, economic, and political participation is "an inherent component, if not requisite, of both sustainable human development and human security" [ibid.]. Today, more than ever, the connection between human development and human security and the impact of globalization on this relationship dominate discourse and practice throughout the U.N. system [see R. Coate, Chapter IV, in this edition of *A Global Agenda:Issues/57*, 2002]. At the 2002 World Economic Forum (held in New York to show support following September 11), Secretary-General Kofi Annan emphasized the urgency of alleviating poverty and ill-health around the world to prevent further resentment and terrorism:

I think we all have a sense today of having come to a turning point in history. . . . last September we found ourselves entering the new millennium through a gate of fire. . . . You all know that you are sharing this planet with well over a billion people who are denied the very minimum requirements of human dignity, and with four or five billion whose choices in life are narrow compared to yours. . . . Left alone in their poverty, these countries are all too likely to collapse, or relapse, into anarchy, a menace to their neighbors and potentially—as the events of September 11 so brutally reminded us—a threat to global security. [*The Earth Times*, February 5, 2002]

The concept of human security is therefore interrelated to, and complementary with, other fundamental notions in international affairs and contemporary dialogue, including human development, human rights, peace, and political stability. "The basic idea is that people are made safer by an open, tolerant, and responsive state capable of ensuring protection of a limited 'vital core' of human rights and basic capabilities. At the same time, enhancing human security reinforces the state by strengthening its legitimacy and stability" [see P. Danchin, Chapter I, *A Global Agenda:Issues/57*, 2002].

"One can perceive a new unity of purpose as most world leaders acknowledge that security in the twenty-first century means human security. AIDS, poverty, terrorism, and other social maladies . . . are [intrinsically] linked and cannot be solved alone or in isolation of each other" [R. Coate, ibid.]. As such, the United Nations will likely increase attention on the pursuit of human security and its intersection with other issues such as human development, human rights, and international peace. In the Age of Human Security, these priorities will likely dominate the global agenda this year and in years to come.

In the Shadow of HIV/AIDS

While the U.N. agenda may now be viewed through the lens of human security, it is operating under the shadow of HIV/AIDS. HIV/AIDS has become not only a global health crisis, but also an obstacle to human development and a threat to international peace and security.

Now the fourth-largest cause of death in the world, HIV/AIDS has infected over 60 million people worldwide [UNAIDS, AIDS Epidemic Update, December 2001, UNAIDS/01.74—WHO/CDS/CSR/NCS/2001.2]. Of the 40 million people now living with the disease, an estimated 95 percent are located in the developing world; 70 percent live in sub-Saharan Africa [UNAIDS, AIDS epidemic update: December 2001; www.unaids.org/epidemic_update/report_dec01/index.html]. Throughout Africa, the worst hit region, HIV/AIDS has created a state of emergency. The disease is now spreading at an alarming rate in the Caribbean region, Asia-Pacific, and Central and Eastern Europe [www.unaids.org/whatnew/others/un_special/Declaration020801_en.htm, April 21, 2002].

Considered the most devastating disease humankind has ever known, HIV/AIDS poses unprecedented hurdles for the international community to overcome. As the pandemic ravages populations across the globe, its invasive reach permeates the U.N. agenda, affecting the scope and capacity of the Organization's work across all sectors. Indeed, the impact of HIV/AIDS is visible in U.N. programs addressing human rights, humanitarian assistance, peacekeeping, development, environment, population, health, women, children, and drug control. Since 1996, U.N. efforts to fight the disease have been coordinated under the umbrella of the Joint U.N. Programme on HIV/AIDS (UNAIDS) that draws on the resources and expertise of specialized agencies throughout the U.N. system. Over the past year, there has been a surge of activity in the ongoing struggle against HIV/AIDS, reinforced by a historic special session of the General Assembly, the priorities of the Secretary-General, and a "sense of collective responsibility" among most of the world's nations [see V. K. Somvongsiri, Chapter V, *A Global Agenda:Issues/57*, 2002].

The General Assembly's special session on HIV/AIDS (June 2001) resulted in a *Declaration of Commitment on HIV/AIDS*, which established a strategic framework for action. According to this framework, "each government pledged to pursue . . . benchmark targets relating to prevention, care, support and treatment, impact alleviation, and children orphaned and made vulnerable by HIV/AIDS" [ibid.]. Meeting these goals within the time-bound targets (by 2005) will require "substantial sustained increases in financial and other resources" [R. Coate, ibid.]. Though the World Bank has recently "doubled its financial support . . . from $500 million to $1 billion, the international community's response to AIDS pales in the face of the pandemic onslaught" [ibid.].

HIV/AIDS is particularly catastrophic for children and those who provide their care. So far, 13 million children have already been orphaned by AIDS, and nearly 600,000 infants are infected every year through mother-to-child transmission [A/S-27/19/Rev.1]. In addition, millions of HIV-positive young people live with the stigma of HIV, but lack access to adequate counseling, care, medicine, and support. "As a result of the devastation wrought . . . by HIV/AIDS, the family structure and social fabric of entire societies are being undermined," according to Peter McDermott, a consultant on HIV/AIDS [www.unicef.org/specialsession/activities/hiv.htm]. "And," he added, "we are still on the upward curve of the pandemic. Never before has the world faced the possibility of so many orphans."

One major obstacle to fighting HIV/AIDS is discrimination against women. Though women are more vulnerable to HIV/AIDS and play a critical role in its transmission to infants and children, gender discrimination stymies efforts to protect women and enlist their support in HIV/AIDS prevention programs. To address this, the United Nations is calling on governments to challenge the gender stereotypes and inequalities in relation to HIV/AIDS [E/CN.6/2002/L.3/Rev.1, and CSW Press Release, WOM/1332, March 15, 2002]. Member states need to increase the capacity of women and girls to protect themselves from HIV/AIDS; expand information, counseling, and services available to pregnant women through prenatal care; provide health (including sexual and reproductive health) care and services; and provide prevention education programs that promote gender equality and encourage the participation of men and boys [ibid.].

In recent years, HIV/AIDS has been increasingly linked with human rights, a trend identified in the *Declaration of Commitment on AIDS*. At the 2001 World Conference against Racism held in Durban, South Africa, Peter Piot, head of UNAIDS, emphasized the role of discrimination and stigma in spreading the disease and impeding access to health care and medication [V. K. Somvongsiri, ibid.]. This emphasis is evident in the theme of the World AIDS Campaign (2002–2003)—"Stigma and Discrimination"— and the focus on access to HIV/AIDS medicine as part of the human right to health.

The disease is also interconnected with U.N. peace operations and humanitarian assistance. The Security Council has continued to confront the issue of HIV/AIDS among U.N. troops and in countries with peace-keeping missions [B. Weil, Chapter II, *A Global Agenda:Issues/57*, 2002]. HIV/AIDS has been especially problematic for peacekeeping in Africa, where local "military troops could become too debilitated" by the disease to support U.N. peacekeeping operations (PKOs) [ibid.]. The Security Council has requested that "all peacekeeping personnel receive and follow appropriate guidance on HIV/AIDS" and that the United Nations "integrate HIV/AIDS awareness, prevention and care into emergency, humanitarian and post-conflict programmes" [S/Res/1379/(2001)].

In his remarks on World AIDS Day (December 1, 2001), Secretary-General Annan recognized the connection between AIDS and development, international security, and political stability. He identified HIV/AIDS as "one of the biggest obstacles to development itself. It affects regional and global stability and risks slowing democratic development. In this way, AIDS not only takes away the present. It takes away the future. That is the toll of AIDS" [www.unaids.org/worldaidsday/2001/index.html].

While the international community has not yet been able to cure or contain HIV/AIDS, all indications forecast dire consequences if its spread cannot be stemmed. If left unchecked, this pandemic will kill millions more people; thwart sustainable human development; decimate economic and social systems; widen the gender gap; and threaten to undermine virtually every sphere of U.N. activity. Undoubtedly, until the blaze of HIV/AIDS is extinguished, it will need to remain front and center on the agenda of the United Nations.

The Gender Dimension

Gender equality and the empowerment of women have been recognized as effective means to stimulate sustainable development and combat poverty, hunger, and disease [see Peng and Sylla, Chapter V, *A Global Agenda: Issues/57*, 2002]. Though women "often bear the greatest burden of extreme poverty," when given the opportunity they are instrumental in improving economic conditions for themselves, their families, and communities [ibid.]. Too frequently, women are denied the benefits of programs and policies designed to relieve external debt and debt-servicing problems of developing countries. Efforts to eradicate poverty must provide women with adequate and appropriate skill training and equal access to control over resources, technologies, credit, and finance.

Grievous disparities between men and women in "economic power-sharing, unequal distribution of unremunerated work," and lack of technological and financial support contribute to a so-called "feminization of poverty" [www.un.org/esa/socdev/ageing]. This is especially pronounced among older persons, the majority of whom are women. Increasingly, older women lack traditional family support structures and "many find their poverty exacerbated by cultural norms that resist their economic empowerment" [E. Wiideman, Chapter V, *A Global Agenda: Issues/57*, 2002]. In general, older women are far more likely than men to be marginalized and perceived as weak and ineffective with little to contribute to society. While the United Nations addresses the eradication of poverty among older persons as a goal in its *International Plan of Action on Ageing 2002*, it still needs to mandate specific steps to reverse the feminization of poverty and protect older women. The gender dimension of ageing requires immediate attention to prepare for the exploding population growth of persons over the age of 60, a group which is expected to double in size within the next 50 years.

Consideration of women's health is another important aspect of human development efforts. To achieve sustainable human development, it is critical to provide women with decent reproductive, sexual, prenatal, and post-partum health care and services. Improving women's health education and treatment helps reduce the transmission of HIV/AIDS; lower infant mortality; control population growth; and reduce malnutrition, hunger, and related illness and disease.

Environmental degradation and natural disasters often impact women more directly than men; at the same time, women play a critical role in mitigating disasters by aiding in response and recovery. Nonetheless, women still do not fully participate in natural resource management, planning, and decision-making. Therefore, global actors are urged "to develop and implement gender-sensitive laws, policies, and programs" that promote gender equality in "land-use, environmental management, and integrated water resources management" [Peng and Sylla, ibid.].

In recent years, the Economic and Social Council (ECOSOC) has endorsed "gender mainstreaming" as a strategy to consider the gender dimension of "legislation, policies, or programs, in all areas and at all levels" [A/52/3, 1997]. By considering the concerns and experiences of both women and men, gender mainstreaming hopes to achieve its goal of gender equality. Progress on gender mainstreaming within the U.N. system has concentrated on "policy and strategy development, program and operational activities, as well as coordination and information sharing" [E/CN.6/ 2002/2]. While ECOSOC's gender mainstreaming strategy remains a watershed in the struggle for gender equality, "sustained and active attention to its progress, constraints, and challenges" is paramount for it to achieve its goal [Carolyn Hannan, Statement at the Commission on the Status of Women, 46th Session, March 4–15, 2002].

2. A Global Agenda: Current Issues Before the United Nations

The underlying themes of human security, HIV/AIDS, and gender equality cut across the U.N. agenda and underscore the inherent linkages between issues of global concern. With these themes in mind, the 2002–2003 edition of *A Global Agenda* analyzes current issues before the 57th General Assembly, with a focus on U.N. activity in seven key areas. Specifically, *A Global Agenda* examines U.N. work in the areas of (1) Humanity (human rights and humanitarian affairs), (2) Peace (peace operations in Africa, Asia, Europe, Latin America, and the Middle East), (3) Security (disarmament, arms control, and counterterrorism), (4) Global Resources (trade, development, environment, and population and food), (5) Society (drugs and crime prevention, health, women, children, ageing, disabled persons), (6) Law and Justice, and (7) Finance and Administration.

Humanity

In this past year, acute politicization hampered the effectiveness of the Commission on Human Rights, the main U.N. Charter-based forum for examining human rights matters. A number of countries with dubious human rights records (Algeria, Burundi, China, Cuba, the Democratic Republic of Congo, Indonesia, Kenya, Libya, Malaysia, Nigeria, Russia, Saudi Arabia, Sudan, Syria, Togo, and Vietnam) now comprise a significant bloc of votes on the Commission. In addition, without the leadership of the United States, which was controversially not re-elected as a member last year, key country situations were simply not addressed. As a result, the Commission failed to pass resolutions condemning human rights violations in countries such as China, Indonesia, Iran, Russia, Saudi Arabia, Togo, and Zimbabwe. It also failed to produce an effective way to protect human rights in the context of a "global war on terrorism." High Commissioner for Human Rights Mary Robinson echoed concerns from nongovernmental organizations (NGOs) warning that increased politicization of the Commission could jeopardize its mandate and significantly reduce its relevance. "This is a time to remind ourselves of [our] . . . essential role . . . in protecting human beings against gross violations of human rights violations through highlighting and publicizing those violations" [Dale Gavlak, "UNHRC Receives Mixed Reviews at Conclusion of Geneva Session," *VOA News*, April 26, 2002].

Despite what many perceived as an erosion of the Commission's capacity and legitimacy, it was able to achieve progress in a few areas. Specifically, it recommended a draft Optional Protocol to the Convention Against Torture (CAT), aimed to strengthen compliance with the treaty. In addition, it "requested a Working Group to draft a new and binding treaty on enforced or involuntary 'disappearances,' called again for a moratorium on all executions, and appointed a new Special Rapporteur on the Right to Health" [P. Danchin, ibid.].

U.N. endeavors in the field of humanitarian assistance over the past year reflect an increasing overlap with U.N. peacekeeping operations. Traditionally, humanitarian efforts were carried out independently from military and diplomatic activity, so as to preserve their political neutrality and impartiality. Humanitarian operations focused on the protection of refugees and the provision of food, water, shelter, and medicine during crises caused by natural disaster or interstate conflict. However, the 1990s witnessed a spate of "internal" conflicts that necessitated concurrent peacekeeping and humanitarian assistance [see D. Dijkeul, Chapter V, *A Global Agenda: Issues/57*, 2002]. As a result, humanitarian and peacekeeping action fundamentally changed in character [ibid.]. Many peacekeeping operations have become in effect "peace-building with a security component" [ibid.] (rather than pure military action), and humanitarian aid workers frequently interact with peacekeepers, military actors, and diplomats. Over the past year, the United Nations provided humanitarian assistance in many parts of the world. In particular, humanitarian assistance took place in Afghanistan, the Democratic Republic of Congo (DRC), Burundi, Sierra Leone and its neighbors, Sudan, Angola, Ethiopia and Eritrea, the Federal Republic of Yugoslavia (FRY), Kosovo, Macedonia, Colombia, Sri Lanka, Indonesia, East Timor, and Chechnya, as part of Russia [ibid.].

Peace

In 2001, the U.N. Department of Peacekeeping Operations (UNDPKO) guided and supported over 35,000 military officers and soldiers and 8,000 civilian police while simultaneously "conceptualizing and implementing its internal review process" [A/56/732, December 21, 2001]. The internal review, presented in a groundbreaking assessment known as the *Brahimi Report* [Report of the Panel on U.N. Peace Operations A/55/305, S2000/809], set a new agenda for the UNDPKO with concrete recommendations to improve the "speed of deployment, administrative support of missions, and coordination among member states" [J. Stedman, Chapter I, *A Global Agenda: Issues/56*, 2001].

Resonating throughout all U.N. peacekeeping operations is the effect of armed conflict on children. Not surprisingly, civil war and other violent campaigns pose extremely traumatic and dangerous situations for children. During armed conflicts,

> children have been the victims of many of the same crimes to which women have been subjected—rape, sexual slavery, torture, mutilation, genocide—yet they are even less able to protect themselves against the adult males who most often perpetrate these acts. In addition to permanent injury and death, children are also vulnerable to HIV/AIDs and other sexually transmitted infections. Even where children recover from or escape abuse, they are often menaced by the presence of landmines. [B. Weil, Chapter II, *A Global Agenda: Issues/57*, 2002]

Abduction into armed combat is another equally serious danger for children. By conservative estimates, at least 300,000 child soldiers are involved in armed conflicts at any given time [*Global Report from the Coalition to Stop the Use of Child Soldiers*, 2001]. To explain why children are so often forcibly conscripted into armed conflicts, the coordinator of the Coalition to Stop the Use of Child Soldiers reports that children "are cheap, obedient and can be easily brainwashed to commit acts of extreme violence" [*Independent*, February 13, 2001]. The U.N. Fund for Children (UNICEF) further explains that children "may be abducted or recruited by force or driven to join armed groups in order to escape poverty or to find the assurance of food or perceived security" [*UNICEF Actions on Behalf of Children Affected by Armed Conflict*, 2002, p.11]. An international treaty banning the use of children under 18 for combat came into force in February 2002, representing an important step in efforts to end this practice.

In nearly all of the African countries with ongoing PKOs, risks for children are particularly high. In the Democratic Republic of Congo (DRC), "of the 2.5 million civilians estimated to have died . . . between 1998 and 2001, one-third were children under five. For each child killed in armed conflicts, three received injuries or permanent disabilities" [B. Weil, ibid.]. The Security Council's attention was repeatedly drawn to Africa in 2001–2002, where it monitored disputes in the DRC, Eritrea and Ethiopia, Sierra Leone, and Western Sahara.

The U.N. Organization Mission in the Democratic Republic of Congo (MONUC) is working on the implementation of the cease-fire agreement, release of prisoners of war, disengagement and redeployment of forces, and facilitation of humanitarian assistance and human rights monitoring in the DRC [S/Res/1291 (2000)]. The U.N. Mission in Ethiopia and Eritrea (UNMEE), deployed in the two countries, is mandated to monitor the cessation of hostilities, ensure compliance with the peace agreement, and coordinate and provide technical assistance to humanitarian and de-mining activity [S/Res/1320 (2000)]. Overcoming major setbacks in 2000, the U.N. Mission in Sierra Leone (UNAMSIL) has been instrumental in decreasing the fighting there. UNAMSIL is the largest PKO with over 17,000 troops currently deployed [*New York Times*, March 21, 2002; www.un.org/peace/bnote010101.pdf]. The 11-year-old U.N. Mission for the Referendum in Western Sahara (MINURSO) is responsible for monitoring "all aspects relating to a referendum in which the people of Western Sahara would choose between independence and reintegration with Morocco" [S/Res/690 (1991)].

In Asia, U.N. involvement in East Timor has been widely praised as an example of a peacekeeping success story. The U.N. Transitional Administration in East Timor (UNTAET) was mandated to establish, coordinate, and support capacity-building for East Timor's eventual transition to self-rule [S/Res/1272 (1999)]. On May 20, 2002, UNTAET formally handed over authority to the East Timorese government. UNTAET "succeeded in maintaining basic security and establishing the administrative and economic structures necessary to create a sustainable state" [see N. Birnback, Chapter II, *A Global Agenda: Issues/57*, 2002]. The U.N. Mission of Support in East Timor (UNMISET), the successor to UNTAET, will provide "substantive assistance and support to East Timor's civil, political, judicial, and security infrastructures" over the next two years [ibid.].

The U.N. Verification Mission in Guatemala (MINUGUA) is the only active PKO remaining in Latin America. MINUGUA's mandate has been extended so that it may continue to verify compliance with the Peace Accords "until the process concludes in 2003" [A/55/973, para. 78]. Meanwhile, the February 2002 collapse of the peace process in Colombia, followed by escalating drug and guerilla-related violence, has the United Nations on heightened alert in the event that increased international involvement becomes necessary.

Peacekeeping in the Balkans focused on Macedonia, Kosovo, and Bosnia. "In Macedonia, peace was maintained with the help of a limited, surgical NATO intervention. In Kosovo, a fledgling effort at self-rule finally took shape. In Bosnia, security remained the constant priority and persistent challenge" [see G. Goldstein, Chapter II, *A Global Agenda: Issues/57*, 2002].

In the Middle East, the Security Council was kept busy with activity concerning Iraq, which refused entry to U.N. arms inspectors for the third consecutive year. Given current diplomatic tension and increasingly bellicose posturing from the United States, the Security Council will likely remain focused on Iraq, especially if tensions flare into full-blown conflict. In the region's other hot zone, continuous bloodshed among

TO: POSC463-010-02F@UDel.Edu
Subject: Global Agenda Readings

Please add the following sections of Global Agenda to your reading assignments:

Under "Peace and Security": Sections II,III, and Section VI, part 1.

Under "Humanitarian Affairs and Human Rights": Sections I and VI, parts 2-8.

Under "Sustainable Development": Sections IV & V.

Under "Administering the UN System": Section VII.

You should read the "Introduction" immediately.

All the best,
Jim Oliver

Israelis and Palestinians in the first half of 2002 captured the world's attention, though the "impact of the United Nations on this volatile conflict was almost nonexistent" [ibid.]. Meanwhile, post-Taliban Afghanistan leaves the United Nations with an enormous challenge in state-building. It remains uncertain what role the Organization will play in this process.

Security

In the field of disarmament and arms control, modest progress (the U.N. Conference on Illicit Trade in Small Arms and Light Weapons in All Its Aspects and a new U.S.–Russia draft treaty on nuclear warhead reduction) was offset by serious setbacks, largely marked by U.S. withdrawal from multilateral commitments. Specifically, the United States withdrew from international efforts to draft a verification system for the 1972 Biological Weapons Convention, refused to resubmit the Comprehensive Test Ban Treaty to the U.S. Senate for ratification, and nullified its Treaty on the Limitation of Ballistic Missile Systems (the ABM Treaty) with Russia. It also restricted the outcome of the U.N. conference on small arms trade, began preparation to orbit weapons in space, and indicated in its January 2002 Nuclear Posture Review that "further nuclear tests might be necessary" [see J. Dean, Chapter III, *A Global Agenda: Issues/57*, 2002].

The major strides taken to combat terrorism affected U.N. efforts on disarmament and arms control. Understandably, the post-September 11 U.N. focus on terrorism overshadowed the agenda of the General Assembly's First Committee (Disarmament and International Security) and dominated discussion in the Committee as members attempted to demonstrate solidarity with the United States. This climate substantially inhibited any criticism of, or confrontation with, the United States over other security issues. Thus, U.S. withdrawal from major international disarmament commitments met with less opposition than otherwise would have been expected [ibid.].

Global Resources

The two most significant events for the world trading system in 2001 and early 2002 were China's entry into the World Trade Organization (WTO) at the end of 2001 and the Ministerial Conference of the World Trade Organization held in Doha, Qatar, in September 2001. While these developments signaled increased openness for global trade, they occurred against a backdrop of trends and events that indicated the opposite [see D. Lynch, Chapter IV, *A Global Agenda: Issues/57*, 2002]. Specifically, international discord on trading issues, economic slowdowns, and terrorism countered the movement toward trade openness. These recent developments, and their implications, are the primary issues that trade policy-makers will face in the coming year.

On the heels of the Doha Round of multilateral trade negotiations, the summit-level U.N.-sponsored International Conference on Financing for Development was held in Monterrey, Mexico, in March 2002. The purpose of the Monterrey conference was to "consider macroeconomic reforms that might ease poverty, slow population growth, and safeguard the environment" [see C. Reardon, Chapter IV, *A Global Agenda: Issues/57*, 2002]. The outcomes of both events indicated an increased verbal commitment to fight poverty [R. Coate, ibid.]. Significantly, the elimination of poverty and promotion of sustainable development were endorsed as the highest priority through the Millennium Development Goals (MDGs) set forth by the Secretary-General at the historic Millennium Summit. "The main challenge now is building the capacity, political will, and commitment required to mount an effective response" [ibid.]. Accordingly, the international community now faces the task of matching its rhetoric with financial commitment to rescue billions of people from poverty.

The next major event on the U.N. development calendar is the World Summit on Sustainable Development (August–September 2002, Johannesburg, South Africa). As articulated by the Secretary-General, the central question underlying the summit is "Can the people now living on this planet improve their lives, not at the expense of future generations, but in a way from which their children and grandchildren will benefit?" [Speech of the Secretary-General, February 2002, London School of Economics]. To implement the sustainable development agenda, it is critical to reform trade, aid, investment, and debt relief policies. How to carry out such changes will be the "primary topics for the World Summit on Sustainable Development" [see G. Karlsson, Chapter IV, *A Global Agenda: Issues/57*, 2002].

Summit preparations have led to numerous evaluations of progress achieved in the past ten years since the 1992 U.N. Conference on Environment and Development (UNCED, or the "Earth Summit"). Achievement highlights in the area of the environmental protection include the adoption of a widely applied plan of action (the so-called *Agenda 21*); a new ethic of conservation and stewardship emphasized in the MDGs; several international treaties on environmental concerns; and the establishment of a U.N. Forum on Forests. Such treaties include the Kyoto Protocol to the Climate Change Convention, the Convention on Biological Diversity, and the Convention to Combat Desertification. Other environmental issues on the U.N. agenda include conserving fish stocks, protecting the ozone layer, and chemical management.

Population growth complicates human development and environmental protection efforts, though its effect is uneven throughout the planet. Over the next 50 years, the 49 least developed countries are expected to triple in size, while the 39 most affluent countries experience negative population growth. As such, though current projections estimate that the global population will swell from 6.1 billion to 9.3 billion by 2050, 85 percent of that population will reside in today's developing countries [C. Reardon, ibid.]. Meanwhile, the U.N. Population Fund (UNFPA) is urging policy-makers to address the enormous "consumption gap" between the populations of different countries. According to the UNFPA's 2001 report, "A child born today in an industrialized country will add more to consumption and pollution over his or her lifetime than 30 to 50 children born in developing countries."

At the same time, 2 billion people (a third of the world's population) lack basic food security, and 1.1 billion people lack access to safe water. Though "the world produces enough food to feed everyone on the planet" [C. Reardon, ibid.], the international community has yet to put into place the "policies, institutions, technologies, and logistics to both prevent and eradicate hunger" [FAO/IFAD/WFP joint paper, February 2002; www.fao.org/docrep/003/y6265e/y6265e00.htm]. The eradication of world hunger is essential to secure "peace and political stability, overall development, and prosperity" [ibid.]. With this in mind, the Food and Agricultural Organization (FAO) is holding a World Food Summit in June 2002. As a follow-up to the 1996 World Food Summit, its goals are to ensure adherence with past international agreements and identify more reliable financial means to eradicate hunger. In the coming years, the international community will also need to address the challenge of producing more crops with less water. To do so, policy-makers will need to invest in innovative water and irrigation technologies, reform national water policies, and ensure equitable water access.

Society

While the global crisis of HIV/AIDS dominates the U.N. health agenda, the World Health Organization (WHO) and other U.N. agencies address a host of other lower profile, yet life-threatening, health issues. Other diseases targeted by the United Nations include malaria, tuberculosis, and polio (which is close to being eliminated worldwide). Priorities also include countering malnutrition and environmental hazards, providing vaccinations [WHO Press Release, March 12, 2002], and improving reproductive health and sexual health care, which are considered critical to control the spread of HIV/AIDS and manage population growth. An emerging concern is child mental health. According to a recent report released by WHO and UNICEF, up to 20 percent of the world's children suffer from mental or behavioral problems, and depression and suicide have increased significantly among children and adolescents [news.bbc.co.uk/hi/english/health/newsid_1867000/1867410.stm, March 12, 2002].

The main U.N. body addressing the advancement of women, the

Commission on the Status of Women (CSW), considered two thematic issues in its annual session (March 2002): the gender perspective in environmental management and the eradication of poverty through the empowerment of women. In preparation of its 2002–2006 multiyear plan, the CSW will address "women's access to and participation in the media, information, and communication technologies; women's human rights and the elimination of all violence against women and girls; the role of men and boys in achieving gender equality; women's equal participation in conflict prevention, management, and resolution; and equal participation in decision-making processes at all levels" [Peng and Sylla, ibid.]. As gender mainstreaming throughout the U.N. system continues, these issues are likely to gain prominence on the global agenda.

The General Assembly held an unprecedented special session on children (May 2002) to assess progress made since the 1990 World Summit on Children, renew commitments, and determine the next steps to be taken on behalf of the world's children. As an outcome, the General Assembly adopted the document: *A World Fit for Children* [A/S-27/19/Rev.1]. The outcome document presents a plan of action with specific goals, strategies, and actions in four areas: promoting health; providing education; ending abuse, exploitation, and violence; and combating HIV/AIDS. The guiding principles and objectives of the outcome document closely mirror the priorities of the Global Movement for Children, a coalition of UNICEF and several nongovernmental organizations working with children. The Global Movement's "Say Yes for Children" campaign (launched in 2001) aims to mobilize support for ten imperatives: (1) end discrimination against children, (2) respect children's rights, (3) provide basic care for every child, (4) protect children, adolescents, and their families from HIV/AIDS, (5) stop violence, abuse, and exploitation of children, (6) respect free expression of children and youth and facilitate their participation in decision-making that affects them, (7) educate every child, (8) protect children from war, (9) protect the earth for children, and (10) eradicate poverty.

At the other end of the human life span, the world population is experiencing a so-called *agequake* with the number of people over age 60 growing at unprecedented rates. The United Nations now faces the "staggeringly complex implications of an increasingly older world population that is diminishingly self-sufficient" [E. Wiideman, ibid.]. Continuing advances in biomedical technology and health care are likely to extend human life "even longer than our most generous estimates" [ibid.]. Human life expectancy has grown by approximately 20 years since 1950. The number of people over the age of 60 (the majority of whom are women) is expected to double in the next 50 years. Accordingly, whereas today about 10 percent of the world's population is over the age of 60, by 2050 that number will swell to 20 percent. As such, issues of welfare schemes, socioeconomic participation, self-fulfillment, and education of older persons will require greater attention in coming years. To address some of these challenges, the Second World Assembly on Ageing (held in April 2002) adopted an International Plan of Action on Ageing (which updated the original Plan adopted in 1982 at the first World Assembly on Ageing). The 2002 Plan addresses various aspects of ageing including security; empowerment and societal participation; self-fulfillment and well-being; economic, social, and cultural rights; gender equality; intergenerational interdependence, solidarity, and reciprocity; health care; partnership among all levels of government, civil society, and the private sector; and scientific research. "The immense impact of global ageing (and the significant resources and commitment necessary to respond effectively)" is likely to affect future generations and feature prominently on the U.N. agenda [ibid.].

Among the most vulnerable and marginalized in societies across the globe, disabled persons comprise a diverse and growing population in need of U.N. attention and member state support and protection. Nearly 10 percent of the world's population is disabled, from vastly different conditions such as mental illness, physical impairments, and amputation from landmines. The World Programme of Action (WPA), which addresses the plight of disabled persons, undergoes its fourth five-year review in 2002. The WPA has a two-fold mission: (1) to ensure the full and equal participation of disabled persons in society and (2) to present strategies for the prevention of disability and the rehabilitation and equalization of opportunities for people with disabilities. The results of the WPA review will likely determine the agenda priorities and strategies to support and protect disabled people.

Increasingly, the illicit "drug trade and transnational crime are entwined with . . . violent conflict and terrorism" [see N. Rosen, Chapter V, *A Global Agenda: Issues/57*, 2002]. In Colombia, the world's leading cocaine supplier, coca production (and the cocaine economy) is inextricable from the escalating civil war and flagging peace process. War in Afghanistan coincided with the rebirth of the opium drug business; the 2002 poppy harvest "was expected to put Afghanistan back at the top of world heroin production" [Associated Press, February 28, 2002]. Given the security lens through which the international community increasingly views drug control, it is especially important to construct alliances against drug trafficking, organized crime, and the growing linkage between terrorism and criminal enterprise. In this context, the Organization's challenge is not just to overcome this "emerging 'dark side' of global integration, but to foster the political will and cooperation [needed] . . . for the preservation of law, order, and security in the days ahead" [N. Rosen, ibid.]. With this challenge in mind, preparations are now underway for the forthcoming 2005 U.N. Congress on Crime Prevention and Criminal Justice, whose proposed theme is "Synergies and Responses: strategic alliances in criminal prevention and criminal justice."

Law and Justice

The field of international law and justice is in the midst of extraordinary development marked by a proliferation of dispute resolution bodies within the U.N. system. These entities now include: the nascent International Criminal Court, ad hoc war crimes tribunals, special courts for Sierra Leone, U.N.-assisted courts for Kosovo and East Timor, the International Tribunal for the Law of the Sea, and the International Court of Justice. Through these bodies, international law plays an increasingly dynamic and prominent role in addressing human rights, terrorism, crimes against humanity, genocide, environment, ocean affairs, and new and diverse challenges such as "war-like terrorist attacks, electronic commerce, and the possibility of human cloning" [see M. Drumbl, Chapter VI, *A Global Agenda: Issues/57*, 2002]. The international ad hoc criminal tribunals "continue to issue watershed judgments" on mass atrocity in Rwanda and the former Yugoslavia. Most significantly, the International Criminal Court (ICC) is poised to enter into force on schedule in July 2002. The ICC is a permanent standing court with jurisdiction over "the most serious breaches of international humanitarian and human rights law" [ibid.]. These developments and the imminent challenges ahead make this a truly a historic year for international law and justice.

Finance and Administration

Finally, in order to manage its hefty agenda, the United Nations will continue efforts to improve its organizational finance and administration, thereby enhancing institutional capacity and effectiveness. In this regard, the 57th Session will focus on personnel-related issues. In particular, it will consider reports on how to strengthen the international civil service and on human resource management. Additional issues to be addressed include financial reports; audited financial statements and related reports; the financial situation of the Organization; the first performance report on the program budget for 2002–2003; administrative and budgetary coordination of the United Nations with its specialized agencies; and the financing of peacekeeping operations [see A. Mango, Chapter VII, *A Global Agenda: Issues/57*, 2002].

Conclusion

In the Age of Human Security, the global agenda of the United Nations takes on greater significance than ever. *A Global Agenda* attempts to clarify the current issues before the 57th General Assembly, by presenting an overview of U.N. activity across various sectors. In so doing, it hopes to enhance the effectiveness of U.N. efforts in the areas of human rights, humanitarian assistance, peacekeeping and peace-building, disarmament, arms control, counterterrorism measures, trade, development, environment, population, food, health, women, children, ageing, disabled persons, drugs and crime prevention, law and justice, and finance and administration. Taken as a whole or in parts, *A Global Agenda* provides the reader with a deeper understanding of global concerns and analysis of the challenges facing the international community today.

I
Humanity

1. Human Rights
By Peter Danchin

A little over a decade ago, Louis Henkin suggested that ours was the "age of rights" and that human rights was the "idea of our time" [Louis Henkin, *The Age of Rights*, New York: Columbia University Press, 1990, p. xvii]. Building from a few terse phrases in the U.N. Charter, the last half century has witnessed the steady universalization and internationalization of the 1948 Universal Declaration of Human Rights and the consequent transformation of international law and politics. Today, the U.N. human rights regime consists of a web of Charter-based and treaty-based institutions and mechanisms and an expansive body of international human rights norms. Its reach and effectiveness is further supplemented, shaped, and increasingly challenged by a proliferation of domestic and international nongovernmental organizations (NGOs). Faced with these developments, some states have resisted the public airing of charges of their own human rights violations, on the grounds that these are domestic matters not subject to U.N. or other external intervention. Under the terms of its Charter, the United Nations is forbidden "to intervene in any matters which are essentially within the domestic jurisdiction of any state" [Article 2(7), U.N. Charter]. As Henkin has observed, however, U.N. practice long ago rejected that objection and arrived at the conclusion that human rights violations are not a matter of domestic jurisdiction or that U.N. discussion of them is not intervention or both.

If all of this had been settled practice, then the Age of Rights was dramatically and tragically confronted on September 11, 2001, with what some now see as the emergence of the "Age of Terrorism." For example, while acknowledging that since the end of the Cold War human rights had become the "dominant moral vocabulary in foreign affairs," Michael Ignatieff questioned whether after September 11 "the era of human rights has come and gone." He noted that "Rome has been attacked, and Rome is fighting to re-establish its security and hegemony." Accordingly, he continues, the international human rights movement will have to engage soon in "the battle of ideas: it has to challenge directly the claim that national security trumps human rights" [Michael Ignatieff, "Is the Human Rights Era Ending?" *New York Times*, February 5, 2002].

That battle of ideas has begun in earnest and is being waged in a number of different fora and in relation to a number of issues, each raising its own problems and implications for the future promotion and protection of human rights. Several interrelated areas of concern underlie this discourse and are likely to shape the U.N. human rights agenda over the coming years. Specifically, these issues are (1) collective security measures (*jus ad bellum* and the new "Bush doctrine"), (2) the relationship between human rights and humanitarian law (*jus in belli*) in the "war on terrorism," and (3) the emerging concept of "human security."

Terrorism and Human Rights: A New Paradigm?

Following the events of September 11, 2001, the Sixth Committee (Legal Affairs) of the General Assembly urgently recommended their efforts to draft a comprehensive treaty on international terrorism. The relationship between international terrorism and human rights has, however, been on the U.N. agenda for some time. In its resolution 1996/20 of August 29, 1996, the Sub-Commission on the Prevention and Protection of Minorities requested Greek professor of international law Kalliopi Koufa to prepare a working paper on the question of terrorism and human rights for consideration at its 49th session [E/CN.4/Sub.2/1997/28]. Subsequently, Koufa was appointed as a Special Rapporteur by the Commission on Human Rights in its decision to conduct a more comprehensive study on this issue [1998/107, April 17, 1998]. Koufa prepared a preliminary report for the Sub-Commission's 51st session in 1999 [E/CN.4/Sub.2/1999/27] and a progress report for its 53rd session in 2001 [E/CN.4/Sub.2/2001/31]. Koufa's reports provide a striking backdrop to the state actions subsequently taken following the September 11 terrorist attacks in New York and Washington, D.C.

Koufa's 2001 progress report begins by noting that the General Assembly adopted a *Declaration on Measures to Eliminate International Terrorism* as early as December 9, 1994 [A/Res/49/60 (1994)]. He also notes that on December 17, 1996, it established an Ad Hoc Committee to develop a comprehensive legal framework of conventions dealing with international terrorism [A/Res/51/210 (1996)]. Nearly three years later, on October 19, 1999, the Security Council voted unanimously to condemn "all acts, methods and practices of terrorism as criminal and unjustifiable, regardless of their motivation, in all their forms and manifestations, wherever and by whomever committed, in particular those which threaten international peace and security" [S/Res/1269 (1999)]. This resolution called for member states to strengthen international cooperation in the fight against terrorism on the basis of the principles of the U.N. Charter and relevant norms of international human rights and humanitarian law and to ratify and implement the numerous international and regional antiterrorist conventions.

Subsequently, on December 17, 1999, the General Assembly adopted a resolution on "Human Rights and Terrorism" in which it condemned terrorism for creating "an environment that destroys the right of people to live in freedom from fear" and for violating the right to life, liberty, and security [A/Res/54/164 (1999)]. It also condemned the incitement of ethnic hatred, violence, and terrorism. Finally, the resolution condemned acts of terrorism as "activities aimed at the destruction of human rights, fundamental freedoms, and democracy; and as threatening the territorial integrity and security of states, destabilizing legitimately constituted governments, undermining pluralistic civil society, and having adverse consequences for economic and social development" [ibid.].

Despite this proliferation of U.N. activity, however, the definition of "terrorism" has remained controversial among states. As far back as 1937, an international effort launched under the auspices of the League of Nations failed to reach agreement on an International Convention for the Prevention and Punishment of Terrorism. Today, there exist many conflicting definitions and piecemeal attempts to regulate specific criminal acts (rather than a single comprehensive convention). According to a Dutch study, 109 different definitions of terrorism have been used in official documents between 1936 and 1983 [Alex Schmid, *Political Terrorism: A Research Guide to Concepts, Theories, Databases and Literature* (1983)]. In this respect, perhaps the most volatile issue is the distinction suggested by some states between "terrorists" and "freedom fighters." At its 26th session held in Burkina Faso in July 1999, the Organization of the Islamic Conference (OIC) adopted the Convention of the Islamic Conference on Combating International Terrorism [A/54/637-S/1999/1204 (2000)]. Soon afterward, the OIC stressed its concerns about the need to distinguish terrorism from a people's struggle for "national liberation . . . and the elimination of foreign occupation and colonial hegemony as well as for regaining the right of self-determination" [OIC, Ninth Summit Conference (Qatar, 2000), Doha Declaration].

Another highly political issue is the suggested conceptual distinction between "state terrorism" (or terrorism promoted or tolerated by states) and "terrorism emanating from irregular armed groups and other groups and organizations" that is directed against the state [E/CN.4/Sub.2/1997/SR.33, para. 42]. It was precisely this issue that confronted the Security Council in the wake of September 11, setting in motion a range of normative and military responses that have had profound ramifications for the protection of human rights in what is now referred to as the "post post-Cold War" era.

Jus Ad Bellum: The New "Bush Doctrine"

On September 12, 2001, the Security Council adopted a resolution unequivocally condemning the September 11 attacks, declaring them to constitute a "threat to international peace and security" and recognizing the "inherent right of individual or collective self defense in accordance with the Charter" [S/Res/1368 (2001)]. The Security Council (on September 28) unanimously adopted a historic resolution directed toward combating terrorists and all states that support, harbor, provide safe haven to, finance, supply weapons to, help recruit, or aid terrorists [S/Res/1373 (2001)]. The resolution required all member states to cooperate in a wide range of areas—from suppressing and financing terrorism to providing early warning, cooperating in criminal investigations, and exchanging information on possible terrorist acts [ibid.]. It also provided for the establishment of a new "terrorism committee" of the Security Council, consisting of all members of the Council, to which all member states were required to report within 90 days on the steps they had taken to implement the resolution. Thus, **Resolution 1373** quickly established a comprehensive legal framework for states to address the threat of international terrorism through mutual cooperation and coordination of their criminal justice systems.

A week later, on October 7, the U.S. Ambassador to the United Nations, John Negroponte, delivered a letter to the President of the Security Council stating that it, together with other states, had "initiated actions in the exercise of its inherent right of individual and collective self-defense." These actions were taken against al-Qaeda terrorist training camps and military installations of the Taliban regime in Afghanistan, on the basis of "clear and compelling information" that al-Qaeda, supported by the Taliban regime in Afghanistan, had a "central role in the attacks." The letter further stated that while still at the early stages, the United States "may find that our self-defense requires further actions with respect to other organizations and other States." Thus was born the "**Bush Doctrine**"—the asserted right of a state (or at least the United States) to use military force in "self-defense" against any state that aids, harbors, or supports international terrorists or terrorist organizations.

This doctrine raises profound implications for international law, justice, and the human rights movement. First, how close must the connection be between the host-state and terrorist organization and who ultimately is to decide this issue in order to justify military force in self-defense? Is presence alone of a terrorist group on a state's territory sufficient and is Security Council approval required before any military action may be taken in self-defense? In this regard, it should be recalled that, despite the absence of any threat of veto by the other permanent members, the United States initiated its military offensive in Afghanistan without seeking Security Council authorization. It chose instead to rely upon its "inherent right" to individual and collective self-defense.

Second, in the case of international terrorist networks—which by definition operate across and within the territories of many states—how far and for how long does this right to self-defense extend? Would it extend, for instance, to a suspected al-Qaeda cell outside of Afghanistan in Somalia, Syria, or the Sudan? Would it extend to other terrorist organizations in third states that have not attacked the United States, but that may be planning or supporting future terrorist attacks? If this broader notion of "anticipatory" self-defense is accepted, does it extend to a "terrorist" or "rogue" state suspected to be developing weapons of mass destruction (as in the case of Iraq)? If so, this would represent a radical change to the norms controlling the use of force under the U.N. Charter—a change that could pose potential threats to both the stability of the interstate system and the international protection of human rights.

The reason for this is that an expanded conception of "anticipatory" self-defense against nonstate terrorist groups opens the way for a new and dangerous exception to the Charter's basic prohibition on the unilateral threat or use of force [Article 2(4)]. The framers of the Charter recognized that Article 2(4) was fundamental in order to "save succeeding generations from the scourge of war" and to secure peace. As the supreme value of the interstate system, it is regarded as more compelling than competing values, even human rights. While at various times states have asserted "benign" exceptions to Article 2(4), none of these exceptions have been accepted by the majority of states. For instance, Brezhnev's assertion of a right to intervene to protect socialism in Czechoslovakia in 1968 and Reagan's assertion of a right to intervene by force to protect democracy in Panama in 1989 were both widely condemned. In relation to the doctrine of humanitarian intervention, the international community does appear to have accepted the so-called "Entebbe exception"—the right to liberate hostages if the territorial state will not or cannot. But it has not accepted a unilateral right to intervene by force to topple a government or occupy its territory, even if that were truly necessary to terminate atrocities or liberate detainees.

The broadening of the *jus ad bellum* (the legality of the resort to use of force by states) poses new dangers for the international protection of human rights. Responding to terrorism with counter-terrorism, or other forcible intervention in another state, inevitably leads to an escalation of violence and, in time, full-scale armed conflict with the certainty of gross human rights violations on both sides. The deplorable situation in Israel and the Occupied Territories over the last year—where a succession of suicide bombings and extra-judicial executions in anticipatory self-defense have become routine—is perhaps the clearest illustration of this vicious cycle of spiraling violence. Even in the case of suggested "humanitarian interventions," the use of force must be tightly constrained. The reasons for this are apparent. Human rights violations occur in all states, and in many states, gross human rights violations are evident. Even international human rights proponents recognize that these violations can serve as a pretext for invasion; that the Entebbe hostage situation apart, it is rare for a state to intervene for an authentic humanitarian purpose; and that such military intervention may result in greater injury to human beings and human rights than do the violations they seek to terminate. Accordingly, this is not a choice that the U.N. Charter has left to individual states to make, establishing instead a comprehensive framework for the collective use of force "in the common interest" under the aegis of the Security Council.

For well-known reasons of self-interest and *real politik*, the permanent members of the Security Council have failed to discharge their responsibilities under Chapter VII of the Charter, especially in the case of gross violations of human rights. Indeed, in the wake of NATO's 1999 bombing campaign in Kosovo without Security Council approval, some scholars began to argue for a new distinction between "legality" and "legitimacy" for the purposes of humanitarian intervention in the case where a coalition of states is acting to halt ethnic cleansing. But now, in the Age of Terrorism, a second and equally complex question confronts the international state system: may a state or coalition of states intervene in anticipatory self-defense, without Security Council authorization, in another state that is alleged to be aiding, harboring, or supporting terrorists? Ambassador Negroponte's letter of October 7 appears to leave open this possibility. Unless the international system moves to develop effective lawful responses to the scourge of terrorism, target states will be tempted to seek unilateral solutions by force—often the "instinctive" response—although it rarely serves its alleged purpose and is often destructive of state as well as human values.

From the perspective of human rights, this creates two dangers. First, it leaves the door open for any state that is the victim of a terrorist attack to use *military* force in response (whether in the territory of other states or on its own territory). This encourages the resort to international or internal armed conflict, rather than other legal and diplomatic measures. Even if increased adherence to international human rights and humanitarian norms *durante belli* by states and combatants is possible, this can only ever serve as damage control once the *jus ad bellum* threshold has been crossed. One need only think of the recent terror attacks on the Indian parliament by suspected Pakistani militants—and of a host of other terrorist bombings in Colombia, Indonesia, Israel, the Philippines, and Russia—to foresee the consequences of an unrestrained right of self-defense in the context of an ongoing, global "war against terrorism." Indeed, many states have already co-opted the language of self-defense to justify the use of military force against "terrorists." For example, "India is already using President Bush's own logic on terrorism to justify its own implicit threat to attack militant training camps in Pakistan territory" [Celia Dugger, "India Calls a Speech by Pakistan's President 'Dangerous,'" *New York Times*, May 29, 2002, p. A8].

Second, this approach conceptualizes responses to international terrorism in a "war" rather than "justice" paradigm, thereby changing the normative legal framework governing the conduct of states' antiterrorist activities, a matter with profound human rights consequences. Both Special Rapporteur Koufa pre-September 11 and High Commissioner for Human Rights Mary Robinson post-September 11 have warned—in the strongest of terms—about the consequences of such a paradigm shift. A failure properly to distinguish acts of war from acts of terrorism is likely to have its greatest consequences in internal conflict situations where significant "gaps" remain in the law. For example, in situations short of armed conflict (i.e., where Common Article 3 and Protocol II of the Geneva Conventions do not apply) internal violence may lead a state to derogate from its obligations under international human rights treaties. This allows the state to engage in conduct forbidden to it in normal times *and* in the more serious conditions of civil war. Thus, states that are engaged in struggles with internal armed groups such as Spain (in relation to the ETA), Turkey (in relation to the PKK), Indonesia (in relation to the GAM in Aceh), Russia (in relation to Chechen rebels), the Phillipines (in relation to the Abu Sayyaf), Pakistan (in relation to numerous militant groups in Pakistan and Kashmir), Israel (in relation to groups such as Hamas in the Occupied Territories), China (in relation to the Uighurs in Xinjiang province) and Colombia (in relation to the FARC) are likely to rely on this grey zone between war and peace in the name of antiterrorism measures.

This danger has for some years led to calls for minimum humanitarian standards to close the "gap" in cases of internal conflicts that fall below the Protocol II threshold and that are insufficiently coverered by either humanitarian or human rights protections. Indeed, this issue has been on the agenda of the Commission on Human Rights since 1994 [Comm. on H.R. Res. 1998/29, *Minimum Humanitarian Standards*, April 17, 1998; Comm. on H.R. Res. 1999/65, *Fundamental Standards of Humanity*, April 28, 1999], has generated two reports by the Secretary-General [E/CN.4/1998/87; E/CN.4/1999/92], and has led to a series of expert meetings. Such minimum humanitarian standards would apply in at least four situations: first, where the threshold of applicability of international humanitarian law is not reached or disputed; second, where the state is not a party to the relevant international instruments; third, where derogation from specific standards is invoked; and fourth, where the relevant actor is not a government, but some other group. In an Age of Terrorism where armed force is employed by states both internationally and internally, the need is greater than ever for an irreducible core of nonderogable humanitarian and human rights norms. This must include core due process guarantees, limitations on excessive use of force and on methods of combat, prohibition of deportation, rules pertaining to detention and humane treatment, and guarantees of humanitarian assistance (see further below).

Neither of these dangers has escaped the attention of the Secretary-General. Upon receipt of Negroponte's letter and after the initiation of extensive U.S. and U.K. military operations in Afghanistan, Kofi Annan stated that while the "states concerned have set their current military action in Afghanistan in [the context of self-defense]" to defeat terrorism we need a "sustained effort and a broad strategy to unite all nations . . . working together and using many different means—including political, legal, diplomatic and financial means" [www.un.org/News/Press/docs/2001/sgsm7985.doc.htm]. The next day, October 9, Annan made a brief statement indicating that he and other diplomats were "disturbed" by the statement in the U.S. letter to the Security Council claiming a legitimate right to extend military attacks beyond Afghanistan. "There is one line in that letter that disturbed some of us," Annan stated. "I think the one sentence which has caused some anxiety amongst the membership—which I have also asked about—was the question that they [the United States] may find it necessary to go after other organizations and other states, beyond al-Qaeda and Afghanistan. Basically, it is a statement that they are at early stages and keeping their options open," he said. At that time, the U.S. State Department's list of "terrorist states" included Iraq, Iran, Syria, Sudan, Libya, North Korea, and Cuba.

While it is perhaps too early to assess the *opinio juris* of states toward the Bush Doctrine, the politics of state practice have quickly revealed a host of problems and double standards. The United States has emphatically urged restraint on the use of force by both India against Pakistan and by Israel against the Palestinians and neighboring states, despite evidence that various states have been supporting, financing, and harboring terrorist groups. Furthermore, in the case of U.S. economic or strategic "allies," clear evidence of financing or supporting terrorist groups appears not to have activated the Bush Doctrine. Such is the case in Saudi Arabia (from whom it receives annually 17 percent of its crude oil imports and nearly half a trillion dollars in investments and to whom it exports the largest amount of arms among developing countries) and Pakistan (which is providing strategic assistance to the U.S.-led military coalition against terrorism).

The Convergence of Human Rights and Humanitarian Law (Jus in Belli)

For some years, both scholars and practitioners have been observing the gradual convergence of international human rights and humanitarian law

[Theodor Meron, *The Humanization of International Humanitarian Law*, 94 A.J.I.L. 239 (2000)]. Indeed, today we no longer refer to the "laws of war" but rather to "international humanitarian law," reflecting the influence of the human rights movement and principles of humanity. The older body of humanitarian law derives historically from medieval notions of chivalry and reciprocity guaranteeing "fair play" and minimizing unnecessary suffering in times of armed conflict. In many respects, this is now being "humanized" to accord with the modern conception of individual human dignity that is thought to prevail in all circumstances.

This process can be seen in a number of areas. As compared with the Lieber code and early Hague law, the guarantees against torture, arbitrary arrest and detention, and discrimination and of due process in the 1949 Geneva conventions and 1977 Additional Protocols reflect the unmistakable influence of the *Universal Declaration of Human Rights* (UDHR). The domain of legitimate reprisals (collective responsibility of the many for violations by a few) has diminished and been influenced by the emphasis in human rights law on individual responsibility. Violations of humanitarian law are increasingly subject to prosecution in third states under the principle of universal jurisdiction. The classic distinctions in thresholds of applicability between "international" [Art. 2, 1949 Geneva Conventions and Protocol I] and "noninternational" [Common Art. 3, 1949 Geneva Conventions and Protocol II] armed conflicts has begun to break down. There are now increasing calls for the formulation of fundamental standards of humanity that protect an "irreducible core of nonderogable norms." We have also seen the emergence of the notion of "crimes against humanity" with no a priori nexus to armed conflict.

While these convergences are welcome developments, it is important to realize that there remain important differences between human rights and humanitarian law. Humanitarian law (the law of armed conflict) regulates aspects of a struggle for life and death between contestants who operate on the basis of formal equality. It allows the killing of "combatants" and tolerates the killing and wounding of innocent civilians not directly participating in the armed conflict as "lawful collateral damage." It also permits deprivations of personal freedom without convictions in a court of law, allows an occupying power to resort to internment and to limit the appeal rights of detained persons, and permits far-reaching limitations on freedoms of expression and assembly. Thus, while humanitarian law attempts to impose constraints on the savagery of war, especially regarding unnecessary suffering of civilians and inhumane methods and means of warfare, it nevertheless permits violations of fundamental human rights. It is of critical importance, therefore, to determine whether or not an international or internal "armed conflict" meets the threshold requirements to apply humanitarian law. If not, then states remain bound by the full array of international obligations that exist under human rights law and other regimes providing for the protection of the rights of the individual.

The danger of an expanded right of states to self-defense in response to actual or anticipated terrorist acts is that it indefinitely places antiterrorism actions of states in the framework of an international armed conflict. This allows for the killing of any persons meeting the definition of "combatants" and means that international humanitarian law primarily will govern the rights of prisoners and civilians in the target state(s). International human rights law continues to apply in such situations of armed conflict and to fill any "gaps" in the humanitarian law regime. However, it may be limited or derogated from by states leaving only a small "core" of human rights law applicable [Advisory Opinion, *Legality of the Threat or Use of Nuclear Weapons*, 1996 I.C.J. 226, para. 25]. Where there is a conflict between the two bodies of law, the law of armed conflict, as the *lex speclialis*, will prevail [Meron, 266–73].

The initiation of the global "war against terrorism" by a U.S.-led coalition of states has blurred the relationship between these two bodies of law and, in many instances, has weakened individual protections. As seen above in the discussion of *jus ad bellum*, this is partly a function of the new type of armed conflict that does not fit easily into a normative framework designed for conflicts between states or between states and internal insurgent groups. But it is also a function of a pervasive attitude of unilateralism, exceptionalism, and general disregard for international law that has characterized U.S. actions since the start of its military offensive in Afghanistan. The consequences of these two factors for the global protection of human rights is well illustrated by the U.S. treatment of persons detained in Afghanistan and on its own territory since commencement of U.S. military operations in Afghanistan on October 7, 2001.

On November 13, 2001, President Bush issued an Executive Order regarding the "Detention, Treatment, and Trial of Certain Non-Citizens in the War against Terrorism." Section two of the Order seeks to define a broad class of persons who may be subject to detention for involvement in acts of "international terrorism." Specifically, it provides for the trial in military commissions of any non-U.S. citizen whom the President determines is, or was, a member of al-Qaeda, or has engaged in, aided or abetted, or conspired to commit acts of international terrorism that have damaged (or threaten to damage) U.S. citizens, national security, foreign policy, or the economy. It also targets any individual who has knowingly harbored any such persons and can be activated when "it is in the interest of the United States that such individual be subject to this order." The unprecedented scope of this order allows for detentions of persons of different nationalities with varying degrees of involvement in the fighting in Afghanistan, association with al-Qaeda or the Taliban, and connection to the events of September 11 or future acts of international terrorism.

According to the U.S. Department of Defense, as of January 28, 2002, 482 prisoners—about one-fifth of whom are Saudi nationals—are being held by U.S. forces in Afghanistan and at Guantanamo Bay, Cuba.

Apart from its obligations under international humanitarian law, the United States is also bound by norms of conventional and customary human rights law in its treatment of these detainees. In 1992, the United States ratified the International Covenant on Civil and Political Rights (ICCPR), which requires state's parties to respect and ensure the rights of "all individuals within its territory and subject to its jurisdiction" [ICCPR, Art. 2]. The ICCPR applies at all times—in times of war and peace—although states may derogate from certain provisions during a "public emergency which threatens the life of the nation," but only to the extent "strictly required by the exigencies of the situation." Any state wishing to derogate must immediately inform the Secretary-General [ibid., Art. 4].

While the United States proclaimed a national emergency [Proclamation 7463, Declaration of National Emergency by Reason of Certain Terrorist Attacks] on September 14, 2001, it has not officially sought to exercise its right of derogation under Article 4 of the Covenant. Accordingly, human rights scholars and NGOs have argued that the President's November 13 Executive Order providing for the detention of certain individuals and the establishment of military commissions is in violation of various provisions of the ICCPR. The vague scope of section 2 of the Order arguably violates the right to security and liberty of the person and the prohibition on arbitrary arrest and detention [ICCPR, Art. 9(1)]. The denial of minimum due process rights to the detainees, including *habeas corpus*, the right to challenge the lawfulness of their detention in a civilian court, and the entitlement to trial within a reasonable time, also arguably violate the ICCPR [Art. 9(3)–(4)]. As indicated above, while some of these provisions may be subject to lawful derogation, the United States has not sought to rely on any such right, and these obligations must therefore be held to be in full force and effect. Furthermore, the Human Rights Committee has stated that even in times of national emergency, the right to *habeas corpus* and judicial review of detention cannot be suspended [General Comment No. 29, States of Emergency (Art. 4), August 31, 2001]. Under the U.S. Constitution, *habeas corpus* may only be suspended in the case of "rebellion" or "invasion" and only then by Congress (although this presumably only applies to persons held on U.S. territory). Finally, the failure to specify those criminal acts encompassed by the term "international terrorism" may place the United States in violation of the Covenant's nonderogable prohibition on the imposition of "ex-post facto laws" [ICCPR, Art. 15]. This issue may become especially relevant if it is sought to convict individuals for international crimes on the basis of membership alone in a terrorist organization, such as al-Qaeda, without proof of any direct involvement in specific acts.

Further questions have been raised regarding the fairness of future trials conducted by U.S. military commissions, especially given the likelihood of imposition of the death penalty. The ICCPR requires a "fair and public hearing by a competent, independent and impartial tribunal established by law." This includes the presumption of innocence, the right to be informed of charges, the right to adequate time for the preparation of a defense, the right to legal assistance of one's own choosing, and the right to examine witnesses. Whether the commissions, which remain wholly subject to the discretion of the U.S. executive, will satisfy these standards is a matter of current controversy [Aryeh Neier, "The Military Tribunals on Trial," *New York Review of Books*, February 11, 2002, p. 13]. The Covenant also guarantees that anyone convicted of a crime shall have the right to his or her conviction and sentence being reviewed "by a higher tribunal according to law." Whether the military review board established by the rules issued by the U.S. Secretary of Defense satisfies this obligation is similarly an open question. Given that the Third Geneva Convention guarantees final appeals to the civilian courts (and ultimately to the U.S. Supreme Court) for POWs interred by the United States, it would be incongruous for the ICCPR to establish a lower standard.

The November 13 Executive Order on military commissions sets a dangerous precedent by the world's reigning superpower and long-standing champion of human rights worldwide. It sets a differential standard of justice for citizens and noncitizens; seeks to derogate from both constitutional and international standards of due process; and, by situating detention facilities outside of the United States, seeks to deny the availability of any judicial fora able to provide effective remedies. This sends a strong message to an increasing number of states, such as China, Myanmar (Burma), Colombia, Egypt, Kyrgyzstan, Malaysia, Nigeria, Peru, Russia, Sudan, and Turkey, as they wage their own "wars against terrorism." It also reverses the consistent and long-standing opposition of the United States to the use of military tribunals in other countries in the name of states of emergency and national security [HRW, *Past U.S. Criticism of Military Tribunals*, Washington, D.C., November 28, 2001]. It also ignores the availability of other domestic and international alternatives. Indeed, various commentators have suggested other preferable fora to prosecute and try international terrorists. Anne-Marie Slaughter has suggested that al-Qaeda "should be tried before the world" and has advocated the establishment of an international tribunal to try accused terrorists [*New York Times*, November 17, 2001]. Conversely, Harold Koh has suggested that "we have the right courts for bin Laden" and that the United States should try suspected international terrorists in its own federal courts, as it has done on numerous prior occasions (including in relation to the 1993 bombing of the World Trade Center and the August 1998 bombings of the U.S. embassies in Tanzania and Kenya) [*New York Times*, November 23, 2001].

The confusion of the war and justice paradigms in combating international terrorism, as represented by the move to establish military tribunals, has potentially far-reaching and devastating effects for the international human rights movement. It threatens to undermine efforts over the last half a century to create a "culture of rights" and respect for human dignity in all parts of the world. As Slaughter has stated, "[s]imply to try all suspected terrorists before U.S. military tribunals intended for emergency battlefield conditions would put America at odds not only with its own domestic constitutional safeguards, but with international conventions on the treatment of prisoners of war. In the long run, this would jeopardize alliances, put Americans at risk, and set back our own values" [Anne-Marie Slaughter, "Tougher Than Terror," 13(2), *The American Prospect*, January 28, 2002].

Apart from suspected terrorists detained on the battlefield in Afghanistan and beyond, more than 1,100 persons, mainly non-U.S. nationals, have been taken into custody in the United States during criminal investigations in the wake of September 11. The U.S. government has released little public information regarding these detentions (including refusing to release the names or whereabouts of detainees to families or to the embassies of states of nationality). Many are being held under new and far-reaching "antiterrorist" legislation [Uniting and Strengthening America by Providing Adequate Tools Required to Intercept and Obstruct Terrorism (USA PATRIOT) Act] adopted on October 26, 2001. Again, this represents a new and worrying threat to the protection of human rights in a country founded on principles of individual liberty and security of the person.

The further danger, of course, of these counter-terrorism measures is the message they send to other states that historically may have been less protective of individual liberty. Post-September 11, similar counterterrorism legislation has already been, or is in the process of being, enacted in many states around the world. For example, on October 15, 2001, the Indian Union Cabinet approved the new Prevention of Terrorism Ordinance, which gives Indian police sweeping powers of arrest and detention. In the United Kingdom, the Anti-Terrorism, Crime and Security Act (enacted on December 14, 2001) permits the detention of nonnationals without charge or trial for an indefinite period of time when the Home Secretary states that he reasonably believes and suspects (including on the basis of secret evidence) a person to be a national security risk and a suspected "international terrorist."

In Africa alone, Mauritius has recently passed the Prevention of Terrorism Act of 2002; Nigeria currently has a bill titled the Anti-Terrorism, Economic and Financial Crimes Act before its parliament; and South Africa is considering a new Anti-Terrorism bill to replace the apartheid era Internal Security Act. And in Egypt, the penal code includes a definition of terrorism that the Human Rights Committee has stated is "so broad that it covered a wide range of acts of different gravity." Furthermore, in Egypt the death penalty may be imposed for the crime of terrorism and, under a 1981 Emergency Law, special military courts may be used for the prosecution of alleged terrorist activity. These courts are headed by military officers appointed by the Minister of Defense and their decisions are reviewed by other military judges and subject to confirmation by the President (who in practice delegates this task to a senior military officer).

The situation in Egypt reveals most starkly the danger—and hypocrisy—of establishing U.S. military commissions as the means by which to combat international terrorism. Since September 11, the Egyptian government has ordered some 285 suspected Islamists—many of whom have been imprisoned for years—to be tried in three separate cases before the Supreme Military Court despite their civilian status. Citing the U.S. decision to establish special military tribunals to try suspected captured terrorists, the Egyptian president recently asserted that "there is no doubt that the events of 11 September created a new concept of democracy that differs from the concept that Western states defended before these events, especially in regard to the freedom of the individual" [Joint Oral Statement, HRW and AI, *Item 4: Report of the U.N. High Commissioner for Human Rights and follow-up to the World Conference on Human Rights*, March 2002]. In spite of its own proposed military commissions, on March 4, 2002, the U.S. State Department Country Report on Human Rights Practices in Egypt stated that these courts "infringe on a defendant's normal right under the constitution to a fair trial before an independent judiciary." The Egyptian emergency law also permits detention without charge for up to 30 days; no maximum limit to the length of detention if a judge upholds the detention order; and the executive to issue a warrant of arrest for any individual who poses a danger to security and public order. Again, the State Department has said that "this procedure nullifies the constitutional requirement of showing that an individual likely has committed a specific crime to obtain a warrant from a judge or prosecutor."

Finally, one of the most controversial issues has been where suspected terrorists will be tried—either by special military commission or in U.S. or foreign civilian courts—and on what basis these determinations will be made. By November 2001, at the urging of the CIA, foreign intelligence services and police agencies in over 50 countries had arrested and detained about 360 suspects with alleged connections to al-Qaeda or other terrorist groups [*Washington Post*, November 22, 2001]. In the United States itself, the "20th hijacker" Zacarias Moussaoui, a French national of Moroccan origin, arrested on August 17 in Minneapolis, is being tried in federal court, rather than a military tribunal. Similarly the "U.S. Taliban," John Walker Lindh, is being tried in a civilian court. This appears to leave military commissions applicable only to non-U.S. nationals apprehended on the battlefield or in the context of military operations, although in the context of the ongoing war on terrorism it is not at all clear how far this notion extends. Will a suspected terrorist, for example, apprehended by U.S. special forces or covert operatives in a state such as the Philippines, Georgia, Pakistan, Yemen, or Indonesia be tried before a U.S. military commission or before national courts of that country or be extradited to the United States or another country that is willing to prosecute?

In order to ensure respect for human rights standards in all states, trials must be conducted in civilian courts in accordance with all of the due process and individual liberty and security of the person guarantees enshrined in international human rights law. As at least one human rights NGO has observed, "the sobering lesson for human rights activists is that even in a highly developed industrialized country, like the United States, with a deeply imbedded tradition of constitutional rights protection, the impulse to impose draconian measures is strong when security concerns come to the fore" [Lawyers Committee for Human Rights, *The Impact on Civil Rights in the United States of the September 11 Attacks*, Working Paper, January 28, 2002]. It is now clear that September 11 represented a setback for human rights globally; the dangerous idea that restricting human rights will contribute to national security has gained in ascendancy both in the United States and around the world. This has led to renewed efforts to better understand the concept of "security" and, in recent times, a new conception of "human security" is emerging on the global agenda.

Human Security

"Human security" was described in 1999 by Japan's Prime Minister Obuchi Keizo as the key idea in "comprehensively seizing all of the menaces that threaten the survival, daily life, and dignity of human beings and to strengthening the efforts to confront these threats" [Obuchi Keizo, "Opening Remarks," in *The Asian Crisis and Human Security*, pp. 18–19 (1999)]. According to Amartya Sen, co-director with Sadako Ogata of a new U.N. Commission on Human Security, this concept can thus be understood as the protection and preservation of human "survival" and "daily life" (presumably against premature death, avoidable ill-health, illiteracy, etc.). It also means the avoidance of various indignities that can shower injury, insult, and contempt on our lives (related, for example, to destitution, penury, incarceration, exclusion, illiteracy, etc.). On this basis, the concept of human security, according to Sen, is underpinned by at least four elements. First, a focus on *individual human lives* (as opposed to the aggregately technocratic notion of "national security" that is favored in the military context). Second, an appreciation of *the role of society and of social arrangements* in making human lives more secure (avoiding a socially detached view of individual human predicament). Third, a reasoned concentration on the *downside risks* of human lives, rather than on the overall expansion of effective freedom in general (contrasting with the broader objective of the promotion of "human development"). And fourth, an emphasis on the *more elementary human rights* (rather than the entire range of human rights) [Amartya Sen, "Basic Education and Human Security," Background Paper, Commission on Human Security, January 4, 2002].

The concept of human security is thus interrelated to, and complementary with, other fundamental notions in international affairs and contemporary dialogue, including "human rights," "human development," and "national security." The basic idea is that people are made safer by an open, tolerant, and responsive state capable of ensuring protection of a limited "vital core" of human rights and basic capabilities. At the same time, enhancing human security reinforces the state by strengthening its legitimacy and stability. It represents an attempt to identify a certain class of objectives among others, which have a particular claim to our attention in the contemporary world. As the international community moves forward in its struggle against international terrorism, the concept of human security would require, for example, greater efforts in securing human capability in areas such as basic education and health, as opposed to the ever-increasing use of military force. In other words, it would seek to lead to the "humanization" of security, much as the idea of human rights has over the last 50 years led to the humanization of the laws of war. These ideas, which require extensive further research and evolution, correlate closely with views already expressed by the Secretary-General [Kofi Annan, We the Peoples: The Role of the United Nations in the Twenty-first Century (2000)] and will no doubt continue to shape the debate regarding human rights in these pages over the years ahead.

The U.N. Role in Human Rights

One of the four purposes of the United Nations is "to achieve international cooperation . . . in promoting and encouraging respect for human rights and for fundamental freedoms for all without distinction as to race, sex, language or religion" [Art. 1(3), U.N. Charter]. Member states, and the United Nations itself, have pledged jointly and separately to promote "universal respect for, and observance of, human rights and fundamental freedoms" [Arts. 55(c) and 56, U.N. Charter]. There are three principal ways in which the United Nations pursues this objective. First, by standard setting—that is, by articulating and elevating international human rights norms to the status of international law. Second, by promoting human rights—that is, by educating different communities, promulgating human rights standards, and disseminating relevant information. Third, by implementing human rights. It is the third objective that has proven the most elusive to realize in practice.

The process of implementation involves at least three subtasks: monitoring, response, and deterrence of violations. Monitoring violations of human rights includes efforts to anticipate and prevent violations through early warning, mediation, or reconciliation and through publicity of alleged violations. In response to violations, the United Nations applies diplomatic pressure and the "mobilization of shame." Finally, it can take stronger action to deter or reduce violations, such as imposing sanctions or other punitive measures and ensuring effective legal remedies to secure relief for victims.

U.N. Human Rights Machinery

There are two principal types of human rights implementation "machinery": the Charter-based and treaty-based bodies. Before reviewing recent activities of these bodies, this section assesses the function and interrelationship of the Commission on Human Rights, the Office of the High Commissioner for Human Rights, and the human rights treaty system.

The main Charter-based organ is the *Commission on Human Rights,* which is a functional commission of the Economic and Social Council (ECOSOC) and the only subsidiary body mandated by the Charter itself. The Commission is comprised of 53 member states, each elected for four-year terms, and is responsible for developing and overseeing all international human rights instruments. The Commission meets annually to hear reports and make recommendations regarding the human rights performance of selected states. It also oversees numerous "extra-conventional mechanisms," which have become a rapidly evolving means to monitor and protect human rights outside the traditional judicial and quasi-judicial monitoring mechanisms. Often referred to as "ad hoc human rights machinery," this includes the thematic and country-specific Special Rapporteurs and Working Groups of the Commission, various activities and operations of the High Commissioner for Human Rights, and country verification missions.

The 1967 ECOSOC Resolution 1235 authorizes the Commission to "make a thorough study of situations which reveal a consistent pattern of violations of human rights" [E/Res/1235 (XLII), E/4393 (1967)]. Although not initially intended as such, the 1235 procedure soon became a vehicle for the establishment of country-oriented study groups and thematic Special Rapporteurs. The 1235 procedure was soon augmented by the introduction of the confidential procedure established by Resolution 1503 [E/Res/1503 (XLVIII) of 27 May 1970, E/4832/Add.1 (1970)]. Under the 1503 procedure, a five-member Working Group of the Sub-Commission on the Prevention and Protection of Minorities (the Sub-Commission) annually receives both thousands of communications alleging violations of human rights and corresponding replies from governments. The Working Group confidentially considers whether particular situations "appear to reveal a consistent pattern of gross and reliably attested violations of human rights and fundamental freedoms," and this determination is often used as a precursor to action under the 1235 procedure. Over 50 countries have been reported to the Commission since 1972, and many governments regularly respond to so-called "1503 communications."

The other main Charter-based organ is the *Office of the High Commissioner for Human Rights* (OHCHR), which oversees and coordinates all U.N. human rights activities [Vienna Declaration and Programme of Action; A/Res/48/141, December 20, 1993]. In connection with the 1997 program for U.N. reform [A/51/950, July 14, 1997, para. 79], the OHCHR and the Center for Human Rights were consolidated into a single office as of September 15, 1997. (The Center was previously the office of the U.N. Secretariat charged with conducting fact-finding and producing reports in connection with the activities of the Commission and the Human Rights Committee.)

The post of High Commissioner, which became a reality after the 1993 World Conference on Human Rights, was intended to be a visible and effective platform to speak out against, and take actions to prevent, serious violations of human rights worldwide. Many observers believed that the first High Commissioner, José Ayala Lasso of Ecuador (appointed in 1993), failed to establish a strong profile for human rights within the U.N. system. The second High Commissioner, however, quickly demonstrated new leadership and a strong moral voice on human rights violations. Appointed in 1997, Mary Robinson, the former head of state of Ireland, continues in that position today.

In dramatic terms, however, Robinson announced at the opening session of the 2001 meeting of the Commission that she would not run for a second four-year term, citing frustration at the many "constraints" inherent in the U.N. system of rights protection. Having been persuaded by the Secretary-General to remain in the post for at least another year, Robinson announced again at the start of this year's meeting of the Commission that it would be her last. According to Reed Brody of Human Rights Watch, "Mary Robinson paid a price for her willingness to stand up to powerful governments that violate human rights" [HRW, *U.N.: Robinson's Departure a "Disappointment"—Human Rights Commissioner Was a Target of U.S.*, March 18, 2002]. Robinson has raised the ire of the United States for her criticism of civilian casualties from air strikes in Afghanistan and the handling of detainees in Guantanamo Bay. She has also been most critical of Russia for abuses in Chechnya and of China for abuses in Xinjiang. It is uncertain at this stage who will replace Robinson as the next High Commissioner for Human Rights.

In addition to the Charter-based mechanisms, *treaty-based bodies monitor compliance with international human rights treaties.* There are currently six major human rights treaties—addressing economic and social rights, civil and political rights, racial discrimination, discrimination against women, torture, and the rights of the child—and each treaty establishes its own monitoring and implementation mechanisms. Many states have ratified all six treaties. The *Convention on the Rights of the Child* (CRC) has the highest number of states parties with 191 ratifications (leaving only Somalia and the United States as nonparties). As of June 17, 2002, there are 148 ratifications of the ICCPR, 145 of the *International Covenant on Economic, Social, and Cultural Rights* (ICESCR), 129 of the *Convention against Torture* (CAT), 162 of the *Convention on the Elimination of all forms of Racial Discrimination* (CERD), and 169 of the *Convention on the Elimination of all forms of Discrimination Against Women* (CEDAW). [The United States has ratified the ICCPR, CAT, and CERD, but in each case, ratification is subject to extensive reservations, declarations, and understandings (RUDs).]

Treaty-based monitoring and supervisory mechanisms have evolved in principally three spheres of procedure—state reporting, individual complaints, and interstate complaints. The last of these mechanisms has not been relied upon by states and has been superseded by the first two. Indeed, in the space of just over 50 years, reporting, supervision, and individual complaint procedures have revolutionized the international protection of human rights. These procedures usually involve periodic reports by states, in accordance with detailed guidelines; review by a committee, accompanied by questions to the reporting states; in some cases, detailed inquiry by a subcommittee or individual rapporteur; and a committee report noting discrepancies between states' conduct and the requirements of the treaty or applicable law. The opportunity for individuals or governments to initiate complaints before international treaty supervisory bodies has been achieved largely by the addition of optional protocols to the human rights covenants. Today, individuals can bring "communications" to four of the treaty monitoring bodies (under CERD, CAT, ICCPR, and CEDAW). Recently, there have been some moves toward introducing an optional protocol to the ICESCR to allow for individual complaints.

In recent years, there have been calls for a major overhaul of the U.N. human rights treaty system. Scholars such as Anne Bayefsky have suggested that the system has a "credibility" problem [Anne Bayefsky, ed., *The UN Human Rights Treaty System in the 21st Century* (2000)]. The main criticisms of the treaty system point to its inability to provide effective remedies for victims, poor quality and delayed response in state reporting, the politicization of the treaty bodies, lack of resources and personnel, and an inability to respond to many complaints. Factors such as these that have led to calls for the consolidation of all the treaty individual complaint mechanisms into a single, full-time, professional body in order to create a more effective long-term international petition system.

For example, Thomas Buergenthal has suggested that the six existing treaty bodies be replaced by two consolidated committees: one to review state reports under all six treaties and the other to deal with individual and interstate communications. He has also suggested the establishment of a "U.N. Court of Human Rights." Buergenthal proposes that the court initially would have only jurisdiction to render advisory opinions, rather than binding judgments, in contentious cases [Thomas Buergenthal, "A Court and Two Consolidated Treaty Bodies," in Bayefsky, ed., *The UN Human Rights Treaty System in the 21st Century* (2000), pp. 299–302]. Reform proposals such as these need to be seriously considered and should be an integral part of the U.N. human rights agenda in the coming years [see also Alexander Downer, *Keeping the United Nations Relevant: International Peace and Security, and Reform*, Statement to the 55th Session of the G.A., September 18, 2000].

The Fifty-eighth Session of the Commission on Human Rights

This year's session of the Commission on Human Rights has been heralded as the "toughest ever." This was the first session held since the World Conference against Racism in Durban and the September 11 terrorist attacks and against the backdrop of spiraling violence in the Middle East [Amnesty International, Press Release, *UN Commission on Human Rights Wraps Up*, May 2, 2002]. This was also the first session without the United States as a member. Controversially, it was not re-elected to a three-year term in May 2001 (apparently reflecting irritation by other member states over U.S. exceptionalism on a host of issues, such as missile defense, the Kyoto Protocol, and nonpayment of U.N. dues). With the United States on the sidelines, Felice Gaer questioned in these pages last year whether the new composition of the Commission would mean that "the outspoken U.S. leadership role on key country situations may be missing next year" [*A Global Agenda: Issues/56*]. This question was soon answered in the affirmative with many observers accusing the Commission of having become "hostage to human rights abusers" and a "forum for defending government's records rather than examining them" [HRW, Press Release, *United Nations: Rights Commission Shields Abusers*, April 26, 2002]. To many, the Commission's most effective tool, its capacity to name and shame human rights violators, was dangerously eroded in this session. Acute politicization was also evident in relation to both country situations and thematic areas, and a clear north/south divide created polarized voting on many resolutions.

On the more positive side, the Commission recommended a draft Optional Protocol to the CAT, which would authorize investigative prison visits by U.N. experts "whenever necessary and without prior consent." This recommendation will now go to ECOSOC and the General Assembly for adoption. It also requested a Working Group to draft a new and binding treaty on enforced or involuntary "disappearances," called again for a moratorium on all executions, and appointed a new Special Rapporteur on the Right to Health. As a testament to the power of civil society, the CAT Optional Protocol initiative was led by Costa Rica and Switzerland, at the urging of a joint appeal launched by ten international NGOs. Despite long-term opposition by states such as China, Cuba, Egypt, Saudi Arabia, and the United States, the resolution was adopted 29 votes in favor, 10 against, and 14 abstentions.

Countries with questionable human rights records now command a significant bloc of votes on the Commission. These countries include Algeria, Burundi, China, Cuba, the Democratic Republic of Congo, Indonesia, Kenya, Libya, Malaysia, Nigeria, Russia, Saudi Arabia, Sudan, Syria, Togo, and Vietnam [ibid.]. This limited the effectiveness of the Commission in several ways. First, the Commission failed to pass country resolutions condemning situations of gross and widespread violations of human rights in countries such as China, Indonesia, Iran, Russia, Saudi Arabia, Togo, and Zimbabwe. Second, the Commission failed to produce an effective response to protect human rights in the context of the new global war on terrorism.

On the question of terrorism and human rights, Mexico proposed a resolution calling for counterterrorism measures to be compatible with international human rights and humanitarian law. It further called for the High Commissioner to monitor and analyze counterterrorism laws and to make recommendations to governments and U.N. bodies, including the new Security Council Counter-Terrorism Committee. Despite receiving broad support, however, this proposed resolution was withdrawn on the final day in the face of a wrecking amendment from Algeria and other governments, concerted pressure from the United States, and general reluctance on the part of the European Union. Authoritarian states such as Algeria, Egypt, Pakistan, and Saudi Arabia—which routinely employ counterterrorist measures to suppress dissent and maintain order—derailed the Mexican initiative. At the same time, the United States strongly opposed the proposed resolution, apparently on the basis that it would unduly limit the work of the Security Council. U.S. opposition also stemmed from concern that it could lead to potential criticism of U.S. policies and measures taken post-September 11 (including its use of military commissions and refusal to grant POW status to Taliban detainees). And the European Union, faced with political pressures and domestic problems of its own (especially Spain, France, and the United Kingdom) failed to maintain a united position on this issue.

While the country-specific situations that arose at the Commission are discussed in more detail below, the overall situation may be summarized as follows. The 2002 session saw the unprecedented use of "no action" motions, which prevent the Commission from even debating the subject matter of a resolution. Calls for "no action" were used before voting on resolutions on Zimbabwe (by Nigeria in response to an E.U.-sponsored resolution), Cuba, and the draft Optional Protocol to the CAT.

Previously, this tactic had been employed only by China in an effort to prevent scrutiny of its human rights record. An African-sponsored resolution on the human rights situation in Equatorial Guinea terminated the mandate of the Special Representative and sought to shift the Commission's focus from monitoring to technical assistance. Despite allegations of numerous extra-judicial killings in Togo in 1998 and despite being a Commission member, Togo was removed from consideration under the confidential 1503 procedure. A resolution on Sudan, however, was passed by one vote and extended the mandate of its Special Rapporteur for one more year. A resolution on Iraq was also passed, extending the mandate of its Special Rapporteur for another year.

For the last two years, the Commission has voted to criticize Russia for abuses of human rights and humanitarian law in Chechnya. Despite complete disregard by Moscow for these resolutions and continuing accounts of atrocities in the region, this year the Commission voted (again by only one vote) not to criticize Russia on Chechnya. The draft resolution on the human rights situation in Chechnya would have deplored the lack of cooperation by the Russian Federation with the special mechanisms of the Commission, while at the same time affirming the right of Russia to defend its territorial integrity. The Commission also voted (also by one vote) to end the mandate of the Special Rapporteur on Iran, even though reformist groups in that country have faced intensified pressure and threats from more hard line elements since U.S. President Bush's now infamous "Axis of Evil" speech. And for the first time in many years, no member of the Commission even introduced a resolution criticizing China for human rights abuses. Commission member Saudi Arabia, which has been criticized by the U.S. State Department as a place where "freedom of religion does not exist" and where rights abuses (including one of the highest numbers of executions) continue to persist, also escaped scrutiny.

Importantly, the Commission again chose not to act in relation to the situation in Indonesia, despite accounts of atrocities and grave human rights violations that include unlawful killings and torture. While the Commission adopted a Chairperson statement on East Timor, no reference was made to serious violations by Indonesia's security forces in the provinces of Aceh and Papua (many of which fall into the "gap" or "gray zone" between human rights and humanitarian law discussed previously). However, the Commission did adopt a Chairperson statement on the human rights situation in Colombia; the statement extended the mandate of the OHCHR in Bogota and urged the Colombian government to develop further their cooperation with that office.

In her closing remarks to the Commission, High Commissioner Mary Robinson warned that the Commission could lose its mandate if it does not do more to protect people whose rights are being violated.

I hear distress and concern voiced by the human rights movement over allegations of increased politicization of issues in the Commission to the detriment of true human rights concerns. This is a time to remind ourselves of the essential role of the Commission on Human Rights in protecting human beings against gross violations through highlighting and publicizing those violations. [Dale Gavlak, "UNHRC Receives Mixed Reviews at Conclusion of Geneva Session," *VOA News*, April 26, 2002]

Report of the High Commissioner for Human Rights

At the opening of the Commission, the High Commissioner delivers an annual report. This year Mary Robinson's report focused on one theme: the importance of human rights as a "uniting framework" for states in the face of human insecurity created by international terrorism [*Human Rights: a uniting framework*, Report of the U.N. High Commissioner for Human Rights, E/CN.4/2002/18, February 27, 2002]. The report begins by stating that the September 11 attacks, which were directed at a largely civilian population, qualify as crimes against humanity making them crimes under international criminal law subject to universal jurisdiction. While terrorism is a clear threat to human rights, an effective international strategy to counterterrorism must not itself violate the human rights of innocent persons:

> The suggestion that human rights violations are permissible in certain circumstances is wrong. The essence of human rights is that human life and dignity must not be compromised and that certain acts, whether carried out by State or non-State actors, are never justified no matter what the ends. International human rights and humanitarian law define the boundaries of permissible political and military conduct. [ibid., para. 5]

In this regard, the report points to three areas of concern: recent antiterrorism legislation, the targeting of particular groups, and discrimination [ibid., para. 8].

The report notes that Security Council Resolution 1373 creates an important legal framework for counterterrorism cooperation between states to ensure that there should be no safe haven for those who plan, support, or commit terrorist acts. The Counter-Terrorism Committee of the Security Council has issued guidelines for the submission of reports on the steps taken to implement this resolution. To assist the Committee in this process, OHCHR has formulated proposals for "further guidance" for states in complying with their international human rights obligations [Annex, E/CN.4/2002/18, p. 17–21]. These guidelines set out detailed criteria for the balancing of human rights protection and the combating of terrorism.

Robinson's report endorses the concept of "human security," for the reason that it places "individuals and their universal rights at the centre of national and global security policies" and encourages a "comprehensive strategy to address the causes of insecurity, not only its consequences and manifestations" [ibid., para. 27–28]. In response to Ignatieff's challenge mentioned at the start of this chapter, the High Commissioner concludes by stating that "[i]n the aftermath of 11 September, some suggested that human rights could be set aside while security was being achieved. Now, however, there is wide recognition that ensuring respect for human rights and dignity throughout the world is the best long-term guarantor of security" [ibid., para. 59].

Country-Specific U.N. Human Rights Actions

While it is not possible to review the full scope of U.N. human rights-related activities in all parts of the world, this section considers a few of the most visible country-specific situations that arose both at the Commission and at the United Nations more generally over the last year.

Afghanistan

The most difficult and daunting country-specific situation on the U.N. human rights agenda is, of course, Afghanistan. The attacks of September 11, and the ensuing U.S.-led military campaign in Afghanistan, have focused world attention on this shattered nation. For the past 23 years, Afghanistan has been subject to foreign interventions leading to a series of brutal wars that have entrenched the power of unaccountable warlords, divided the country along ethnic lines, and destroyed its already weak infrastructure and economic base. During this period, the Afghan people experienced systematic and widespread violations of human rights ranging from political killings to desperate impoverishment. The reconstruction of Afghanistan is now an urgent priority and is being seen as a "litmus test for whether universal values of human rights and development will help define the parameters of global security, or whether the narrow military interests of powerful states will predominate." At stake is "not only the ability of Afghans to enjoy their fundamental rights, but the very legitimacy of the United Nations as the unbiased guardian of international law and guarantor of peace and security for all peoples of the world" [Center for Economic and Social Rights (CESR), *Human Rights and Reconstruction in Afghanistan*, May 2002, p. 1–2].

The United Nations has in fact long been engaged in the country, both in trying to end the inter-Afghan fighting that followed the Soviet withdrawal in 1989 and in delivering humanitarian assistance to large numbers of people in Afghanistan and in refugee camps in neighboring countries. On December 5, 2001, the Bonn Conference concluded successfully, and members of the Security Council received the text of the "Agreement on provisional arrangements in Afghanistan pending the reestablishment of permanent government institutions" (Bonn Agreement) [S/2001/1154], which the Council fully endorsed the following day [S/Res/1383 (2001)]. According to the Secretary-General, the Bonn Agreement represents a "historic opportunity for the people of Afghanistan to emerge from a cycle of conflict and devastating poverty into a future in which there can be reconstruction and peaceful development" [Report of the S.G., *The situation in Afghanistan and its implications for international peace and security*, A/56/875-S/2002/278, March 18, 2002].

The implementation period of the Bonn Agreement is envisaged to last for two to three years and is intended to lead to a full-fledged government chosen freely by the entire electorate of Afghanistan. As of this writing, the Interim Authority chosen at Bonn is headed by Chairman Hamid Karzai and is to be succeeded by a Transitional Authority, selected through an emergency *loya jirga* that is convening in mid-2002. Working with Lakhdar Brahimi, the Secretary-General's Special Representative for Afghanistan, Karzai has already commenced the arduous and wide-ranging work of rebuilding the country. The Bonn Agreement calls for the United Nations to assist in the establishment of an independent Human Rights Commission and a Judicial Commission. Together these bodies will have the task of ensuring that international human rights law and standards are implemented in the particular social, political, and cultural context of Afghanistan. The advancement of the rights and participation of women—and the integration of a gender perspective—will be a primary focus for these institutions. In this regard, the OHCHR has seconded a human rights adviser to the Office of the Special Representative in Kabul to provide advice in the initial stages of developing a human rights program. In addition, the ongoing work of the Special Rapporteur on Afghanistan, Kamal Hossain, is integral to this process.

On March 9, 2002, a national workshop on human rights, opened by Mary Robinson, was convened in Kabul with participants representing a wide spectrum of Afghan society, numerous human rights NGOs, and institutions. The workshop produced four working groups to formulate proposals for (a) the establishment of the independent Human Rights Commission; (b) the development of a national program of human rights education; (c) approaches to human rights monitoring, investigation, and remedial action; and (d) the advancement of the rights of women. Difficult questions of accountability for human rights and humanitarian law violations, and transitional justice more broadly (including proposals for the establishment of a Truth Commission to uncover the atrocities committed over two decades of war), are sure to be a major part of these proposals. Interestingly, the Security Council has sought to link development aid to improved human rights performance [S/Res/1401, March 28, 2002]. It is clear that the $4.5 billion reconstruction process will be a test case for a rights-based development approach that prioritizes basic needs, guarantees local participation, addresses the root causes of poverty, and establishes effective procedures for accountability and remedies for victims.

Beyond Kabul, the overall human rights situation in Afghanistan remains appalling. There have been reports of civilian massacres involving reprisal killings, summary executions, and the taking and retaking of areas by warring factions. In many areas of the country, gross violations of the human rights of women and girls continue, including rape and other forms of sexual violence, abductions and kidnappings, as well as forced marriages and trafficking. The existence of millions of Afghan refugees and internally displaced persons is also creating great insecurity and instability in the country. Pending the creation of a national army, U.S. and U.K. unwillingness to expand the International Security Assistance Force (ISAF) beyond Kabul to other major cities and surrounding areas has allowed these violations to continue largely unchecked.

Each of these factors has been recognized by the General Assembly [*Question of human rights in Afghanistan*, A/Res/56/176, February 7, 2002] and the 2002 Commission on Human Rights [*The situation of human rights in Afghanistan*, Commission on H.R. Res/2002/19, E/CN.4/2002/L.31, April 22, 2002]. The Secretary-General has also urged the Security Council to "support the wish of the Afghan people for the expansion of the [ISAF]" so as to minimize the "likelihood of large-scale hostilities erupting again between existing armed factions" [A/56/875-S/2002/278, pp. 9, 21]. According to a recent independent mission to Afghanistan, "without an international force to maintain peace, disarm warlords, oversee the transition to a more representative government, and establish mechanisms for human rights accountability, Afghanistan is likely to slide into renewed war once the world's attention shifts to the next global crisis" [CESR, Human Rights and Reconstruction in Afghanistan, May 2002, p. 2]. Thus, until the overall human security situation in the country is adequately addressed, the broad scope of activities of the U.N. Assistance Mission in Afghanistan (UNAMA)—political, human rights and rule of law, gender, relief, recovery, and reconstruction—will remain at risk of unraveling.

China

For only the second time since 1990, a China resolution was not introduced at the Commission on Human Rights. On March 11, 2002, the E.U. foreign ministers met in Brussels and expressed concern about the "lack of respect for human rights in China, including the freedoms of expression, religion, and association," but at the Commission the European Union declined to sponsor a resolution. Without a seat on the Commission, the United States could not be an original sponsor of a resolution. Despite the conspicuous absence of a China resolution, many argue that China warrants increased U.N. attention as its human rights record has deteriorated over the past year. According to one NGO, the "Chinese government's preoccupation with stability in the face of continued social

and economic upheaval has fueled an increase in human rights violations"
[*Principal Concerns of Human Rights Watch for the 58th Session of the United Nations Commission on Human Rights*, Memorandum to Member States and Observer States of the CHR, 2001].

Russia (Chechnya)

For a number of years, separatist rebels have been seeking control of the province of Chechnya in the southeast region of the Russian Federation, with a view to political and legal independence from Russia. In response to Chechen armed incursions into the neighboring republic of Dagestan and several bombings in Russia, in September 1999 the Russian government launched what it termed an "antiterrorist" operation in Chechnya based on its 1998 Law on the Suppression of Terrorism. Section 3 of that law defines such operations as "special activities aimed at the prevention of terrorist acts, ensuring the security of individuals, neutralizing terrorists and minimizing the consequences of terrorist acts." Thus, well before the events of September 11, the militarization of counterterrorism efforts and the shadowy line between "terrorists" and "freedom fighters" were already controversial and urgent questions on the human rights agenda in Russia.

For the purposes of the Chechen operation, the Russian government has deployed Ministry of Defense troops and riot police. The riot police units are also called "temporary police" as they are staffed by police officers sent to Chechnya for limited periods from various regions in Russia. The regular police departments are staffed by Chechen police officers, who do not directly participate in antiterrorist operations. These police departments are weak; many Chechen police officers have neither weapons nor access to vehicles or other equipment. The 1998 Law gives extensive powers to antiterrorist units. It allows officials involved in antiterrorist operations to perform random identification checks and detain indefinitely individuals without proper identity documents. It allows them to freely enter homes, search vehicles, perform body searches, restrict or prohibit the movement of persons and vehicles, and use any means of communication and transportation belonging to private individuals.

In this context, the failure of the Commission this year to pass a resolution condemning the Russian Federation's ongoing military and police actions in Chechnya represents arguably the greatest casualty of the events of September 11. The Russian government has rejected the Commission's previous resolution requiring steps to be taken to curb serious abuses in Chechnya (including forced disappearances, extra-judicial executions, and torture) and to start a meaningful domestic accountability process [H.R. Comm. Res. 2001/24]. Russia has also failed to establish an independent commission of inquiry or invite several of the Commission's ad hoc monitoring mechanisms (including the Special Rapporteurs on torture and extra-judicial, summary, or arbitrary executions) [Report of the High Commissioner in accordance with Res. 2001/24, E/CN.4/2002/38, February 26, 2002]. This follows Russia's rejection of a similar resolution passed at the 56th Commission. It has also been noted that Chechen rebels have ignored the Commission's calls to respect international humanitarian law [HRW, Oral Statement at UNHCR 58th Session, Item 9 of Provisional Agenda: Russia/Chechnya]. As a result, civilians in Chechnya suffer from both ruthless sweep operations by Russian troops and brutal guerrilla tactics employed by rebel fighters. Human rights groups have continued to document the arbitrary detention of thousands of people and the torture and ill treatment of many of them.

These failures have created a situation of almost complete impunity in relation to the Chechen conflict. As of May 2001, of the 358 cases of alleged abuses against civilians under investigation for the Council of Europe, 11 have been brought to trial resulting in only five prison sentences. The majority of investigations into widespread and systematic rights abuses by Ministry of Defence personnel conducted by the military procuracy have been suspended or closed. In "disappearance" cases, as many as 79 percent of the investigations have been suspended; the criminal investigation list does not include a single case of torture or inhuman treatment. The high profile trial of Yuri Budanov, a former colonel and tank commander charged with abducting and murdering an 18-year-old Chechen woman in March 2000, has been recessed on numerous occasions. Following the finding by a psychiatric institution that Budanov was "emotionally distressed" at the time of the murder, the charge was reduced to manslaughter opening the way for Budanov to receive amnesty.

Cuba

For several years, the U.S. government has sponsored and gathered co-sponsors for resolutions critical of the human rights situation in Cuba. Cuba has a deplorable track record with regard to U.N. human rights monitoring mechanisms, having denied access to the U.N. Special Rapporteur on Cuba for several years (until the rapporteur's mandate was finally discontinued). At the 56th Commission last year, Cuba sought to discredit the report of the Special Rapporteur on Violence against Women, Radhika Coomaraswamy [E/CN.4/2000/131]. Nevertheless, a resolution was passed expressing concern about continuing human rights violations in Cuba, the ninth such resolution passed since 1991. It urges the government to invite the U.N. Special Rapporteurs on torture and on freedom of expression to visit the country. In the resolution, the Commission noted that Cuba had made "no satisfactory improvements" in the area of human rights. It expressed particular concern at the "continued repression of members of the political opposition." The resolution also expressed concern about the "detention of dissidents and all other persons detained or imprisoned for peacefully expressing their political, religious, and social views and for exercising their right to full and equal participation in public affairs." (An early draft of the resolution criticized the U.S. economic embargo on Cuba, but that language was omitted from the final version [HRW, *Cuba* chapter in *World Report 2002*].) The resolution, which was sponsored by the Czech Republic, passed by a 22–20 vote, with a number of abstentions.

At this year's session of the Commission, a resolution on Cuba was again narrowly passed by 23 votes to 21, with 9 abstentions [H.R. Comm. Res. 2002/18, April 19, 2002]. The resolution invited Cuba to make similar efforts to achieve progress in the area of "human, civil and political rights," as it had to give "effect to the social rights of the population despite an adverse international environment [which were] to be recognized." The resolution further requested the High Commissioner for Human Rights to send a personal representative with a "view to cooperation between her Office and the Government of Cuba in the implementation of the present resolution" [ibid.].

During the session on Cuba on April 19, 2002, the statement of Cuban delegate Juan Antonio Fernandez reflected the politics of the Commission. Palacios stated that the United States needed the Cuban resolution to "justify its genocidal policy of economic blockade against Cuba, and had secretly and conspiratorially drafted" other Latin American countries reflecting their "full surrender and complete subordination to Washington's dictates." After the passage of the resolution, Cuba's foreign relations with Mexico (which had voted for the resolution, rather than abstaining as usual) were thrown into turmoil when Cuban President Fidel Castro released a tape of a March 19 private telephone conversation that he had with Mexican President Vicente Fox. Apparently at the urging of the United States, Fox asked Castro "to help me as a friend," by cutting short his visit to the U.N. International Conference on Financing for Development (held March 18–22 in Monterrey, Mexico). While it appears unlikely that diplomatic relations will be severed between the two countries, on April 22, Castro labeled the Uruguayan government a "stale and abject Judas" for its sponsorship of the resolution against Cuba. Uruguayan President Jorge Batlle responded the next day by breaking off diplomatic relations with Cuba until such time as "the Cuban people have peace and freedom."

Finally, without specifically mentioning the long-standing U.S. trade embargo on Cuba, the Commission this year passed a resolution by 38 votes to 6 on "Human Rights and unilateral coercive measures" [Comm. on H.R. Res. 2002/22, April 22, 2002]. The resolution urged all states to "refrain from adopting or implementing unilateral measures not in accordance with international law and the Charter of the United Nations, in particular those of a coercive nature with extraterritorial effects, which create obstacles to trade relations among States" [ibid.]. In particular, the resolution rejected the application of such measures as "tools for political or economic pressure against any country, particularly against developing countries, because of their negative effects on the realization of all human rights of vast sectors of their populations" [ibid.]. On November 27, 2001, the General Assembly adopted the tenth resolution in as many years by 167 votes in favor, 3 against (Israel, Marshall Islands, and the United States), with three abstentions on the need to "end the economic, commercial and financial embargo imposed by the United States on Cuba" [A/Res/56/9 (2001)].

Iraq

A significant breakthrough was achieved in the context of U.N. relations with Iraq when in January 2002 the Iraqi government announced that it would accept a visit by the Special Rapporteur on the situation of human rights in Iraq. (The visit occurred from February 11–15, 2002.) The subsequent report of the Special Rapporteur makes various recommendations, including calls for a moratorium on executions; reductions in the number of crimes that carry the death penalty, including the trafficking of women and exploitation of women for prostitution; the improvement of conditions on death row and prison conditions in general; greater respect for freedom of religion; continuation of dialogue between the Ministry of Foreign Affairs and the Special Rapporteur; the abolition of the Special Courts and adherence at all times to international human rights law; and the elimination of discrimination against ethnic or religious groups [E/CN.4/2002/44, March 15, 2002]. The Special Rapporteur also considered the humanitarian situation in the country and expressed concern about the effects of ongoing U.N. sanctions. He noted that while the oil-for-food program provided the population with sufficient food, "general poverty still exists in the country, and many persons suffer from malnourishment as they are forced to sell their food rations to purchase medicines, clothing etc." The lack of water, sanitation, and electricity were also highlighted as serious problems.

At the Commission this year, a resolution on the situation of human rights in Iraq was adopted by a roll-call vote of 28 in favor, 4 opposed, with 21 abstentions. The Commission strongly condemned the systematic, widespread, and grave violations of human rights and international humanitarian law by the government of Iraq (including summary and arbitrary executions, the use of rape as a political tool, enforced disappearances, arbitrary arrests, and systematic torture). It called upon the government to cooperate with the U.N. human rights mechanisms and decided to extend the mandate of the Special Rapporteur for a further year.

Finally, on the blurred distinction between "international terrorism" and "freedom fighters," Iraq has consistently argued before the United Nations that it is the victim of two acts of "terrorism." First, it is a victim of the "continued and unjust sanctions imposed by the United States through the Security Council" resulting in the loss of "more than a million and six hundred thousand of its innocent children, women and the elderly" [G.A./9927, October 4, 2001]. Second, as a result of U.S.-trained groups of mercenaries carrying out "terrorist operations inside cities, such as explosions and assassinations aimed at destabilizing Iraq" [ibid.]. Iraq has further argued that it cannot consider the "legitimate struggle of the Palestinian people against occupation, and Zionist aggression as terrorism."

On August 14, 2001, Iraq sent a *note verbale* on the issue of "terrorism and human rights" to the Sub-Commission on the Promotion and Protection of Human Rights. In it, Iraq alleged that in 1998, the U.S. Congress "passed the so-called 'Iraq Liberation Act' under which $97 million were allocated to fund a group of mercenaries, hirelings of the United States intelligence services, so that they could carry out acts of terrorism and sabotage inside Iraq with a view to disrupting order and security and killing its innocent civilians" [E/CN.4/Sub.2/2001/37]. Iraq further alleged that the ongoing aerial bombardment of "residential areas and civilian infrastructure" by U.S. and U.K. aircraft had resulted in the death or injuries of "more than 350,000 civilians" [ibid.].

Israeli-Occupied Territories

Over the last year, the situation between the Israelis and Palestinians has deteriorated rapidly creating a tragedy characterized by total disregard on both sides for human rights and humanitarian law.

On March 6, 2002, the Special Rapporteur on the situation of human rights in the Palestinian territories occupied by Israel since 1967, John Dugard, issued a report on the basis of visits made to the area in August 2001 and February 2002 [E/CN.4/2002/32]. Dugard was appointed by the Commission in July 2001 to investigate violations of international humanitarian law and human rights in the context of military occupation. The report begins by noting that while terrorism is a "scourge that threatens Israelis and Palestinians alike, . . . it is important to stress that the main explanation for the acts of terrorism committed by Palestinians against Israelis is the military occupation," which is "responsible for most of the violations of humanitarian law and human rights in the region" [ibid.]. The report recommends the urgent need for an international peacekeeping mission in the region; the cessation of the continuing expansion of existing settlements and the demolition of houses in Palestinian territory (in the Gaza Strip alone, over 400 houses have been completely destroyed leaving over 5,000 persons homeless); the easing of restrictions on freedom of movement resulting from checkpoints and "closures" that have caused great personal, social, and economic hardships to civilians in violation of the Fourth Geneva Convention; and better measures to ensure the safety and welfare of schools and schoolchildren [ibid.].

In response to this and related reports, the Israeli government has challenged the mandate of the Special Rapporteur. It argues that the situation in the Palestinian Territory is not one of *military* occupation and that the Rapporteur is only empowered to investigate violations of humanitarian and not human rights law [E/CN.4/2002/129]. Israel has further refused to allow the High Commissioner for Human Rights to undertake a visiting mission to the Palestinian Territories, a situation that has undermined the Commission's credibility and competency. Israel has also refused to cooperate with a fact-finding mission initiated by the Secretary-General and authorized by the U.N. Security Council on April 19, 2002, to investigate the "unknown number of deaths and destruction" in the Jenin refugee camp [S/Res/1405 (2002)]. While the Security Council has officially endorsed a "vision of a region where two States, Israel and Palestine, live side by side within secure and recognized borders" [S/Res/1397 (2002)], that vision remains as elusive as ever, with tragic consequences for human rights on both sides.

Other Countries and Thematic Issues
Other pressing country-specific situations of concern to the U.N. human rights system include several African countries, such as Algeria, Democratic Republic of Congo (DRC), Egypt, Sierra Leone, Sudan, and Zimbabwe. In particular, there is an urgent need in the DRC to investigate and ensure responsibility for grave violations of human rights and humanitarian law, especially in relation to sexual and gender-based violence [S/Res/1376 (2001)]. Other countries such as Colombia, Iran, Saudi Arabia, Turkmenistan, and Uzbekistan also pose enormous challenges and obstacles to the more effective promotion and protection of human rights. Finally, the issue of widespread and systematic violations of international human rights and humanitarian law in Indonesia remains a volatile situation. Perhaps more than any other country-specific situation, various conflicts in Indonesia fall squarely into the "gap" discussed previously between an internal armed conflict (which falls below the Protocol II threshold) and a state of emergency (which opens the possibility for derogations of fundamental human rights).

In relation to thematic issues, the reports of the various Special Rapporteurs and other officials presented to this year's Commission reveal the full breadth of U.N. human rights work. Thematic areas include violence against women and the integration of the human rights of women and the gender perspective [E/CN.4/2002/83/Add.1]; promotion and protection of human rights defenders [E/CN.4/2002/106]; religious intolerance; rights-based development; economic, social, and cultural rights; minority rights; indigenous rights; racism, racial discrimination, xenophobia, and all forms of discrimination; torture and detention; disappearances and summary executions; freedom of expression; independence of the judiciary; states of emergency; self-determination; and the rights of the child.

On the issue of children's rights, from May 8–10, 2002, world leaders gathered for the U.N. General Assembly Special Session on Children, which is a follow-up to the 1990 World Summit on Children. At both the special session and preparatory committee meetings, the U.S. negotiating position generated great concern among other countries, participating NGOs, and civil society actors. In particular, the United States consistently sought to eliminate or minimize references to the Convention on the Rights of the Child (CRC) in the Declaration and Plan of Action. It has also refused to accept language that refers to the CRC as the primary international standard for the promotion and protection of children's rights. (The CRC is the most universally ratified treaty in history, with 191 states parties; as noted above, only the United States and Somalia are not currently parties.) The United States has further sought to roll back international agreements to provide adolescents with sexual and reproductive health education and services, arguing that the word "services" is another word for "abortion." The basis of the U.S. position appears to center on the claim that the CRC will undermine parental authority, interfere with the parents' ability to raise and discipline their children, and elevate the rights of children above the rights of parents. The most serious conflict between the CRC and U.S. law, however, is in relation to the death penalty for offenses committed before the age of 18. In the last five years, nine executions of juvenile offenders were carried out in the United States. (The DRC and Iran are the only other states to have carried out such executions in the last three years.)

With the need greater than ever before for a truly universal and international human rights regime, it is hoped that the U.S. attitude of exceptionalism and unilateralism will give way to greater multilateral cooperation and respect for international law. As Human Rights Watch argues in the introduction to its 2002 World Report:

> hypocrisy matters because it is profoundly more difficult to promote values of human rights if some of the most visible and powerful proponents seek to exempt themselves from these same standards. This exceptionalism remains strong after September 11, as governments seek to justify extraordinary constraints on rights in the name of combating extraordinary threats. Yet in the long term, this trend is counterproductive. If the logic of terrorism, not just immediate terrorist threats, is ultimately to be defeated, governments must redouble their commitment to international standards, not indulge in a new round of excuses to ignore them.

2. Humanitarian Assistance
By Dennis Dijkzeul

The relationship between humanitarian assistance and security has shifted rapidly since the terrorist attacks of September 11, 2001. To better understand this new and intertwined relationship, it is important to examine the background of humanitarian activities during the past decade in several humanitarian crises, especially in Afghanistan.

Since the end of the Cold War, the world has witnessed an outbreak of "internal" conflicts, in contrast to the earlier pattern of conflicts between states with standing armies. Initially, it appeared that these conflicts stemmed from ethnic or religious tensions with the goal to exterminate or disempower certain populations. Later analysis revealed that small but powerful individuals and groups, such as warlords, militias, and governing elites, manipulated many of these conflicts for economic gain [see D. Keen, *The Benefits of Famine,* 1994; M. Kaldor, *New and Old Wars: Organized Violence in a Global Era,* 2001]. Examples of predatory war economies include Sierra Leone with timber and blood diamonds, Angola with oil and blood diamonds, the Democratic Republic of Congo (DRC) with illegal mining and timber, and Colombia with drugs. In addition, as states have disintegrated, disciplined armies, controlled by either a strong government or a dominant ideology, have become increasingly rare. The fragmentation of warring groups has made them difficult to control. Frequently, the distinction between armed forces and civilians, between perpetrators and victims has blurred. As a result, the number of civilian casualties, refugees, and Internally Displaced Persons (IDPs) has increased dramatically. Through refugee flows, economic decline, and arms trafficking, several conflicts have spilled over into neighboring countries, spreading instability regionally (for example, Western Africa, the Great Lakes region, and Central Asia). Many conflicts became chronic emergencies [see J. Macrae, *Aiding Recovery: The Crisis of Aid in Chronic Political Emergencies,* 2001].

Not surprisingly, the U.N. system has faced huge operational challenges while addressing these conflicts. On the one hand, it had to alleviate the immediate humanitarian needs of local populations. On the other, it had to achieve sustainable peace, through prevention, peacekeeping, or developmental work. This resulted in the break down of ingrained, institutional division within the U.N. system, previously structured into separate short-term, humanitarian relief organizations, security institutions, and long-term development agencies.

In response to these mounting challenges, many humanitarian organizations—both nongovernmental organizations (NGOs) and U.N. agencies—decided in the early 1990s that they should involve security elements more than before. Thus, they attempted to influence member state representatives on the Security Council, asked for military protection in certain conflicts, and, in their advocacy, paid more attention to the security establishment in their respective countries. In essence, they aimed to "humanitarianize" the security agenda that had hitherto focused on interstate war.

As a consequence, peacekeeping and humanitarian action fundamentally changed in character. Before the end of the Cold War, so-called "first-generation peacekeeping" put lightly armed Blue Helmets on a demarcation line once the fighting ended. Diplomats would then work out peace accords [Ratner, *The New U.N. Peacekeeping,* 1994]. Some of these operations, for example on Cyprus, have continued for years. In these contexts, humanitarian action was generally not part of the peacekeeping mandate. Humanitarian organizations focused independently on the protection of refugees, as well as on the provision of food, water, shelter, and medicine. The success of their actions depended crucially on rapid response, political neutrality and impartiality, and the provision of relief on the basis of need and without discrimination [J. Barry and A. Jefferys, *Bridge Too Far: Aid Agencies and the Military in Humanitarian Response,* HPN Network Paper 37, 2002, p. 11]. The humanitarian organizations would quickly come in, do their job, save lives, and leave. To optimize their aid delivery, humanitarian actors tried to remain independent of political and military actors.

In the 1990s, however, peacekeeping and humanitarian action increasingly overlapped and took place *during* conflicts. In this new generation of peacekeeping, military actors, humanitarian organizations, and diplomats interact more intensely over longer periods of time. However, most activities remain organizationally under the U.N. umbrella and were based on Chapter VI of the U.N. Charter. So-called "second-generation peacekeeping" is generally more about rebuilding with a security component than about pure military action. The characteristics of these interstate conflicts caused great operational problems, in particular with linking relief and reconstruction, and with understanding local actors in their political context. Member states often abdicated responsibilities to the United Nations and international NGOs and did not provide sufficient diplomatic and financial support. At the same time, the U.N. system often lacked management capacity. So, despite ambitious agendas for peace, the actual capacity to secure peace was often inadequate.

Specific problems occurred with peace enforcement under Chapter VII of the U.N. Charter. In Somalia, for example, peace enforcement backfired. The Security Council approved other peacekeeping operations (PKOs) for the Gulf War and for the conflicts in Rwanda, Haiti, Bosnia and Herzegovina, Albania, Kosovo, and East Timor.

> [T]he UN did not control the Chapter VII enforcement operations; they have always been implemented by either a single country or a group of countries. In addition to UN-sanctioned operations, there have been several "unilateral interventions" that have not enjoyed Security Council authorization. NATO's Operation Allied Force against Yugoslavia in March–June 1999 is perhaps the [best]-known recent example of such a unilateral intervention, which was essentially "self-mandated" by the NATO Council, the Alliance's political leadership.

Only after the air strikes ended on 10 June did the Security Council retrospectively authorize the operation. [ibid., p. 3]

NATO justified its military attacks in the Federal Republic of Yugoslavia (FRY) as a humanitarian intervention. When the bombings ended and NATO forces entered Kosovo, the military also played a large role in the provision of humanitarian aid. This has raised issues as to what constituted a "humanitarian intervention." The first question is whether an intervention via military *means* should properly be termed "humanitarian." The second question involves the *ends* sought by the intervention [*A Global Agenda: Issues/56*, p. 191]. Put differently, is there such a thing as a "humanitarian war"? The principles, objectives, and effectiveness of military involvement need to be studied in detail. In particular, military attacks under the heading of humanitarian intervention deserve close scrutiny. The positions in the debate on military involvement varied from a principled decline of a military role in humanitarian crises to a working out of an optimal division of labor and the establishment of a better mutual understanding of civil and military actors.

The military operations in Afghanistan in response to the September 11 terrorist attacks went another step further. The United States and United Kingdom bypassed NATO, but notified the U.N. Security Council about their operation in Afghanistan. During the bombings, before the ground operations, the United States also carried out "humanitarian" airdrops. Was this a humanitarian action to alleviate human suffering, or was it the final indication that security concerns trumped the humanitarian agenda? Does it imply that humanitarian action has become a means to win war? Or does it imply that some states have become serious about assisting and protecting vulnerable populations, even with military force? Combining attacks with food relief goes beyond an optimal division of labor between military and nonmilitary actors. For humanitarians, the use of military force has ominous implications for neutrality and impartiality. Without multilateral U.N. Security Council approval and consent of the warring parties, such military action hampers humanitarian activities on the ground. Even humanitarian organizations that operate independently from the military may then risk being perceived locally as partners to the foreign military presence.

The fall of the Taliban regime also gave rise to a new set of questions regarding the rebuilding of Afghanistan. In short, who wins the peace in Afghanistan? Should the military have a role in reconstruction? Can soldiers carry out humanitarian work while fighting continues? If they have a humanitarian role, can they carry arms while dressed as civilians? In this context, the role of the military in linking relief and development comes to the fore. Once again, speed, neutrality, and impartiality can be compromised. This is also relevant to other complex emergencies with military involvement, such as in Kosovo, Macedonia, and other countries where the "war on terrorism" might continue.

Management and Funding

Funding is a major determining factor in the success or failure of humanitarian actions. If neutrality and impartiality were fully realized, humanitarian assistance would be provided solely on the basis of need, determined on a case-by-case basis. However, needs are not objective realities; they always imply a judgment about the state of the victims and their society.

Generally, all U.N. agencies and some international NGOs cooperate in the Consolidated Appeal Process (CAP) to obtain voluntary funding. Some U.N. agencies also rely partly on assessed contributions. The CAP appeals are made to donor governments for individual countries or specific situations where humanitarian relief is needed. The CAP process originated in the early 1990s to integrate all of the different proposals from different organizations in a more common approach. The U.N. system, in particular the Office for the Coordination of Humanitarian Affairs (OCHA), has worked hard to improve the CAP process. Today, CAPs provide in-depth country information on the humanitarian situation. The 2002 Inter-Agency Consolidated Appeals funding indicates that resources made available to U.N. agencies and NGOs over the course of the last ten years have consistently and severely fallen short of the stated requirements. This year is certainly no exception to this rule of chronic underfunding.

From 1992 through 2000, total funding mirrored the pattern of requirements, but leading into 2002, in the wake of the events of September 11, 2001, many humanitarian organizations and regions have found themselves marginalized and in greater need than ever. Consuming as the crisis in Afghanistan has been, however, some sectors have maintained funding, some even seeing moderate increases, though not in proportion to their respective requirements. In other words, the rate increase of requirements outpaced the rate increase in funding.

Between 2001 and 2002, funding made available to OCHA and the World Food Programme (WFP) has decreased, but in step with their decreasing stated requirements. In contrast, funding for the U.N. High Commissioner for Refugees (UNHCR) has increased, but at a decreasing rate relative to its requirements. From a sector perspective (see chart), agriculture, economic recovery and infrastructure, education, mine action, and family shelter and nonfood items have realized moderate increases in funding. However, funding has eroded in the areas of coordination and support services, food, health, protection of human rights and the rule of law, security, and water and sanitation [2002 Inter-Agency Consolidated Appeals].

Figure I-1

Total Requirements Vs. Total Funding 1992 – 2002

As of March 26, 2002 (Data source: UNOCHA, Consolidated Inter-Agency Appeals 2002)

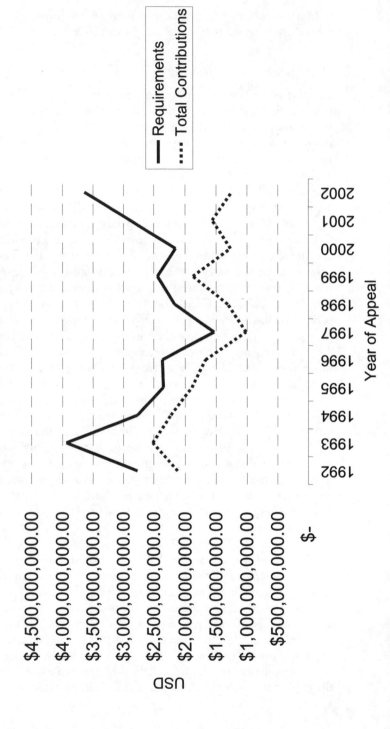

Table I-1: 2002 Consolidated Inter-Agency Humanitarian Assistance Appeals Summary of Requirements and Contributions by Affected Country/Region

As of March 26, 2002

Compiled by OCHA on the basis of information provided by the respective appealing organizations.

Affected Country/Region	Requirements (US$)	Contributions/Pledges (US$)	Carry Over (US$)	Total resources available (US$)	Shortfall (US$)	Requirements covered (%)	Implementation period
Angola	232,768,666	23,773,759	0	23,773,759	208,994,907	10.20	Jan-02–Dec-02
Burundi	107,865,224	1,667,106	0	1,667,106	106,198,118	1.50	Jan-02–Dec-02
Democratic Republic of the Congo	194,140,365	12,979,943	0	12,979,943	181,160,422	6.70	Jan-02–Dec-02
DPR Korea	258,136,111	22,013,539	0	22,013,539	236,122,572	8.50	Jan-02–Dec-02
Eritrea	120,463,547	1,616,156	0	1,616,156	118,847,391	1.30	Jan-02–Dec-02
Great Lakes Region and Central Africa	13,062,255	698,643	0	698,643	12,363,612	5.30	Jan-02–Dec-02
Guinea	58,470,746	1,521,650	0	1,521,650	56,949,096	2.60	Jan-02–Dec-02
Indonesia	40,795,472	7,395,501	0	7,395,501	33,399,971	18.10	Jan-02–Dec-02
ITAP for the Afghan People	1,763,894,630	660,304,521	0	660,304,521	1,103,590,109	37.40	Jan-02–Dec-02
Liberia	17,232,575	143,287	0	143,287	17,089,288	8.00	Jan-02–Dec-02
North Caucasus	31,946,549	4,339,766	0	4,339,766	27,606,783	13.60	Jan-02–Dec-02
Republic of Congo	33,935,923	766,572	0	766,572	33,169,351	2.30	Jan-02–Dec-02
Sierra Leone	88,624,925	2,745,127	0	2,745,127	85,879,798	3.10	Jan-02–Dec-02
Somalia	83,683,971	6,412,954	0	6,412,954	77,271,017	7.70	Jan-02–Dec-02
Southeastern Europe	236,654,801	2,917,348	806,764	3,724,112	232,930,689	1.60	Jan-02–Dec-02
Sudan	250,177,962	10,022,367	0	10,022,367	240,155,595	4.00	Jan-02–Dec-02
Tajikistan	76,556,685	894,045	0	894,045	75,662,640	1.20	Jan-02–Dec-02
Uganda	68,103,410	1,087,567	0	1,087,567	67,015,843	1.60	Jan-02–Dec-02
West Africa	5,873,538	88,273	0	88,273	5,785,265	1.50	Jan-02–Dec-02
Grand Total	**3,682,387,355**	**761,388,124**	**806,764**	**762,194,888**	**2,920,192,467**	**20.70**	

Historically, it appears that donor responses to crises have been clouded by regional bias and an inequitable relationship between the severity of crises and the funding made available to address them. High profile or nearby crises drew more from donor coffers than less well-publicized crises, and many areas have suffered dramatically as a result, indicating at least in part the effects of "donor fatigue." Burundi, for example, saw the percentage of its funding decrease from 47.83 to 16.85 percent; Angola, 50.01 to 27.68 percent; Democratic Republic of Congo, 66.74 to 11.16 percent; and Sudan, 61.81 to 6.46 percent [ibid.]. Although more funding is anticipated this year, it is unlikely that the decrease will be offset by new donations. In addition, most donors prefer not to fund overhead costs, although such funding is necessary to build management capacities and substantive competencies, for example, in public health and water and sanitation.

Tracking the amounts of funding is the most practical way to distinguish donor government rhetoric from action. It is plausible, if not altogether likely, that the trend of decreasing funding will continue into 2003 as the world's attention fixes on the events unfolding in the Middle East and Afghanistan. At the same time, crises in other regions of the world may grow more pronounced in the absence of humanitarian funding and international political attention. As a result, institutional imperatives such as access to resources, substantive competencies, and managerial capacity influence the decisions of humanitarian organizations to launch a humanitarian intervention. "Perhaps contrary to the rather utopian Red Cross/NGO Code of Conduct, which states that 'aid priorities are calculated on the basis of needs alone,' the final decision will always require a principled choice, involving careful consideration of 'in-country' humanitarian imperatives in relation to 'external' institutional imperatives" [M. Oxley, *Measuring Humanitarian Need, ODI HPN Report*, January 7, 2002]. For organizations that want to operate independently or at arms-length from the military, these choices have become harder, especially when donor governments tie their aid to conditions about types of projects, vendors, and cooperating partners (including the military).

U.N. Humanitarian Assistance Around the World

The United Nations provides humanitarian assistance in many parts of the world, in particular Afghanistan, the Democratic Republic of Congo (DRC), Burundi, Sierra Leone and its neighbors, Sudan, Angola, Ethiopia and Eritrea, the Federal Republic of Yugoslavia (FRY), Kosovo, Macedonia, Colombia, Sri Lanka, Indonesia, and East Timor. Chechnya, as part of Russia, receives less international attention.

Afghanistan

In its 23 years of civil conflict, Afghanistan has become the quintessential example of the consequences of both international neglect and attention. During the Soviet invasion, one of the more heated episodes of the Cold War, "humanitarian assistance . . . was parallel to and became inextricably linked with U.S. covert operations and, to a lesser extent, [with] . . . other western governments to provide military assistance to the mujahidin" [A. Donini, *The Politics of Mercy: UN Coordination in Afghanistan, Mozambique, and Rwanda*, Occasional Paper #22, Watson Institute, Brown University, Providence, RI, p. 26]. The mujahidin included fighters who set up al-Qaeda and the Taliban. After the overthrow of the communist regime, internecine fighting continued, but international neglect set in. "By the end of 1993, the United States had decided that Afghanistan was no longer of strategic interest and abruptly left the scene, creating formidable problems for its NGO implementing partners," in health care, for example [ibid., p. 51]. The conditions for the ultimate blowback had slowly been created; by 1996, the Taliban had risen to power; only in the North did the alliance under Massoud still hold control. In the late 1990s, "reports mounted of drug trafficking, the export of terrorism, and grave human rights abuses" in Taliban-controlled Afghanistan [SC/7824]. Aid to Afghanistan diminished, even though it faced the longest drought in living memory, and the Security Council imposed sanctions [S/Res/1267(1999); S/Res/1333(2000)]. To a surprising extent, however, the Taliban did cut down on opium production in 2000 and 2001.

When the United States and its allies attacked al-Qaeda and the Taliban, they responded by closing off the country and evicting foreign humanitarian officials, further aggravating the dire humanitarian situation. During air raids, U.S. forces dropped both bombs and humanitarian food packages. This raised serious fears in the humanitarian community about "mixing arms with aid." The air drops were criticized in terms of their legitimacy—this was not a proper role for the military and constituted a propaganda tool that negatively affected impartiality, neutrality, and effectiveness. Airdrops were extremely expensive and did not reach the neediest (women, children, elderly, and handicapped). Only the strongest people, frequently armed men with means of transport, were able to collect the packets. Nor were the food contents (e.g., peanut butter) adapted to the local culture. In addition, finding the packets was dangerous, as they could have landed in minefields. Moreover, the packets were of the same yellow color as cluster bombs. Other military actions also gravely concerned humanitarians; one Red Cross compound was actually bombed twice. Warring factions and bandits also stole a considerable amount of humanitarian supplies and equipment.

When the Taliban regime collapsed sooner than originally expected, sleeping Taliban cells, as well as active pockets of resistance, remained inside Afghanistan and across the border in Pakistan. Despite the ongoing insecurity, humanitarian workers hurried to get in and take action "in response to the approaching Afghan winter and the millions who were without food and shelter" [SC/7266].

In the meantime, the Security Council had approved the strategy of the Secretary-General's Special Representative, Lakhdar Brahimi, to create a stable, peaceful Afghanistan through a broadly based political reconstruction process. Under his guidance, the Bonn Conference, a meeting of the Northern Alliance and other Afghan groups, convened. On December 5, they signed an agreement on provisional political arrangements, pending the reestablishment of permanent government institutions. Amid accusations that some ethnic groups had not been adequately represented in the interim government, its new chair, Hamid Karzai, a Pashtun tribal leader and military commander, arrived in Kabul on December 12, 2001 [ibid.].

The interim government chosen at Bonn will be succeeded by a Transitional Authority, selected by an emergency *loya jirga*, a traditional Afghani council of elders. The *loya jirga* will convene in June 2002. "There have been reports of money being distributed and widespread lobbying by political groups and powerful figures who are trying to get large numbers of their supporters into the emergency *loya jirga*" [A/56/875-S/2002/278, para. 39]. Officially, a conventional *loya jirga* is to ratify a new constitution within 18 months of the establishment of the Transitional Authority [ibid., para. 8]. The Bonn Agreement also provided for an International Security Assistance Force to Afghanistan (ISAF) [S/Res/1386 (2001)].

The tasks that the interim government faced were and continue to be daunting. Ill-equipped, cash-strapped, and inexperienced, it had to deal with the continuing humanitarian crises and it needed to rebuild a deeply divided and impoverished society. The interim government presented its first priorities and proposals to the International Conference on Reconstruction Assistance to Afghanistan in Tokyo in January 2002. More money was pledged at the conference than expected ($4.5 billion pledged for $10 billion requested over the next five years [SG/SM8108, AFG/183 (2002)]), yet only a small amount of the promised money has trickled in [*The Economist*, March 23, 2002, p. 40]. In addition, $1.3 billion was requested for immediate humanitarian needs [United Nations, *Immediate and Transitional Assistance Programme for the Afghan People 2002: Updated financial requirements,* February 2002]. Requests to expand ISAF to other cities [SC/7284 (2002)], which would increase the power of the central government in other regions and enhance security, have not been granted due to resistance by the United States and the United Kingdom. As if these challenges were not enough, in March 2002, Afghanistan had to deal with a locust pest and three earthquakes.

The government is now rebuilding the civil service, but cannot pay recurrent costs, including salaries, without support from the international community. It is also creating a national army, police, and judiciary system. Together with U.N. Children's Fund (UNICEF), U.N. Education, Scientific, and Cultural Organization (UNESCO), and many NGOs, the government launched a back-to-school program on March 23, 2002. "The plan was for a total of 1.8 million children [both boys *and* girls] to return to school on this day and a later million at a later date" [*OCHA Afghanistan Brief*, May 2, 2002].

Still, the international focus and internal progress cannot obscure the fact that millions of Afghans remain dependent on the United Nations and other international organizations for basic lifesaving assistance. Security has improved, but remains compromised with continued fighting, ethnic clashes, and banditry. By May 2002, the United Nations was able to travel in as much as 85 percent of the country [ibid.].

The return of refugees and Internally Displaced Persons (IDPs) went faster than UNHCR and the International Organisation for Migration (IOM) expected, partly because rainfall was better than during the previous three years. Still, many returnees arrived in regions where they face chronic poverty, lack of employment opportunities, and weak social services. Approximately four million refugees still remained in Pakistan and Iran. Within Afghanistan, there were about 785,000 IDPs [ibid.]. Unfortunately, there were also new refugees, mainly Pashtun minorities fleeing persecution in the North.

Chronic malnutrition remained a problem in many parts of Afghanistan. The World Food Programme (WFP) now attempts to secure that additional food items are included in the food packages. Rapid assessment missions by WFP in rural areas also indicated an increasing need for food aid in the pre-harvest hunger period. About 80 percent of the Afghani population depends on subsistence farming, which makes the population vulnerable to the scourges of drought and war. Improving agriculture, through such measures as livestock vaccination, irrigation, crop improvement, and pest control, is essential to the long-term well-being of many returnees. The drought, combined with unsustainable water exploitation, has led to an alarming drop in the water table. "As many as two-thirds of all wells have a low yield or have dried up. Shortages of potable water have negatively impacted on health, hygiene, and food security" [ibid.]. Some humanitarian organizations have protested the role of American soldiers, armed but dressed as civilians, helping to build irrigation projects near Herat.

In May 2002, health monitoring and vaccination (for example, with measles, TB, and polio) were improving. The mine action program also expanded. In addition, new area-based development programs were being developed that combined immediate intervention to alleviate suffering and rebuild livelihoods with longer-term, development-oriented activities.

The U.N. presence in Afghanistan has also begun to restructure in order to achieve greater integration of its expanded activities. The new U.N. Assistance Mission in Afghanistan (UNAMA) absorbed the functions of the former U.N. Office for the Coordination of Humanitarian Affairs to Afghanistan and the U.N. Special Mission to Afghanistan. UNAMA is supposed to work closely with the interim government, in particular the Afghan Assistance Coordination Authority (AACA), which coordinates international assistance [L. Minear, *Humanitarian Action in an Age of Terrorism, Background Paper International Expert Conference*, Arden House, May 24–25, 2002]. Such coordination is necessary with 18 U.N. agencies and several hundred national and international NGOs working in Afghanistan [United Nations, *Immediate and Transitional Assistance Programme for the Afghan People 2002: Updated financial requirements*, February 2002].

The need for humanitarian assistance remains large and the arduous task of rebuilding is a long-term endeavor. Countries around the world have stated that, this time, they will not abandon the people of Afghanistan [A/56/875-S/2002/278, para. 130]. Hopefully, they will follow up on their rhetoric. The situation in Afghanistan illustrates how dangerous it is to neglect countries deemed "strategically irrelevant." Nowadays, the violence of failed states can spread beyond neighboring countries. In addition, earlier action of the great powers can come back to haunt them. A sustained effort by the international community to make peace and create stable, economically viable societies may be the best antidote to terrorism and humanitarian crises.

Democratic Republic of Congo (DRC)

Although the humanitarian situation in the DRC remains dire, the political situation has improved somewhat with international negotiations. There are three main political forces in the DRC: (1) the government under President Joseph Kabila, which receives support from Angola, Zimbabwe, and Namibia, controls the western and southern part of the country; (2) the Movement for the Liberation of Congo (MLC), under Jean-Pierre Bemba, which used to be supported by Uganda, controls the northern region; and (3) the Rwandan-dominated Congolese Rally for Democracy (RCD) controls the East. In addition to these three entities, which are given to internal fighting, there are also many other armed groups, such as the *Interahamwe* (the ex-Rwandan forces) and the *Mayi-Mayi* (local rebels who frequently fight the RCD). Finally, different ethnic groups also fight each other. As a result, the violence is hard to control with many warring factions, which often lack a clear hierarchy and sometimes fragment or shift alliances for short-term economic gain and survival.

The Security Council has asked the international supporters to withdraw from the conflict. The Namibians have done so, while the Ugandans initially pulled back some troops to reinforce them later. Burundi and Angola have also withdrawn some forces. Zimbabwe and Rwanda, however, seem intent on staying [S/2002/169, para. 4].

In April 2002, the peace talks in Sun City, South Africa, broke down over power sharing. The Congolese government did reach an agreement with the MLC, but the RCD rejected the agreement. According to the agreement, Joseph Kabila will remain president and Jean-Pierre Bemba will become Prime Minister in a transition government. Together the government and MLC control about 70 percent of the DRC's territory. Both Uganda and South Africa argued that the RCD was erroneously excluded from the agreement [NRC Handelsblad, April 19, 2002]. The RCD protested strongly and later teamed up with opposition figures from western DRC. Many observers now fear a further escalation of the violence.

In the meantime, the U.N. Observer Mission in Congo (MONUC) has focused on controlling the cease-fire and monitoring the withdrawal of forces by 15 kilometers from their forward positions. In December 2001 and January 2002, MONUC experienced a setback when the RCD and the Congolese army fought over the city of Moliro in South Kivu. Both parties later withdrew from the city [USAID, *Complex Emergency Situation Report*, May 2, 2002]. Currently, MONUC is expanding its tasks to support the total withdrawal of foreign troops from the DRC; advance disarmament, demobilization, repatriation, resettlement, and reintegration; foster confidence-building and direct dialogue between the Rwandan government and the Congolese government; demilitarize Kisangani—an important trading center on the Congo river; and reopen the Congo river for commercial and humanitarian traffic [S/Res/1376 (2001)]. MONUC also carries out humanitarian, human rights, and child protection activities. Its progress has been haphazard at best. Safety to cross the Congo river has increased, but only one humanitarian convoy has made it from Kinshasa to Kisangani and back since it was reopened [S/2002/169, paras. 19–21]. There has also been some progress with the demobilization of child soldiers, but repatriation of former Rwandan combatants has stalled. Violations of the cease-fire occur on a regular basis.

"The overall humanitarian situation continues to be characterized by grievous human rights violations, chronic food [in]security, population displacement, and outbreaks of infectious diseases. Poor security conditions significantly limit the access of humanitarian agencies, and the humanitarian situation in the east . . . remains particularly precarious" [ibid., para. 71]. Not surprisingly, the DRC has an extremely high mortality rate with outbreaks of cholera and meningitis, as well as widespread AIDS. Malnutrition, especially among children under five, is common [ibid., para. 74]. In addition, the eruption of the Mt. Nyirangongo volcano destroyed large parts of the eastern city of Goma, further straining the already limited humanitarian resources.

It is estimated that there are "more than 2.2 million displaced persons in the DRC as a result of both the conflict and natural causes" [USAID, *Complex Emergency Situation Report*, May 2, 2002]. For the country as a whole, this number is relatively constant, but the situation in the East is getting worse. With its extension, MONUC is supposed to become more active in this part of the country [SC/7266]. Hopefully, the international effort to create peace will continue. Only peace can bring the security needed for alleviating humanitarian suffering and economic rebuilding.

Burundi

An eight-year civil war and continued ethnic tensions between the Hutu majority and Tutsi minority continue to make Burundi one of the most volatile countries in the Great Lakes region. In accordance with the *Arusha Agreement on Peace and Reconciliation in Burundi*, signed in August 2000, a transitional, power-sharing government has been in place since November 2001. Nevertheless, fighting intensified last year, and two rebel groups that did not participate in the peace process continue to thwart efforts to reach a cease-fire agreement [2002 Inter-Agency Consolidated Appeals]. Simmering ethnic tensions and escalating violence prompted Nelson Mandela, as a member of the U.N.-led Implementation Monitoring Committee, to convince the South African government to send 1,400 peacekeeping troops to the capital Bujumbura last year.

The conflict has displaced more than 400,000 people who are living in internal displacement camps and caused another 400,000 Burundians to seek refuge in neighboring countries, the majority in Tanzania [ibid.]. Last year 28,000 people repatriated, significantly more than in 2000 when less than 7,000 returned home. The Tripartite Commission, comprised of representatives from the Tanzanian and Burundian governments and UNHCR, met in January and concluded that repatriation of Burundian refugees should occur as soon as possible. Nevertheless, the Commission decided not to promote a full-fledged, organized repatriation, due to continued security concerns. UNHCR is, however, providing transportation to those refugees who have decided to return to Burundi on their own, because making the trip on foot has proved a harrowing and hazardous experience for refugees who are frequently harassed by rebel groups [ibid.]. Burundi hosts some 27,000 refugees from the Democratic Republic of Congo (DRC). At the same time, some of its armed factions operate from Congolese soil. In response, the peace processes in both countries can be linked more explicitly [S/2001/970, para. 103].

A malaria epidemic that lasted from November 2000 to August 2001 is dissipating. Three campaigns headed by UNICEF and the World Health Organization (WHO) to vaccinate against measles, tetanus, and polio are underway [OCHA Burundi: Update on the humanitarian situation, January 2002]. Food insecurity remains a serious problem with more than two million children at risk of dying from a combination of chronic malnutrition, low birth weight, and high disease burden [2002 Inter-Agency Consolidated Appeals]. The food insecurity is heightened by an ongoing drought that began in 1998 [*UNHCR briefing notes,* March 12, 2002]. To conclude, "[w]hile the environment for the delivery of humanitarian and post-humanitarian assistance has improved . . . the humanitarian situation and the living conditions of the people have not" [2002 Inter-Agency Consolidated Appeals].

Sierra Leone, Liberia, and Guinea

Sierra Leone has been experiencing internal conflict, population displacement, massive human rights abuse, economic collapse, and severe food insecurity since March 1991 [M. Young, *Practicing principled humanitarian assistance in conflict: the experience of ActionAid-Sierra Leone,* HPN, February 22, 2002]. 45,000 people have been killed and many more maimed as a result of the conflict [*The Economist,* May 18, 2002, p. 12]. Whereas in years past, the situation in Sierra Leone seemed hopeless, the recent aggressive peacemaking by bilateral British troops, supported by rearguard U.N. troops, has effectively ended the war, opened up the northern and eastern parts of the country, and allowed a peaceful election.

A continuing concern is the role of the illicit trade of diamonds in the Sierra Leonean conflict. However, the implementation of U.N. Security Council Resolution 1306 [S/Res/1306 (2000)] combined with the continuing efforts of the Economic Community of West African States (ECOWAS) and the establishment of a Certificate of Origin program are helping curb the flow of conflict diamonds out of Sierra Leone.

A recent report (by UNICEF and Save the Children–U.K.) expressed concern over the condition of children in West African Refugee camps, where many become victims of sexual abuse. To address the issues raised in the report, Olara Otunnu, the Special Representative of the U.N. Secretary-General for Children and Armed Conflict, has compiled an extensive list of preventative measures; a committee has also been established with representatives from U.N. agencies, U.N. Mission in Sierra Leone (UNAMSIL), NGOs, and members of civil society [ibid.].

Disarmament initially ended in December 2001, but was extended to mid-March with over 40,000 former fighters disarmed and more than 7,000 weapons collected [OCHA, *Sierra Leone Humanitarian Situation Report,* February 1–28, 2002]. The U.N. Mission is implementing the first phase of its program to provide sustainable income-generating opportunities for 7,000 ex-combatants and 35,000 dependents. The International Office for Migration (IOM) reported that more than 1,200 ex-fighters are currently employed in projects to improve sanitary systems and provide access to safe drinking water.

While the security situation in Sierra Leone has improved, anxiety over the hostilities in neighboring Liberia has heightened. There have been reports that Sierra Leonean ex-combatants have been drawn into the fighting between Liberian dissidents and the Armed Forces of Liberia.

Also, Sierra Leone is currently hosting 18,000 Liberian refugees. On March 8, 2002, ministers from Sierra Leone, Liberia, and Guinea decided to strengthen the security along their borders. The joint security body's Technical Committee was given a mandate to begin implementation and deployment of a Joint Border and Security force along their common borders [ibid.]. While collective progress is being made to secure the region, fighting between the government and the rebels in Liberia's Lofa county continues to intensify and has displaced more than 5,000 Sierra Leonean and Liberian nationals, particularly women and children.

Sudan

At first glance, Sudan shares striking similarities with Afghanistan. Like the Taliban, the Khartoum government is an internationally isolated Islamic regime engaged in a long war with an internal region, in this case the South. Neither the regime nor the armed opposition groups are able to defeat each other. The political alliances in the North and the South are continuously feeble and shifting. The country also suffers from severe droughts. Upon closer scrutiny, however, the similarities stop.

First, although the South is predominantly animist and Christian, the war is actually "more like a clash of civilizations than a battle of religions. . . . [I]f northerners had their way, war in the South would ultimately be resolved in the same way as the one in America's West: through the subjugation of the native peoples and relinquishment of local resources to the northern conquerors" [R. Martin, "Sudan's Perfect War," *Foreign Affairs*, March/April 2002, p. 121]. Second, in contrast to the Taliban, the Khartoum regime seems increasingly able to overcome its isolated international position. It is now closer with its neighbors than it has been in years. The regime also condemned the attacks of September 11, 2001. Third, the war has become self-sustaining; the oil fields, which almost lie exclusively in the South, provide the government with resources to continue warfare and arms production. At the same time, governments and corporations now have an economic interest to look the other way when human rights abuses occur. Because of the oil fields, the government "has redoubled its efforts to wipe out resistance in the area and consolidate its control" [ibid., p. 119].

Because Sudan is such a large country, it is difficult to make generalized statements about the humanitarian situation. Currently, drought emergency relief is taking place in the states of Northern and Southern Darfur and in the Red Sea State [IFRC, *Sudan: Drought Appeal No. 11/01 operations update No. 4*, March 13, 2002].

Considerable humanitarian assistance in the war-torn areas is provided through Operation Lifeline Sudan (OLS), in which UNICEF plays a coordinating role. OLS is a tripartite agreement of negotiated access among the government of Sudan (GOS), the Southern Peoples Liberation

Movement (SPLM), and the United Nations. "Under this framework, a consortium of U.N. agencies and more than 40 international and indigenous NGOs provide emergency relief and rehabilitation assistance" [USAID, *Sudan—Complex emergency situation report #3 (FY 2002)*, March 6, 2002, p. 1]. However, insecurity frequently hampers access and operations in opposition-held areas. The conflict in the oil-rich, western Upper Nile and the Nuba Mountains has led to large displacements and food insecurity, which is further aggravated by droughts as well as floods. Organizations provide food aid, execute polio eradication programs, and implement disease surveillance programs.

In early 2002, the Khartoum government made a few peace overtures (for example, a GOS/SPLM cease-fire in the Nuba Mountains on January 22, 2002). It also improved its relationship with Uganda, so that both countries would not support opposition forces on each other's soil [*The Economist*, April 20, 2002, p. 44]. Since the government wanted to improve its international standing in order to obtain loans from international financial institutions, the United States was increasingly able to play a brokering role. However, in February 2002, the Khartoum government carried out bombardments on two different WFP emergency food distributions [USAID, *Sudan—Complex emergency situation report #3 (FY 2002)*, March 6, 2002, p. 1]. In the past, the government, counter to its OLS commitments, often bombed health centers and food distribution points in the south and denied humanitarian flights access to specific locations. The recent bombings place the government's commitment to peace in doubt [U.N. OCHA Integrated Regional Information Network, *Focus on oil-related clashes in western Upper Nile*, February 28, 2002].

Angola

The humanitarian situation in Angola did not improve in 2001. Many areas remained inaccessible to humanitarian agencies, and emergency programs were overburdened by triple the projected number of displaced individuals. In addition, humanitarian program funding was reduced substantially. Some agencies were able to "stabilize acutely distressed populations in accessible areas, [but] little progress was made in reducing the emergency caseload and virtually no improvement occurred in social indicators" [2002 Inter-Agency Consolidated Appeals]. The humanitarian effort remained large, however, consisting of "ten U.N. agencies, 100 international NGOs and more than 340 national NGOs either active or registered" [ibid.].

Despite expectations of only slightly lower levels of displacement in 2002 [ibid.] and given unexpectedly high mortality and malnutrition rates [Médecins Sans Frontières, May 7, 2002], there is an air of optimism for the near future of Angola. After the death of the National Union for the Total Independence of Angola (UNITA) strongman Jonas Savimbi, UNITA's new leaders entered a cease-fire agreement with the Angolan government on

April 4, 2002. This resurrected previous government offers of "amnesty for rebels who surrender and an old proposal to integrate some of UNITA's 50,000 troops into the national army" [*The Economist*, April 4, 2002].

In April, U.N. agencies and NGOs conducted rapid assessments in newly accessible areas and discovered emergency conditions in 4 of 38 locations assessed [OCHA, *Humanitarian Situation in Angola*, April 30, 2002]. High levels of malnutrition in many provinces and increasing mortality rates at IDP camps and elsewhere highlighted the need for humanitarian action. In a review of lessons learned in 2001, OCHA reported "the marked increase in reported violations of human rights has underlined the need for a rights-based strategy to humanitarian assistance" [ibid.]. In 2002, food agencies plan to shift from general distributions to targeted assistance. The Angolan government has promised to ensure that humanitarian activities are linked to strategies for poverty alleviation and national reconciliation [ibid.]. The primary concern is whether the cease-fire will hold. International support for demobilization is crucial in this respect. The government contends that it is willing to work for national reconciliation [*The Economist*, February 28, 2002], but suspicions run high on both ends of the bargaining table.

Ethiopia and Eritrea

Though conditions have improved in the Horn of Africa, where a recent drought (1999–2000) and border war (1998–2000) between Eritrea and Ethiopia are fresh in people's memories, there are still a host of humanitarian concerns, including potential food shortages, landmine casualties, and other health-related issues.

The two countries signed a *Comprehensive Peace Agreement* in December 2000. The U.N. Mission in Ethiopia and Eritrea (UNMEE), deployed in July 2000 to monitor the Temporary Security Zone (TSZ) separating the two countries, will remain to oversee the implementation of the border decision and facilitate a number of other measures specified in the Agreement. In Ethiopia, demobilization of 150,000 troops is underway. Since UNMEE operates after the cessation of hostilities in a security zone between the two countries, it resembles more traditional U.N. peacekeeping than the other, more multidimensional missions described in this chapter.

Repatriation of refugees and the return of IDPs to their homes continued throughout 2001 in Ethiopia. Toward the end of the conflict, in December 1999, there were almost 350,000 IDPs. Last summer, 50,000 people remained displaced [*IDPs in Ethiopia: Population Profile and Figures*, Global IDP project, May 12, 2002]. Eighty percent of the IDP population in northern Ethiopia has returned to their home communities. Though the repatriation effort in the eastern region of Ethiopia is expected to finish by mid-2002, the country still hosts more than 170,000 refugees, particularly in the west and north where there are a significant number of Sudanese and Eritrean refugees [2002 Inter-Agency Consolidated Appeals].

In Eritrea, the conflict and drought affected 1.6 million people, including 900,000 IDPs [ibid.]. Since 1999, substantial progress has been made to repatriate and return people to their homes [*IDPs in Eritrea: Population Profile and Figures,* Global IDP Project, May 12, 2002]. By year's end, it is anticipated that UNHCR will have assisted another 140,000 Eritreans in returning home, mostly from Sudan. The United Nations Development Programme (UNDP) and UNHCR continue to address social and economic reintegration needs of returning refugees and IDPs [S/2002/245], though economic development and food distribution are seriously hampered by a high population growth rate and a fractured road infrastructure.

Within Ethiopia, increased rainfall in the Somali region has shifted UNICEF's emphasis from providing emergency assistance to sustainable programming. Although a better harvest is expected this year, famine caused by drought conditions is a constant threat that will need ongoing monitoring. Despite more rain, food shortages remain a concern in several areas of the Somali and Bale regions and will require monitoring throughout 2002 [2002 Inter-Agency Consolidated Appeals]. Food assistance will continue this year, especially in the regions where there was a particularly poor crop yield in 2001 [S/2002/245]. Eritrea also saw more rain in the past year, but drought continued to affect more than 500,000 people by the end of 2001 [2001 Inter-Agency Consolidated Appeals].

Landmines take the lives of several civilians and children each month [5th UNICEF/RaDO Tigray Quarterly Mine/UXO Victim Information report]. Nevertheless, mine clearance teams have made headway with mine risk awareness and landmine removal during the past year. UNMEE, in close cooperation with UNICEF, has been conducting mine risk education programs with volunteers who will continue to educate in their local communities.

Despite the problems, conditions were less urgent in 2001 than in previous years and are expected to continue to improve in the region. U.N. agencies are working to smooth the transition from emergency operations to development. In addition, a series of meetings with Eritrean and Ethiopian religious leaders has been held. In February 2002, meetings facilitated by UNMEE and the Norwegian Church brought together Eritrean and Ethiopian leaders to discuss a common message of peace [S/2002/245]. Nevertheless, nerves remain raw. When a group of journalists (that included Eritreans) visited the disputed town of Badme, the Ethiopian Prime Minister asked for the resignation of the UNMEE commander. The United Nations apologized, but this failed to satisfy the Ethiopians [*NRC Handelsblad,* May 4, 2002].

Southeastern Europe

The general trend toward stability and development in Southeastern Europe is gaining force, although ethnic tensions can still flare up and set back the processes of reconciliation and social-political transition. Most U.N. and other international organizations (NATO, OSCE, and EU) try to harmonize their approaches in this region.

> The conditions in the region are in place to: (1) increase the pace of return of refugees and IDPs to their original homes, and of local integration for those who choose this option; (2) facilitate rehabilitation and promote peace and social cohesion in southern Serbia, Kosovo, and the former Yugoslav Republic of Macedonia; and (3) move the development agenda forward, supporting sustainable economic progress and transfer of responsibility for care of the most vulnerable groups to the appropriate government social welfare structures. [2002 Inter-Agency Consolidated Appeals]

International support for peacekeeping, development cooperation, and humanitarian assistance remain necessary.

Bosnia and Herzegovina enjoys relative political stability, which facilitates a continued high rate of refugee and IDP returns. Economic growth, however, is slow to resume and the capacity of both government and civil society need to be strengthened further [ibid.]. In ***Croatia*** the number of returning refugees is also increasing. The democratic government has reformed some discriminatory legislative and administrative provisions and committed itself to resolving property and housing problems faced by returnees [ibid.]. ***Albania*** was not greatly affected by the civil conflict in neighboring Macedonia last year and most of its Kosovar refugees have returned. However, the country shows many signs of chronic underdevelopment [ibid.].

During Milosevic's reign, the economy of the ***Federal Republic of Yugoslavia*** (FRY) went into a steep decline. His removal by the end of 2000 improved access for international organizations and ensured, for the first time in ten years, that the FRY contributed again to regional stability and economic growth [OCHA, *Humanitarian Situation, Protection and Assistance: Internally Displaced Persons in Serbia and Montenegro*, Humanitarian Risk Analysis No. 18, OCHA Office in Belgrade, p. 33]. Many donors condition their aid on the government's cooperation with the International Criminal Tribunal in The Hague. An increasing number of indictees are now going to The Hague, several voluntarily, although General Mladic, one of the central war criminals, remains at large in Serbia. (Radovan Karadzic is still hiding out in eastern Bosnia and Herzegovina.)

One large problem remains the status of ***Montenegro*** within the FRY. At the moment, a "looser federation called simply Serbia and Montenegro" is in the works, but it is not sure what the final situation would look like. If Montenegro secedes, in itself a very contentious issue, then Kosovo may in response also reinforce its claim to independence, which can create a highly combustible situation [*The Economist*, March 23, 2002, p. 50].

The 231,000 IDPs from Kosovo are the main humanitarian concern in the FRY. Serbia wants the refugees to return to Kosovo to strengthen its political claims on Kosovo. The Kosovars do not trust the IDPs/refugees because they are believed to have cooperated with the Yugoslav army and make the possibility of independence more remote. The situation of the IDPs is complicated. Many IDPs, especially the Roma, are not registered. They lack housing and income security (52 percent unemployed, while the average household lives below the poverty level) [OCHA, *Humanitarian Situation, Protection and Assistance: Internally Displaced Persons in Serbia and Montenegro*, Humanitarian Risk Analysis No. 18, OCHA Office in Belgrade, p. 3]. The possibility of return hinges on whether Kosovo remains in the FRY. As a result, many of the IDPs live in limbo, and the return process is very slow and unpredictable [2002 Inter-Agency Consolidated Appeals].

The U.N. Interim Administration in *Kosovo* (UNMIK), established in 1999 [S/Res/1244 (1999)], is now slowly handing over tasks to the Kosovo government. "On 28 February, the three major Kosovo Albanian parties reached agreement on forming a coalition government. . . . The same agreement put forward Ibrahim Rugova, a moderate leader, as candidate for President" [S/2002/436]. The final status of Kosovo remains extremely contentious. Most Serbs live in enclaves protected by KFOR. The humanitarian situation, however, has improved. Maternal and infant mortality rates are falling, while agricultural production continues to improve. The transition from food aid to social welfare support is nearing completion and de-mining is making progress. Still, lack of funding meant that many programs had to be canceled, reduced, or readjusted [2002 Inter-Agency Consolidated Appeals]. Despite the international attention and U.N. involvement, no solution has been proposed to the fundamental question of sovereignty vis-à-vis Serbia, which means that interethnic conciliation will remain problematic too.

In 2001, *Macedonia* had the dubious distinction of being the most unstable country in the Balkans with ethnic Albanians fighting government forces. As in many armed conflicts, these armed groups also engage in serious criminal behavior such as drug smuggling and trafficking in women. In recent months, conflict has decreased significantly, partly because of international intervention and the deployment of NATO troops. The ethnic Albanian armed groups were disarmed in September 2001. Since then, 134,500 of the 170,000 people who fled their homes have returned [OCHA, *Humanitarian Update FYR of Macedonia*, March 9, 2002]. The Macedonian government has adopted constitutional minority rights, for example, with the Albanian language. Nevertheless, the returnees and remaining IDPs face several humanitarian obstacles: a tense security situation, mines and unexploded ordnance, destroyed homes, nonfunctioning basic services, and closed or damaged health-care facilities and schools. In response, UNHCR and other U.N. agencies have stepped up their activities to bring communities together by supporting bus lines, providing legal assistance, and promoting the acceptance of international legal standards (e.g., Convention of the Rights of the Child). Other U.N. agencies focus on demining (U.N. Emergency Mine Action Project in Sudan [UNMAS]); shelter, water, and sanitation (UNHCR); the rebuilding of health structures (WHO); education (UNICEF); and food (WFP with Action Against Hunger) [ibid.].

If peace continues to hold in southeastern Europe, humanitarian assistance can be phased out during the next few years. To this end, the international community will increasingly have to focus on development activities to improve governance, promote economic growth, and foster reconciliation and regional cooperation.

Chechnya

Russian forces are continuing a bloody clampdown on rebel activities in this breakaway republic, which is trying to secede for the second time since 1994. Human rights groups report frequent abuses by Russian troops, accusing them of torturing and disappearing civilians during roundups of alleged terrorist and rebel forces. Still, since September 11, international criticism has died down. Meanwhile, Russian forces also suffer losses in ambushes set by rebel fighters.

The conflict has caused huge displacement, and a political solution does not seem imminent, though a meeting last November with negotiators from the Russian and Chechen governments sent a signal that Russia is nowhere near winning the war [*The Economist*, November 22, 2001]. In the meantime, violence, landmines, and food shortages have disrupted the lives of hundreds of thousands, causing a flood of Chechens to seek refuge in Georgia, Kazakhstan, and the neighboring Republic of Ingushetia. As of this April, Ingushetia hosted 150,000 IDPs from Chechnya, and more continue to flow in, seriously testing the capacity of Ingushetia's own fragile infrastructure. The number of Chechens residing in Georgia, however, went down 50 percent to less than 4,000, according to the United Nations Association of Georgia [S. Jashi and C. Georgia, *Georgia: Chechen refugee number decreases*, United Nations Association of Georgia, May 2, 2002]. Without a cease-fire in sight, many of the 310,000 IDPs are reluctant to return to their home communities. Furthermore, humanitarian aid organizations have been faced with problems accessing trouble spots, which exacerbates the situation.

Despite the obstacles, several U.N. agencies—UNICEF, UNHCR, WHO, and WFP—together with the aid community are involved in a number of activities to improve the lives of IDPs and ameliorate conditions in the capital Grozny. Measures include providing education, food, and other necessities to IDPs; helping those Chechens who wish to remain in Ingushetia and other areas of the Federation find housing outside camps and become integrated in their new communities; and pushing to get more freedom of movement for the international aid community, which has been hampered by Russian troops with little regard for international humanitarian or human rights law [2002 Inter-Agency Consolidated Appeals].

UNICEF is involved in projects addressing education, health and nutrition, mine awareness, and clean water and sanitation. It has been successful in its effort to coordinate other NGOs in the region to provide the majority of IDP children with two years of schooling in tents and other makeshift facilities.

In Chechnya, mines have injured as many as 10,000 people, including 4,000 children. It is estimated that 500,000 mines have been laid and that more continue to be planted [*U.N. Mine Action report on the Russian Federation*, www.mineaction.org, May 12, 2002]. Through its Action Programme, UNICEF has been working to bring risk awareness to schools and IDP camp populations through the training of educators and psychologists who will in turn educate in local communities. UNICEF, in cooperation with UNHCR, WHO, and the International Committee of the Red Cross (ICRC), is also helping support a prosthesis workshop and provide psychosocial services for victims of mine injuries. UNICEF reports that the "latest information on the number of child mine victims and their mental health status is so pessimistic that, unless some serious financial support is extended, it will be impossible to tackle this major and long-lasting problem" [UNICEF, *Humanitarian Action: Northern Caucasus Donor Update*, April 22, 2002]. Together with the Polish Humanitarian Organisation and ICRC, UNICEF has also been able to provide drinking water to more than 40,000 people and has helped offset the outbreak and spread of disease by installing a sewage and garbage collection service in Grozny.

So far, an end to the fighting is not in sight. Although U.N. agencies are working to address primary needs, such as providing food, shelter, and education, UNICEF warns that conditions could deteriorate without sustained support. "Needs in Chechnya remain largely unmet and current insecurity is hindering access to beneficiaries, and worsening some already grave problems" [ibid.].

Colombia

The humanitarian situation in Colombia remained dire throughout 2001 and will likely be exacerbated by a rupture in the three-year peace process between the Colombian government and the Revolutionary Armed Forces of Colombia (FARC) that occurred in February 2002.

In the past 15 years alone, two million people (particularly women, children, and indigenous groups) have been displaced by fighting between the military, leftist insurgents, and paramilitaries. According to Colombian government figures, the basic needs of almost 30 percent of the population are not being met [U.N. Mine Action, Colombia country profile, www.mineaction.org]. Furthermore, people (often IDPs) without proper documentation are denied services such as medical care.

Increased hostilities in the western and northeastern regions, following the derailment of the peace process, are causing border countries to see a dramatic rise in asylum applications and people seeking refuge [*Outgoing U.N. official highlights "scourge" of displacement,* March 24, BBC Monitoring International Reports].

Colombia remains the only country in Latin America where mines continue to be laid on a regular basis. There were more than 200 victims of landmines last year. At the request of the government, UNMAS will conduct an interagency mission to assess the problem during 2002. Meanwhile, UNICEF, together with a number of national and international organizations, continues to coordinate mine awareness training and advocate "for the comprehensive implementation of the Mine Ban Convention" [U.N. Mine Action, Colombia country profile, www.mineaction.org].

Whether a possible change in government, to be determined in elections in May 2002, will bring the derailed peace negotiations back on track is uncertain. But now, in cooperation with the Bush administration's "Plan Colombia" initiative to wipe out the drug trade, the United States is going to step up support for the Colombian military. Specifically, it will allow a portion of the more than $1.1 billion in aid it gives to the "War on Drugs" to be used to fight insurgents and paramilitary groups. The humanitarian impact of "Plan Colombia" could be severe.

Sri Lanka

With peace talks scheduled to take place in Thailand (May 2002) between the recently elected Sri Lankan government and the Liberation Tigers of Tamil Eelam (LTTE), an end to the conflict in Sri Lanka seems plausible for the first time in 19 years. Almost 70,000 people have died in the conflict, which has internally displaced more than 800,000 [Global IDP Database, www.idpproject.org].

To address the humanitarian needs that stem from this conflict and a prolonged drought, UNICEF has asked the donor community for $3.6 million. A recent assessment cited areas of particular concern as education, health, and nutrition. The lion's share, however, will go to "special protection," which in 2001 comprised mine awareness programs, psychosocial support for widows and children, as well as rehabilitation centers for mine victims [UNICEF, *A Humanitarian Appeal for Children and Women,* January–December, 2002, Sri Lanka].

Last year, following a one-month landmine assessment trip to the country, UNMAS drafted a proposal to address the situation. The mission found that both parties in the conflict lay mines [*UNMAS Missions Report, Sri Lanka*, June 2001]. Because landmines affect such a wide area, UNMAS recommends a nationwide approach. U.N. agencies, as well as aid organizations and the Sri Lankan government, will be involved in this initiative to set up rehabilitation clinics and conduct mine awareness campaigns.

The recruitment and abduction of children and women as fighters by the LTTE has been particularly prevalent during this conflict. To address the psychological and social ramifications from this, UNICEF helps socially rehabilitate and integrate former child combatants; it also conducts awareness campaigns on the Convention on the Rights of the Child and its Optional Protocol on the involvement of children in armed conflict.

A prolonged drought has affected food supplies, especially in the south of Sri Lanka, prompting WFP to initiate an emergency operation from October 2001 to this year's harvest season in March 2002. The agency distributed food and nutritional supplements to 300,000 people in Sri Lanka and introduced work schemes involving 225,000 people who will, among other projects, help clean irrigation canals [*Sri Lanka: U.N. food agency to help 300,000 drought victims*, U.N. News Centre, www.un.org].

Despite the peace process, as of March 2002, the situation was still too sensitive and potentially volatile to repatriate some 100,000 Sri Lankan refugees living in southern India [*UNHCR says Sri Lanka still fragile*, BBC News, March 19, 2002]. Even with the obstacles of landmines, damaged communities, and food shortages, a number of the estimated 800,000 IDPs have begun to return to their homes. "[I]t is envisaged that 200,000 IDPs would be returned or resettled by the end of 2002 and the remaining 600,000 by end 2004" [Global IDP Database, Sri Lanka, www.idpproject.org].

Indonesia

The end of Abdurrahman Wahid's presidency (July 2001) did not lead to the widely feared violence people expected. Even though the new administration under Megawati Sukarnoputri has taken little action to address the root causes of the internal conflicts that have beleaguered Indonesia, the country has stabilized somewhat. Most Indonesians are wary of the political turmoil of recent years [*The Economist*, April 13, 2002, pp. 41–42]. The country still has large separatist movements in Aceh, West Papua, and to a lesser extent the Malukus. As in East Timor, democratic control of the military remains an issue.

The number of IDPs in Indonesia has grown from less than 350,000 in August 1999 to more than one million in September 2001 [2002 Inter-Agency Consolidated Appeals]. Although some IDPs are victims of natural disasters, most are victims of different conflicts.

The Islamist movement in Aceh wants to separate from what it perceives as its Javanese colonial overlords. Control of natural wealth, in particular oil and gas, is an important issue in this respect. In Irian Jaya (West Papua), the indigenous population argues that they have been unjustly incorporated into Indonesia and demand independence. In both Aceh and Papua, the human rights situation has continued to deteriorate as the security forces against pro-independence movements have intensified their operations. Grave human rights violations have been committed, including extra-judicial executions and torture and the destruction of houses and means of livelihood in both provinces as a form of collective punishment. The armed opposition groups are also responsible for serious human rights abuses, including unlawful killings and abductions [Amnesty International, 58th U.N. Commission On Human Rights (2002) Background Briefing]. The situation in the Malukus is even more complex, with Muslim and Christian Moluccans fighting each other: "The so-called religious conflicts . . . are deeply rooted in economic-political differences between two groups who happen to belong to different religions. . . . [E]xternal religious extremists have 'religionised' the conflict in the Malukus" [2002 Inter-Agency Consolidated Appeals].

Many of the IDPs face hunger and disease and are deprived of the basic necessities of life, as they struggle to survive away from their homes. However, because of the widespread nature of IDP requirements and the lack of available capacity and resources, it has been difficult to respond adequately to the Indonesian crisis. U.N. agencies such as WHO, UNICEF, and the Food and Agriculture Organization of the United Nations (FAO) have been providing assistance to IDPs (with health and food security projects, for example). UNHCR is supporting police-training programs on human rights and refugee laws. OCHA, in collaboration with other U.N. agencies and NGOs, continues to monitor the situation and advance efforts to ensure awareness of and compliance with the Guiding Principles on Internal Displacement [ibid.]. The government has made public a new policy for the management of IDP situations and hopes to complete its implementation by the end of December 2002. International humanitarian assistance agencies believe that this is overly optimistic and that it will take at least another year to solve the crisis [ibid.].

East Timor

The East Timorese elected their first president in a free and fair election with universal suffrage on April 14, 2002. The ballot marked the placement of the last major democratic institution in East Timor before independence. The Legislative Assembly—popularly elected in a U.N.-administered ballot in 2001—will transform itself into a National Parliament on May 20, and the new East Timor Government, including President-elect Xanana Gusmão, will be sworn in the same day.

Since August 7, 2000, the U.N. Transitional Administration in East

Timor (UNTAET) has been working to establish a functioning administration and the transfer of administrative power to Timorese control. While noting that many important political advances have been made, and steady gains achieved, UNTAET has pointed out that

> the comparative fragility of the political foundations of this new country, its very limited pool of professional and administrative expertise, lack of strong independent security mechanisms and nascent state of economic development mean that [it] will continue to require significant assistance from the international community well after independence, in order to ensure stability and realize the potential for progress that has been generated over the past two years. [S/2002/80]

An important aspect to ensuring security in East Timor is facilitating the return of refugees. 17,900 refugees returned in 2001 (bringing the total to 192,000), but an estimated 60,000–75,000 remain in West Timor [ibid.]. The Indonesian government, UNTAET, UNHCR, IOM, and other humanitarian organizations are involved in efforts to facilitate returns. Continued protection of returnees is necessary to ensure a high rate of returns, although UNTAET has observed that the most significant deterrents to further returns are now economic concerns rather than security issues and militia intimidation [ibid.].

Conclusions

The list of humanitarian crises in this chapter is not exhaustive. Some hidden, or less noticed, humanitarian crises include Nagorno Karabakh (Azerbaijan), Burma, North Korea, and Somalia. Several other countries, like Guatemala and Zimbabwe, are teetering on the brink of potential disaster.

It is crucial to note the differences among the crises. Some humanitarian crises occur in capable states, such as Colombia and Sri Lanka, which are fighting a battle against insurgents and terrorists. "Others— Congo, Angola, and Sudan—are resource-rich states whose elites are incapable or unwilling to use resource revenue to develop their countries and end civil wars. Still others—Afghanistan, Somalia, and Sierra Leone— are weak states, with poor resource endowments, and have proved incapable of providing effective governance at all" [M. Ignatieff, "Intervention and State Failure," *Dissent*, Winter 2002, p. 117]. All of these crises, however, share at least two factors: (1) a regime or government that is or has been insufficiently accountable to the local population, and (2) the state is unable to maintain a monopoly on internal means of violence [ibid.].

Addressing these crises generally implies some kind of "nation-state building," which is exactly what the United Nations has been doing with varying degrees of success in Kosovo, Bosnia and Herzegovina, East Timor, Afghanistan, and so on. The humanitarian values of impartiality and neutrality, however, function best when there is a well-functioning, accountable state, which is temporarily unable to provide succor, due to an earthquake, for example. In these cases, humanitarians do not have to worry about the political implications of their actions; saving lives will be the overriding concern. Similarly, with war among standing armies, humanitarian organizations can by and large maintain their impartiality and neutrality, because the roles of the states, the military, and the humanitarian organizations are well defined. However, a breakdown of states often blurs the roles of different actors in a conflict. With nation-state building, humanitarian and other organizations generally need to remain in the country over an extended period and are often forced, sooner or later, to take sides in a conflict, which inevitably has political ramifications. It becomes difficult not to ask the question: which faction would do best in nation-state building to get a well-functioning, inclusive state? Because U.N. agencies take on so many tasks with political implications, their neutrality and impartiality are likely to become compromised. Both civilians and warring factions will carefully monitor, and often manipulate, humanitarian organizations to their own advantage.

It would greatly help U.N. humanitarian efforts, if rich countries would provide funding and diplomatic support. Then, at least, the humanitarian agencies and their donors would have distinct, but complementary roles, in relief and rebuilding. However, this is not happening. Declining trends in funding, neglect of so-called marginalized or "strategically irrelevant" areas, and insufficient or irregular international political attention mark the chronic crises of humanitarian assistance efforts. Currently, Afghanistan is crowding out other crises, whereas Africa remains the basket case. Hence, "humanitarianism must always be as much an emblem of political failure as it is an expression of human decency" [D. Rieff, "Moral Imperatives and Political Realities," *Ethics and International Affairs*, Vol. 13, p. 39]. Humanitarian actors "occupy the central role in these crises precisely because [these] are otherwise of so little geostrategic or economic [interest] to the powers that could intervene militarily, or use their diplomatic clout to change the situation on the ground for the better far more effectively than the most dedicated humanitarians can ever hope to do. To put it starkly, MSF has a place at the table about Rwanda because so few institutions care about Rwanda" [ibid.]. Humanitarian organizations depend on donor support for funding and, paradoxically, it is often the neglect of a crisis that allows them to take on a prominent role. Yet, without support of the rich states, the neutrality and impartiality of U.N. and humanitarian agencies gets easily compromised, as they take on more tasks and have to face the concomitant political implications.

Military attacks occur when the powerful countries realize that they do have an interest after all. Politically, the military are not the first problem; they essentially carry out orders. The problem lies more in the capitals of the western countries, where domestically perceived, geopolitical considerations take the upper hand, currently under the heading of "security" and "war against terrorism." The politicians in these capitals do not invest sufficiently in conflict prevention and nation-state building. Their scarce development cooperation dollars are outweighed by corporate welfare, agricultural subsidies, and import quotas that hamper the developing economies. They also regularly foster arms sales and prop up corrupt regimes. They too often neglect crises until the media, and now also terrorists, point out that neglect has distinct political disadvantages. The military generally come in after the crisis has already unfolded.

The mixing of arms and aid in Afghanistan, which is a major development since September 11, 2001, goes one step too far. "Food bombings" are first and foremost a propaganda tool, with perhaps the saving grace of inefficiently saving some lives, but they should not be called "humanitarian." In general, military attacks against a regime that abuses its population, as in Serbia/Kosovo, are difficult to judge, because there is a moral calculus involved—oftentimes an imperfect calculus dominated by domestic concerns from the rich capitals. In these cases, humanitarians must keep a distance so that they can maintain (a modicum) of neutrality and impartiality apart from the domestic concerns; they must prevent a blurring of roles in order to function optimally.

In cases with little or no combat, but with a military presence, a more mutually supportive relationship is possible. First, the military can foster a secure environment for civilians and humanitarian agencies, as happened in Sierra Leone. Second, the military can also support the protection and assistance work of the agencies. Finally, they can provide direct assistance to civilians in need. In these three cases, humanitarian and military action should not be integrated but complementary to preserve as much as possible the ideals of neutrality and impartiality. Humanitarians should recognize their limitations in nation-state building and the political consequences of their actions. They can be manipulated by local factions or sidelined by western policy-makers. Yet they should oppose their incorporation into the security concerns of the rich countries and protest against military attacks disguised as humanitarian interventions. National security concerns of the rich countries do not need to trump the humanitarian agenda. Humanitarian organizations should carry out more advocacy to international decision-makers, emphasizing the negative consequences for international security if failed states are neglected. As the military are increasingly confronted with the difficulties in rebuilding, they may actually become receptive to such advocacy.

II
Peace

1. Africa
By Benjamin Weil

"The countries of sub-Saharan Africa have always had to fight for America's attention," reported Rachel Swarns of the *New York Times*. "Lately, most have fallen off the map" [December 23, 2001]. Referring no doubt to the aftermath of September 11, 2001, Swarns accurately noted the reduced coverage of Africa by the American press in the months following the terrorist attacks in the United States. Yet some of the U.N. peacekeeping operations in Africa made progress in 2001 and into the early months of 2002, and the African continent was not without its proponents from other nations during the same period.

One such proponent was British Prime Minister Tony Blair. In 2001, Blair promised long-term involvement in Africa to help heal "a scar on the conscience of the world." British Foreign Secretary Jack Straw defended the Prime Minister against allegations that his plans for the international community to resolve Africa's problems were "overambitious" and "overidealistic," saying, "It really is a serious initiative. Africa matters. It matters if you want to produce a stable world. You can't have four continents going forward and one going backwards" [*Guardian*, January 24, 2002]. Proving his resolve, Blair undertook an intensive four-day journey to Nigeria, Ghana, Sierra Leone, and Senegal in February 2002, with the goal of drawing up a plan for conflict prevention in Africa to be presented at a spring 2002 meeting of the Group of Eight in Canada [ibid., February 7, 2002].

Another champion of sub-Saharan Africa has been Secretary-General Kofi Annan. His own Ghanaian origins have made Annan a hero for the entire continent, while his frequent trips to African nations have underscored his commitment. In addition to focusing on poverty as the cause of many of Africa's problems, Annan has pressured pharmaceutical companies to make HIV/AIDS-related drugs available to some of the 25 million Africans living with the virus. As the former head of U.N. peacekeeping operations, the Secretary-General has also kept conflict in Africa high on his agenda. Under the "Annan Doctrine," he has stated that "governments should not hide behind sovereignty to commit atrocities and industrialized nations should consider military intervention in civil wars on purely humanitarian grounds, where no strategic interest exists" [*Boston Globe*, April 22, 2001]. With disputes to monitor in the Democratic Republic of Congo, Eritrea and Ethiopia, Sierra Leone, and Western Sahara, in addition to the related problems of HIV/AIDS and children affected by armed conflict, Africa has succeeded in holding the attention of Kofi Annan and the U.N. Security Council in 2001–2002.

Armed Conflict and Children

One theme that resonates throughout all peacekeeping operations in Africa—and beyond—is **the effects of armed conflict on children**. Events occurring in 2001 and into 2002 in African countries with U.N. peacekeeping missions highlight the traumatic and dangerous situation of children caught in the throes of civil wars and other violent campaigns. Children have been the victims of many of the same crimes to which women have been subjected—rape, sexual slavery, torture, mutilation, genocide—yet they are even less able to protect themselves against the adult males who most often perpetrate these acts. In addition to permanent injury and death, children are also vulnerable to HIV and other sexually transmitted infections. Even when children recover from or escape abuse, they are often menaced by the presence of landmines. The risks for children are particularly high in nearly all of the African countries with ongoing peacekeeping operations, including Sierra Leone and the Democratic Republic of Congo. Of the 2.5 million civilians estimated to have died in Congo between 1998 and 2001, one-third were children under five. For each child killed in armed conflicts, three received injuries or permanent disabilities [G. Machel, *The Impact of War on Children*, Hurst and Company, 2001, p. 67].

A further and equally serious danger for children living in situations of armed conflict is being forced into combat. At least 300,000 child soldiers are estimated to be involved in armed conflicts at any given time, but the actual figure may be much higher [*Global Report from the Coalition to Stop the Use of Child Soldiers*, 2001]. In February 2002, an international treaty signed by 94 countries and banning the use of children under 18 for combat came into force. "They are cheap, obedient and can be easily brainwashed to commit acts of extreme violence," reported the coordinator of the Coalition to Stop the Use of Child Soldiers, by way of explaining why children are so often abducted into armed conflicts [*Independent*, February 13, 2001]. The U.N. Fund for Children (UNICEF) reports that children "may be abducted or recruited by force or driven to join armed groups in order to

escape poverty or to find the assurance of food or perceived security"
[*UNICEF Actions on Behalf of Children Affected by Armed Conflict*, 2002, p. 11].

Developments in West Africa in early 2002 demonstrated that the abuse of children during situations of armed conflict remains a burning issue for the United Nations. In March, the U.N. High Commissioner for Refugees (UNHCR) and Save the Children reported the shocking news that there was "evidence of extensive sexual exploitation of refugee children in Liberia, Guinea and Sierra Leone—much of it allegedly perpetrated by workers locally employed by national and international nongovernmental organizations, as well as by U.N. agencies, including UNHCR" [Agence France Presse, March 9, 2002]. The report was based on testimony from 1,500 children and adults living in the camps and stated that locally hired camp officials were "demand[ing] sex in exchange for the food and medicine the children need to survive" [*New York Times*, February 27, 2002]. The abused children—mainly girls aged 13 to 18—were quoted as believing that surrendering to sexual demands was "the only option they had in order to receive food and other basic necessities." The abuse suffered by girls in the West African refugee camps also exposed them to the risk of HIV infection, the report noted [ibid.].

The report prompted statements of outrage and concern by many U.N. officials, including the Secretary-General, who pledged to "act forcefully, should any of these allegations be confirmed" [*Boston Globe*, February 28, 2002]. Special Representative of the U.N. Secretary-General for Children and Armed Conflict Olara Otunnu assured the public that the United Nations would "ensure that the rules of conduct concerning children are clear for all field staff and that [the] United Nations in conflict areas are equipped with the training materials and the supervision necessary to oversee and address transgressions" [U.N. Press Release, HR/4581, March 8, 2002]. The U.N. Special Rapporteur for Violence against Women, Radhika Coomaraswamy, "called on Sierra Leone to draw up measures to combat rape and domestic violence," saying women were the main victims of the country's gruesome ten-year civil war. A survey conducted in June 2001 found that, of 733 Sierra Leonean women and girls questioned, 72 percent had had their human rights violated, and more than half reported survivng sexual violence, rape, and gang rape [Agence France Presse, March 20, 2002].

The head of the U.N. peacekeeping mission in Sierra Leone immediately ordered base commanders to extract guarantees that local staff members were in no way implicated in the abuse of women and children and that punishment would ensue if these orders were not respected [ibid., March 9, 2002]. In its resolution 1400 of March 28, 2002, the Security Council expressed its "serious concern at the violence, particularly sexual violence, suffered by women and children during the conflict in Sierra Leone," as well as concern about "allegations that some United Nations personnel may have been involved in sexual abuse of women and children in camps for refugees and internally displaced people in the region," in addition to voicing its support for the Secretary-General's policy of zero tolerance for such behavior.

HIV/AIDS

The issue of **HIV/AIDS** among U.N. troops and in countries with peace-keeping missions continues to confront the Security Council, especially in Africa. Richard Cornwall, a military analyst with the South African Institute of Strategic Studies, sounding a note of warning in April 2001, asserted that military troops could become too debilitated to support U.N. peacekeeping operations if steps were not taken to halt the spread of the virus within African armies, among which HIV infection rates soared as high as 40 percent among soldiers in Angola and South Africa and 70 per cent among Zimbabwean militia members [*San Diego Union-Tribune*, April 15, 2001]. By May, an unpublished U.N. study reported that as many as two out of every three Sierra Leonean soldiers could be living with HIV infection. This prompted Major James Samba, chairman of the HIV/AIDS committee of the Sierra Leone armed forces, to admit that "[w]e've done absolutely nothing, we have no policy. It's a disaster. There will have to be a continuous high level of army recruitment because of this disease" [*Guardian*, May 12, 2001].

In November 2001, the Security Council passed resolution 1379, which requested the Secretary-General to "ensure that all peacekeeping personnel receive and follow appropriate guidance on HIV/AIDS and training in international human rights, humanitarian, and refugee law relevant to children." It also requested the "agencies, funds and programmes of the United Nations to integrate HIV/AIDS awareness, prevention and care into emergency, humanitarian and post-conflict programmes" [S/Res/1379 (2001)]. The U.N. General Assembly Special Session on HIV/AIDS, held in June 2001, also addressed the issue of HIV/AIDS in conflict and disaster-affected regions in its declaration of commitment [June 27, 2001]. Other entities within the United Nations, including UNICEF, have acted to deal with both HIV/AIDS and children affected by armed conflict, which has related programs in Angola, the Democratic Republic of Congo, Eritrea, Ethiopia, Guinea, Liberia, Sierra Leone, and Somalia, among other countries [*UNICEF Actions on Behalf of Children Affected by Armed Conflict*, 2002].

Democratic Republic of Congo

In January 2001, Laurent Kabila, liberator of the Congolese people from longtime dictator Mobutu Sese Seko and self-proclaimed president of the newly named Democratic Republic of Congo, was fatally shot by one of his bodyguards, Rashidi Muzele. Within a few days, Kabila's 29-year-old son, Joseph, appeared on the scene and assumed tactful but unmistakable control of the government. As of late April 2002, a month into a murder trial that will examine as many as 135 suspects, no clear conclusion has emerged about the mastermind behind the killing of Laurent Kabila [*New York Times*, April 24, 2002], though members of either of two Congolese rebel movements (Rally for a Democratic Congo and Movement for the Liberation of the Congo), at least a half dozen neighboring countries, and disillusioned members of Kabila's own entourage may have wanted him dead. But Joseph Kabila still holds the country's presidency, and by Congolese standards the past 15 months have been relatively quiet.

Relative quiet in the Democratic Republic of Congo, a country the size of Western Europe, does not mean a lack of turmoil for its 50 million inhabitants [*Washington Post*, August 15, 2001] nor the absence of challenges for the 5,500 members of the **U.N. Organization Mission in the Democratic Republic of Congo (MONUC)**. MONUC, which has existed on paper since February 2000 but required more than a year to deploy its military troops, was created to "develop . . . an action plan for the overall implementation of the Ceasefire Agreement by all concerned," "work with the parties to obtain the release of all prisoners of war," "supervise and verify the disengagement and redeployment of the parties' forces," and "facilitate humanitarian assistance and human rights monitoring," among other tasks [S/Res/1291 (2000)].

Soon after taking office, Joseph Kabila began to impress foreign leaders—especially those from Western countries—with his sobriety and dedication. "I always back my words with action; when I promise something, I have to do it," said Kabila [*Financial Times*, May 9, 2001]. To prove that these were not empty words, he replaced most of his father's cabinet and repealed some of the elder Kabila's problematic economic policies, rescinding, for example, the monopoly granted by his father to Israel's International Diamond Industries (IDI) diamonds. Kabila's economic strides—including floating the country's currency and raising the artificially low price of fuel—were sufficient to regenerate interest from the International Monetary Fund, which has waxed positive about renewing relations with Congo [ibid., May 10, 2001; May 29, 2001]. He also initiated prompt cooperation with the United Nations, finally paving the way for the deployment of MONUC staff members, as well as making overtures to rebel leaders and other Congolese political factions [ibid., May 9, 2001]. By May 2001, Kabila had allowed the key opposition leader, Etienne Tshisekedi, to return from exile and reinstated former Botswana President Ketumile Masire—earlier barred by Laurent Kabila from carrying out his duties—as the Organization of African Unity's mediator in Congo [*Scotsman*, May 10, 2001]. Before the month had ended, Joseph Kabila had lifted restrictions on political parties in Congo [*Financial Times*, May 24, 2001] and agreed to a July meeting with political rivals to discuss democratic rule in the country [*Christian Science Monitor*, May 24, 2001].

Despite these positive developments, Congo has not been free of strife or controversy since Joseph Kabila ascended to the presidency. In April 2001, six Red Cross workers were killed in the country's Goma region [*Financial Times*, April 27, 2001]. Six months after Kabila assumed office, the effects of Congo's three-year civil war remained firmly entrenched: two million people were displaced, 18.5 million had no access to formal health care, 16 million had critical food needs, infant mortality had reached 41 percent in the east, four out of ten children were not in school, and only 45 percent of the population had access to safe drinking water (only 3 percent in rural areas). The interest of neighboring countries in Congo's resources—including vast diamond reserves—had not waned, fueling the continued backing of rebel forces by Uganda and Rwanda [ibid., August 8, 2001]. The *New York Times* reported that "[r]oads, schools and medical clinics barely exist" and that "[m]alnutrition and poverty have brought back diseases, like sleeping sickness, that had been under control" [August 12, 2001]. Analysts estimated that the war had caused up to 2.5 million deaths and that the country would need $350 million per year in aid to reverse negative health and mortality trends [*Washington Post*, August 15, 2001].

In January 2002, a natural disaster struck Congo. Goma's 11,380-foot Nyiragongo volcano erupted, demolishing 40 percent of the town and causing 350,000 of its 400,000 residents to flee across the border into Rwanda. The eruption ruined Goma's airport, lake port, and numerous roads; gutted stores and residences throughout the town; and knocked out the electricity and water supply [*Christian Science Monitor*, January 22, 2002]. The United States flew in thousands of blankets, water jugs, dust masks, and plastic sheeting, but Congo's Washington-based ambassador, Faida Mitifu, noted that "[t]he international response has been quite slow. . . . It has taken five days before food started getting to people" [*New York Times*, January 24, 2001].

MONUC found itself proportionately challenged by its task of demilitarizing rebel groups across Congo's vast expanse. In February 2002, Secretary-General Annan described the situation as "very volatile" (due particularly to increased fighting between rebel groups in the country's northeast region), conceded the impossibility of MONUC's task, and recommended an increase in the number of troops stationed in Congo [U.N. News Centre, February 19, 2002]. Nevertheless, by the end of the month 100 troops had arrived in Kindu, in eastern Congo, to prepare for the arrival of an additional 2,000 MONUC troops tasked with disarming 30,000 rebels [Deutsche Presse Agentur, February 28, 2002]. The MONUC mandate is currently in effect until June 15, 2002 [S/Res/1355 (2001)].

On February 25, after a delay of two years, an official "inter-Congolese dialogue" was finally convened in Sun City, South Africa. Three hundred representatives of the Congolese government, three rebel groups, and other organizations met for 45 days of negotiations [*New York Times*, February 26, 2002]. By the scheduled end of the talks, on April 11, no agreement had been reached on who would head the country's interim government during a period leading up to national elections [*Guardian*, April 12, 2002]. The current government proposed that Joseph Kabila remain president for a period of 18 to 24 months. The Congolese Liberation Movement, backed by Uganda, voiced no objection to this arrangement, but the Rwanda-supported Congolese Rally for Democracy refused to accept Kabila as the head of a transitional government [*New York Times*, April 11, 2002]. The dialogue was extended for a week, but ended without a full consensus, though the pact between the current government and the Congolese Liberation Movement remained intact [ibid., April 20, 2002].

Sierra Leone

After more than ten years of civil war in Sierra Leone, the past year has witnessed significant progress toward peace in the West African nation. The **U.N. Mission in Sierra Leone (UNAMSIL)**, after suffering humiliating setbacks in 2000, has been instrumental in setting the stage for decreased fighting between the Sierra Leone government and the **Revolutionary United Front (RUF)**. With 17,400 troops currently deployed, UNAMSIL is the largest peacekeeping mission in operation [*New York Times*, March 21, 2002]. The mission's mandate specifies that it should: "assist the Government of Sierra Leone in the implementation of the disarmament, demobilization and reintegration plan," "monitor adherence to the ceasefire in accordance with the ceasefire agreement of 18 May 1999," "facilitate the delivery of humanitarian assistance," "provide support, as requested, to the elections, which are to be held in accordance with the present constitution of Sierra Leone," and "guard weapons, ammunition and other military equipment collected from ex-combatants and to assist in their subsequent disposal or destruction," among other tasks [S/Res/1270 (1999); and S/Res/1289 (2000)].

During the first months of 2001, the situation in Sierra Leone appeared bleak, with RUF rebels "raping, killing and abducting Sierra Leonean refugees fleeing desperate conditions," according to Human Rights Watch [April 3, 2001]. But UNAMSIL peacekeepers soon began to assert their force against rebel forces, deploying in April 2001 to the town of Makeni, a former RUF headquarters [BBC News, April 17, 2001]. By May, the *New York Times* reported that rebel forces had begun to release child soldiers, one of RUF's principal and cruelest weapons. However, sources suggested that neighboring Liberia and Guinea were now bearing the brunt of the conflict, with the same forces simply "moving to new ground." Fighting remained entrenched in the eastern region of Sierra Leone, home to the diamond mines that financed the Liberian-backed RUF militia [May 26, 2001].

In January 2002, while UNAMSIL troops procured the disarmament of over 47,000 former RUF combatants [Agence France Presse, January 17, 2002], Secretary-General Annan and the Security Council pressed forward with plans to set up a war crimes tribunal in Sierra Leone. Scaled down from its original design, the tribunal would target the prosecution of approximately 20 accused ringleaders of the country's civil war [*New York Times*, January 4, 2002], including Foday Sankoh, the RUF leader in detention in a secret location since early 2000. As the London *Guardian* noted, "[t]here is a compelling case against Mr. Sankoh as the head of a force which systematically raped, enslaved and mutilated thousands of people by cutting off their arms. Children were a favoured target: boys were taken as bearers or to fight, while thousands of girls were kidnapped for sex" [January 17, 2002]. The Sierra Leone war crimes tribunal is set to begin operations in the fall of 2002 and will be jointly run by Sierra Leonean judges and lawyers and "prominent jurists from outside the country" [*New York Times*, March 21, 2002].

In March 2002, although the sexual abuse scandal in West African refugee camps had cast a shadow on locally hired UNHCR staff members, the Security Council extended the UNAMSIL mandate through September 30, 2002. UNAMSIL's expressed goal is maintaining a secure environment for national elections to be held in May 2002 [S/Res/1400 (2002)]. By the end of March, increasing numbers of refugees began to return to Sierra Leone from Guinea [U.N. News Centre, March 22, 2002], and April saw the approval by the election commissioner of the RUF Party's candidate for president, Paolo Bangura [*New York Times*, April 12, 2002].

Ethiopia and Eritrea

In July 2000, the United Nations established its most recent peacekeeping operation, the **U.N. Mission in Ethiopia and Eritrea (UNMEE)**. With 4,200 troops deployed in the two countries, UNMEE is mandated to "monitor the cessation of hostilities," "monitor the temporary security zone (TSZ) to assist in ensuring compliance with the agreement on Cessation of Hostilities," and "coordinate and provide technical assistance for humanitarian mine-action activities in the TSZ and areas adjacent to it," in addition to other duties [S/Res/1320 (2000)].

In many ways, UNMEE has proven itself to be the least volatile of the current African peacekeeping missions. Despite many difficult conditions, the U.N. Mission in Ethiopia and Eritrea is "considered a model mission" in which "there are more offers for peacekeepers than there is space" [*New York Times*, April 6, 2001]. Eritrea had existed as an Italian colony, but was annexed by Emperor Haile Selasse of Ethiopia in 1962. Rebels from both countries joined forces to defeat another Ethiopian dictator,

Mengistu Haile Mariam, in 1991, and Eritrea became an independent nation. But the 620-mile border between the two countries remained ill defined, and full-scale war erupted in 1998 over the small border town of Badme [ibid., April 14, 2002]. Over the next two years, 100,000 soldiers died. Yet for the last six months of 2000, both countries observed a cease-fire with no assistance from peacekeepers [ibid., April 6, 2001].

Despite relative calm in the region, there was no shortage of problems connected to fallout from the war. Exports of products such as shoes, clothing, and salt fell from $100 million in 1997 to $20 million in 2001 [ibid., April 24, 2001]. Total costs of the war reached $2.9 billion, with defense spending increasing from $95 million in 1997–1998 to $777 million in 1999–2000, while only 47 of 217 foreign investment projects approved before the war were still operational at the end of 2000 [*Financial Times*, August 8, 2001]. In April 2001, 135,000 people remained displaced from the war [*New York Times*, April 24, 2001], and the World Food Program reported in May that a million Eritreans were jeopardized by hunger due to delays in establishing the buffer zone between Ethiopia and Eritrea [ibid., May 24, 2001]. At the same time, the Ethiopian government, dominated by the Ethiopian People's Front for Democracy and Justice, took a hard line toward its own citizens. It ordered a brutal suppression of student protests, which resulted in at least 30 deaths in April 2001 while also rounding up hundreds of suspected dissidents, including opposition leaders and well-known academics. Other citizens, frustrated by widespread poverty and unemployment, responded with riots and looting [*Financial Times*, May 29, 2001]. On the other side of the nondemarcated border, Eritrea expelled the Italian ambassador after he expressed concern over government attacks on dissenters. "It is very difficult to see where Eritrea is going," said Ambassador Mario Baldi. "It seems as though it is isolating itself from the rest of the world" [ibid., October 2, 2001].

In December 2001, *Le Monde Diplomatique*'s Jean-Louis Peninou described the situation as "tense but generally under control," ascribing much of the tension to the U.N.'s "hasty" rendering of the Temporary Security Zone, based mainly on reference points provided by Ethiopia. In March 2002, the Secretary-General was able to assure the Security Council that the situation in Ethiopia and Eritrea "remained generally calm," although both parties were still "essentially defensive." Secretary-General Annan reminded the council of the enormous threat posed by landmines in the region, although mine clearance teams succeeded in clearing 2,133,369 square meters of minefield and battlefield areas in the Temporary Security Zone between December 2001 and February 2002. "[T]he leaders of Eritrea and Ethiopia should be commended for having left much of the war legacy behind them," he concluded [S/2002/245, March 8, 2002]. The Secretary-General's Special Representative for Children and Armed Conflict also found reasons for optimism, when, following a mission to Eritrea and Ethiopia in March 2002, he reported having found very little use of child soldiers and "no evidence of child abuse in refugee camps," in stark contrast to other conflict zones monitored by the United Nations [U.N. News Centre, March 26, 2002].

With UNMEE mandated to remain in the area through September 15, 2002 [S/Res/1398, March 15, 2002], Eritrea and Ethiopia made the news again in April 2002, when an international commission presented its ruling on the new permanent border. "Whatever the Ethiopian government has announced is a lie," said a state television announcer in Eritrea [*Washington Post*, April 14, 2002]. The *New York Times* reported that "[t]ensions between the two countries remain so high that the United Nations peacekeepers . . . patrolling . . . the disputed border went on a heightened state of alert" [April 14, 2002]. Badme, the small border town over which the war between the two countries had originally exploded, also found its way back into the international news. "I'm a seventh-generation descendent of Badme, and I'm an Ethiopian," the *New York Times* quoted Mamuye Legesse as saying, when informed that Badme now fell on the Eritrean side of the border. But Legesse declined to resume armed conflict over the border dispute, according to the *New York Times*. "I will claim in the right way, through the commission, that this is my land," he stated. "If that doesn't work, I won't fight. War is too destructive. That war destroyed our land" [April 16, 2002].

Western Sahara

The oldest peacekeeping operation in Africa is the **U.N. Mission for the Referendum in Western Sahara (MINURSO)**. The main task of MINURSO, which has been in existence for 11 years, is to monitor "all matters relating to a referendum in which the people of Western Sahara would choose between independence and reintegration with Morocco" [S/Res/690, April 29, 1991]. The dispute in Western Sahara harkens back to the end of Spanish colonial rule in 1976, when Morocco annexed the territory. For the past 25 years, the Saharawis, descended from nomadic desert tribes, have lived in exile in southwest Algeria. Their homes are tent cities that have burgeoned into functioning societies with 90 percent literacy and equal rights for women. Under the auspices of the Popular Front for the Liberation of the Saguia de Hamra and Rio de Oro (POLISARIO Front), with support from Algeria, Cuba, and Libya, Saharawis fought against Morocco—supported by the United States—for the 15 years, leading up to the U.N.-brokered cease-fire in 1991 [*Independent*, June 12, 2001]. Since then, MINURSO has faced a situation so intractable that the Secretary-General recently pondered whether "it might be time to write off the UN's 11-year bid to solve the dispute between Morocco and the Algerian-based Polisario Front" [Agence France Presse, February 20, 2002].

Even to the mildest of critics, U.N. handling of the Western Sahara situation has often been puzzling. As recently as June 2001, the United Nations through its envoy to Western Sahara, former U.S. Secretary of State James Baker, was preparing to propose "substantial autonomy" under Moroccan sovereignty to the beleaguered territory. The arrangement would have involved elections of an executive to run the territory's internal affairs, while Morocco handled defense, foreign affairs and the "preservation of territorial integrity against secessionist attempts," pending a referendum on final status to be held after five years [*Financial Times*, June 28, 2001]. Some weeks later, Morocco signed deals allowing a French energy company, TotalFinaElf, and a U.S.-based operation, Kerr-McGee, to engage in oil exploration in an area totaling 90,000 square miles off the coast of Western Sahara. "After protests from Polisario," reported the *Financial Times*, "UN experts are looking into the legality of the oil licences" [September 14, 2001]. Not until late January 2002 did the U.N. Under-Secretary for Legal Affairs deliver his opinion that "if further exploration and exploitation activities were to proceed in disregard of the interests and wishes of the people of Western Sahara, they would be in violation of the international law principles applicable to mineral resource activities in Non-Self-Governing Territories" [S/2002/161, February 12, 2002].

Critics such as European Union Member of Parliament Margot Kessler pointed out "a direct link between Morocco's persistent refusal to abide by international legality in relation [to] its occupation of Western Sahara, and the gross violations of human rights this regime perpetrates on a daily basis against the Saharawi population." Kessler cited the Moroccan bombing of Saharawis with napalm in 1975, the poisoning of Saharawi wells, the killing of their camel herds, and widespread slaughter campaigns. "To this day," she continued, "living under Moroccan occupation means to live with the fear of arbitrary arrest, torture, detention without trial, unfair trial, disappearance, and summary execution" [article published by the Institute of Human Rights, Potsdam University, October 2001].

In December 2001, a number of institutions and individuals, including five recipients of the Nobel Peace Prize, wrote letters to Secretary-General Kofi Annan, congratulating him on being awarded the Nobel Peace Prize for 2001, and reminded him that the "abandonment of the referendum in Western Sahara would constitute a betrayal of the inalienable right of the Saharawi people to self-determination" and that the same act "would also be a defeat for the United Nations' proud history of support for decolonization and respect for international legality" [letter to Kofi Annan from José Ramos-Horta, Rigoberta Menchú Tum, Oscar Arias Sánchez, Adolfo Perez Esquivel, Máiread Maguire, and Cora Weiss, December 12, 2001].

In January 2002, the *Washington Post* reported that the POLISARIO Front had released a group of 115 Moroccan soldiers, after 25 years of captivity [January 18, 2002], but the *Financial Times* stated in March 2002 that

Morocco had increased its diplomatic efforts to convince Western governments to oppose any proposal to partition Western Sahara. "The issue is between Morocco and Algeria," said Morocco's foreign minister, Mohammad Benissa [March 14, 2002]. By the end of March, with the MINURSO mandate under the latest in a series of two- and three-month extensions [S/Res/1394, February 27, 2002], the Security Council was reported to be considering four options, including moving forward with a referendum for self-determination; revising a plan for Western Sahara autonomy under Moroccan rule; presenting each side with a nonnegotiable division of the territory; and withdrawing the MINURSO troops [Agence France Presse, March 26, 2002].

2.   Asia: Keeping the Peace in East Timor
By Nick Birnback

After hundreds of years of Portuguese rule, 24 years of Indonesian occupation, and almost 3 years under U.N. transitional administration, East Timor became an independent nation on May 20, 2002. It has been a long and devastating struggle for the East Timorese, and undoubtedly more hardship lies ahead. Nevertheless, for the first time since the 16th century, the fate of *Timor Loro Sa'i* is in the hands of the territory's true sovereign: the East Timorese people. The international community played an indispensable role in this process, and in many ways East Timor remains a U.N. success story.

UNTAET

By the end of October 1999, the political situation radically changed for East Timor. The Indonesian Assembly (the MPR) had ruled that the "integration" of East Timor was officially null and void; pro-independence leader Xanana Gusmão had returned triumphantly to Dili; U.N. Security Council Resolution 1272 (October 25, 1999) had created the U.N. Transitional Administration in East Timor (UNTAET); and the last Indonesian representatives had left East Timor. The Australian-led International Force for East Timor (INTERFET) began preparations for its withdrawal; in February 2000, it was officially replaced by UNTAET.

At a terrible cost of human suffering and bloodshed, the determination and bravery of the East Timorese people finally paid off, though Herculean obstacles to anything approximating normalcy still remained. UNTAET inherited a territory literally razed to the ground, with the majority of the population homeless or dislocated or both, a massive refugee problem, and a constant lingering threat from militia groups that had simply moved locales and now operated from across the border in West

Timor. This later threat was made painfully clear when militia groups brutally murdered three UNHCR staff members in their office in Atambua, West Timor, in September 2000. What little civil infrastructure had existed prior to the popular consultation had been destroyed. There was an acute shortage of East Timorese with any type of professional training, and even the provision of the most basic of services proved daunting. UNTAET's mandate, passed under Chapter VII of the U.N. Charter, was to establish an effective administration for East Timor; to coordinate humanitarian, rehabilitation, and development assistance; and to support capacity-building for East Timor's eventual transition to self-rule [S/Res/1272, October 25, 1999]. Since the arrival of UNTAET, the International Community has spent over $2.4 billion to protect and rebuild East Timor [*Sydney Morning Herald*, April 18, 2002]. The road had been bumpy and UNTAET and the East Timorese have faced many challenges over the almost three years, but at the time of writing, the future looks comparatively bright.

First and foremost, UNTAET and its almost 9,000 peacekeepers and over 1,000 civilian police (CivPol) succeeded in keeping the peace following the departure of INTERFET. This was assisted greatly by the signing of an April 2000 Memorandum of Understanding between the West Timor Indonesian Military (TNI) Commander and UNTAET's Force Commander [U.N. News Service, April 11, 2000]. The Mission has made great strides in the complex task of establishing a public and civic administration for East Timor. With UNTAET's help, siginifcant progress has been made. A fully-Timorese Council of Ministers is already running the majority of the transitional government, almost 10,000 East Timorese have been recruited as civil servants, over 200,000 refugees have returned to East Timor since October 1999 (UNHCR estimates less than 60,000 remain), a customs service has been established, a battalion of former-FALINTIL fighters have been trained and re-formed as the nucleus of an East Timor Defence Force, and over 1,450 East Timorese have been trained and are now members of the East Timorese Police Service. An official language has been chosen (controversially, Portuguese), and an official currency selected (the U.S. dollar). With the cooperation of Jakarta, UNTAET has also established a Joint Border Commission to facilitate the institution of neighborly relations between East Timor and Indonesia [See S/2002/80, Report of the Secretary-General on the U.N. Transitional Administration in East Timor, January 19, 2002; Fact Sheets #1, #2, and #10, UNTAET Office of Communications and Public Information, February 2002].

East Timorese Foreign Policy

East Timor has also moved toward closer ties with its Asian neighbors. President-elect Gusmão has consistently advocated reconciliation with Indonesia, and his attitude has been echoed for the most part by the diplomacy of Nobel laureate and current East Timorese Foreign Minister Jose Ramos Horta. This policy of reconciliation was greatly assisted by then Indonesian President Abdurrahman Wahid's February 2000 apology for "Indonesia's history of atrocities in East Timor" [Associated Press, March 1, 2000].

In addition to improved relations with Jakarta, East Timor has maintained its close ties with Canberra, signing a number of agreements and co-ventures with Australia. Notable among these are the Timor Sea Arrangements (July 5, 2001) concerning energy exploration in the potentially vastly lucrative Baya-Undan fields under the Timor Sea between East Timor and Australia [*New York Times*, July 6, 2001]. This represented the first time in its history that the United Nations negotiated a bilateral treaty on behalf of a soon-to-be independent nation.

East Timor has also pursued expanded diplomatic ties with other regional powers, requesting observer status in Association of Southeast Asian Nations (ASEAN), a traditional first step to membership [*Financial Times*, July 25, 2000]. Malaysia, Thailand, and the Philippines have all contributed troops to the peacekeeping effort. Japan, a long-time financial donor to peacekeeping operations, has sent the largest ever, overseas military deployment, around 700 all ranks (including for the first time, female personnel) of its self-defense forces [Deutsche Presse Agentur, March 22, 2002].

Elections

Following the completion of a comprehensive voters registry of over 737,000 people on August 30, 2001 (not-coincidentally, the two-year anniversary of the Popular Consultation), the East Timorese elected an 88-member "Constituent Assembly." In March 2002, the body overwhelmingly adopted the Constitution of the "Democratic Republic of East Timor," ending a 17-month-long process of negotiation [Associated Press, March 22, 2002]. With a legislative body and a Constitution in place, in mid-April 2002, the East Timorese went to the polls and chose their first President in "the third and last U.N.-organized election to be held in East Timor" [Independent Electoral Commission Chief Electoral Officer Carlos Valenzuela, Press Statement, April 17, 2002]. Long-time independence leader Xanana Gusmão won easily with 82 percent of the popular vote, campaigning on a platform of "national reconciliation, investment, national development, democracy, good governance and freedom of the press" [Xanana Gusmão, *Themes of the Presidential Campaign*, March 15, 2002]. Disagreements reportedly remain, however, between Gusmão and East Timorese Prime Minister Mari Alkateri over the latter's rejection of the President-elect's plans for a government of National Unity [Associated Press, April 18, 2002].

Justice

The issue of justice, both current and retrospective, remains one of the single greatest concerns to both the international community and the East Timorese people. On the domestic front, the East Timorese and UNTAET have made significant strides in establishing a functioning criminal justice system. Despite an initial lack of trained personnel, UNTAET has succeeded in establishing a Prosecutor General's Office, a public defender's service, district and appeals courts, and a prison system [UNTAET Fact Sheets #8, February 12 and 13, 2002]. Through the East Timorese-led Office of the General Prosecutor, modest progress has also been made in the prosecution of serious crimes committed in East Timor from January 1 to October 25. This has included the expansion of the Serious Crimes Unit and the handing down of a number of indictments for crimes against humanity. The successful December 2001 prosecution of the "Los Palos case" defendants marked the first international application of laws originally created for the International Criminal Court. However, UNTAET itself admits that limited resources and a lack of trained personnel have slowed the process down to a near crawl [ibid.]. Some observers have suggested that the judicial system is still "only partly functioning and is fragile and vulnerable to interference" ["East Timor: Justice at Risk," Amnesty International Press Release, July 27, 2001]. "Law and order is barely maintained; justice in not being administered effectively; and the human rights of the East Timorese people cannot be guaranteed" [ibid.].

In addition to the development of the criminal justice system, a fully-East Timorese Commission for Reception, Truth, and Reconciliation was chartered in Dili (in January 2002). Six regional offices were established soon after. The Commission is chartered to "seek the truth" regarding human rights violations in East Timor during the Indonesian occupation and up until the arrival of UNTAET and to establish community reconciliation through a truth-telling mechanism at the local level. Through local mediation panels, the Commission will also address past cases of "lesser crimes such as looting, burning and minor assault . . . to reach agreement on an act of reconciliation to be carried out by the perpetrator." The Commission does not address major criminal acts, which are referred to the Serious Crimes Unit [UNTAET Fact Sheet #10, February 2002]. President-elect Gusmão has also indicated his desire to see amnesties granted to former militia members [Associated Press, April 23, 2002].

The pursuit of justice is also proceeding on the international front. While the human rights community had been decrying the brutality of the Indonesian occupation since the 1970s, the wholesale destruction of East Timor in 1999 by pro-Indonesian forces finally provoked a public outcry demanding some kind of accountability. This charge was led by the U.N. Secretary-General, who spoke about possible "crimes against humanity" and declared that "the individuals who have ordered and carried out these crimes must be held accountable" [*New York Times*, September 11, 1999; U.N. Press Release, SG/SM/7127, September 11, 1999].

INTERFET's mandate, although passed under the peace enforcement section of the U.N. Charter, was justified on largely humanitarian grounds and specifically "demanded" that those responsible for such acts of violence be brought to justice [SC/1999/1264, September 15, 1999]. Initially the process seemed to be headed toward the establishment of an international tribunal along the lines of those that had been established for Rwanda and the former Yugoslavia. The U.N. Commission on Human Rights called on the Secretary-General to establish an international commission of inquiry to conduct investigations into violations of human rights and humanitarian law in East Timor since January 1999 [Ian Martin, "Self-Determination for East Timor," LynneReiner, 2001, p. 114]. U.N. legal experts visited East Timor at the end of 1999 and proposed further investigations. However, after weighing the geostrategic importance of repairing damaged relations with Indonesia, the international community soon lost interest and, instead, pushed for redress through Indonesian judicial processes [Geoffrey Robinson, "If you leave us, we will die," *Dissent* winter 2002, p. 11]. Indonesia has established an Ad Hoc Human Rights Court and has charged a number of high-level Indonesian officials with crimes related to activities in East Timor [*New York Times*, November 4, 2001]. However, sentences thus far have amounted to little more than slaps on the wrist, and the Prosecutor General in Jakarta has yet to cooperate with judicial authorities in Dili. Following the light sentences handed down for the murderers of the UNHCR workers and the failure of Jakarta to charge the TNI Commander General Wiranto with any crime, most legal observers have little faith in the objectivity or competency of Indonesian courts with regard to East Timor.

"Free at Last, Free at Last": Post-UNTAET East Timor

Though UNTAET formally handed over authority to the East Timorese government on May 20, 2002, the U.N. presence will not disappear from the island. UNTAET's successor mission, the U.N. Mission of Support in East Timor (UNMISET), will last for a two-year period and will continue to provide substantive assistance and support to East Timor's civil, political, judicial, and security infrastructures [Secretary-General's Report, April 23, 2002]. The United Nations has succeeded in maintaining basic security and establishing the administrative and economic structures necessary to create a sustainable state. However, the institutions are fragile and underresourced, and it will take a continuing and serious commitment on behalf of the international community to ensure that East Timor takes its rightful place in the community of nations.

The United Nations has a great deal to be proud of in East Timor. "Of the recent international efforts to put failed states or contested territories under some kind of international trusteeship," the *Economist* writes, "East Timor seems among the most successful" [April 17, 2001]. The international community kept the issue alive until the political dynamic in Indonesia shifted sufficiently to allow an act of self-determination to take place. The United Nations planned, organized, and carried out a complex electoral exercise in adverse conditions and within an exceptionally compressed timetable. Following the Indonesian failure to live up to its security obligations under the May 5 Agreements, the United Nations was able to mobilize international support to the point where the Indonesians allowed a Chapter VII-mandated multinational force to be deployed inside their "sovereign" territory. This, too, was done at an accelerated pace and with an unprecedented level of international consensus for action.

For almost three years, UNTAET has fulfilled the functions of a government in East Timor, filling the gap and assisting while the territory prepared to become an independent and self-sustaining state. Law and order has been maintained and the basic structures of government and administration are in place. All these accomplishments would not have been possible without the intervention of the United Nations. But there are more sobering lessons as well. Perhaps as much as a third of the East Timorese population died as a result of the Indonesian occupation, but because of Indonesia's strategic significance as the world's fourth largest nation (and significantly, the largest "pro-Western" Muslim country), the international community could not generate the political will to act. The United Nations signed onto an agreement whereby security for the ballot would be provided by the very institution responsible for wide-scale abuses and repression. Later, a U.N. mission stood by blind, trapped, and helpless as murderous thugs carried out "an orchestrated scorched-earth policy commanded by Indonesia's military" [*New York Times*, February 25, 2002], killing hundreds if not thousands, looting, raping, burning, and ultimately dislocating most of an entire terrified population. Had FALINTIL commanders not steadfastly refused to allow their troops to be provoked into attacking the militia groups, the situation could have easily degenerated even further, with Indonesia credibly claiming that the killing was the result of a civil war within East Timor.

The United Nations leaves behind a population unsure of whether they will ever see justice for the crimes committed against them. East Timor enters the international community as the poorest state in Southeast Asia. By its own admission, UNTAET's "Timorization" policy has progressed slowly and has not succeeded in fully preparing the East Timorese people to take the reigns of government. And yet, through an act of almost unimaginably courageous self-determination, East Timor stands on the brink of realizing the goal of an almost 500-year-old struggle. In the end, the only heroes of the story are the East Timorese people themselves.

3. Peace in Latin America and the Caribbean
By Cristina Eguizábal and Diana Ayton-Shenker

During the 1990s, U.N. peacekeeping operations (PKOs) were instrumental in ending civil wars in El Salvador and Guatemala and restoring stability in Haiti (following President Aristide's return to power). However, their success in bringing a lasting peace to the region over the long term has been less clear-cut. Several constraints have hindered the effectiveness of the PKOs: limited mandates, lackluster support from the international community, a disinterested international media, and difficulty obtaining pledges from donors. Most of all, powerful sectors within post-conflict societies have been unwilling to make the sacrifices required to sustain peace based on social justice and respect of human rights.

In recent years, the region has enjoyed significant democratic advances; free elections, civilian governments, and political party alternation have become the norm. Unfortunately, institutional weakness, economic inequality, and increased personal insecurity continue to plague the region and seriously threaten the political gains of the last decade.

With the exception of the U.N. Verification Mission in Guatemala (MINUGUA), no U.N. PKOs are currently active in Latin American and the Caribbean. Though many Latin American countries are confronting some kind of political crisis and several border issues persist throughout the region, most civil conflicts have been contained, if not resolved. The case of Colombia stands out with its internal violence and instability, raising implications for potential U.N. peacekeeping efforts in the near future.

Guatemala: Is the Work Done for MINUGUA?

In 1996, the government of Guatemala and the National Revolutionary Army of Guatemala (URNG) signed Peace Accords ending over three decades of civil war. At the same time, the U.N. Verification Mission in Guatemala (MINUGUA) was established to support the peace process and oversee its implementation. Its mandate was originally intended to span four years ending in 2000, by which time specific commitments of the peace agenda were supposed to be met. However, when it became evident that progress was lagging far behind schedule, the parties involved requested MINUGUA to maintain its mission in Guatemala through 2003 [A/55/389].

Despite the initial optimism expressed at the January 2000 election of President Alfonso Portillo, after two years in office his government has been unable to revitalize the peace process in Guatemala. The international donor community, Guatemalan civic groups, and human rights organizations have all denounced the governing *Frente Republicano Guatemalteco*'s (FRG's) limited commitment or capacity to implement the electoral, military, and fiscal reforms identified in the peace agenda.

Secretary-General Annan asserted that the sustainability and strength of the peace process were threatened because it was still having "little impact on the lives of Guatemala's people" [A/55/973, para. 6, June 1, 2001]. He expressed concern at the growing "deterioration of public security" and "climate of intimidation," citing the rise of crime, "actions by armed criminal groups," and threats against judicial officials, human rights advocates, public figures, and journalists [ibid.]. Unfortunately, this recent trend has prompted fears of a new wave of political violence [*New York Times*, May 3, 2002].

The Timetable Agreement of the Peace Accords specified commitments to be met in four thematic areas: (1) resettlement, integration, and reconciliation; (2) comprehensive human developments; (3) sustainable development of production; and (4) modernization of the democratic state [ibid., para. 25]. Three additional areas "cut across the entire peace agenda: indigenous peoples' rights, commitments on women, and the strengthening of social participation" [ibid.]. Unfortunately, by the start of 2002, most of the rescheduled commitments (extended from December 2000 to December 2004) had not yet been implemented [MINUGUA, *Informe para el grupo Consultivo para Guatemala*, Guatemala de la Asuncion, January 18, 2002, p. 4].

For Guatemalans, the Peace Accords provided "a national agenda of democratization and development aimed at overcoming poverty, promoting reconciliation, and reducing the historic social debt still borne by the State toward major segments of the population" [MINUGUA, Press Release, REF.05–2002; Message of Gerd Merem, the Special Representative of the U.N. Secretary-General to the Consultative Group for Guatemala, Washington, D.C., February 11, 2002].

Sadly, the most marginalized and excluded sectors in Guatemala (indigenous peoples, women, and peasants) have yet to realize the "hopes that accompanied the signing of the Peace Agreements" [ibid.] and live in poverty or extreme poverty. To overcome this inequity, it is urgent to close the "continuing gulf in access to education, justice, and health, especially between the indigenous and non-indigenous population and between the urban and rural population" [ibid.]. To counter discrimination against indigenous and rural populations, MINUGUA has recommended incorporating an increased number of indigenous people in the civil service [MINUGUA, *Informe para el grupo Consultivo para Guatemala*, Guatemala de la Asuncion, January 18, 2002, p. 6].

MINUGUA acknowledges that sufficient public spending is necessary to implement "the most important peace priorities, including education, health, housing, justice, public security, rural development and special attention to the uprooted and demobilized sectors of the population" [MINUGUA, Press Release, REF.05–2002; Message of Gerd Merrem, Washington, D.C., February 11, 2002]. However, it cautions that "implementation of many of the pending commitments . . . will be impossible in 2002 with the [insufficient] finance resources that have been assigned" [ibid.]. Fierce opposition from the business sector has blocked all attempts to enlarge the tax base through the establishment of income and capital taxes. To address this situation and provide resources to the state, MINUGUA advocates the "comprehensive implementation of the Fiscal Pact," making public spending prioritized and transparent [ibid.]. Special Representative of the U.N. Secretary-General to the Consultative Group for Guatemala Gerd Merem adds, "macroeconomic stability must be reconciled with political stability, social spending and public investment, especially in a post-conflict society" [ibid.].

In concluding his report on MINUGUA's efforts to verify compliance with the peace agreements, the Secretary-General noted that "much has been achieved but much remains to be done . . . [to overcome] the profound social inequalities that still exist" in Guatemala [A/55/973, para. 79]. In particular, the Secretary-General highlighted gender inequity, lack of access to basic services, unequal employment opportunity, poverty, "extreme poverty," and ethnic discrimination as threats to the peace process. According to the Secretary-General, resolving this social inequity is "the basic prerequisite for guaranteeing peace and eliminating the considerable potential for conflict that still characterizes Guatemalan society" [ibid.].

MINUGUA will continue to verify compliance with the Peace Accords according to the new timetable for implementation "until the process concludes in 2003" [ibid., para. 78].

Colombia: How to Pursue the Peace Effort?

During his 1998 political campaign, former President Pastrana declared his intention of "internationalizing peace" and outlined the different roles that the international community could play: as facilitator of pre-negotiation conditions, proponent of negotiating formulas, witness of future accords, and verifier of their implementation. Once in office, however, neither the government nor the largest guerilla group, the **Revolutionary Armed Forces of Colombia (FARC)**, encouraged the international community to participate in negotiations [Fernando Cepeda, *La dimension internacional del proceso de paz*, Summit of the Americas Center; *Conflicto armado: perspectivas de paz y democracia*, Miami, Latin American and Caribbean Center, 2001, pp. 81–85].

Indeed, it was only after the peace process was already unraveling, in January 2002, that the Group of Facilitating Countries (Canada, Cuba, France, Italy, Mexico, Norway, Spain, Sweden, Switzerland, and Venezuela) was able to observe the aftermath of the talks. Pastrana's government never accepted offers from the United Nations, the European governments, or the United States for technical assistance to define strategy or devise negotiating tactics for the process. Nonetheless, the international community's participation has been increasing in terms of resources invested, effective participation, and ground presence in Colombia [ibid.].

Incrementally, specialized U.N. agencies have been upgrading their field activity on the ground in Colombia. This has been the case, for example, of the UNHCR, UNICEF, and the U.N. High Commissioner for Human Rights (UNHCHR). Periodically, special rapporteurs have informed the international community about the plight of Colombia's internally displaced persons or child soldiers and have documented specific human rights abuses, such as the use of torture and the use of forced disappearances as a war tactic. The most active U.N. involvement with peacemaking has been through the office of the U.N. Secretary-General Special Adviser, a position currently held by James LeMoyne. (James LeMoyne, a former journalist with U.N. Development Programme [UNDP] experience, replaced the Norwegian diplomat, Jan Egeland, following Egeland's resignation in January 2002.)

By the beginning of 2002, Colombians had become increasingly vocal in their criticism of the demilitarized zone in Southern Colombia, which was being used as a safe haven for the insurgents. (As a goodwill gesture ostensibly aimed at jumpstarting the peace negotiation process, President Pastrana ceded territory to the FARC, declaring the traditional rebel stronghold to be a demilitarized zone [DMZ] on November 7, 1998.) Originally intended for a period of 90 days, the DMZ, an area roughly the size of Switzerland, remained in place until February 2002.

At this point, the FARC were in complete control of the DMZ, where they rested and trained; kept their abduction victims; grew and processed coca; and stored stolen goods, such as cars, heavy machinery, and cattle [International Crisis Group, *Colombia's Elusive Quest for Peace*, March 26, 2002, p. 21]. The international community's criticism of the DMZ had also been mounting during the last months of 2001. The European Union was particularly distressed by the abduction of three German citizens by the FARC in July 2001. By the end of the year, peace negotiations were at a complete standstill. During the entire time that the FARC had been in control of the DMZ, only one agreement was reached: a limited humanitarian accord (signed on June 2, 2001) on the release of 242 soldiers and police held hostage by the FARC.

On January 10, 2002, in the midst of campaigns for legislative elections in March and presidential elections in May, the FARC invited James LeMoyne, Daniel Parfait (the French Ambassador and coordinator of the Group of Facilitating Countries), and a representative of the Catholic Church to discuss ways of saving the peace process. This was a drastic departure from FARC's strong opposition to any mediation effort what-soever and its long held distrust vis-à-vis the international community.

Thanks to the mediation of this group, an agreement was reached on January 20 establishing an extremely ambitious timetable to discuss such difficult issues as a cease-fire, paramilitaries and kidnapping, and interna-tional verification. Large sectors of Colombia reacted with outrage and thought that the agreement gave undeserved recognition of the FARC's legitimacy as a reliable negotiating partner. They were particularly critical of the high profile roles played by LeMoyne and Parfait in securing the accord [*Los Angeles Times*, January 15, 2002].

However, negotiations resumed, and on February 7, a second proce-dural agreement was reached on the permanent presence of the U.N. Spe-cial Adviser, the Group of Facilitating Countries, and the Catholic Church in the negotiations. Less than a week later, on February 20, a FARC commando highjacked the plane carrying Senator Eduardo Gechen (President of the Colombian Senate Peace Commission, who was flying back to Bogotá), apprehended him, and took him hostage. For Pas-trana, it was the last straw; that same day, he ordered the Army to regain control of the DMZ.

(Less public, parallel peace negotiations were conducted during the Pastrana administration with the other major rebel group, the National Liberation Army [ELN]. Facilitated by Cuban authorities and held in Havana, these talks broke down at the end of May 2002 [BBC News, June 1, 2002].)

On May 26, 2002, Alvaro Uribe Velez, an ultraconservative running as an independent, was elected president of Colombia, narrowly avoiding a run-off by capturing 53 percent of the vote. His law and order message struck a chord among voters who were disappointed by the fruitless peace talks and wary of FARC's increasing use of kidnapping as a war tactic [*Le Monde Interactif*, May 28, 2002]. (As of this writing, FARC holds 1,300 hostages, including 1 presidential candidate and 5 elected officials [ibid.].)

As soon as he learned of his victory, President Uribe asked the United Nations to form a mediation team to assess the possibility of a new round of negotiations with the insurgents, providing they agree to a cease-fire and halt terrorism and kidnappings. While the United Nations responded cautiously [*Pais*, May 29, 2002], the United Self-Defense Groups (AUC) immediately supported the proposal [*Washington Post*, May 29, 2002]. Dur-ing his presidential campaign, Uribe promised to double the security forces and create a militia of a million citizens [BBC News, May 27, 2002]. Critical observers question Uribe's request for U.N. involvement as a ploy to jus-tify military build-up and the possibility of total war [*Guardian*, May 28, 2002].

Since the breakdown of the peace process in February 2002, violence has escalated dramatically and is expected to continue rising in the near future. Drug- and guerilla-related violence may spread further to Colombia's neighbors, who are facing their own difficult times. The potential of violence spilling over Colombia's borders may necessitate a regional approach, or at least a regional component, to international peacekeeping efforts in Colombia.

4. Europe: Peacekeeping in the Balkans
By Gordon Goldstein

During the past year, U.N. and international engagement in the Balkans has been a narrative with several strands. In Macedonia, peace was maintained with the help of a limited, surgical NATO intervention. In Kosovo, a fledgling effort at self-rule finally took shape. In Bosnia, security remained the constant priority and persistent challenge. And at the International War Crimes Tribunal in the Netherlands, the rapid progression of war through the Balkans was dramatically revisited through the trial of several former protagonists in the fighting, most significantly Slobodan Milosevic.

Macedonia

Throughout the 1990s, compared to its neighbors, Macedonia was a small island of relative political stability, contained from the ethnic strife that had torn apart Bosnia and Croatia. But in 2001, that balance quickly eroded. In early June, the Macedonian army renewed attempts to retake a rebel-held village in the mountainous northeast, continuing a month of government efforts to drive ethnic Albanian insurgents out of Macedonia.

The stand-off was exacerbated by the presence of at least 8,000 mostly ethnic Albanian villagers, who had been trapped in the battle zone for a month. The government said that the villagers were being used as human shields by a guerrilla group, the National Liberation Army. The armed group had been waging a five-month-long campaign seeking greater rights for Macedonia's Albanian minority. The UNHCR reported that since the start of the conflict in February 2001, about 20,000 ethnic Albanian refugees had crossed into Kosovo, the Serbian province where ethnic Albanians predominate [*New York Times*, June 2, 2001].

Eager to diffuse the crisis, the NATO alliance announced it was prepared to send up to 3,000 European troops to Macedonia to help disarm the ethnic Albanian rebels if a peace agreement could be reached. Ambassadors from the 19 NATO countries expressed willingness to contribute to a brigade-size force, with the United States providing potential support for logistics, communications, and intelligence. In a joint statement, the allies emphasized "the urgent need for a successful outcome of the political dialogue between the different parties in the former Yugoslav republic of Macedonia and the cessation of hostilities as one essential precondition for any NATO assistance" [*Washington Post*, June 21, 2001].

Fighting flared again on June 22, 2001, when Macedonian forces launched a heavy offensive against Albanian rebel positions just north of the capital, Skopje, breaking a tentative cease-fire and leaving a diplomatic initiative for a peace agreement in tatters. NATO Secretary-General Lord Robertson denounced the military action as "complete folly." The renewed fighting caused another surge of refugees fleeing into Kosovo. The UNHCR said 1,450 Albanians had crossed from Macedonia into Kosovo, bringing the total over the previous six months to more than 50,000 [*New York Times*, June 23, 2001].

As the conflict continued in the last week of June, Macedonia remained "perched between peace and war. . . . The sinews of ethnic tolerance . . . stretched precariously thin" [*Los Angeles Times*, June 29, 2001]. A fragile cease-fire gave way to intense fighting in the town of Tetovo, even as negotiators struggled to close a deal between Macedonia's Slavic majority and an ethnic Albanian minority that represented close to one-quarter of the country's two million people [ibid.].

On July 4, 2001, President Boris Trajikovski said peace talks had been resumed even though shelling and shooting continued around the northern mountains, where government troops and Albanian rebels had now been fighting for four months. "I do not doubt that we will continue to face armed provocations by those who oppose peace," the president said. "Yet I assure that together with the international community, we are firmly determined to persist along the path to which, you have to believe me, there is no alternative" [*New York Times*, July 5, 2001].

The NATO operation was envisioned to last no more than 30 days, and its primary purpose would be to supervise the disarmament of the ethnic Albanian rebels, who were to surrender their weapons voluntarily at 15 collection centers. "Everybody is absolutely determined that there must be no question of mission creep in Macedonia," a senior NATO diplomat said. "It would be politically and militarily dangerous for the alliance to get bogged down in yet another operation in the former Yugoslavia."

Britain, whose government has been particularly sensitive to fears that a war in Macedonia could reignite fighting elsewhere in the region, indicated its willingness to contribute about one-third of the proposed 3,500 troops. Italy, France, and Greece had pledged to be the other main contributors [*Washington Post*, July 14, 2001]. When summer came to a close, the NATO peacekeepers were finally on the ground, as British transport planes ferried in the first contingent of allied soldiers [*New York Times*, August 19, 2001].

Once more, Macedonia retreated from the brink, a fact noted with satisfaction by the U.N. Security Council, which passed a resolution welcoming the Framework Agreement, signed in Kopje on August 13, by the government and the leaders of four political parties. Resolution 1371 rejected "the use of violence in pursuit of political aims" and stressed that "only peaceful political solutions can assure a stable and democratic future for the former Yugoslav Republic of Macedonia" [S/Res/1371 (2001)].

Kosovo

The province of Kosovo, whose fate in 1999 unexpectedly prompted NATO's first sustained military intervention, is today essentially a ward of the international community—a U.N. protectorate held together with the reinforcement of 38,000 allied troops, including 3,000 Russians. Thousands of the Americans serving in Kosovo enthusiastically cheered President George W. Bush when he visited the largest U.S. military camp in the province and proclaimed that "America's contribution is essential, both militarily and politically" [*New York Times*, June 25, 2001].

Less than a year earlier, Mr. Bush questioned whether American troops should remain in the Balkans at all. Presumably the responsibilities of global power have been sobering to the Bush administration. Without troops from the United States and its NATO partners, Kosovo would almost certainly slip into a state of anarchic disorder even more acute than its current, constant hum of violence. Bombings, grenade attacks, house-burnings, and other forms of intimidation remain daily events in Kosovo. Most of these acts are aimed at driving out the estimated 60,000 to 100,000 remaining members of the minority Serb population—a reversal of the Serb repression of Albanians that preceded NATO's arrival [*Washington Post*, July 29, 2001].

The task of law enforcement is complicated by the frequently conflicting and overlapping jurisdiction of the peacekeeping troops and the 4,386 U.N. police. But even a more rational organizational scheme for law enforcement would not be sufficient to address the deeply systemic influence of organized crime. As Balkans scholar Misha Glenny wrote:

> The former Yugoslavia is a jumble of chronically weak states and quasi-protectorates run by the international community's ill-disciplined army of acronyms—SFOR, KFOR, and the rest. The greatest beneficiaries of this disorganization are criminal mafias, that have constructed huge networks based on the trade in illegal immigrants, prostitutes, weapons, drugs and, above all, cigarettes. These mafias do not recognize national boundaries. The Serbian underworld cooperates as happily with Albanian gangsters as it does with Bosnian or Croat tough guys. So influential has this web of crime become that the Sicilian mafia has retreated from its operations in central and northern Italy, which are now dominated by Balkan gangs. [*New York Times*, October 16, 2001]

Compounding the threat of organized crime is the influence of organized political corruption. Throughout the region, public safety is being increasingly challenged by powerful alliances between ethnic nationalist politicians and organized criminal groups. These groups have penetrated the banking system, municipal government functions, and various industries. They stage riots, engage in looting, and stage car-jackings. American and European troops who came to Bosnia in 1995 to keep warring armies apart are now confronting a new hybrid of ethno-criminal political violence, not easily ameliorated through conventional peacekeeping [*Washington Post*, June 24, 2001].

It is in this atmosphere of pervasive danger that the U.N. Mission in Kosovo (UNMIK) must operate. In an effort to gain support from Belgrade for elections in Kosovo, the UNHCR reversed its position on the return of Serbian refugees to the province, which it had previously opposed as too risky. "I think it will add to Kosovo's credibility to allow this to go ahead," said Ruud Lubbers, the U.N. High Commissioner for Refugees.

U.N. support for the repatriation of Serbian refugees to Kosovo was another reflection of the shifting politics surrounding the international administration of the province. The Special Representative of the Secretary-General in Kosovo, Hans Haekkerup (the former Danish defense minister who succeeded Bernard Kouchner as the top U.N. official in Kosovo) drafted a new constitutional framework for Kosovo that dampened Albanian expectations for independence.

The framework lays out the legal basis for a system of self-government, including elections to a ruling assembly and the nomination of a president, which will be in effect until a final settlement on Kosovo's status is reached. But it does not say when or how the final status will be decided, and Mr. Haekkerup refused Albanian requests for a referendum on independence, a directly elected president, and a constitutional court. When consultations with Albanian leaders became locked in disagreement, Mr. Haekkerup overruled their objections and signed the framework into being. The Serbs were presented with the framework as well and had no authority to veto its provisions [*New York Times*, June 8, 2001].

To encourage the nascent process of self-governance in Kosovo, the Security Council issued a statement calling upon all men and women of Kosovo to vote in the November 17 elections. The Council also called on all of Kosovo's elected leaders to publicly condemn violence and ethnic intolerance. Briefing the Council, Mr. Haekkerup said "We are standing on the threshold of fulfilling core objectives of Security Council resolution 1244—the establishment of substantial autonomy and functioning self-government in Kosovo" [SC/7165, October 5, 2001].

A party led by moderate ethnic Albanian Ibrahim Rugova won Kosovo's landmark general election, but without a sufficient margin to form a majority. Rugova's Democratic League of Kosovo won 46 percent of the votes for a 120-seat provincial assembly, while the Kosovo Democratic Party (led by former guerrilla chief Hashim Thaqi) came in second with almost 26 percent. A coalition representing Kosovo's Serbian minority won about 11 percent of the votes [*Washington Post*, November 20, 2001].

The election was part of the U.N. blueprint to establish self-rule while keeping the province under the overall authority of its international administration. "The final status of Kosovo will be decided at a later time," said Mr. Haekkerup, who supervised the balloting. "That was not part of this election, and that's not part of the powers of the assembly elected here" [ibid.]. As one editorial comment concluded:

> The Kosovo elections succeeded first and foremost because 36,000 NATO troops, including 5,400 Americans, are still deployed there as peacekeepers after Mr. Milosevic's own downfall. The peacekeepers have not stopped all violence between Serbs and Albanians, but . . . [b]acked by NATO's muscle, a UN administration has been able to restore basic services, begin reconstruction and organize the elections, even while postponing the fundamental—and still explosive—question of whether Kosovo will remain part of Serbia and Yugoslavia in the long term, or become an independent state. [*Washington Post*, November 23, 2001]

Holding free and fair elections was a signal event in the political life of Kosovo. Creating a coalition government on the basis of the balloting's outcome would prove to be a more elusive achievement. The ethnic Albanian leader, Ibrahim Rugova, twice failed to win enough support in the province's new legislature. The outcome deprived Kosovo of a president or a government almost two months after its historic first election to create self-rule under the aegis of the United Nations [*New York Times*, January 11, 2002]. By the middle of February, a government had still not been formed. Talks with the second-largest group, the Democratic Party of Kosovo (PDK), proved fruitless. The party's leader, Hashim Thaqi, demanded the post of Prime Minister, a request that was rejected. Thaqi was formerly the head of the Kosovo Liberation Army, a brutal and reportedly corrupt guerrilla force that fought a two-year war for Kosovo's independence [*Washington Post*, February 16, 2002].

On March 1, 2002, the deadlock was broken. "After more than three months of political stalemate, this is good news for Kosovo," said U.N. Secretary-General Kofi Annan. "I am glad that the political leaders appear to have put their difficulties behind them. . . . I am very pleased with the nominations of Dr. Ibrahim Rugova as President of Kosovo and Dr. Bajram Rexhepi as Prime Minister. I know that both are committed to building a positive future for all of Kosovo, and both can count on my support" [SG/SM/ 8145, 3/1/2002].

Bosnia

For the **U.N. Mission in Bosnia and Herzegovina (UNMIBH)**—like the other internationally administered territories of the Balkans—the greatest challenge was providing security. In a report issued in late 2001, Secretary-General Annan observed:

> UNMIBH continues to progress towards the goal of completing its core mandate. Significant achievements since my last report include a qualitative improvement in inter-Entity and regional police cooperation, which now focuses on anti-terrorism activities; the effective work of the State Border Service, which has reduced by two-thirds suspected illegal migration to Europe; the launching of the Police Commissioner project; the success of the STOP project in tackling human trafficking; the introduction of a disciplinary code to improve internal management systems and accountability in the police force; and the intensive preparatory work to establish a State Information and Protection Agency, legislation for which is now before State bodies. In the politically difficult environment of Bosnia and Herzegovina, these achievements have not come easily. UNMIBH has had to overcome strong resistance and, sometimes, defiance. [U.N. Security Council S/2001/1132]

While Bosnia's present remained stable enough—its ethnic conflicts held in relative check by patrolling international forces—the past came rushing back through the proceedings of the International War Crimes Tribunal in the Netherlands. In November 2001, the tribunal convicted a Bosnian Serb General, Radislav Krstic, of genocide for overseeing the 1995 massacre of as many as 8,000 Muslim men and boys after Bosnian Serb forces overwhelmed the "safe haven" declared by the United Nations in Srebrenica. The massacre at Srebrenica was the worst mass killing in Europe since the Holocaust, and the conviction was the first formal finding of genocide to arise from the Balkan wars of the 1990s. "In July 1995, General Kristic, you agreed to evil and this is why today this trial chamber convicts you and sentences you to 46 years in prison," Judge Almiro Rodrigues told the defendant [*Washington Post*, August 3, 2001; and *New York Times*, August 3, 2001].

In its first major trial to address the prison camp set up by Serbs during the Bosnian war, the tribunal convicted five Bosnian Serbs for their role in the notorious Omarska camp. The camp was a place of death and torture, set in an old, iron ore mine in the village of Omarska. What happened there in the summer of 1992, the court said, was a "hellish orgy of persecution." The five men, four of them former policemen, were all found guilty as the court concluded they had known about or participated in rape, torture, and killing of Muslim and Croat men and women under their control [*New York Times*, November 3, 2001].

The most important trial of the Balkan wars was set in motion on an early summer evening in 2001, when Slobodan Milosevic was spirited away from Belgrade to the tribunal in the Netherlands. The surprise extradition was engineered by leaders of Yugoslavia's Serb Republic in defiance of a Belgrade court [*Washington Post*, June 29, 2001]. Their motivation was simple, and their incentive was compelling. After Serbia turned over Mr. Milosevic last year, international donors pledged $1.2 billion in desperately needed, reconstruction aid, including about $130 million from the United States. Despite his legacy of nationalistic demagoguery and the wave of violence he incited with a mythic vision of a Greater Serbia, the end-game for Mr. Milosevic revolved around nothing more complicated than cold cash [*Washington Post*, February 16, 2002].

The handover of Mr. Milosevic—the first former head of state to be surrendered to an international tribunal—marked "an important day for international criminal justice," said chief prosecutor Carla Del Ponte [*New York Times*, June 30, 2001]. In his first appearance before the tribunal to stand trial for crimes against humanity, Mr. Milosevic disdainfully dismissed the court as "an illegal organ." The image of the fallen head of state now incarcerated and isolated in The Hague was a striking one for reporters. "Jutting chin raised contemptuously, Mr. Milosevic sat flanked by two guards before seven empty chairs intended for his lawyers. The former Serbian leader, who plunged the Balkans into four brutal ethnic wars, chose to appear without counsel and to deliver his own rebuttal, in English: 'I consider this tribunal a false tribunal and indictments false indictments'" [*New York Times*, July 4, 2001].

In late November 2001, the prosecution significantly broadened the case against Mr. Milosevic, charging him with committing genocide during the 1992–1995 war in Bosnia. Mr. Milosevic would be the first head of state to ever be taken to court on charges of genocide—plotting the full or partial destruction of an ethnic group—the most grievous of all war crimes. The indictment, the third filed against Mr. Milosevic at the tribunal, claims that he orchestrated a brutal ethnic-cleansing campaign carried out by the Yugoslav army and Bosnian Serb militias. The drive left 200,000 dead and spawned one million refugees.

According to the indictment, "Slobodan Milosevic participated in a joint criminal enterprise, the purpose of which was the forcible and permanent removal of the majority of non-Serbs, principally Bosnian Muslims and Bosnian Croats." It holds him responsible for the expulsion of thousands of people from Bosnia, and the killing of more than 7,000 Muslims in July 1995 in Srebrenica. The prosecution claimed that "[t]he total number of people expelled or imprisoned is estimated at over a quarter million."

The indictment claims that prisoners were held in "conditions of life calculated to bring about the partial physical destruction of those groups, namely through starvation, contaminated water, forced labor, inadequate medical care, and constant physical and psychological assault" [*Washington*

Post, November 24, 2001; and *New York Times*, November 24, 2001]. At a pretrial hearing in late January 2002, Mr. Milosevic again dismissed the charges and lashed out at the prosecution and judges presiding over the tribunal. "Serbian politics, Serbia and I myself were involved in creating peace in Bosnia and Croatia. We were not involved in making war," he insisted [*New York Times*, January 31, 2002].

The trial of former President Milosevic, which is expected to last two years, opened on February 12, 2002. "One must not seek ideals underlying the acts of the accused," Ms. Del Ponte explained during the prosecution's opening statement. "Beyond the nationalist pretext and the horror of ethnic cleansing, beyond the grandiloquent rhetoric and the hackneyed phrases he used, the search for power is what motivated Slobodan Milosevic." As a wave of violence orchestrated by Mr. Milosevic spread across the Balkans, "some of the incidents revealed an almost medieval savagery and a calculated cruelty that went beyond the bounds of legitimate warfare" [*New York Times*, February 13, 2002].

In his energetic four-hour opening statement, Mr. Milosevic largely ignored the charges made against him and continued to denounce the tribunal's legitimacy. "This court is illegal," he said, "because it is financed through donations by, for example, Saudi Arabia, that also finances international terrorism." Saudi Arabia is 1 of 28 countries donating money to the tribunal. "You basically have nothing," said Milosevic, "and that is why you have to concoct things, you have to invent things." Milosevic added: "The real crime was the killing of Yugoslavia and crucifying me here." Of the indictments accusing him of war crimes, Milosevic described them variously as a "terrible fabrication," a "nebulous construction," and a "miserable opus" [*Washington Post*, February 15, 2002; and *New York Times*, February 15, 2002].

"I shall indeed avail myself of my right to examine and cross-examine witnesses," Mr. Milosevic said during the second day of his opening statement, promising to prove that it was the United States and NATO—rather than his leadership—that had carried out policies of genocide in the Balkans. Mr. Milosevic said he would seek testimony from former President Bill Clinton, former Secretary of State Madeleine Albright, U.N. Secretary-General Kofi Annan, former Senator Bob Dole, former German Chancellor Helmut Kohl, and the entire U.S. negotiating team at the 1995 Bosnian peace talks in Dayton, Ohio [*Washington Post*, February 16, 2002].

In March 2002, the United States indicated its willingness "to permit some U.S. officials to provide testimony in The Hague if it's necessary," a senior State Department official said. But Americans would be called as witnesses for the prosecution to strengthen the case that Mr. Milosevic directly and explicitly targeted Muslims and Croats for acts of genocidal violence. Richard Holbrooke, the Clinton administration's chief envoy to the Balkans, disclosed that he had agreed to testify if asked by prosecutor Carla Del Ponte [*Washington Post*, March 21, 2002].

While his indictment on charges of genocide is historic, prosecutors will try to prove that Mr. Milosevic's brutality assumed a variety of forms. "Mr. Milosevic faces charges not only for murder and ethnic cleansing, but also for command responsibility for rape and other sexual violence," noted Martina Vandenberg of Human Rights Watch. "After centuries of invisibility, these brutal crimes against women have emerged from the shadows and into the courtroom. That the . . . indictment of Mr. Milosevic includes rape and sexual violence charges marks a victory for women everywhere" [*New York Times*, February 18, 2002].

5. The Middle East
By Gordon Goldstein

Peacekeeping and security missions in the Middle East in 2001–2002 reflected a potent irony for the United Nations: in a region where practical engagement was ostensibly needed most, multilateral action was reduced to its least meaningful form. In Iraq, for a third consecutive year arms inspectors were barred from making a visit, the Security Council busied itself with resolutions stamping the status quo, and the expectation took root that a major U.S. military intervention to topple Saddam Hussein was increasingly probable. In the region's other major story, continuous bloodshed among Israelis and Palestinians—a vicious cycle of suicide bombings and reprisals—became the new norm in one of world's most troubled inflection points of religion, history, and geopolitics. Meanwhile, the impact of the United Nations on this volatile conflict was almost nonexistent. And in Afghanistan, the rout of the Taliban after the September 11 attacks left the United Nations with an enormous new challenge in state building; it remains to be seen whether or not the U.N. system is up to the task.

Iraq

On June 1, 2001, the Security Council reached agreement to extend for one month its so-called oil-for-food program, which places the revenues from Iraqi oil exports into a U.N.-administered escrow account for the purchase of food commodities and medicines [S/Res/1352]. With its extension, the Council deferred a decision on a joint American–British proposal to overhaul the full scope of the Iraq sanctions regime. That proposal was designed to ease restrictions on almost all of Iraq's civilian imports while cracking down on oil smuggling. It was also intended to expand the list of prohibited items that might be used to enhance Baghdad's military capabilities and its program for the development of nuclear, chemical, and biological weapons [*New York Times*, June 1, 2001]. Technical experts and officials from the Council's five permanent members met in Paris on June 12, 2001, to review a list of goods that the United States proposed to prohibit for import [*New York Times*, June 13, 2001].

Two arms control experts, combing through unpublished reports of the disbanded U.N. Special Commission on Iraq, found evidence that Iraq continued to buy prohibited weapons and parts throughout the period that sanctions were in effect. Many of the items, which included missile components and high-technology machine tools, were purchased in central and eastern Europe, said Gary Milholin, director of the Wisconsin Project on Nuclear Arms Control in Washington, D.C. "What this shows is that Saddam's procurement network is alive and well and has been working steadily despite the sanctions" [*New York Times*, June 18, 2001].

Negotiations collapsed as Russia and the United States failed to agree on an expanded list of prohibited *dual-use* items (goods with both a civilian and military application). Russian Foreign Minister Ivan Ivanov warned U.S. Secretary of State Colin Powell that Moscow would block a U.S.–British Security Council resolution to introduce new sanctions against Iraq, because it would damage their commercial relations with Iraq. "We see in the new scheme a major threat to Russian trade and economic interests in Iraq," Ivanov wrote in a letter to Powell. "We cannot allow it to pass" [*Washington Post*, June 26, 2001]. Despite Russia's resistance, Powell lobbied other Council members, winning agreement from China and France for the new list of items to be reviewed [*New York Times*, June 30, 2001].

Iraq's oil trade with Turkey, Jordan, and Syria generates for Baghdad an estimated $1 billion a year in unrestricted revenue. This money can be used to buy and develop biological weapons, shop for fissile material on the black market, or to build ornate palaces (all activities that Hussein has been known to undertake). For Iraq's neighbors engaging in illegal trade, oil is purchased at a steep discount of up to 40 percent below market value. Both Iraq and its neighbors opposed the replacement of such lucrative, but illegal, trade outside the aegis of the oil-for-food program. Russia, which has been awarded billions of dollars in future contracts to develop Iraq's oil fields, has had its own rationale for opposing a more durable system of so-called smart sanctions [*New York Times*, July 1, 2001].

As Iraq's oil trade has grown, so too has its diplomatic leverage. Baghdad's oil revenue surged from $4 billion in 1997 to $18 billion in 2000. To punish France for its sporadic support of U.S. policy, Baghdad cut its imports of French goods to $310 million in the second half of 2000, down from $616 million from the previous six months [*Washington Post*, July 3, 2001]. Iraq also threatened retaliation against Turkey and Jordan if they supported the American and British proposal to tighten their borders and halt Iraqi smuggling. Syrian President Bashar Assad told U.N. Secretary-General Kofi Annan he would not allow U.N. inspectors into his country to enforce the American and British plan. And Jordanian Prime Minister Ali Abu Ragheb sent Annan a letter warning that Jordan's cooperation "might very well threaten its social, economic, and political stability."

"Politics is about interests. Politics is not about morals," said Iraq's U.N. Ambassador, Mohammed Douri, in early July 2001. "If the French and others will take a positive position in the Security Council, certainly they will get a benefit. This is the Iraqi policy." The acting U.S. Ambassador to the United Nations at the time, James B. Cunningham, rebuked Baghdad's machinations. "Iraq is using money and oil as a weapon against the international community," he said. "My government is accustomed by now to Iraq's cynicism towards its own people, and to its bluster and threatening policies. We find it harder to understand, however, why others would join in playing that game when the status quo is clearly not satisfactory" [*Washington Post*, July 3, 2001].

As Colin Powell assumed his new role of Secretary of State, he made the overhaul of the Iraqi sanctions regime one of his top priorities. His effort came to a disappointing end on July 2, 2001, when in the face of a Russian veto the United States and Britain were forced to abandon their joint resolution and settle for a five-month extension of the oil-for-food program [S/Res/1360]. "It strikes us as illogical for the Russians to take this position when it is so clear that there is a basis in the Council for an agreement—an agreement that would help the Iraqi civilians," said Ambassador Cunningham. He called the collapse of the new sanctions resolution "a defeat for the Iraqi people" [*New York Times*, July 3, 2001].

The defeat of the smart sanctions initiative was a victory for Russian industry and oil producers, who were lavishly rewarded for their nation's support of Iraq in the Security Council. In late September, days after President Vladimir Putin cast Russia's lot with the "war on terrorism" and the Bush administration began expressing its concern about Iraq, Baghdad announced plans to award Russian companies another $40 billion in contracts as soon U.N. sanctions were lifted [*New York Times*, February 3, 2002].

When it came time for a vote, the Security Council unanimously approved the routine five-month extension of the oil-for-food program. Russia insisted that all references to the British–American proposal be deleted from the draft resolution before it could be adopted [*New York Times*, July 4, 2001]. Iraq, which had temporarily halted oil exports earlier in the month to protest the proposed British–American resolution, formally agreed to the terms of the resolution [*New York Times*, July 10, 2001]. Two days later, Iraq resumed its oil exports [*New York Times*, July 12, 2001].

The sanctions regime was again put on the table for Council consideration at the close of November 2001. The United States had no choice but to extend the status quo for another six months [S/Res/1382]. The events of September 11 had put a premium on U.S. and Russian cooperation in the war against terrorism. In this climate, Washington was reluctant to revive its previous differences with Moscow over the so-called goods review list that would be the key to a new sanctions program [*New York Times*, November 28, 2001].

Along with the implementation of a new sanctions regime, the resumption of arms inspections in Iraq was another central but elusive goal pursued within the Security Council. In November 2001, Iraq reiterated its rejection of a U.N. resolution that would lift sanctions in return for the resumption of international weapons inspections. Iraq's Foreign Minister Naji Sabri renewed his country's opposition to the resolution in talks with the Secretary-General [*New York Times*, November 16, 2001].

President George W. Bush warned Hussein that if he did not admit the U.N. inspectors, he would face serious consequences. In a comment that seemed to convey a threat of action, President Bush said: "If anybody harbors a terrorist, they're a terrorist. If they fund a terrorist, they're a terrorist. If they house terrorists, they're terrorists. I mean, I can't make it any more [clear] to other nations around the world. If they develop weapons of mass destruction that will be used to terrorize nations, they will be held accountable" [*New York Times*, November 27, 2001].

Although President Bush brandished ambiguous threats, U.N. diplomats said that U.S. officials rarely discussed the President's desire to see inspectors return to Iraq. Hans Blix, the Swedish Executive Director of the U.N. Monitoring, Verification, and Inspection Commission (UNMOVIC), the arms inspection unit for Iraq, said that he had seen no sign that Washington had "accelerated" its efforts in this regard [*Washington Post*, January 11, 2002].

As the drumbeat for military action to topple Hussein emanated more loudly from Washington, the Secretary-General warned the United States not to expand its war against terrorism into Iraq. "Any attempt or any decision to attack Iraq today will be unwise and could lead to a major escalation in the region," Mr. Annan said at a news conference in Oslo, where he accepted the Nobel Peace Prize in December 2001. "It seems almost indecent to be accepting a prize for peace when peace and security are denied to so many people in so many parts of the world" [*New York Times*, December 10, 2001].

Following President Bush's dramatic allusion to an "axis of evil" in his state of the union address on January 29, 2002, Iraq instructed the Arab League to extend an offer of dialogue "without preconditions" with Secretary-General Kofi Annan. According to the cautious official statement in response, "The Secretary-General indicated that he was prepared to receive a delegation from Iraq to discuss implementation of relevant

Security Council resolutions. He will check his calendar to find a mutually convenient time" [*New York Times*, February 5, 2002].

When talks were held one month later, it marked the first time in a year that Iraq had engaged in discussions with the United Nations. Dr. Blix attended the meeting along with Major General Hussam Mohammed Amin, the Baghdad official responsible for working with inspectors inside Iraq. The meeting produced no tangible results, although the Iraqis called the exchange "constructive and positive," while the Secretary-General's spokesman said the discussion was "frank and useful" [*New York Times*, March 8, 2002]. Following a closed-door briefing to the Security Council, Mr. Annan told reporters that Council members "would hope that these talks will move on expeditiously and yield results that will send in the inspectors" [U.N. News Service, April 15, 2002].

In a speech in Geneva to prospective inspectors, Dr. Blix described his intent to implement an aggressive monitoring program that was immediate, unconditional, and unrestricted. "For the credibility of future inspections, it is important that there are no sanctuaries and that access is without any delay that might permit the removal of evidence" [*New York Times*, March 9, 2002].

News reports suggested that the Bush administration was divided over the political utility of resuming U.N. inspections. Some administration officials argued that inspections would pose a potential trap, providing Iraq with yet another opportunity to stall, frustrate, and obstruct the U.N. monitors. Others argued that, as the probability of American intervention increased, the United States would come under acute pressure (particularly from its European allies) to allow a final diplomatic effort to reinstate inspections before initiating military action. Failure to comply fully with inspections might then strengthen the American case for military action. Vice-President Dick Cheney, meeting with Prime Minister Tony Blair in London, seemed to acknowledge such a possibility. "So if the issue of inspectors is to be addressed," said Mr. Cheney, "we feel very strongly as a government that it needs to be the kind of inspection regime that has no limitations on it, that is a 'go anywhere, any time' kind of inspection regime, so that, in fact the outside world can have confidence that he is not hiding material that he has promised to give up" [*New York Times*, March 12, 2002].

Although U.N. inspectors remained banned from Iraq, a different U.N. mission on the Iraq–Kuwait border continued. The U.N. Iraq–Kuwait Observation Mission monitors the demilitarized zone between the two countries. The force is comprised of 1,097 total uniformed personnel, including 192 military observers and 905 troops [UNIKOM Facts and Figures, www.un.org/Depts/DPKO/Missions/unikom/unikomF.htm]. The peacekeeping force contributes to calm and stability and should be maintained, according to a report by the Secretary-General released at U.N. Headquarters in New

York [U.N. News Service, April 3, 2002]. (Established on April 9, 1991 [S/Res/689 (1991)], following the forced withdrawal of Iraqi forces from the territory of Kuwait, the termination of the U.N. Iraq–Kuwait Observation Mission [UNIKOM] is subject to the concurrence of all the permanent members of the Council [www.un.org/Depts/DPKO/Missions/unikom/unikomM.htm].)

Israeli–Palestinian Conflict

In the Israeli–Palestinian conflict, tensions reached a new peak in March 2002, when Israeli forces retaliated against a wave of suicide bombings by deploying as many as 20,000 troops to hunt down terrorists in the West Bank. In the shadow of escalating violence, the Security Council approved a resolution endorsing a Palestinian state and calling for a cease-fire in the conflict [S/Res/1397 (2002)]. In a statement to the U.N. Security Council, the Secretary-General delivered some of his most outspoken remarks to date on the difficult question of the peace process and its all but complete collapse:

> To the Israelis I say: you have the right to live in peace and security within secure internationally recognized borders. But you must end the illegal occupation. More urgently, you must stop the bombing of civilian areas, the assassinations, the unnecessary use of lethal force, the demolitions and the daily humiliation of normal Palestinians.
>
> To the Palestinians I say: you have the inalienable right to a viable state within secure internationally recognized borders. But you must stop all acts of terror and all suicide bombings. It is doing immense harm to your cause, by weakening international support and making Israelis believe that it is their existence as a state, and not the occupation, that is being opposed. [*New York Times*, March 13, 2002]

In April 2002, with no imminent withdrawal of Israeli tanks and troops, Arabs stepped up demands to the Security Council for a punitive resolution against Israel and the dispatch of an international monitoring force. But the U.S. veto would make such a resolution improbable; the U.S. Ambassador to the United Nations John Negroponte observed, "We do not need any more resolutions" [*New York Times*, April 10, 2002].

Afghanistan

As to the fate of Afghanistan, the Secretary-General said in December 2001 that the situation was "very complex and very difficult" and would not be resolved "for a long time to come" [*New York Times*, December 10, 2001]. Following the swift American defeat of the Taliban in response to the attacks of September 11, U.N. talks in Bonn led to the establishment of an interim governing administration for Afghanistan [*New York Times*, December 10, 2001].

The Security Council voted unanimously to authorize a British-led peacekeeping force in Afghanistan that would maintain order and assist with the transfer of power to the new interim government headed by Hamid Karzai, the Pashtun tribal leader backed by the United States. The Security Council resolution [S/Res/1386 (2001)] authorized the peacekeepers to use force in order to protect the new government and U.N. personnel in Kabul [*Washington Post*, December 21, 2001]. One month later, U.N. and U.S. military officials warned aid groups working in Afghanistan that the country was becoming more unstable and dangerous, even in Kabul where a British-led peacekeeping force was trying to maintain stability [*Wall Street Journal*, January 21, 2002].

On the eve of the Secretary-General's arrival in Afghanistan to show support for the leadership of Hamid Karzai, the official who was the second-in-command for the U.N. mission there resigned. He argued that the international security force must be increased to as many as 35,000 [*New York Times*, January 25, 2002]. Weeks later, U.S. and U.N. diplomats acknowledged that the peacekeeping force would not be expanded. Despite pleas from the country's interim government for tens of thousands of additional troops to provide security in provincial cities [*Washington Post*, March 20, 2002], Afghanistan would not receive the requested assistance.

III
Security
By Jonathan Dean

The modest progress achieved in disarmament during the past year (May 2001–May 2002) coincided with a number of serious reverses to multilateral arms control and disarmament.

Following the September 11 attacks in New York and Washington, D.C., the Bush administration added over $48 billion to the U.S. defense budget, as well as nearly $40 billion to "homeland defense." While only future developments and analysis can determine whether this reaction was justified, the size of the U.S. defense budget continues to alarm those who believe military budgets should become smaller. Indeed, the U.S. defense budget is now larger than the combined total of the ten next largest national defense budgets [Richard Norton-Taylor, "Top Gun—and the rest," *The Guardian*, February 13, 2002]. The Bush administration increased its budget for missile defense to $8.6 billion annually [Christopher Hellmann, "Highlights of the FY '03 Budget Request," *Center for Defense Information*]. It also financed, for the third consecutive year, the development of two missile defense weapons for space orbit, with testing in space to take place in five to six years.

In many ways, 2001 was marked by U.S. withdrawal from international arms control commitments. In July 2001, the United States withdrew from an ad hoc group attempting to draft a verification system for the 1972 **Biological Weapons Convention**. During the review conference for the Convention in November 2001, the United States blocked continuation of the ad hoc group, although it also proposed some specific verification measures. In December 2001, President Bush gave the required six-month notice of the U.S. intention to withdraw from the **Treaty on the Limitation of Anti-Ballistic Missile Systems (ABM)** with Russia. The ABM Treaty limits missile defenses against ballistic missiles. Russia protested. In October 2001, the United States announced in the U.N. First Committee that it would not resubmit the **Comprehensive Test Ban Treaty** to the U.S. Senate for ratification. In the January 2002 Nuclear Posture Review, the Bush administration indicated that further nuclear tests might be necessary.

Nevertheless, moderate progress was achieved when the United

States and Russia signed a draft treaty (on May 23, 2002) reducing the number of each side's deployed intercontinental-range nuclear warheads from about 6,000 each to 1,700–2,200 for each country over a ten-year period. This approximated the reductions foreseen in the unratified START II Treaty signed in 1993 by Presidents George H. Bush and Boris Yeltsin, and in the uncompleted START III talks between Presidents Clinton and Yeltsin. In July 2001, participants in a U.N.-sponsored conference reached the first international agreement in the field of global arms transfers to tighten controls on the illicit traffic in small arms. **The U.N. Conference on Illicit Trade in Small Arms and Light Weapons in All Its Aspects,** and the nonbinding political agreement it produced, responded to a series of bloody, civil, and ethnic wars fought mainly with small arms. While the agreement was modest, it was at least a beginning in this important new field of multilateral cooperation.

1. First Committee (Disarmament and International Security)

The *Disarmament and International Security Committee,* or First Committee of the General Assembly, convened its annual meeting in the fall of 2001 to assess the world security and disarmament situation and to review all disarmament issues on the agenda of the General Assembly. The 2001 sessions of the First Committee were preceded by a week of general debate in the General Assembly (56th session). Following this debate, the First Committee considers draft resolutions submitted by member states, backed in most cases by a varying group of co-sponsoring member state governments.

The general discussion in the First Committee (October 8–November 6, 2001) was completely overshadowed by the September 11 attacks, which occurred just as the General Assembly was convening. Police barriers blocked off all streets leading to the United Nations, and internal security was intensified. Understandably, the First Committee debate took second place to the debate on terrorism in the General Assembly and to ongoing work of the Security Council on terrorism [see final section below]. Within the First Committee itself, discussion was dominated by the desire of U.N. member states to show solidarity with the United States. Confrontation between the United States and other governments—over topics like the U.S. intention of withdrawing from the ABM Treaty—was deliberately subdued by member states. Significantly, the "New Agenda Coalition," a group of medium-sized states that have led the drive for action on nuclear disarmament, abstained from introducing a resolution this year that would have brought it into confrontation with the United States.

There were 92 statements in the general First Committee debate.

These statements were followed by discussion and votes on 45 resolutions and 6 decisions ("decisions" are primarily procedural, such as referring an issue to next year's First Committee), a little less than the average number for First Committee resolutions.

Under-Secretary-General for Disarmament Affairs Jayantha Dhanapala set the tone in his opening remarks at the First Committee session by stating that the September 11 attacks would have been even worse in their effects if they had used weapons of mass destruction. He added that the attacks increased the urgency of decisive action on disarmament. Meanwhile, the U.N. Department for Disarmament Affairs (UNDDA), headed by Dhanapala, is the smallest U.N. department and was denied the 4 percent budget increase given to all others. (A number of nongovernmental organizations appealed to the Fifth Committee of the General Assembly, the finance and administration committee, to reverse this decision.)

Ambassador Andre Erdos of Hungary, this year's First Committee chair and an active proponent of disarmament, tabled a new resolution (56/24T) on the essential role of effective multilateral disarmament and nonproliferation measures in the action against terrorism. Ambassador Erdos wanted the resolution to be adopted by consensus without change, but was obliged by member pressure to add a reference to *multilateralism* as a core principle in disarmament and to call on member states to fulfill their arms control obligations. The resolution was then adopted without a vote. The references to multilateralism and to fulfilling obligations were directed at the United States without naming it and indicated considerable emotion [Jenni Rissanen, *Disarmament Diplomacy*, October/November 2001, pp. 19–20].

As always, *nuclear disarmament,* including creation of nuclear-free zones, dominated the First Committee roster of resolutions, with 16 of 45 resolutions addressing the topic. This priority was followed by eight resolutions on regional disarmament and arms control. These resolutions included a proposal by India calling on the Conference on Disarmament [see below] to negotiate an international treaty prohibiting the use or threat of use of nuclear weapons. There were several statements of support for Secretary-General Annan's proposal in 2000 to convene an international conference on preventing nuclear dangers, a conference that could bring all nuclear weapon states together at the same table. As they did the preceding year, the United States, the United Kingdom, France, and Israel opposed the proposal to convene such a conference.

In addition to nuclear disarmament, First Committee resolutions dealt with several other issues: the current U.N. study on missiles; support for the ABM Treaty (in the face of the anticipated U.S. withdrawal); prevention of an arms race in outer space; fulfillment of the Non-Proliferation Treaty Article VI obligations for nuclear disarmament; and support for the completion of a verification protocol regarding biological weapons (in the face of U.S. withdrawal from the ad hoc group of officials negotiating the protocol).

Six countries supported the convening of a Fourth Special Session on Disarmament at the 57th General Assembly [A/56/24D, see also Emily Schroeder, *NGO Weekly Report*, week 1, section 9, www.reachingcriticalwill.org]. Support for this idea comes primarily from governments acutely dissatisfied with lack of progress on disarmament. In this context, Under-Secretary-General Dhanapala suggested in his opening speech that member states might wish to consider reform of the U.N. disarmament machinery. The New Zealand representative, a member of the New Agenda Coalition, in his talk to the First Committee, urged basic reform of the restrictive consensus rules under which the Geneva-based Conference on Disarmament operates.

Two other topics that received major attention were (1) a possible convention for the suppression of acts of nuclear terrorism and (2) a resolution introduced by Colombia [A/56/24V] calling on all states to implement the program of action adopted at the July 2001 U.N. Conference on Illicit Trade in Small Arms and Light Weapons. The resolution called for a review conference scheduled for 2006 and for transparency in arms transfers, U.N. Register of Conventional Arms, and defense budgets. Iraq presented a resolution on the effects of the use of depleted uranium in armaments, asking the Secretary-General to seek the views of member states on this topic [A/56/536C]. The resolution was defeated (Yes 45, No 54, Abstain 45) [see A/56/536, Report of the First Committee].

The energetic treatment at the United Nations of terrorism post-September 11, together with the continuation of unilateral action by the United States in many arms control areas, reinforced the impression of many observers that the First Committee and its disarmament resolutions had been marginalized more than ever. But this has happened before in the past half century, and the First Committee has repeatedly proven itself to be an indispensable forum of international discussion, providing a good opportunity each year to measure evolving international opinion.

2. Conference on Disarmament

The 66-member *Conference on Disarmament*, an independent body based in Geneva, determines its own rules and agenda, but reports annually to the General Assembly, and discusses topics referred to it by the General Assembly. The Conference on Disarmament, repeatedly referred to by the General Assembly as the "single multilateral disarmament negotiation forum of the international community," negotiated the Chemical Weapons Convention (1993) and the Comprehensive Nuclear Test Ban Treaty (1996). In its earlier incarnation as the "Eighteen Nation Disarmament Committee," it negotiated the Non-Proliferation Treaty in 1968. Thus, the Conference has demonstrated that it can work successfully. But in order for that to happen, the major powers have to agree and the United States has to take the lead.

Since 1996, the Conference has been stalled because of lack of agreement on the agenda, which must be adopted by consensus, a consensus renewed at the beginning of each negotiating year in January [Jenni Rissanen, *Disarmament Diplomacy*, December 2000, March 2001]. During most of this period, China, backed by Russia and Pakistan, has insisted that the Conference negotiate on preventing an arms race in outer space, as well as on a possible treaty ending production of fissile material for nuclear weapons [Wade Boese, "Conference on Disarmament Starts 2001 Session in Stalemate," *Arms Control Today*, March 2001].

In February 2001, the Chinese representative proposed that the Conference agree to negotiate treaties on nuclear disarmament, fissile cut-off, security assurances to non-nuclear states, and prevention of an arms race in outer space. The U.S. position has been that it is willing to "discuss" nuclear disarmament and prevention of an arms race in outer space, but not to "negotiate" on these topics [Rissanen, ibid.]. Brazilian Ambassador Celso Amorim, a devoted supporter of disarmament, proposed in August 2000 that the Conference establish four ad hoc committees. Specifically, he proposed two to deal with nuclear disarmament and prevention of an arms race in outer space, one to negotiate a treaty to end production of fissile material, and another to negotiate security assurances to non-nuclear states [Wade Boese, "C.D. Session Ends in Deadlock; Coordinators Appointed," *Arms Control Today*, July/August 2001]. Discussion in the Conference on Disarmament has since focused on Amorim's proposal.

In June 2001, the Chinese representative presented a proposal listing the possible components of a treaty to prevent the weaponization of space, an indication that China took this issue seriously. Also in June 2001, the (by now, seriously frustrated) C.D. participants once again selected three ambassadors from their own ranks to act as Special Coordinators to try to get the Conference moving [Jenni Rissanen, *Disarmament Diplomacy*, June 2001]. One Special Coordinator was to review the items currently on the C.D. agenda to see whether some inactive issues could be dropped. Another was to review expansion of membership. And the third was to examine improved and effective functioning of the Conference. The Sri Lankan Ambassador, in reporting on the last point, found strong support for dropping consensus in establishing the agenda and for retaining it in matters of substance. Several other countries, among them Russia, Iran, and Pakistan, wanted to retain the consensus rule for all C.D. decisions [Jenni Rissanen, *Disarmament Diplomacy*, July/August 2001]. The Special Coordinator on C.D. membership found that all 22 current applicants still wanted membership [Press Release, DCF/412, January 18, 2002]. New Special Coordinators were appointed for the next round.

Discussion of the Amorim proposal in the first C.D. session of 2002 indicated that Russia and Pakistan were easing their insistence on linking negotiation of a treaty to prevent an arms race in space with a fissile cut-off, but that China was remaining firm on this position. China evidently considered the issue important enough to stand alone in opposition to U.S. plans to move missile defense weapons into space and possibly to keep open its own option to produce more fissile material, if it decides on major expansion of its nuclear arsenal [Personal communication to author from direct observer of C.D. activities].

3. The Disarmament Commission

The 2002 session of the *Disarmament Commission* was postponed to April 2002 because of the U.N. focus on terrorism [Press Release, DC/2829, April 17, 2002]. However, a brief note on the Commission may be useful.

The Disarmament Commission was established by the General Assembly in 1952 with a mandate to address the regulation, limitation, and balanced reduction of all armed forces and armaments, as well as measures for elimination of weapons of mass destruction. As the United States and the USSR moved in 1959 to establish the Ten Nation Committee on Disarmament (a precursor of the present Conference on Disarmament), the Disarmament Commission fell into disuse. However, it was reestablished by the 1978 Special Session on Disarmament (SSOD) of the General Assembly, as the follow-on mechanism for the Special Session. The main task of the Disarmament Commission is to prepare for a further Special Session on Disarmament. To do so, the Commission has carried out studies of major disarmament themes. There has been continual pressure, especially from developing countries, for such a session, which would approach disarmament from a comprehensive point of view. The larger countries, especially the United States, have blocked these pressures, claiming that a new SSOD would incur considerable cost with little gain.

The result has been a three-week session of the Disarmament Commission each April at the United Nations. Although sessions of the Disarmament Commission are open to all 190 U.N. member states, the main figures at the session are ambassadors and other officials of the Conference on Disarmament. The work of the Commission has continued to be organized in two working groups, one on "Ways and Means to Achieve Nuclear Disarmament" and the other on "Practical Confidence-Building Measures in the Field of Conventional Arms."

4. Action and Inaction on Nuclear Weapons

U.S.–Russian Reductions

The past year brought an important U.S.–Russian agreement *for reduction of strategic nuclear arsenals.* Meeting at the Bush ranch in Crawford,

Texas, on November 13, 2001, President George W. Bush pledged to reduce deployed U.S. strategic warheads to between 1,700 and 2,200 over a ten-year period; President Vladimir Putin indicated he would reciprocate by reducing the Russian nuclear arsenal. Each country is credited with about 6,000 deployed strategic warheads at present. Ensuing negotiations culminated in the signing of a brief treaty on May 23, 2002.

In the negotiations leading up to this outcome, President Bush conceded to Russian desires to have a written treaty and to the desire of Senators Biden and Helms to have a treaty ratified by the U.S. Senate. In the course of the negotiations, Russia dropped proposals that warheads withdrawn from operational deployment should be dismantled and that there be a transparent information exchange on warheads of each country. Both points had been under discussion between Presidents Clinton and Yeltsin in connection with uncompleted talks on a possible START III agreement. (START II, signed by Presidents Yeltsin and George H. Bush in January 1993, was never finally ratified.) Russia also dropped proposals to limit the number of missile defense interceptors deployed by each country and to prohibit the weaponization of space. These were Russian efforts to retain the main features of the ABM Treaty, voided by President Bush as of June 13, 2002.

Verification of the new agreement will occur through procedures taken over from the START I Treaty, which remains in force. The Clinton administration never resubmitted the START II Treaty (bringing U.S. and Russian deployed warhead levels to 3,000–3,500) to the U.S. Senate for final ratification, in the face of Senator Helms' threat to use the ratification proceedings to eliminate the ABM Treaty. Therefore, START II is in abeyance. The START III negotiations, kicked off with a Yeltsin–Clinton agreement at Helsinki in 1997, had the target of reducing to a level of 2,000–2,500 operationally deployed warheads for each country, with provision for monitored dismantling of warheads withdrawn from deployment and exchange of information on remaining warhead holdings. These steps, together with cut-off of production of fissile material and transfer of surplus material to storage monitored by **the International Atomic Energy Agency** (IAEA), were to be the beginning of "irreversible nuclear disarmament."

The chief criticisms of the May 2002 draft treaty are that the levels of deployed weapons could have been still lower and that it is not irreversible. In fact, the United States has stated the intention of maintaining a large portion of its withdrawn warheads in "active storage" from which warheads can be remounted on delivery systems. There is no mention in the new agreement of tactical-range nuclear weapons, of which Russia is supposed to have superiority.

The Nuclear Posture Review

The May 2002 U.S.–Russian agreement on nuclear reductions took place against the background of the Bush administration's **Nuclear Posture Review,** a brief, unclassified version of which was issued, six months late, on January 9, 2002.

The content of the Review will ultimately be reflected in a new Presidential Directive on Nuclear Weapons. The Review forecast the sizable 4,000 warhead reduction in deployed weapons contained in the May 23 agreement and proclaimed the end of the Cold War. Nevertheless, Russia and China remain targeted by U.S. strategic weapons, and five new countries were added to the pretargeted list: Libya, Syria, Iraq, Iran, and North Korea. The threat to use U.S. nuclear weapons if the United States, its troops, or allies are attacked with nuclear, chemical, or biological weapons is more explicit in the Review than it has been in the past. The Review further states that U.S. nuclear weapons may also be used in unforeseen circumstances, opening up the possibility of the use of nuclear weapons as general-purpose weapons. Most of the weapons downgraded from operational deployment will be stored in operational condition and can be reloaded on delivery vehicles relatively rapidly.

According to the Review, facilities for production of new warheads and of tritium gas, used to boost explosion of hydrogen weapons, will be established. As far as is known, there is no mention in the Review of the U.S. obligation to eliminate nuclear weapons under the Non-Proliferation Treaty. To the contrary, there are references in the Review to measures intended to make the U.S. nuclear arsenal effective for 20–30 years in the future and longer.

One feature of the Review that has been particularly questioned is the repeated implication that the United States will resume testing nuclear weapons and will undertake the first studies to develop a bunker-penetrating warhead. All in all, the impression created by the Review was that the Bush administration was more ready to use nuclear weapons on a wider range of potential targets than any preceding administration [Phillipp C. Bleek, "Nuclear Posture Review Released, Stresses Flexible Force Planning," *Arms Control Today*, January/February 2002].

First Committee Action

First Committee resolutions addressed several nuclear weapon issues in the fall session of 2001.

Japan again presented its omnibus proposal for step-by-step action to eliminate nuclear weapons [A/Res/56/24N]. Only the United States, Micronesia, and India voted against. Myanmar, with co-sponsorship from *Non-Aligned Movement* states [for a full list, see *Disarmament Resolutions and Decisions of the*

Fifty-Sixth Session of the General Assembly] called for an international conference on nuclear disarmament and also supported Secretary-General Annan's call for an international conference to reduce nuclear dangers [A/Res/56/24R]. Mexico placed the Secretary-General's proposal for an international conference on the First Committee agenda for September 2002 [A/C.1/56/L.16]. India's resolution [A/56/24C] called for de-alerting and steps to reduce risks of the unintentional use of nuclear weapons. This resolution also supported the Secretary-General's call for an international conference to reduce nuclear dangers. In addition, India reintroduced its resolution [A/56/25B] calling for an international convention prohibiting the use or threat of use of nuclear weapons. Malaysia referred to the advisory opinion of the International Court of Justice on nuclear weapons and called for immediate international negotiations leading to the early conclusion of a Nuclear Weapons Convention to eliminate nuclear weapons [A/56/24S].

Pakistan reintroduced its resolution [A/56/22] calling for strengthening of negative security assurances by nuclear weapon states to protect nonweapon states, including a treaty on this subject. Nonweapon states, especially Non-Aligned Movement states, are pressing for an international treaty incorporating and strengthening the assurances given by nuclear weapon states at the conclusion of the Non-Proliferation Treaty (NPT) in 1968, and its extension conference (1995), not to use nuclear weapons against nonweapon states. (The exception to the agreement is if the latter were allied with a weapon state.) This goal is opposed by the United States, Russia, United Kingdom, and France, all of whom abstained in the vote for Resolution 56/22 [A/56/22; see *Disarmament Resolutions and Decisions*].

Discussion was intensified at the Conference on Disarmament and in the NPT Prepcom, by indications in the U.S. Nuclear Posture Review that the United States is targeting Iran, Libya, and Syria, as well as Iraq, with nuclear weapons. These countries are nonnuclear parties to the NPT, and there have been no official charges that they have violated that treaty.

Nuclear-Free Zones

Nuclear-free zones were also a recurrent First Committee theme. One resolution called on all African states to sign and ratify the African Nuclear Weapon Free Zone Treaty (Treaty of Pelindaba) [A/56/17]. Another resolution introduced by Mexico asks those who have signed but not ratified the Treaty of Tlatelolco establishing a Nuclear-Free Zone in Latin America (Cuba) to ratify as soon as possible. Egypt again proposed a resolution on a Middle East Nuclear-Free Zone [A/56/21]; Israel, which was called on to agree to a nuclear weapon-free zone, again stated (for the 21st time) that it would act on this resolution after completion of the Middle East peace process. Brazil's resolution [A/56/24G] for a nuclear weapons-free Southern Hemisphere called for establishing a nuclear-free zone in the entire hemisphere to include the Middle East and South Asia. Uzbekistan proposed a Nuclear-Free Zone in central Asia (a decision was reached to place this issue on next fall's First Committee agenda). Finally, a resolution on the Indian Ocean as a Zone of Peace, introduced by South Africa [A/56/16], asks for a security dialogue in the area.

Comprehensive Test Ban Treaty (CTBT)

A First Committee Resolution (New Zealand Decision [A/C.1/56/L. 10/Rev. 1]) asking only that the subject of the Comprehensive Test Ban Treaty be placed on next year's agenda was adopted by 140 to 1. The United States cast the "no" vote against consideration of the CTBT on the agenda, stating that it "had no plans to seek reconsideration of the Senate's action" in rejecting the treaty while also stating that it intended to maintain its moratorium on nuclear testing [*Disarmament Diplomacy,* October/November 2001, p. 28].

A conference on facilitating entry into force of the CTBT was held November 11–13, 2001, at the United Nations, demonstrating international support for the treaty. Delegates from 118 treaty states participated. The United States declined to attend. The number of states that have signed the treaty is 164; 89 states have ratified, including 31 of the 44 nuclear-capable states whose ratification is required by the text of the treaty. North Korea, India, and Pakistan have not signed the treaty. The United States, China, Israel, and seven other states have not ratified. In August 2001, the United States announced that it would not provide technical or financial support for on-site inspections in support of the treaty. Despite this, at the November conference, Wolfgang Hoffmann, executive secretary of the preparatory commission for the treaty, reported good progress in establishing the treaty's verification system [Phillipp C. Bleek, *Arms Control Today,* December 2001, pp. 21, 26].

On January 5, 2001, General John M. Shalikashvili issued his report to President Clinton stating that advantages of the CTBT outweigh any disadvantages and calling for treaty ratification. General Shalikashvili suggested instituting a periodic joint executive–legislative review after ratification, which could trigger U.S. withdrawal if there were actual difficulties [for text of the report, see *Arms Control Today,* January 2001].

5. Non-Proliferation Treaty: Preparatory Committee for the 2005 Review Conference (NPT Prepcom)

The **2002 Preparatory Committee for the 2005 Review Conference of the Non-Proliferation Treaty** (full review conferences take place every five years) held its discussion April 8–19, 2002, at the United Nations.

The three main objectives of the Non-Proliferation Treaty (which now has 187 treaty parties) are to prevent the spread of nuclear weapons, promote nuclear disarmament, and promote peaceful uses of nuclear energy. The Prepcom (further sessions will be held in 2003 and 2004) is expected to review performance of each article of the treaty and to begin discussion of the main topics that will be handled in the 2005 Review Conference. Review conferences are in essence report cards on the progress made toward fulfillment of treaty goals, chief among them, the elimination of nuclear weapons.

Under-Secretary-General Dhanapala opened the April 2002 Prepcom, pointing out that the terrorist attacks of September 11, 2001, had significantly changed the international climate since the year 2000 Review Conference. (This was also the first Prepcom to take place during the Bush administration, with its negative views on multilateral disarmament.) Dhanapala referred to the fact that the CTBT had still not entered into effect five years after its conclusion. Furthermore, 51 states still did not have safeguards agreements with the IAEA; only 24 states had committed themselves to the expanded, post-UNSCOM (the U.N. Special Commission established after the 1991 Persian Gulf War to remove weapons of mass destruction) safeguards proposed by the IAEA for 61 states. Ambassador Henrik Salander of Sweden presided over the Prepcom, which was attended by representatives of 137 states parties. The NPT Review Conference and Prepcoms are exceptionally open to nongovernmental organizations (NGOs), which regard them as the focal point of U.N. work on disarmament. Representatives of 62 NGOs attended this Prepcom session; one meeting of the session was actually given over to 14 NGO presentations.

During the Prepcom, the United States, whose previous representative had agreed to the 2000 Review Conference Document, objected to reports called for in that document, indicating that it would not be bound by the 2000 vote under the Clinton administration. This was confirmed by the new U.S. representative, Eric Javits, who stated that the United States no longer supported some of the Article VI conclusions from the year 2000 Review Conference, including calls to support the ABM Treaty and to ratify the CTBT. Egypt, as spokesman of the New Agenda Coalition, called for transparency, verification, and irreversibility in all disarmament measures; legally binding security assurances; no-first-use commitments; cuts in tactical nuclear weapons; and the avoiding of a new arms race in outer space. The E.U. representative made similar points and said that pending U.S.–Russian nuclear reductions should be embodied in a legally binding instrument providing for irreversibility, verification, and transparency. Russia urged the United States to ratify the CTBT and opposed the weaponization of outer space, again asking for a moratorium on putting weapons into space.

The Chairman's Report for the Prepcom called on Cuba, Israel, India, and Pakistan to accede to the NPT as nonweapon states [NPT/CONF. 2000/MC. III/1, section VI]. The Report said the most important means of combating terrorism was to strengthen nonproliferation measures, especially those of the IAEA. The Report supported the continuing validity of the 2000 Review Document; expressed support for the CTBT; expressed concern over U.S. withdrawal from the ABM Treaty and over the possibility of an arms race in outer space; welcomed the prospective U.S.–Russian agreement on nuclear reductions; and called for provisions ensuring irreversibility, verification, and transparency. The Chairman also called for further reductions in tactical nuclear weapons and for the beginning of negotiations on a fissile cut-off treaty. He called for strengthened security assurances against nonweapon states, full compliance with IAEA safeguards, and resumption of inspections in Iraq. It was a succinct list of *desiderata* for nuclear disarmament.

6. Missiles, Missile Defense, and Space Weapons

Antiballistic Missile (ABM) Issues

Moves of the Bush administration to reject the 1972 U.S.–Russian ABM Treaty limiting antiballistic missile systems culminated in President Bush's formal declaration of withdrawal from the Treaty on December 13, 2001, to take effect on June 13, 2002. The central content of the Treaty was its limitation on the number of deployed antimissile interceptors. With this limit gone, the United States can deploy an increasing number of missile defenses of all kinds. The combining of defense with offense serves to augment offensive capability. As such, the expansion of U.S. missile defenses (even with founded doubts about the capacity of the interceptors) and increase in U.S. offensive capacity will likely become a source of serious concern to other nuclear weapon states. This is already the case for China, which presently has only about 20 long-range ballistic missiles capable of reaching U.S. territory.

Well-aware of the central importance of this issue, Russia tried in the negotiations leading up to the May 23, 2002, U.S.–Russian nuclear reduction agreement to include in the agreement a provision limiting the number of antimissile interceptors that could be deployed. The second main point of the ABM Treaty was its prohibition on space weapons. Here, too, the Russian government tried and failed to gain U.S. agreement to include a provision banning space weapons in the agreement [Communication to author from the Russian Embassy, Washington, D.C.].

The elimination through nullification of the ABM Treaty of any restriction on the number of antimissile interceptors deployed by the

United States means that the U.S. missile defense program will be an engine for increases in the size of the world's nuclear arsenals in coming decades. The elimination of the prohibition against placing weapons in space means that the only legal barriers to the weaponization of space are the prohibition against orbiting weapons of mass destruction in the 1967 Outer Space Treaty and prohibitions in the START and INF Treaty against interfering with national means of verification. The Bush administration's 2002 and 2003 defense budgets contain funds for development of two space orbiting weapon: a kinetic kill vehicle and a space-based laser. If these weapons are deployed in the next decade, as is the administration's aim, the weaponization of space will have begun. In one sense, weaponization will begin on June 14, 2002, when, as announced by Lt. General Ronald Kadish, director of the Missile Defense Agency, excavation will begin for missile interceptors in Fort Greeley, Alaska. Missile interceptors can be used as antisatellite weapons, or ASATs, to destroy satellites in space orbit.

ABM and Space Weapons in the First Committee

These developments received broad attention from the international community in the 2001 First Committee and in the 2002 NPT Prepcom. First Committee Resolution 56/24A, introduced by Russia and co-sponsored by China and Belarus, calls for efforts to strengthen and preserve the ABM Treaty. It says that measures undermining the Treaty would also undermine global strategic stability and further strategic nuclear arms reductions. The vote on the resolution was 82 for, 5 against (United States, Israel, Micronesia, Albania, and Benin), with 62 abstentions. The figures were a little lower than the previous year, probably because of an ongoing, although fruitless, negotiation between the United States and Russia on a possible successor to the ABM Treaty. This possibility was referred to in the debate over this resolution [*Disarmament Diplomacy*, October/November 2001; Disarmament Resolutions of the 56th Session, U.N. Department for Disarmament Affairs].

Resolution 56/23 calling for prevention of an arms race in outer space was introduced by Sri Lanka and co-sponsored by China, Russia, and a number of other countries. The vote on the resolution, similar to that in previous years, was 156 for, 0 opposed, and 4 abstentions (United States, Israel, Micronesia, and a new recruit, Georgia), which makes it as close to unanimity as possible [*Reaching Critical Will*, Week 1, p. 5]. The resolution urges the Conference on Disarmament to negotiate a treaty preventing an arms race in space as soon as possible. In the debate, Canada pointed out that space is the only environment where weapons are not present; it was imperative that preventive diplomacy keep space free of weapons.

The Chinese draft treaty on preventing the weaponization of space seems to be held up indefinitely in the Conference on Disarmament.

Meanwhile, NGO thinking seems to be going in the direction of propos-
ing partial (rather that total) restriction of weaponization, accompanied
by "rules of the road" to reduce the risk of confrontational incidents in
space [James Clay Moltz, "Breaking the Deadlock on Space Arms Control," *Arms Control Today*,
April 2002].

Missiles

One way to deal with missiles other than missile defense is to seek to
control the missiles themselves. After several attempts, Iran succeeded in
2000 in getting General Assembly approval for a comprehensive study of
missiles. (Presumably, Iran's motivation was the pounding it took from
Iraqi missiles in the Iran–Iraq War.) As a result, Under-Secretary-General
Dhanapala assembled a "Panel of Government Experts on the Issue of
Missiles in All Its Aspects." The Panel met July 30–August 3, 2001, and
in April 2002 at the United Nations; it is scheduled to have its final meeting in July 2002. The Panel will present a report to the Secretary-General
who will submit it to the 57th General Assembly in the fall of 2002.

In the First Committee debate on October 10, 2001, the Indonesian
representative pointed out that the Panel study marked "the first time that
member states have decided to focus their work on the issue of missiles as
a source of instability" [*Reaching Critical Will*, NGO *Weekly Reports*, 2001, Week 1, p. 3].
The Indonesian representative added that the Panel's recommendations
are anticipated to include issues such as "limiting production and deployment of missiles, a global missile warning system and other ways of controlling missile proliferation, incentives to encourage states from producing long-range missiles, and a multilateral regime or convention to
counter missile proliferation" [ibid.]. Indonesia's summary was logical, but
in fact, the Panel is unlikely to make many far-reaching recommendations
owing to widely divergent views among its national experts, some of
whom are reported to claim that "there is no global missile problem"
[Personal account to author by a Panel expert].

Iran's Resolution 56/24B, in the 2001 First Committee call for support of the U.N. study of missiles, was adopted by the General Assembly
by 98 votes for, 0 opposed, with 58 abstentions; many of the latter are
members of the Missile Technology Control Regime [see below]. Iran
commented, correctly, that finally missiles have been included in the international arms control and disarmament agenda. In that sense, the missile study is the counterpart of the July 2001 U.N. Conference on the
Illicit Traffic in Small Arms. These two subjects are now established
within the legitimate scope of those states interested in disarmament. But
missiles are just at the beginning of the road.

Missile Technology Control Regime (MTCR)

As Iran's proposal for a U.N. study on missiles was making its slow progress through the U.N. system, the 33 members of the **Missile Technology Control Regime** (MTCR), led by the United States, were developing their *Code of Conduct*.

The Missile Technology Regime was established in 1987 by the United States and several other NATO member states to brake the proliferation of missiles. Up to then, missile proliferation was aided at least partly through sales by the now 33 member states of the Regime, who together own most of the world's supply of intermediate and long-range ballistic missiles, as well as most of its cruise missiles. By 1999, it was clear that the Regime had reached the limits of its effectiveness. Nonmembers India, Pakistan, Iran, and North Korea were expanding their own missile holdings; member Russia, as well as partial member China (despite many efforts, China has not yet signed on to limitations on export of missile components), and nonmember North Korea were actively selling missiles or missile components. In this situation, members of the Regime conceived of an *International Code of Conduct Against Ballistic Missile Proliferation*, whose final text was approved at the MTCR Plenary in Paris in 2002.

The Code asks "subscribing states" (both MTCR members and those without missiles) to recognize the dangers of missile proliferation, agree that space launch vehicles should not be used to conceal ballistic missiles program, agree to transparency on ballistic missile programs, and adhere to conventions on space, including the 1972 Liability Convention. The Code also asks commitment from subscribing states to exercise "maximum possible restraint in producing missiles" and "where possible to reduce national holdings of such missiles."

There are several problems with the Code. It is being promoted by the main missile producers who do not offer substantial inducements, including much-discussed gratis or low-cost launch of space vehicles, in return for abstaining from obtaining missiles; do not propose prelaunch inspections of their own space launch vehicles to ensure that they are not long-range missile tests or even attacks; and, most of all, do not propose any obligatory reductions in their own missile holdings. As such, there is nothing in the Code that seems likely to cause the main missile offenders to moderate their actions or potential proliferators to hold back.

Little has been heard in recent months of Russian proposals to control long-range missiles, initiated in international conferences in Moscow in 2000 and 2001. Russia was moved by the pending collapse of the ABM Treaty to propose a global warning and information-sharing system for ballistic missile launches. The U.S.–Russian Joint Data Exchange Center in Moscow agreed in 1999 to exchange immediate information on missile launches but has been making conspicuously slow progress through licensing requirements of the Moscow municipal bureaucracy.

The entire topic of controlling delivery vehicles for highly destructive weapons on a global basis is just emerging as an international concern. There is a long way to go before any action will be taken. The necessary steps include moving the Code of Conduct, and perhaps the MTCR itself, to a U.N. framework, rather than leaving it in the hands of the missile producing states and instituting a dependable system of information exchange. If a U.N. missile forum emerges, it could be used to discuss and discourage adverse missile developments. In the long run, if there is to be an effective regime, the main missile producers have to accept restrictions on their holdings and production. A serious complicating factor is the increasing U.S. dependence on missiles of all kinds for its position as the world's leading military power. Furthermore, attack aircrafts (which are highly effective in delivering weapons of all kinds and are another area of U.S. strength) would at some point have to be controlled in addition to missiles [Mark Smith, *The Arms Control Reporter*, March 2002].

7. Biological Weapons

There was much discussion in the 2001 First Committee of withdrawal of the Bush administration in July 2001 from the work of the Ad Hoc Committee seeking to develop a verification protocol or treaty amendment to the 1972 **Biological Weapons Convention**. The Convention had been without agreed verification measures since its entry into force, because at the time most governments considered attacks by biological weapons to be impractical. Adopted by consensus and sponsored by Hungary, resolution 56/414 asks the Secretary-General to help the parties to the Biological Weapons Convention assist in preparing for the Fifth Review conference (November 17–December 7, 2001). At the time this resolution was being discussed, anthrax attacks were taking place in the United States. Member state representatives, including Ambassador Toth of Hungary, chair of the Ad Hoc Group, still hoped the Bush administration would relent and rejoin the work of the Ad Hoc Committee of treaty parties trying to develop a verification system for the convention. Their hopes were to be disappointed.

The background to these events was that, in 1991, the parties to the Biological Weapons Convention established an ad hoc group of governmental experts to examine the question of verification and establish an agreed verification system for the treaty. In 1994, treaty participants established an Ad Hoc Group to develop a verification system. In July 2001, the United States withdrew from the Ad Hoc Group and termed its work a "hopeless failure" [Jonathan B. Tucker and Raymond A. Zilinskas, "Assessing U.S. Proposals to Strengthen the Biological Weapons Convention," *Arms Control Today,* April 2002]. At the Review Conference of the treaty (November 19–December 7, 2001), the United States again opposed the protocol on verification prepared by the Ad Hoc Group and then called for the Ad Hoc Group's negotiation mandate to end and be replaced by annual conferences of states parties. Uncertain about what to do, conference participants decided to adjourn the review conference and to reconvene on November 11–22, 2002.

During the negotiation of the verification protocol in 23 sessions of the Ad Hoc Group, the countries most interested in biological-genetic research (United States, Germany, and Japan) favored strong export controls, strong protection for proprietary commercial and defense information, and non-intrusive verification visits. For their part, governments of developing countries favored relaxation of export controls, generous conditions for sharing new drugs, and tougher inspections. After Ambassador Toth presented the draft text to the Ad Hoc Group in February 2001, the Bush administration review team rejected the draft protocol in May 2001. The administration team said it believed the verification system would not prevent cheating, would be burdensome to U.S. universities and industries, and would make U.S. companies vulnerable to theft of valuable commercial secrets. The United States was concerned by the fact that only a tiny fraction of facilities with biological weapons capability would be covered worldwide, while even small facilities could produce biological weapons; provisions for inspections in the draft protocol had built-in delays that would permit evidence to be covered up.

Especially after the September 11 terrorists attacks and the unsolved October 2001 anthrax attacks in the United States, it emerged with growing clarity that the United States increasingly feared successful espionage of its own experiments with biological weapons defenses. These concerns had intensified as U.S. authorities became more apprehensive about terrorist use of biological weapons; hostile observers might be able to detect which biological weapons the United States most feared and also those it was not working on. At the November 2001 Review Conference, the United States charged Iraq, Iran, North Korea, Libya, Syria, and Sudan with having illicit biological weapon programs. On November 1, 2001, prior to the opening of the Review Conference, President Bush presented U.S. proposals for strengthening the international regime against biological weapons. Chief among them was a procedure whereby the U.N. Secretary-General would approve inspections at short notice and the idea of a code of ethical conduct for bio-scientists, which could bring voluntary abstention from potentially dangerous activities.

The subject is already on the agenda of the First Committee for the fall of 2002 and of the uncompleted Review Conference in November 2002. It is very improbable that the United States will shift its position toward the Convention verification protocol, although it has proposed several individual verification measures. However, protocol supporters have been affronted by what they consider a classic example of Bush administration unilateralism, so it is likely that a standoff will continue for some time [*The Arms Control Reporter* (December 2001) has a good review of the biological weapons controversy].

8. Chemical Weapons

First Committee Resolution 56/24K, adopted by consensus as in earlier years, stresses the necessity to adhere to and fulfill the **Chemical Weapons Convention** and to cooperate with the implementing organization, the **Organization for the Prohibition of Chemical Weapons** (OPCW). In the debate, Israel said it would ratify the convention when and if there was overall improvement of the Middle East security situation.

The Chemical Weapons Convention entered into force in April 1997. It has been ratified by 145 countries and has a generally successful implementing organization, the OPCW, based in The Hague. The organization has carried out an active program of field inspections. However, in late April 2002, the organization's executive council, led by the United States, fired Director Jose Bustani by a vote of 48 to 7, with 43 abstentions. Bustani was criticized for paying too little attention to verification and too much attention to efforts to gain Iraqi membership in the OPCW [*Manchester Guardian*, May 4, 2002].

Both the United States and Russia, the biggest holders of chemical weapons, are behind in their schedules for destruction of these weapons (Russia very much so).

9. Small Arms

The 2001 First Committee considered two resolutions on small arms. The first resolution, adopted by consensus, calls on member states to support the follow-on activities of the July 2001 **U.N. Conference on Illicit Trade in Small Arms and Light Weapons in All Its Aspects**, including the Review Conference in 2006. Resolution L47 was sponsored by Colombia, which chaired the Conference. (The latter part of the conference title expresses the hope, frustrated in practice, for a broader agenda than the illicit arms trade.) A General Assembly vote on this resolution was postponed at the request of the United States to examine its budgetary implications. However, the United States spoke of the July 2001 conference in positive terms. The second resolution, UNGA Resolution 56/124U, introduced by Mali, requests the help of the United Nations and the international community in curbing illicit traffic in small arms and in collecting such weapons.

Background

Since 1995, pressed by African countries that have been suffering terrible bloodletting in internal wars, mainly carried out by small arms and by light weapons like mortars and recoilless rifles served by two–three man crews, U.N. groups have been discussing plans to limit small arms and light weapons. After meetings of experts (in 1997 and 1999) and preparatory committees of interested states (in February 2000, January 2002, and March 2002), the U.N. conference held 23 informal meetings from July 11–19, 2001, one of them devoted to NGO statements.

On July 20, 2001, the Conference adopted a **Program of Action,** which represents a voluntary, nonbinding agreement among the participating countries, rather than an international treaty [U.N. Department of Disarmament Affairs, "Report of the United Nations Conference on the Illicit Trade in Small Arms and Light Weapons in All Its Aspects"]. Many conference participants had hoped to reach agreement on marking and tracing weapons, regulation of arms brokers, strict export criteria, and control on sales to nonstate actors like domestic extremists. Fulfillment of these modest aims was blocked by a few member states, especially China and the United States. China blocked agreement on marking and identifying weapons. Arab states made increased transparency in gun sales hostage to their efforts to include Israeli nuclear weapons in the U.N. Register. The United States blocked establishment of norms and legal standards for gun ownership or measures that might limit domestic gun ownership or oblige changes in U.S. domestic legislation.

Other delegations considered that the U.S. delegation was representing U.S. gun producers, brokers, and the National Rifle Association [Rachel Stohl, "United States Weakens Outcome of U.N. Small Arms and Light Weapons Conference," *Arms Control Today*, September 2001]. However, the Program of Action does establish norms and standards to guide efforts to control illicit trade. It proposes international measures for acting against illicit manufacturing of small arms and, as it says, "promotes responsible action by states with a view to preventing the illicit export, import, transit, and retransfer of small arms and light weapons" [U.N. Department of Disarmament Affairs, "Report of the United Nations Conference on the Illicit Trade in Small Arms and Light Weapons in All Its Aspects"]. It provides for a conference in 2006 to review progress and for various regional conferences in the interim. Despite obstructions, the conference represents a useful beginning on an important subject.

10. Terrorism and the United Nations

The immediate reaction of the U.N. General Assembly, Security Council, and Secretary-General on September 12, the day after the al-Qaeda attacks on New York and Washington, was to declare full solidarity with and support for the United States. The General Assembly on September 12, its first plenary meeting of 2001, condemned the heinous acts of terrorism of September 11, declared its condolences and solidarity with the people and government of the United States, and urgently called for international cooperation to bring the perpetrators to justice [A/Res/5611].

The Security Council in *Resolution 1368* (2001) of September 12 broke a long-standing deadlock in the United Nations by recognizing the right of individual or collective self-defense in retaliation against terrorist acts. The Security Council declared the September 11 attacks a "threat to international peace and security" [S/Res/1368 (2001)], a characterization that authorized collective military action. This decision, taken with the support of China, Russia, France, the United Kingdom, and all members of the Council, legitimized U.S. retaliatory action against the Taliban and al-Qaeda in Afghanistan.

Prior to the September 11 attacks, the United Nations had performed valuable service over the years in negotiating 12 international conventions against terrorism, as well as 6 treaties regarding terrorism against aircraft, vessels at sea, or oil platforms; the protection of diplomatic personnel; hostages; the marking of plastic explosives to aid detection; suppression of terrorist bombings; and suppression of the financing of terrorism. The United Nations also imposed sanctions for acts of terrorism on Libya and Sudan.

On September 24, the Security Council [S/Res/1373 (2001)] reaffirmed the right of self-defense against terrorism, acting under Chapter VII of the Charter. This made clear that the Council was dealing with a threat to international peace and security and that Council decisions are obligatory for member states. The Security Council resolution called on member states to pass their own legislation to block criminal funding of terrorist acts, freeze funds connected with terrorists or terrorist organizations, prohibit funding to terrorists, deny safe haven to terrorists, bring suspected terrorists to justice, and suppress recruitment of terrorists on their soil. This resolution incorporated the action provisions of the U.N. Conventions on Terrorist Bombings and Suppression of Financing for Terrorism, which the United States and other states hastened to ratify.

Resolution 1373 also established a **Counter-Terrorism Committee** in the Security Council to monitor implementation of the program in the resolution. On October 4, the President of the Security Council appointed U.K. permanent representative Sir Jeremy Greenstock as chairman of the Counter-Terrorism Committee, with the permanent representatives of Colombia, Mauritius, and Russia as vice-chairs. The Counter-Terrorism Committee immediately sent out standard checklists and guidelines to all member states, indicating how they should demonstrate compliance with Resolution 1373.

On April 15, 2002, the Security Council heard the required six-month report of the activities of the Counter-Terrorism Committee [S/PV.4512]; Ambassador Greenstock reported that the Committee had received 143 reports from member states and "others" (OSCE, European Union, Cook Islands, and Switzerland). The Committee had reviewed and responded to 62 member states. Fifty member states had not yet submitted reports. Discussion in the Council session indicated that most of the 50 countries that had not responded required financial assistance or advice from technical experts on how to proceed with the necessary legislation.

There was criticism that funding for assistance and an adequate number of expert advisers had not yet been provided. Some concerns were expressed that human rights must be adequately protected in combating terrorism.

All in all, the report evidenced vigorous and effective follow-through of a very broad Security Council resolution that required up to 17 conforming laws or decrees from each member state. That 140 member states had performed all these actions within six months was a remarkable feat, attesting to their recognition of the increased dangers of terrorism and desire for solidarity with the United States. There was no doubt that international barriers against terrorism were now greatly strengthened, to the benefit of all countries, and also that there would be a real follow-up with the 50 states that had not yet complied with Resolution 1373, most of which were developing countries.

The United Nations did more than mobilize the international effort against terrorism. It negotiated and installed a provisional government for Afghanistan, as the Taliban regime was defeated and dispersed. After difficult negotiations culminating in a marathon session of hostile factions in Bonn (November 27–December 5, 2001), the Secretary-General's indefatigable U.N. Envoy Lakhdar Brahimi succeeded in bringing about agreement on a provisional government headed by Hamid Karzai.

Through these efforts, the United Nations has conclusively proven its value in counter-terrorism, both to the United States as well as to other member states. However, evidence is not conclusive for the related question of whether the need for international cooperation against the September 11 terrorists has brought about enduring change in the pattern of unilateralism and independent action apparent in the first months of the Bush administration. Certainly, such change is not evident in the field of disarmament, where the United States has nullified the ABM Treaty; ended the international effort to draft a verification protocol for the Biological Weapons Convention; restricted the outcome of the U.N. Conference on Small Arms; refused to resubmit the Comprehensive Test Ban Treaty to the U.S. Senate while moving toward renewed testing; and begun preparation to orbit weapons in space. No shift toward U.S. multilateralism was evident in President Bush's "Axis of Evil" speech when, without consultation with Congress, the President broadened the war against terrorism to include Iraq, Iran, and North Korea, nor when he rejected repeated pleas of Hamid Karzai and many others to support a broader peacekeeping force for Afghanistan. [An invaluable source for this section is the UNA-USA policy report, "Combating Terrorism: Does the U.N. Matter—and How?" edited by Jeffrey Laurenti, December 7, 2001.]

IV
Global Resources

1. The World Trade Organization (WTO) and Trade
By David A. Lynch

China's entry into the World Trade Organization (WTO) and the Doha Round of trade negotiations were the two most significant events for the world trading system in 2001 and early 2002. Both developments signaled greater openness for world trade. China, among the world's most active traders, formally became a WTO member at the end of 2001, with Taiwan entering shortly afterward. In September 2001, the WTO successfully launched long-awaited and comprehensive multilateral trade negotiations at its biennial ministerial meeting in Doha, Qatar. Symbolically and substantively, Doha was a long way from Seattle, the site of the inconclusive and conflict-ridden biennial ministerial meeting in November 1999.

However, these steps toward openness were themselves contentious and occurred amidst trends and events (international discord on trading issues, economic slowdowns, and terrorism) that diminished trade openness and harmony. The European Union and the United States continued to bicker over a host of trade issues, complete with economic retaliation and threats of greater economic retaliation to come. Developing and developed nations disagreed on many fundamental issues of trading. In addition, the world economy slowed dramatically as the United States tipped into recession with synchronized slowdowns elsewhere. In fact, after years of steady growth, trade growth turned negative in 2001. Trade flows shrank by 1.5 percent in volume and 4 percent in value in 2001, after a 12 percent volume gain in 2000. The 4 percent drop is the largest annual trade volume decrease since 1982. Despite last year's downturn, the WTO does expect trade volumes to grow again in 2002 and early evidence suggests the prediction is correct [WTO Press Release, May 2, 2002]. And finally, the September 11 attacks against the United States underscored the tenuous nature of trade relations in 2001 and early 2002, demonstrating that economic relations are sensitive to peace and security. These are the primary issues facing trade policy-makers in the coming year.

Doha: A Long Way from Seattle and a Long Way to Go

In November 2001, the WTO attempted to redeem itself from the disastrous biennial ministerial meeting in Seattle two years before. The 1999 meeting made headlines for the street battles between police and antiglobalization protesters. While the acrimony outside the meeting hall did not spill over into the meeting, there was already sufficient tension within. Discord among developed nations and between developed and developing nations within the meeting hall halted launching the next comprehensive round of trade negotiations, which had been the meeting's primary goal.

At Doha, 142 member countries agreed to launch the next round of negotiations. It will be a complex and daunting task. There are more members and more issues than during the Uruguay Round, the last set of comprehensive talks. Those negotiations took eight years. At Doha, nations pledged to finish the talks by January 2005.

While agreement was reached at Doha, negotiations were far from smooth sailing. Concerns of developing nations raised issues that came close to sinking the Doha meeting. Poorer nations have long complained that the WTO and its predecessor, the General Agreement on Tariffs and Trade (GATT), have selectively opened the world's trading system to the advantage of developed nations. Accordingly, developed nations' exports face openness, while developing nations' exports face continued protectionism. Their primary evidence is in the industries of agriculture and textiles and apparel. In these areas poorer nations have some economic advantages. For instance, textiles and apparel are among the most labor-intensive industries in the world; thus poorer nations with lower wage levels have a competitive advantage. But textiles and apparel were kept outside of the GATT. While the GATT successfully lowered tariffs and eliminated quotas for many industrial goods, it did not diminish protectionism in textiles and apparel, much to the detriment of developing nations. Agriculture was also excluded from the GATT. Both were finally brought within the GATT/WTO through the Uruguay Round agreement that established the WTO in 1995. But their inclusion in the WTO has been partial, with continued high tariffs on agricultural products and a long phase-in period for textiles and apparel. This has frustrated developing nations and led some to feel they were misled.

Developing nations also accuse richer nations of providing subsidies that poor nations do not have the resources to match and of putting up barriers to trade through the use of antidumping duties and other similar policies. As they face these barriers to exporting into rich nations, developing nations argue that the Uruguay Round forced them to open their economies in economically and politically painful ways. Some say that the Uruguay Round provided developing nations with "too much pain, and little gain."

Initial drafts of the **Doha Declaration**—containing the formal list of negotiating topics and, often, the generally agreed upon goal within each topic—were unpalatable to many developing nations. In fact, the Indian Minister of Commerce and Industry said, "The only conclusion that could be drawn is that the developing countries have little say in the agenda-setting of the WTO" [*Washington Post*, November 11, 2001]. India led other developing nations to campaign for a commitment for an immediate acceleration of textile and apparel tariff reductions. On this particular issue, developing nations did not win. But on numerous other issues, developing nations won concessions about the direction the Doha Round negotiations will take. Despite the Indian Minister's frustration, developing nations have been far more assertive in negotiations about the Doha Round than they were for other rounds; they are no longer a silent majority [*Financial Times*, November 6, 2001].

Developing nations were able to convince developed nations that overriding patents to stem public health crises such as **HIV/AIDS** was acceptable. Generically producing otherwise expensive patented medicines would normally violate patent laws, but the immediate human cost of upholding patent laws was too high in this case. Developed nations, especially the United States, feared that this would weaken the Agreement on Trade-Related Aspects of Intellectual Property Rights (TRIPS Agreement) and discourage pharmaceutical research, but proponents of the change argue it will save millions of lives.

Another contentious set of issues between developing and developed nations were pushed off the immediate Doha Round agenda, but could reemerge on the agenda if there is consensus to do so at the next biennial ministerial meeting in 2003. These issues sought by developed nations, especially the European Union, include investment rules, competition policy (also known as antitrust policy), government procurement, and customs procedures [Associated Press, November 14, 2001].

Agriculture is among the most protected economic sectors in the world. Not only do traditional barriers to trade such as tariffs remain high, but there is also heavy government involvement in agriculture through production and export subsidies. Many developing nations argue that they cannot compete in agriculture given these realities. The Organization for Economic Cooperation and Development (OECD) estimates that agricultural subsidy levels in 2000 were $90.23 billion in the European Union, $59.90 billion in Japan, and $48.96 billion in the United States [Reuters, November 13, 2001]. Developing nations have no hope of keeping up with subsidies such as these and argue that subsidies depress world farm prices, thus threatening their already poor farmers.

The primary effort to avoid more openness in agriculture came from the European Union, especially France. The European Union compromised with developing nations by linking greater agricultural openness to developing nations' acceptance of environmental issues being on the Doha Round's agenda. Developing nations are fearful that developed nations will use environmental arguments to keep out developing nation products; they also want agricultural export subsidies to end. France remained reluctant about opening agriculture, but was placated by noting in the Doha Declaration that negotiations on agricultural export subsidies "with a view to phasing [them] out" would be held "without prejudging the outcome" [*Washington Post*, November 15, 2001]. In other words, France, the most vocal defender of E.U. subsidies, did not yet want to concede defeat.

Developing nations (and the European Union) were also able to get the United States to agree to place antidumping rules on the negotiating agenda [Associated Press, November 14, 2001; *Washington Post*, November 15, 2001]. This made agreeing to a new negotiating round easier for developing nations, and it made the thought of greater agricultural openness less distasteful to the European Union [BBC News, November 14, 2001]. It may, however, make any trade agreement reached in the Doha Round less acceptable to the U.S. Congress.

In the end, the Doha Declaration took six days and two all-night bargaining sessions, followed by more negotiating over amendments to make the Declaration more palatable to developing nations, yet still acceptable to developed nations [Reuters, November 14, 2001]. All nations did agree to the final Doha Declaration. The primary legacy of outgoing WTO Director-General Mike Moore will be reaching agreement on the Doha Declaration and launching the Doha Round, also called the *Doha Development Agenda*. Carrying out the Doha Round will be left to his successor, Supachai Panitchpakdi. It remains to be seen how the concessions leading to the Doha Declaration will play out in negotiations and how they will be greeted in the nations' home legislatures.

China: One, Two, or More Chinas?

After 15 years of reforms and negotiations, China finally became a WTO member in December 2001 [*Doha WTO Ministerial 2001: Summary of November 11, 2001*, www.wto.org; *Economist*, November 10, 2001]. The main question is whether or not China is ready for the WTO. How this question is answered depends largely on whether China is perceived as one nation-state or two (China and Taiwan). This perception has been a matter of ongoing debate, acrimony, and, from time to time, violence. China believes strongly that there is "one China," with Taiwan as a renegade province. Taiwan increasingly views itself as an independent nation. Both are now WTO members with Taiwan (or "Chinese Taipei," as it is known in the WTO's diplomatic parlance) officially entering the WTO in January 2002, one month after China [*New requests and completed accessions 2001–2002*, www.wto.org]. (China insisted that it join first.) Taiwan will clearly face fewer challenges from WTO membership than China, simply because its economy is much more open and developed than China's.

Ultimately, China's preparedness for the WTO varies greatly within mainland China itself. The coastal areas are far more economically developed than much of the interior of China. Confusing matters further, economic distinctions remain between these areas and the very modern and economically open Hong Kong, officially a part of China since mid-1997. Hong Kong's merchandise trade is only slightly smaller than that of the rest of China [WTO Annual Report, 2001, p. 20]. Hong Kong and the coastal regions stand ready to take advantage of China's newly won WTO membership. These areas have long been a site for foreign direct investment and have catapulted China to its status as the world's fourth largest trader, consistently among the fastest growing economies [Counting the European Union as one nation, WTO Press Release, May 2, 2002]. Much of China's interior, however, is much less developed, and many fear that imports will put Chinese producers (often state-run industries) out of business. Many also argue that WTO entry will exacerbate the already growing inequality between regions within China. Rural unemployment and poverty have led millions of Chinese to move to the booming coastal cities. In fact, over 100 million are adrift having left rural areas for work in the cities [*Business Week*, January 13, 2002]. This massive rural-to-urban migration is also likely to be exacerbated by China's WTO entry [*Economist*, September 15, 2001]. Some of the reforms China is facing include a reduction of tariffs from an average of 21 percent to 8 percent, an end to subsidies for farmers and state-owned companies, and fewer restrictions on foreign investment [*Washington Post*, November 11, 2001].

Another question many ask is whether the world is ready for China's WTO membership. China is likely to be an assertive and powerful proponent of developing nations' interests. In fact, one reason China wanted to join the WTO now was to ensure that it was included in, and therefore could shape, the Doha Round negotiations. China's economic development is sufficiently rapid and massive that it is attracting an enormous amount of investment—$45 billion in 2000—and is therefore altering production and trade patterns in much of the world [*Washington Post*, November 11, 2001]. The most significant changes are likely to be felt elsewhere in Asia, where companies will both compete and cooperate with production in China. As if to symbolize this, in November 2001, Taiwan began to allow direct investment and trade with China [ibid., November 8, 2001]. In fact, the anticipation of greater investment and production in China has become a self-fulfilling prophecy.

China also holds great potential as an export market for U.S. and other developed nations' goods. Some estimates predict China will import $264 billion worth of capital-intensive manufacturing goods, such as vehicles and machinery, over the next ten years. Agriculture exports are predicted to increase by $73 billion during the same period. And China is already the world's largest consumer of mobile phones, and mobile phone sales there are expected to double by 2005 [*Business Week*, January 13, 2002].

U.S. Trade Leadership in Steel: Back Tracking, Fast Tracking, or Both?

The United States is the world's largest trader with the world's largest economy and is thus viewed as the leader in global trade negotiations. A number of developments in the United States suggest it will not be leading as forcefully as it might otherwise. Shortly after preaching the benefits of free trade and soothing developing nations' fears about another round of comprehensive trade negotiations in Doha, the Bush administration announced increased tariffs of up to 30 percent on many steel imports [*New York Times*, May 15, 2002]. The Bush administration claims that the increased tariffs, which are to be in effect for three years, are legal under the WTO's 1994 Safeguards Agreement, which allows increased duties to limit a surge of imports that threatens an industry. A group of countries cooperating to fight the U.S. duties argue that the United States has lost every case it has brought to the WTO in which it claimed damage to an industry from an import surge [Reuters, April 12, 2002].

To much of the world, the U.S. steel tariffs are simple hypocrisy; others view them as political realism. The U.S. steel industry, like the steel industry elsewhere, is in deep trouble, and the steel industry is particularly important in two swing states that Bush narrowly won: Ohio and West Virginia, and two that he narrowly lost: Pennsylvania and Michigan. Bush's margin of victory in the 2000 Electoral College vote was as close as his margin of victory in the Florida popular vote. Had Bush lost any of the states that he won, he would not be the U.S. President, even with Florida going his way. Candidate Bush told West Virginia that he would consider raising steel tariffs. His opponent, Vice President Al Gore, conspicuously did not. (Nor did the Clinton administration raise steel tariffs, despite intense pressure.)

The European Union was able to make these same political calculations as they devised their list of $538 million worth of U.S. imports that they would target for retaliation if approved by the WTO's Dispute Settlement Body (DSB). They drew up another list of products worth $364 million, against which they may retaliate before the DSB issues a ruling. The list includes steel products and citrus fruit, the latter being a mainstay of the Florida economy. For the moment, the European Union is not implementing the more immediate sanctions, which may or may not be legal under WTO rules; instead it is using the DSB [*New York Times*, May 15, 2002; *Economist*, May 11, 2002].

The European Union, China, Japan, Norway, South Korea, and Switzerland have each filed cases with the DSB [www.wto.org]. It is China's first-ever complaint to the DSB. Japan announced tariffs on U.S. steel effective before a DSB ruling [*New York Times*, May 18, 2002; *Washington Post*, May 18, 2002]. The European Union, fearing a surge of inexpensive steel that would have gone to the United States, also announced that it too will increase tariffs on some steel imports [Reuters, March 28, 2002]. China then also instituted steel tariff increases from 7 to 26 percent to guard against import surges [ibid., May 22, 2002]. In both cases, the increased duties are not aimed specifically at U.S. steel exports.

Developing nations are notably absent from the list of nations whose steel faces U.S. antisurge duties. Steel from 80 developing nations was exempted, as was steel from Canada and Mexico, the U.S. partners in the North American Free Trade Agreement (NAFTA) [*New York Times*, March 6, 2002]. This will slightly minimize the negative impact the tariffs will have on the U.S. free trade credentials and therefore on its moral authority to lead WTO trade negotiations. Developing nations' exemption from the U.S. steel duties is all the more important given their skepticism about the world trading system.

Clearly, there are domestic electoral benefits that flow to the Bush administration from its decision to grant antisurge tariffs. In addition, steel protectionism might make free trade more politically palatable to the U.S. Congress. This is important in the administration's efforts to obtain fast track negotiating authority from Congress. Fast track, now officially called Trade Promotion Authority (TPA), prevents Congress from amending any negotiated agreement during the ratification process. Both houses of Congress would vote to ratify or reject any final negotiated agreement, but could not change the agreement. To win fast track approval, Bush must convince a majority of both houses and this has proven difficult during the last decade. In fact, the Clinton administration was unable to overcome the Congressional fast track logjam that began when fast track authority ended in 1994 [*Washington Post*, December 12, 2001].

The logjam centers on traditional job loss concerns from both parties and charges from the left that the WTO is unfriendly to the environment, labor, and poor countries. The right generally supports freer trade, but this support would end if the WTO became friendlier to the environment and labor. Bush was able to get TPA approved in the House of Representatives in December 2001, but by only a single vote. Again, it took protectionism—this time for the textile industry and some agricultural products—for the Bush administration to convince wavering members of Congress [*Economist*, May 11, 2002]. The effort in the Senate to pass a clean fast track authorization bill has, to date, failed. Instead a bipartisan bill emerged that allows the Congress to veto portions of trade agreements that change U.S. antidumping and other similar laws [*Washington Post*, May 15, 2002]. (Dumping is selling a product in a foreign market at a price below that in the home market or selling a product below the costs of production.) In order to convince developing nations to engage in another round of comprehensive trade negotiations, the Bush administration specifically agreed to review WTO rules regarding antidumping duties [Associated Press, November 11, 2001]. It is widely believed that TPA is essential to a successful Doha Round.

Thus, the Bush administration has shown great hesitation toward free trade in numerous instances, and the U.S. Congress has echoed this hesitation. If the executive and legislative branches of the world's richest nation are wavering about greater trade openness, one can imagine the trepidation in nations where the margin of error between economic success and poverty is dramatically smaller.

The European Union and the United States: Bickering Siblings

The United States and the European Union are among the richest and most productive traders in the world whose economies are closely intertwined through trade and investment. On many trade issues, they agree with one another. For instance, at Doha they proved very effective in working together to launch the Doha Round of negotiations. Yet, when it comes to implementing many of the trade agreements they have been instrumental in creating, there is much discord. They seem like wealthy siblings bickering over details of a large inheritance that, no matter the outcome, will leave them wealthier still. Other nations aren't as wealthy and will receive a smaller inheritance and therefore find this discord a bit misplaced. Nevertheless, the squabbling continues. A host of issues remain outstanding between the two giant traders, but three currently stand out as the most contentious: U.S. tariffs, corporate tax policy, and agricultural subsidies.

The fight over the U.S. tax code is based on a defunct corporate tax policy that was known as Foreign Sales Corporation (FSC). Under FSC, U.S. corporations could exempt up to 30 percent of their export income from taxation. To the European Union, this was an illegal export promotion, and it took its case to the WTO and won in 1999. The United States then altered its law, but the new version was not sufficiently different and thus wound up as a dispute at the WTO. In early 2002, the WTO's DSB ruled that the new U.S. law also violates WTO rules and that the European Union is entitled to retaliation. This case is significant because of the amount of money involved. The numbers dwarf other cases on which the DSB has ruled since its inception in 1995. Retaliation may be as high as $4 billion according to the European Union or under $1 billion according to the United States [*Los Angeles Times*, January 15, 2002; Associated Press, February 14, 2002]. If the European Union retaliates, the United States has threatened to challenge E.U. tax codes at the WTO, and there is a good chance that the United States could prevail [*Wall Street Journal*, January 15, 2002, and January 17, 2002].

Some analysts argue the European Union will use the ruling as a bargaining chip for other concessions from the United States [Gary Hufbauer, *The FSC Case: Background and Implications*, January 22, 2002]. The fact that E.U. retaliation could lead to noticeably higher prices within the European Union gives it reason to pause before carrying out retaliatory measures. Comments by E.U. Trade Commissioner Pascal Lamy suggest the European Union is not eager to apply sanctions [Associated Press, February 14, 2002].

Another issue the European Union and United States consistently argue about is agriculture. Within this economic sector, there are many smaller disputes such as U.S. and Canadian hormone-fed beef that the European Union keeps out. The European Union lost this argument in the DSB and, instead of complying with the DSB, pays higher duties on some of its exports to the United States and Canada. Also, there is the ongoing debate stemming from the U.S. penchant for, and E.U. aversion to, Genetically Modified Organisms (GMOs).

A much larger and longer-standing farming argument is over agricultural subsidies. The United States has long subsidized its farming sector, but less so than the European Union or Japan. But the European Union argues that its per farmer subsidies are actually lower than those in the United States. While this is true, the farms in Europe are smaller than those in the United States; thus there are higher overall agriculture subsidies. Since 1996, U.S. subsidies have been scaled back, and at Doha, the United States was a vocal advocate for examining agricultural subsidies in the round's negotiations, against stringent E.U. (mostly French) insistence. With the Doha negotiations still in their infancy, the United States is set to increase its farm subsidies by roughly 80 percent. In some ways, this may diminish E.U. and U.S. tension by limiting the pressure that the United States can place on the European Union to reduce its subsidies. That tension will be passed on to developing nations that cannot afford to keep up with developed nations' farm subsidy programs [*Economist*, May 11, 2002]. As the Chinese government put it, the [U.S. farm] bill distorts international farm trade, goes against the U.S. government's commitment of liberalizing farm trade, and damages the ongoing WTO new round of talks on farm trade [Reuters, May 22, 2002].

Reaching Out to Developing Nations: Technical Assistance

Clearly many developing nations could benefit more from the world trading system if they were fully able to participate in setting trade rules and if they were better able to understand and administer the technical aspects of existing trade rules. For instance, if governments know how to meet food safety standards, they will be more likely to successfully export. For many poor nations, a primary hurdle to fully participating in the world trading system is simply a lack of resources. Many nations cannot afford to have a full-time delegation at the WTO in Geneva. Many cannot afford to have a team of lawyers to adjudicate trade disputes within the WTO's DSB. The WTO has made an increasing effort to reach out to developing nations and nations in transition from centrally planned economies to assist them in these matters.

Technical assistance consists of numerous activities to help developing and transitioning nations understand the world trading system. Training sessions on trade policy take place at the WTO in Geneva, and now seminars and courses are offered in various locations around the world. The WTO has established 109 Trade Reference Centres for 88 least developed and other developing nations. These provide the trade ministries with information technology sufficient to access WTO and other related websites [*Fact sheet on technical cooperation*, March 28, 2002; *WTO assistance for developing countries*, www.wto.org]. The WTO also engages in technical missions to help nations draft legislation that will be consistent with WTO commitments [*Activities of WTO technical cooperation*, www.wto.org]. One problem with these programs has been funding. Only 10 percent of technical assistance funding in 1999 came from the regular WTO budget; the other 90 percent came from extra-budgetary donations [WTO Annual Report, 2001, p. 26].

In order to help developing and transitioning nations take part in the Doha Round negotiations, WTO member nations promised to double the 15 million Swiss francs they had already pledged for WTO Trade-Related Technical Assistance (TRTA). Additionally, many governments indicated that they would provide other support such as organizing their own trade training courses [WTO Press Release, 279, March 11, 2002].

To help developing and transitioning nations understand and navigate through trade disputes at the DSB, the WTO makes legal assistance available through the Technical Cooperation Division of the WTO Secretariat. Also, the WTO established the Advisory Centre on WTO Law to provide training and legal advice about the WTO to developing nation members and all least developed nations [WTO Annual Report, 2001, p. 27].

The WTO is also making a concerted effort to increase internal transparency. This means the WTO is trying to do a better job at making decision-making visible to all of its members. Some of this can be done simply by disseminating information about WTO activities to its members, especially those without permanent representatives in Geneva.

WTO's Dispute Settlement Body (DSB)

Some consider the DSB to be the most important element of the WTO, because it helps ensure that trade disputes are resolved by the rule of law, not the rule of the jungle. Still, the more powerful nations have clear advantages. Less powerful nations may be hesitant to challenge the powerful; they may need the powerful nation's assistance in other matters.

The DSB does encourage the resolution of cases by the parties to a dispute through consultation instead of legal battle. Consultations involve negotiations, and powerful nations will always have an advantage. But if a powerful nation violated trade rules, a less powerful nation will have the WTO's DSB to stand with it, in its attempt to change the powerful nation's behavior. However, the lack of resources again makes developing nations disadvantaged compared to wealthier nations. Without permanent representatives in Geneva or the resources to have teams of lawyers argue cases, many developing nations face significant challenges within the DSB. But here, too, the WTO tries to help. The Secretariat will make a legal expert available to any member that requests it. Also, as part of the WTO's technical assistance endeavors, it has organized training courses to make developing nations more aware of the dispute settlement process [*Technical Cooperation: Disputes*, www.wto.org].

The WTO's dispute settlement process has been well used. From the DSB's inception in 1995 through 2000, there were over 200 formal complaints made to the DSB [WTO Annual Report, 2001, p. 27]. Three-quarters of these were from developed nations against other developed nations. The remaining one-quarter of complaints were filed by developing nations. Half of these developing nation complaints were against developed nations and half against other developing nations [WTO Annual Report, 2001, p. 27].

The stages of the WTO's dispute settlement process are as follows: (1) the formal request for a consultation and consultations, (2) the establishment of a panel, (3) the ruling of the panel, (4) the appellate ruling, and, finally, (5) implementation. If implementation is not adequately carried out, then retaliation is authorized. Approximately three-quarters of cases are resolved through consultations before the panel stage [WTO Annual Report, 2001, p. 27]. Most cases that reach a panel ruling go all the way to an appellate ruling, which is final. Most of the appellate rulings are implemented, but there are some formal complaints about "offending" nations inadequately implementing appellate decisions. Through 2000, there were four cases in which the DSB authorized retaliation due to inadequate implementation. Retaliation takes the form of higher tariffs equivalent to the damage done by the offending nation. It has been carried out in three of these instances. Nations are somewhat hesitant to retaliate because it raises prices for their consumers [WTO Annual Report, 2001, p. 28].

As this suggests, the DSB process can be time consuming. For instance, the Bush administration's tariffs on steel products came in March of 2001. Countries immediately turned to the WTO's DSB, but the DSB's decision isn't expected until late in 2003 or early 2004 [*New York Times*, May 15, 2002; Reuters, May 22, 2002]. Meanwhile, the tariffs stand.

Accession: The Road to Join the WTO

With the addition of China and Taiwan (Chinese Taipei), the WTO's membership is 144. Even before they joined the WTO, WTO members accounted for over 90 percent of world trade [WTO Annual Report, 2001, p. 46]. Currently there are 30 nations in line to join [List of applicants to become WTO members, www.wto.org]. These range from significant traders like Russia and Saudi Arabia to tiny countries like Andorra and Vanuatu.

How long does it take to join the WTO? The fastest accession to the WTO took two years and four months by the Kyrgyz Republic [WTO Annual Report, 2001, p. 28]. But the true answer varies with the degree of openness in an applicant's economy. If a nation's economy is open, the process does not require significant economic reforms. The nation desiring WTO entry must, however, reach bilateral agreements with all other WTO members about market access. This can be quite time consuming. For nations whose economies are not open, the time required to enter the WTO depends on their desire and will to open their economies. It can easily take a decade or longer for a country that is not committed to opening its economy. For many nations, this is a difficult process for two reasons. First, as the WTO pushes trade barriers ever lower by covering more issues and economic sectors, the requirements to join require more openness and are more complex. Second, many of the nations now in line to join the WTO are making the transition from centrally planned to market economies [ibid., p. 46].

Much focus about WTO accession is on Russia. It does need further reform to reach the minimal level of economic openness found in WTO members. It has moved considerably in this direction since 1993 when it applied for membership; Russia hopes to join in 2002. This seems doubtful [Agence France Presse, February 8, 2002]. Russian policy-makers are hesitant to reform. Some argue, for instance, that WTO member nations are being too demanding [*Financial Times Information*, February 19, 2002; *Economist*, November 24, 2001]. Many observers think 2003 is too optimistic. The primary reforms that Russia must implement regard agricultural subsidies, the judiciary system, intellectual property rights, and barriers to foreign investment in financial services [Europe Information Service, December 8, 2001; Agence France Presse, February 8, 2002].

The current roster of the 30 applicants is as follows: Algeria, Andorra, Armenia, Azerbaijan, Bahamas, Belarus, Bhutan, Bosnia Herzegovina, Cambodia, Cape Verde, Kazakhstan, Laos, Lebanon, Libya, Macedonia, Nepal, Russia, Samoa, Saudi Arabia, Seychelles, Sudan, Syria, Tajikistan, Tonga, Ukraine, Uzbekistan, Vanuatu, Vietnam, Yemen, and Yugoslavia [List of applicants to become WTO members, www.wto.org].

Regional Trade Agreements: A Complex Puzzle

Regional Trade Agreements (RTAs) are increasing in number and complexity. There were 172 RTAs in force as of July 31, 2000, and 68 more under negotiation or not yet in force; however, some of these will replace existing RTAs [*Mapping of Regional Trade Agreements*, October 11, 2000, www.wto.org].

There are many varieties of RTAs. They vary primarily by the number of members, type of members, geographic scope, and the depth of integration they provide. Membership can be bilateral (between two nations) or plurilateral (among three or more nations). RTAs are typically between nations, but can also be between nations and other RTAs or exclusively between RTAs, such as the proposed E.U.-Common Market of the South (Mercosur) agreement. They can encompass an entire region, like the 34-nation Free Trade Area of the Americas (FTAA); be subregional, like the Andean Community of Nations (CAN); or cross-regional, like the proposed E.U.-Mercosur agreement.

To add another layer of complexity, regional trade agreements vary by the degree to which they integrate their members' economies. Some RTAs promote economic cooperation, but are not free trade agreements; they do not lower trade barriers significantly. Others have low trade barriers in virtually all economic sectors. Customs unions are RTAs that also establish common external tariffs. Some RTAs coordinate their monetary policy or adopt a common currency.

Africa Regionalism: Integrating Toward Disintegration?

Africa's RTAs have been troubled. There are many RTAs in Africa, but often their commitment to openness has been uneven, thus subgroups of RTAs have formed their own RTAs, or joined other RTAs, much to the confusion of everyone. In fact, regional agreements often do not include much free trade. U.N. Under-Secretary Kingsley Amoako contends that crosscutting membership makes true integration in Africa more difficult. Amoako cited the Common Market for Eastern and Southern Africa (COMESA), Southern African Development Community (SADC), the Southern African Customs Union (SACU), and East African Community (EAC) as examples of this problem [Deutsche Presse-Agentur, July 6, 2001].

For instance, five members of SACU—Botswana, Lesotho, Namibia, South Africa, and Swaziland—are also members of the 14-member SADC, which hopes to establish a FTA by 2004 [WTO Annual Report, 2001, p. 39; Agence France Presse, May 21, 2001]. SADC members South Africa and Botswana do not belong to COMESA, but many other nations are in both SADC and COMESA [Agence France Presse, May 21, 2001]. COMESA and the SADC are considering a merger [Agence France Presse, May 21, 2001]. Meanwhile, 9 of COMESA's 20 nations launched the COMESA-FTA in October 2000, which also aims for a common external tariff by 2004. The nine that formed the FTA are Djibouti, Egypt, Kenya, Madagascar, Malawi, Mauritius, Sudan, Zambia, and Zimbabwe [Agence France Presse, May 21, 2001, and October 31, 2001].

The East African Community (EAC), which includes Kenya, Tanzania, and Uganda, was re-launched in January 2001 after collapsing in 1977 from economic and political disagreements. EAC nations seek the formation of the proposed East African Customs Union with common external tariffs as well as a common market. The EAC believes the customs union will be launched in 2002 [Agence France Presse, November 30, 2001, and March 25, 2002]. Rwanda and Burundi have also sought membership to the EAC. Of the three EAC nations, Kenya and Uganda are also COMESA members. (Tanzania had been in COMESA, but dropped out.) Applicants Rwanda and Burundi are also both COMESA members [COMESA website, www.comesa.int].

The Americas: Hemispheric Free Trade, Narrow Integration, or a Jumble?

Regional trade in the Americas is getting more confusing. Having the Andean Community of Nations (CAN), the Caribbean Economic Community (CARICOM), the Free Trade Agreement of the Americas (FTAA), the Common Market of the South (Mercosur), the North American Free Trade Agreement (NAFTA), and various other economic groupings is confusing enough, but there are also intergroup negotiations between many of these groups and with others both inside and outside the Americas. Additionally, bilateral free trade agreements have also proliferated in the region.

Because President Bush has made FTAA his primary trade goal in the Americas and because the United States is the economic giant in the region, there has been momentum toward realizing the FTAA goal of free trade from Canada to Chile. (This would, however, exclude Cuba whose disfavor in Washington, D.C., disqualifies it and French Guyana, which is officially still French.) Other nations in the FTAA have agreed to integrate by 2005, but there are many nations that have shown hesitation. While Venezuela's President Hugo Chavez has been the most outspoken critic of the FTAA, Brazil also has been hesitant about the agreement. Brazil, the primary trading power in South America, would prefer greater integration in South America (and elsewhere) before negotiating with the United States. Toward that end, it has urged greater cooperation between Mercosur—which consists of Argentina, Brazil, Paraguay, and Uruguay, with Chile and Bolivia as associate members—and the Andean Community of Nations (CAN), which includes Bolivia, Colombia, Ecuador, Peru, and Venezuela. The CAN formally agreed to ongoing trade negotiations with Mercosur. The CAN seeks to be a free trade area, have a common agricultural policy, and then, by the end of 2003, establish a custom's union (with a common external tariff) [CAN's Declaration of Santa Cruz de la Sierra, January 31, 2002].

Mercosur has also been negotiating a free trade agreement with the European Union. But Mercosur itself has been struggling, due largely to Argentina's currency crisis. Trade shrank 10 percent among Mercosur nations in 2001. Intra-Mercosur exports accounted for 18 percent of its members' exports in 2000, down from 25 percent in 1998 [*Economist,* January 1, 2002]. Brazil has suggested that Mercosur would be all but dead if Argentina adopts the dollar as its currency [ibid.].

Caribbean nations feel even more vulnerable to U.S. economic power and the world trading system than do South American nations. Thus, they too want deeper integration regionally before hemispheric free trade. The Caribbean Community, CARICOM, seeks greater economic integration, but meetings devoted to this are often short on specifics [Associated Press, December 12, 2001]. The 25 leaders of the Association of Caribbean States did, however, agree to support the FTAA.

Bilateral trade negotiations have been extensive across the Americas. The United States and Chile have been negotiating. Brazil has been negotiating with Mexico, Russia, China, and India [*Economist,* January 5, 2002]. Mexico has entered into bilateral free trade agreements with numerous countries.

While all of this spreads economic openness to a degree, it creates many separate sets of rules that are confusing to keep straight. Thus many WTO proponents call for fewer regional trade agreements and, instead, a stronger WTO.

To opponents of globalization, the FTAA and other regional agreements are, like the WTO, insufficiently responsive to concerns about the environment, labor, and other social issues. They look at NAFTA and see an increase in trade, but also an increase of misery along the U.S.–Mexican border. Many Mexican border towns have extensive slums without sewage or significant public investment of which to speak, despite the thousands of *maqiladora* (assembly) plants that have massively increased production and trade [ibid., February 16, 2002].

Asian Regionalism

Asian regionalism has been different from that found elsewhere because the most economically important nations officially eschewed regional FTAs until recently. For a time, Japan, China, South Korea, and Taiwan were among the few significant economies of the world that were not in any FTAs. These nations have been in the Asian Pacific Economic Cooperation Forum (APEC) for some time now, but the 21-nation APEC, which includes non-Asian nations such as the United States, has not fostered much economic integration. APEC's goal is greater trade integration for developed members by 2010 and for developing members by 2020, but few concrete steps have been taken to get there in recent years [Japan Economic Newswire, October 21, 2001].

In any case, the four nations' aversion to regional FTAs has ended. Japan and Singapore have negotiated an FTA that is likely to be approved in 2002 and begin in 2003. Japan and South Korea are considering negotiations for an FTA, and China has announced plans to form a regional

FTA with the ten nations of the Association of Southeast Asian Nations (ASEAN) [Reuters, November 6, 2001; *Straits Times,* November 30, 2001; and Noboru Hatakeyama, *Japan's New Regional Trade Policy—Which country comes next after Singapore?*, Lecture at the Institute for International Economics, March 13, 2002; www.iie.com].

The original six nations of ASEAN—Brunei, Indonesia, Malaysia, the Philippines, Singapore, and Thailand—agreed to the ASEAN Free Trade Area (AFTA) in 1992. AFTA was scheduled to begin in 2008. This goal, however, was then moved up to 2003, and then, again, to 2002. ASEAN's newer entrants—Cambodia, Laos, Myanmar (Burma), and Vietnam—are scheduled to enter by 2006 [Reuters, November 6, 2001; *Straits Times,* November 30, 2001, and January 1, 2002]. AFTA has not moved very quickly toward integration, but ASEAN did take a step of greater symbolic and perhaps practical significance: ASEAN and China announced that they would join in a free trade area within ten years, the ASEAN–China FTA [Reuters, November 6, 2001; *Straits Times,* November 30, 2001]. Japan is also studying entry into an FTA with ASEAN. Japan, however, is hesitant to open its agriculture market and that would be of great interest to ASEAN members.

Ultimately China would like to create a West Pacific Economic Zone (WPEZ) including China, Japan, South Korea, and the ASEAN nations [*Straits Times,* November 30, 2001]. Japan has called for an East Asian Community, but has done little to put this idea into practice.

The European Union: Deeper and Wider

The 12 E.U. nations that adopted the euro took another step toward deeper integration in early 2002 with elimination of their national currencies. Three E.U. nations remain outside the euro-zone: Denmark, Great Britain, and Sweden.

The European Union is also widening. There are 13 nations in line to join the European Union, and 10 of them may join in a "Big Bang" enlargement in 2004. The ten nations are the three Baltic nations (Estonia, Latvia, and Lithuania), the Czech Republic, Hungary, Poland, Slovakia, Slovenia, and two island nations: Malta and the divided Cyprus. To enter the European Union, the nations will continue economic and political reforms, and the European Union itself must reform its voting system and agricultural and regional poverty aid programs. These programs account for 80 percent of the E.U. budget and cannot be sustained with the additional entrants unless altered [*Financial Times,* November 14, 2001]. Other nations negotiating to join the European Union are Bulgaria, Romania, and Turkey.

Middle East

The six-nation Gulf Cooperation Council (GCC) signed an agreement to establish a customs union (meaning a common external tariff) by 2003 and a single currency by 2010. GCC members include Bahrain, Kuwait, Oman, Qatar, Saudi Arabia, and the United Arab Emirates. The European Union and the GCC have long considered establishing an FTA. The European Union considers the GCC's formation of a customs union a requirement for establishing a FTA with it [*New York Times*, January 1, 2002].

The Arab League, which includes GCC members and Egypt, Iraq, Jordan, Lebanon, Libya, Morocco, Syria, and Tunisia, hopes to establish a common market by 2007 [WTO Annual Report, 2001, p. 39].

2. The United Nations and Development
By Roger A. Coate

In recent years, human development and security have come to be seen as being inextricably linked. Today, more than ever, they dominate discourse and practice throughout the U.N. system. This preeminent role was clearly demonstrated during the debate at the U.N. Millennium Summit in September 2000. The challenges to human development and security posed by forces of globalization dominated and focused much of the global agenda since. The U.N. Secretary-General has summarized the nature of the challenge succinctly:

> As the new century dawns, there can be no task more urgent for the United Nations than that fixed by the Millennium Summit, of rescuing more than one billion men, women and children from "abject and dehumanizing poverty." At that Summit, Governments also agreed that the benefits of globalization—faster and more sustained growth, higher living standards, more employment and large human dividends from advances in technology—require concerted action, at both the national and international levels, and cannot be left to the operation of markets alone. Rather, globalization and its accompanying market energies must be guided and harnessed to become inclusive forces for sustainable, people-centered development. In this effort, Governments, international organizations, private entities, and civil society all have a role to play, in a spirit of true partnership. [U.N. Doc. A/AC.257/12, December 18, 2000, p. 2]

In this context, member states at the Millennium Summit endorsed the elimination of poverty and the promotion of sustainable development as the world organization's highest priority. The main challenge now is building the capacity, political will, and commitment required to mount an effective response.

Formalizing a Global Development Agenda

This consensual priority focus stands in marked contrast to the frequently heated North–South debates of previous decades. Building on the activities of the United Nations' first three development decades (1960–1989), numerous important events over the last dozen years have transformed the global development debate and, indeed, U.N. discourse in general. The Millennium Summit and Millennium Assembly represent just two— albeit two very important—links in a growing chain of multilateral global conferences and activities focusing on development-related issues and problems. These activities over the past decade or so constitute an impressive list of global initiatives that have served to help refocus and redirect the global development agenda:

- South Commission Report (1990)
- World Summit for Children (1990)
- *Human Development Report* (annually since 1990)
- World Conference on Education for All (1990)
- U.N. Conference on Environment and Development ("Earth Summit," 1992)
- Eighth Session of the U.N. Conference on Trade and Development (UNCTAD VIII, 1993)
- World Conference on Human Rights (1993)
- Commission on Sustainable Development (established 1993)
- International Conference on Population and Development (IPDC, 1994)
- *An Agenda for Development* (1995)
- World Summit on Social Development (1995)
- Fourth World Conference on Women (1995)
- Commission on Global Governance Report (1995)
- Second U.N. Conference on Human Settlements (Habitat II, 1996)
- World Food Summit (1996)
- Ninth Session of the U.N. Conference on Trade and Development (UNCTAD IX, 1996)
- Special Session of the General Assembly to Review and Appraise the Implementation of Agenda 21 (1997)
- Special Session of the General Assembly on the International Conference on Population and Development (1999)
- Special Session of the General Assembly on Small Island States (1999)
- Tenth Session of the U.N. Conference on Trade and Development (UNCTAD X, 2000)
- Secretary-General's Millennium Report, We the Peoples: The Role of the United Nations in the 21st Century (2000)
- Special Session of the General Assembly on the World Summit for Social Development and Beyond: Achieving Social Development for All in a Globalizing World (2000)
- Millennium Summit (2000)

- Third United Nations Conference on the Least Developed Countries (2001)
- Special Session of the General Assembly for an Overall Review and Appraisal of the Implementation of the Outcome of the Second U.N. Conference on Human Settlements (Habitat II) (2001)
- Special Session of the General Assembly on HIV/AIDS (2001)
- World Conference Against Racism, Racial Discrimination, Xenophobia and Related Intolerance (2001)
- The Fourth World Trade Organization Ministerial Conference (2001)
- International Conference on Financing for Development (2002)
- Special Session of the General Assembly on Children (2002)
- World Food Summit: Five Years Later (2002)
- The World Summit on Sustainable Development (2002)

Through this ever-evolving discourse, the concepts of human development and sustainable development became fused in the concept *sustainable human development*, which in turn became further entwined with the concept of *human security*. Promoting peace and security, the primary raison d'être of the United Nations, has come to mean promoting and sustaining "human security."

Human Security and Development

In the aftermath of the events of September 11, 2001, it is more widely acknowledged than ever that traditional division of international issues into matters of "war and peace" on one hand and questions of "economic and social" affairs on the other no longer holds credence. Thinking out of the traditional military security "box," however, is not easy for many diplomats and statesmen who were nurtured during the Cold War period. Yet for the most part, people are coming to embrace the proposition that "[t]he concept of security must change—from an exclusive stress on national security to a much greater stress on people's security, from security through armaments to security through human development, from territorial security to food, employment, and environmental security" [UNDP, *Human Development Report 1993*]. Human security is a qualitative condition that entails individual and collective perceptions of low threat to physical and psychological well-being from all manner of agents and forces that could degrade their lives, values, and property. It focuses attention directly on human beings and their circumstances [Thomas Weiss et al., *The United Nations and Changing World Politics*, Third Edition (Boulder: Westview, 2001)].

In order to understand the current approaches to development in the U.N. system, it is important to acknowledge an important underlying assumption: human security emphasizes the psychological as well as physical end state of development, more than the mechanical processes of development [see *Global Agenda: Issues/56,* 2001]. Creating the foundation for sustainable human development entails empowering individuals, groups, and communities to become engaged constructively and effectively in satisfying their own needs, values, and interests, thereby providing them with a genuine sense of control over their own futures. "[P]eople's participation is becoming the central issue of our time," and it is inextricably linked with and is an inherent component, if not requisite, of both sustainable human development and human security [UNDP, *Human Development Report 1993*].

The U.N.-led "people-centered" development agenda that has evolved over the past decade focuses heavily on integrating and empowering relevant stakeholders, including especially women, youth, the poor, and other marginalized elements of society, in addition to civil society more generally and the private sector. The way to eradicate poverty, the UNDP annual *Human Development Reports* have argued, is to empower the poor and marginalized elements of society to provide for the satisfaction of their own basic needs and values. The U.N. Development Programme (UNDP) "promotes the empowerment of people through measures to build their coping and adapting capacities, to increase their productivity and income, and to participate more fully in decision-making" [UNDP, *UNDP Today: Reform in Action,* 1999].

A more or less coherent programmatic framework of development goals, objectives, and sectoral policy paradigms thus emerged and formed the foundation for the U.N. Millennium Declaration. The Declaration was couched in the language of certain shared fundamental values—freedom, equality, solidarity, tolerance, respect for nature, and shared responsibility. It focused on eradicating extreme poverty, creating enabling environments at the national and international levels conducive to development, promoting good governance both domestically and internationally, mobilizing financial resources required for development, addressing the special needs of LDCs (less developed countries), dealing comprehensively and effectively with debt problems, and addressing the special needs of small island and landlocked developing countries. In line with the evolving global development framework, the assembled heads of state and government resolved to promote gender equality and the empowerment of women, develop and implement strategies to increase employment opportunities, encourage the pharmaceutical industry to make essential drugs more widely available in developing countries, develop strong partnerships with civil society, and ensure that the benefits of new technologies, especially information and communication technologies, are available to all [U.N. Doc. A/Res/55/2, September 18, 2000].

Of course, important differences persist. Developed countries generally place greater emphasis on promoting values such as good governance, the priority role of the market, the rule of law, and human rights at the domestic level. Developing countries, on the other hand, tend to focus more on global economic inequalities, structural barriers, resource maldistribution and consumption, and debt and other development finance problems. All in all, however, a general consensus prevailed. It can be summed up in part as follows:

> The primary resource for development is the great untapped reservoir of human creativity and talent of the people of the developing countries themselves; the release of this human potential requires investment in education, infrastructure, public health and other basic social services, as well as in production for the market. . . . [T]he central goal of public policy on financing for development must be to support equitable and sustainable growth in developing countries, reduce risks of systemic crises and make available the resources required for achieving key developmental goals. [U.N. Doc. A/AC.257/12, December 18, 2000]

Also, there appears to be genuine consensus that the eradication of extreme poverty and the promotion of sustainable development should be the major focus of development strategies. Good governance, the empowerment of stakeholders, and popular participation represent means toward these ends.

To attain those ends, a number of specific goals and associated targets and indicators have been established growing out of the extensive series of global conferences and activities over the past decade—most especially the activities surrounding the Millennium Summit.

Millennium Development Goals

These Millennium Development Goals (MDGs) have been commonly accepted throughout the U.N. system, including the Bretton Woods Institutions, as a framework for assessing progress. Whereas the first seven goals focus on ends, the eighth and final goal concentrates on means—creating an effective global partnership for development. These goals, targets, and indicators (bulleted points below) are:

Goal 1: Eradicate extreme poverty and hunger
Target: Halve, between 1990 and 2015, the proportion of people whose income is less than $1 a day.
- Proportion of population below $1 a day
- Poverty gap ratio *(incidence x depth of poverty)*
- Share of poorest quintile in national consumption

Target: Halve, between 1990 and 2015, the proportion of people who suffer from hunger.
- Prevalence of underweight in children (under five years of age)
- Proportion of population below minimum level of dietary energy consumption

Goal 2: Achieve universal primary education

Target: Ensure that, by 2015, children everywhere, boys and girls alike, will be able to complete a full course of primary schooling.
- Net enrollment ratio in primary education
- Proportion of pupils starting grade 1 who reach grade 5
- Literacy rate of 15- to 24-year-olds

Goal 3: Promote gender equality and empower women

Target: Eliminate gender disparity in primary and secondary education preferably by 2005, and in all levels of education no later than 2015.
- Ratio of girls to boys in primary, secondary, and tertiary education
- Ratio of literate females to males among 15- to 24-year-olds
- Share of women in wage employment in the nonagricultural sector
- Proportion of seats held by women in national parliament

Goal 4: Reduce child mortality

Target: Reduce by two-thirds, between 1990 and 2015, the under-five mortality rate.
- Under-five mortality rate
- Infant mortality rate
- Proportion of one-year-old children immunized against measles

Goal 5: Improve maternal health

Target: Reduce by three-quarters, between 1990 and 2015, the maternal mortality ratio.
- Maternal mortality ratio
- Proportion of births attended by skilled health personnel

Goal 6: Combat HIV/AIDS, malaria, and other diseases

Target: Have halted, by 2015, and begun to reverse the spread of HIV/AIDS.
- HIV prevalence among 15- to 24-year-old pregnant women
- Contraceptive prevalence rate
- Number of children orphaned by HIV/AIDS

Target: Have halted, by 2015, and begun to reverse the incidence of malaria and other major diseases.
- Prevalence and death rates associated with malaria
- Proportion of population in malaria-risk areas using effective malaria prevention and treatment measures
- Prevalence and death rates associated with tuberculosis

- Proportion of T.B. cases detected and cured under the Directly Observed Treatment Short-Course (DOTS) initiative

Goal 7: Ensure environmental sustainability
Target: Integrate the principles of sustainable development into country policies and programs and reverse the loss of environmental resources.
- Change in land area covered by forest
- Land area protected to maintain biological diversity
- GDP (Gross Domestic Product) per unit of energy use
- Carbon dioxide emissions (per capita)

Target: Halve, by 2015, the proportion of people without sustainable access to safe drinking water.
- Proportion of population with sustainable access to an improved water source

Target: Have achieved, by 2020, a significant improvement in the lives of at least 100 million slum dwellers.
- Proportion of population with access to improved sanitation
- Proportion of population with access to secure tenure (Urban/rural disaggregation of several of the above indicators may be relevant for monitoring improvement in the lives of slum dwellers.)

Goal 8: Develop a global partnership for development
Target: Develop further an open, rule-based, predictable, nondiscriminatory trading and financial system (includes a commitment to good governance, development, and poverty reduction—both nationally and internationally).
- Net ODA (Official Development Assistance) as a percentage of DAC donors' gross national income
- Proportion of ODA to basic social services (basic education, primary health care, nutrition, safe water, and sanitation)
- Proportion of ODA that is untied
- Proportion of ODA for environment in small island developing states
- Proportion of ODA for the transport sector in landlocked countries

Official Development Assistance (ODA)
Target: Address the special needs of the least developed countries (includes tariff- and quota-free access for exports, enhanced program of debt relief for heavily indebted poor countries (HIPC) and cancellation of official bilateral debt, and more generous ODA for countries committed to poverty reduction).

Market access

Target: Address the special needs of landlocked countries and small island developing states (through the Barbados Programme and 22nd General Assembly provisions).

- Proportion of exports (by value, excluding arms) admitted free of duties and quotas
- Average tariffs and quotas on agricultural products and textiles and clothing
- Domestic and export agricultural subsidies in OECD countries
- Proportion of ODA provided to help build trade capacity

Debt sustainability

Target: Deal comprehensively with the debt problems of developing countries through national and international measures in order to make debt sustainable in the long term.

- Proportion of official bilateral HIPC debt canceled
- Debt service as a percentage of exports of goods and services
- Proportion of ODA provided as debt relief
- Number of countries reaching HIPC decision and completion points

Other

Target: In cooperation with developing countries, develop and implement strategies for decent and productive work for youth.

Target: In cooperation with pharmaceutical companies, provide access to affordable, essential drugs in developing countries.

Target: In cooperation with the private sector, make available the benefits of new technologies, especially information and communications.

- Unemployment rate of 15- to 24-year-olds
- Proportion of population with access to affordable, essential drugs on a sustainable basis
- Telephone lines per 1,000 people
- Personal computers per 1,000 people [www.worldbank.org/data/mdg/].

These MDGs are viewed as being mutually reinforcing with the overarching objective being poverty reduction.

Progress and Challenges to Achieving the MDGs

Progress toward achieving these goals, however, has been mixed, to say the least. As suggested in the World Bank's *World Development Indicators 2002*,

Despite progress in recent years, both poor and rich countries need to do much more, if the international community is to meet its commitment of halving global poverty in all the world's regions by 2015. . . . Current estimates say that brisk economic growth in China and India [which collectively contain 38 percent of the world's population] will enable the world to reach the overall goal of halving global poverty by 2015. But the data . . . say progress is uneven and too many regions and countries are falling far short of the goals. [www.worldbank.org/data; www.worldbank.org/developmentnews/stories/html/042002a.htm]

This new report indicates that, in order for most developing regions to achieve the poverty-reduction goal, an average per capita income growth rate of 3.6 percent per year would be needed. As also pointed out in the report, however, such a rate of growth would be nearly twice the rate achieved over the past decade. The picture is similarly gloomy for the other goals—none of which are likely to be met completely at current rates of progress.

Figure IV-1 and Table IV-1 illustrate, respectively, how countries and people are doing with respect to the MDGs.

As reflected in the *Human Development Report 2001,* for example,

While 66 countries are on track to reduce under-five mortality rates by two-thirds, 93 countries with 62% of the world's people are lagging, far behind or slipping. Similarly, while 50 countries are on track to achieve the safe water goal, 83 countries with 70% of the world's people are not. More than 40% of the world's people are living in countries on track to halve income poverty by 2015. Yet they are in just 11 countries that include China and India. . . , and 70 countries are far behind or slipping. Without China and India, only 9 countries with 5% of the world's people are on track to halve income poverty.

Yet there are signs of hope. Many countries have already achieved, or are well on the way to achieving, universal primary education. However, in sub-Saharan Africa and least developed countries (LDCs), the situation remains rather bleak.

LDCs and Sub-Saharan Africa

The LDCs, including most sub-Saharan African countries, have been struggling economically in recent years. The rate of growth of their gross domestic products (GDPs) has generally declined from its peak of 4.6 percent in 1996 to an estimated 3.0 percent for 1999. "Recent economic growth has not been strong or sustained enough to increase *per capita* income or make an impact on the levels of poverty in the sub-Saharan region. It has been estimated that 44 percent of Africans as a whole, and 51 percent of those in sub-Saharan Africa, live in absolute poverty" [Report by the Secretary-General, *Acceleration of Development in Africa and the Least Developed Countries,* United Nations, A/AC.253/22, February 24, 2000, p. 2].

Most LDCs lack sufficient capacity to integrate productively into the

Figure IV-1

Millennium Declaration goals for development and poverty eradication: how are countries doing?

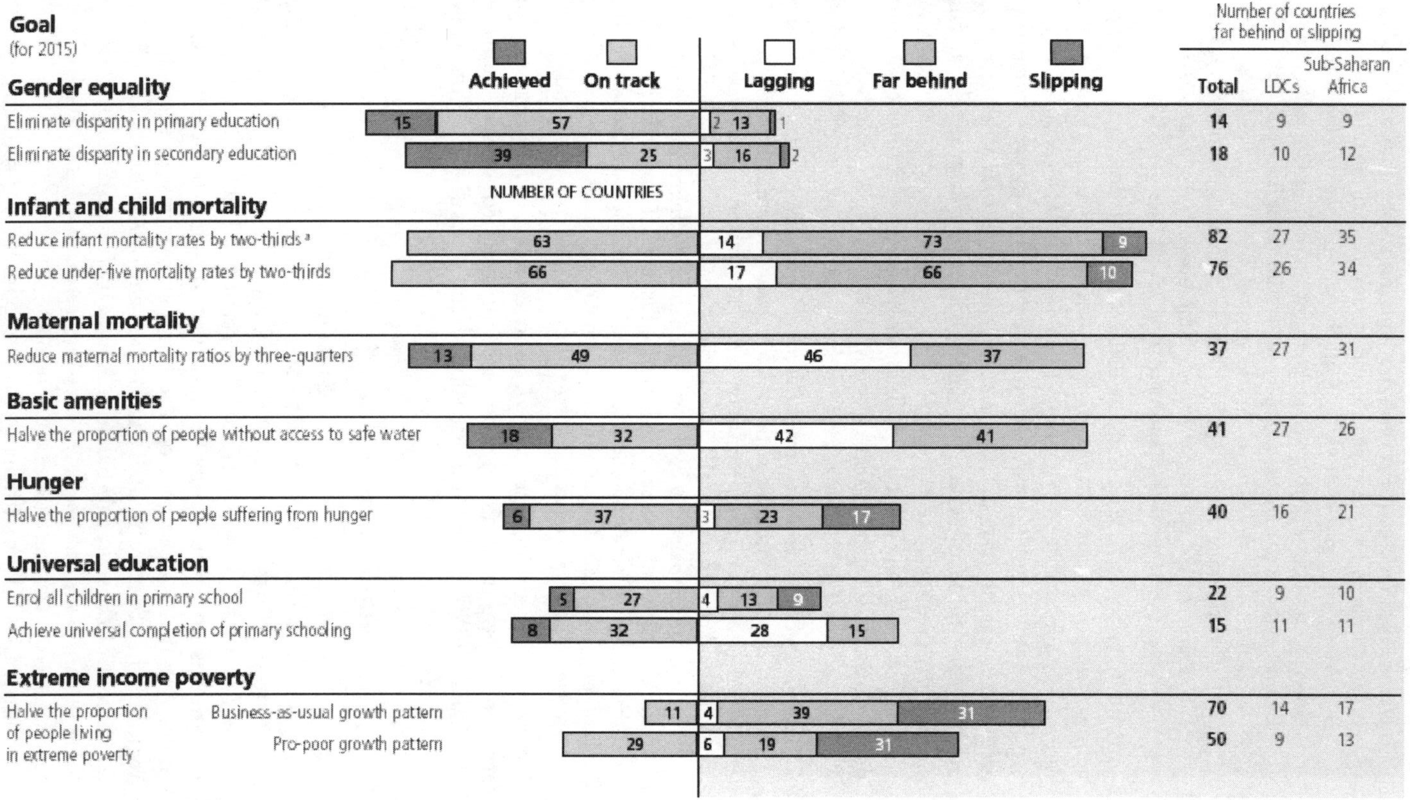

Bar categories (NUMBER OF COUNTRIES): Achieved, On track | Lagging, Far behind, Slipping

Goal (for 2015)	Achieved	On track	Lagging	Far behind	Slipping	Number of countries far behind or slipping — Total	LDCs	Sub-Saharan Africa
Gender equality								
Eliminate disparity in primary education	15	57	2 13	1		14	9	9
Eliminate disparity in secondary education	39	25	3 16	2		18	10	12
Infant and child mortality								
Reduce infant mortality rates by two-thirds [a]	63		14	73	9	82	27	35
Reduce under-five mortality rates by two-thirds	66		17	66	10	76	26	34
Maternal mortality								
Reduce maternal mortality ratios by three-quarters	13	49	46	37		37	27	31
Basic amenities								
Halve the proportion of people without access to safe water	18	32	42	41		41	27	26
Hunger								
Halve the proportion of people suffering from hunger	6	37	3 23	17		40	16	21
Universal education								
Enrol all children in primary school	5	27	4 13 9			22	9	10
Achieve universal completion of primary schooling	8	32	28	15		15	11	11
Extreme income poverty								
Halve the proportion of people living in extreme poverty — Business-as-usual growth pattern		11	4 39	31		70	14	17
Pro-poor growth pattern		29	6 19	31		50	9	13

Note: This analysis excludes high-income OECD countries. See technical note 3 for an explanation of the assessments of progress and for information on the data sources used. LDCs are least developed countries.
a. International development goal.

Table IV-1   Millennium Declaration goals: how are people doing?
Percentage of world population[a]

Goal (for 2015)	Achieved or on track	Lagging, far behind, or slipping	No data
General equality			
Eliminate disparity in primary education	58	5	22
Eliminate disparity in secondary education	42	22	21
Infant and child mortality			
Reduce infant mortality rates by two-thirds[b]	23	62	(.)
Reduce under-five mortality rates by two-thirds	23	62	(.)
Maternal mortality			
Reduce maternal mortality ratios by three-quarters	37	48	(.)
Basic amenities			
Halve the proportion of people without access to safe water	12	70	3
Hunger			
Halve the proportion of people suffering from hunger	62	11	12
Universal education			
Enroll all children in primary school	34	5	46
Achieve universal completion of primary schooling	26	13	46
Extreme income poverty			
Halve the proportion of people living in extreme poverty			
Business-as-usual growth pattern	43	34	8
Pro-poor growth pattern	54	23	8

Note: Population shares do not sum to 100% because the analysis excludes high-income OECD countries.

a. Refer to sum of country population in respective categories as a percentage of world population.

b. International development goal.

Source: FAO 2000b; UNICEF 2001b, 2001c; World Bank 2000c, 2001b; UN-ESCO 2000b; UNFPA 2001; UNAIDS 1998, 2000b; IMF, OECD, UN, and World Bank 2000; Hammer, Healey, and Naschold 2000.

global economy. Many suffer from weak and unpredictable political and economic institutions. Their economies tend to be based on low productivity traditional sectors. And many are extremely disadvantaged with respect to essential development elements such as education, sanitation, transportation, communication, clean water, adequate development financing, and electrical power and energy resources. Moreover, stifling debt burdens, lack of access to developed-country markets, declining official development assistance, and numerous other exogenous factors constrain development progress.

In assessing the progress made over the decade since the Second U.N. Conference on Least Developed Countries, the Third U.N. Conference on LDCs summarized the situation this way:

> Ten years after the adoption of the Paris Programme of Action . . . , the objectives and goals set out therein have not been achieved. LDCs are being bypassed by the process of globalization, leading to their further marginalization. For their part, most LDCs have pursued economic reform programmes set out in the previous Programme of Action, including elimination or substantially reducing tariffs and other trade barriers, liberalizing currency regimes, privatizing public enterprises, establishing and strengthening institutional and regulatory frameworks and adopting liberal investment policies. The results of these reform efforts have been below expectations. Declining availability of financial resources, domestic and external, including ODA, a heavy and unsustainable debt burden, falling or volatile commodity prices, complex trade barriers, lack of economic and export diversification and market access for key products which LDCs benefit from, as well as supply-side constraints, have seriously affected the growth and development prospects for LDCs. [U.N. Doc. A/CONF.191/11, June 8, 2001]

In brief, most LDCs are caught in a vicious circle of poverty—a degenerating circle worsened, especially in Africa, by the HIV/AIDS pandemic.

HIV/AIDS and Poverty

It has now been more than twenty years since the discovery of acquired immunodeficiency syndrome (AIDS). In these short two decades, HIV/AIDS has become the most devastating disease ever known to humankind. More than 60 million people have been infected [UNAIDS, AIDS Epidemic Update December 2001, UNAIDS/01.74E—WHO/CDS/CSR/NCS/2001.2].

HIV/AIDS has become the fourth-largest cause of death in the world. As illustrated in Table IV-2, the impact of the pandemic varies dramatically from region to region with the worst horror based in developing regions.

In 2001, for example, it was estimated that 95 percent of the 40 million people living with the disease were located in the developing world. It has become the leading cause of death in sub-Saharan Africa, where 18 million have died and where 28.1 million, or 70 percent, of the people living with HIV/AIDS reside. The statistics for the region are staggering.

> HIV prevalence rates have risen to alarming levels in parts of southern Africa, where the most recent antenatal clinic data reveal levels of more than 30% in several areas. In Swaziland, HIV prevalence among pregnant women attending antenatal clinics in 2000 ranged from 32.2% in urban areas to 34.5% in rural areas; in Botswana, the corresponding figures were 43.9% and 35.5%. In South Africa's KwaZulu-Natal Prov-

Table IV-2   Regional HIV/AIDS statistics, end of 2001

	Epidemic started	*Adults & children living with HIV/AIDS*	*Adults & children newly infected with HIV*
Sub-Saharan Africa	late 70s early 80s	28.1 million	3.4 million
North Africa & Middle East	late 80s	440,000	80,000
South and South-East Asia	late 80s	6.1 million	800,000
East Asia & Pacific	late 80s	1 million	270,000
Latin America	late 70s early 80s	1.4 million	130,000
Caribbean	early 90s	420,000	60,000
Eastern Europe & Central Asia	late 70s early 80s	1 million	250,000
Western Europe	late 70s early 80s	560,000	30,000
North America	late 70s early 80s	940,000	45,000
Australia & New Zealand	late 70s early 80s	15,000	500
TOTAL		40 million	5 million

Source: UNAIDS, *AIDS Epidemic Update: December 2001;* www.unaids.org/ epidemic_update/report_dec01/index.html

ince, the figure stood at 36.2% in 2000. . . . At least 10% of those aged 15–49 are infected in 16 African countries, including several in southern Africa, where at least 20% are infected. Countries across the region are expanding and upgrading their responses. But the high prevalence rates mean that even exceptional success on the prevention front will now only gradually reduce the human toll. It is estimated that 2.3 million Africans died of AIDS in 2001. [UNAIDS, *AIDS Epidemic Update*, December 2001]

At the same time, it is estimated that 3.4 million new cases occurred in the region in the same year.

The UNAIDS report for 2001 indicated that the economic impact of AIDS in Africa has been profound.

It is estimated that the annual per capita growth in half the countries of sub-Saharan Africa is falling by 0.5–1.2% as a direct result of AIDS. By 2010, per capita GDP in some of the hardest hit countries may drop by 8% and per capita consumption may fall even farther. Calculations show that heavily affected countries could lose more than 20% of GDP by 2020. . . . An index of existing social and economic injustices, the epidemic is driving a ruthless cycle of impoverishment. People at all income levels are vulnerable to the economic impact of HIV/AIDS, but the poor suffer most acutely. One quarter of households in Botswana, where adult HIV prevalence is over 35%, can expect to lose an income earner within the next 10 years. A rapid increase in the number of very poor and destitute families is anticipated. Per capita household income for the poorest quarter of households is expected to fall by 13%, while every income earner in this category can expect to take on four more dependents as a result of HIV/AIDS. [UNAIDS, *AIDS Epidemic Update*, December 2001]

The region has also suffered significant setbacks in life expectancy. In nearly two dozen countries, life expectancy has fallen over the last decade and a half. In six—Botswana, Burundi, Namibia, Rwanda, Zambia, and Zimbabwe—the decline has been more than seven years. In Botswana, Malawi, Mozambique, and Swaziland, life expectancy is now less than 40 years. Overall in sub-Saharan Africa, instead of an average life expectancy of 62 years, which is estimated in the absence of HIV/AIDS, it is only 47 years [UNAIDS, *AIDS Epidemic Update*, December 2001]. In the face of this overwhelming health crisis, Africa is experiencing a profound shortage of manpower in the health-care sector [WHO Press Release, ReliefWeb, February 1, 2002]. Unfortunately, in some countries, like Botswana, the situation may be much wore dire than previously reported. According to Botswana Health Minister Joy Phumaphi, for example, the World Health Organization's (WHO's) projections for her country have been underestimated by 50 percent [U.N. Wire, February 1, 2002].

While sub-Saharan Africa is by far the worst hit region of the world, it does not stand in isolation in terms of implications for development. In fact, the fastest-growing AIDS epidemic is in Eastern Europe—especially the Russian Federation. Of the estimated one million people in the region living with HIV, one-quarter were newly infected during 2001. In Russia, new infections have been almost doubling every year since 1998. The Caribbean is the second-most affected area of the world. Asia and the Pacific is estimated to now have 7.1 million people living with HIV/AIDS, and 435,000 people died of the disease in 2001 [UNAIDS, *AIDS Epidemic Update*, December 2001].

The implications of AIDS for development go far beyond economic factors. One of the most significant impacts has been on educational systems. In the most highly infected countries, "HIV/AIDS kills teachers faster than they can be trained, makes orphans of students, and threatens to derail efforts . . . to get all boys and girls into primary school by 2015." HIV prevalence among teachers, for example, is 30 percent in Malawi, 20 percent in Zambia, and 12 percent in South Africa. Moreover, AIDS has resulted in a widening gender gap. In addition to being more susceptible to infection than boys, girls are more prone to dropping out of school to care for sick family members [World Bank, *Education and HIV/AIDS: A Window of Hope,* www.worldbank.org/developmentnews/stories/html/050802a.htm].

Although HIV/AIDS is only one factor affecting the attainment of the Millennium Development Goals, dealing successfully with the pandemic is one of the most significant factors for achieving wide-scale sustainable human development and security. Unless checked, AIDS threatens to erase the chances of breaking out of the poverty syndrome for a significant portion of humankind.

Making Human Development and Security Sustainable

Ten years ago, heads of government and state meeting in Rio adopted a global policy framework for sustainable development, *Agenda 21.* Now, a decade later, heads of government are meeting again in Johannesburg from August 26–September 4, 2002, to take stock and attempt to move the global development agenda forward. As before, the debate centers on the nexus of issues related to protecting the human environment, reducing poverty, promoting human rights, and building sustainable security. In this context, the Secretary-General has identified ten priority themes: globalization, poverty, health, energy, freshwater, Africa, finance and technology, patterns of consumption and production, international governance, and the management of ecosystems and biodiversity [U.N. Wire, U.N. Press Release, February 13, 2002]. In essence, the summit represents an attempt to integrate the Millennium Development agenda with the Agenda 21 objectives and strategy.

A few of the issues that loom large on the Johannesburg agenda include sustainable energy sources, use, and efficiency; clean water and sanitation; and development finance. Providing electricity and increasing sustainable energy sources and services for the poor is a critical component of building sustainable human security. It is estimated that two billion people, mainly in rural areas, lack access to electricity and must rely on firewood, dung, and other traditional biofuels, when they are available, for heating and cooking. In addition to dealing with the energy needs of the poor, the conferees will address issues related to pollution, greenhouse gas emissions, and mechanisms for financing energy development. And lurking in the background in the context of post-September 11 are energy security issues such as dependence on oil supplies, vulnerability of large-scale energy infrastructures, and similar concerns.

Access to clean water is another important item on the sustainable development agenda. It is estimated that 1.1 billion people are without reasonable access to safe water, 2.4 billion live without improved sanitation facilities, and some 4 billion without adequate wastewater disposal. The yearly death toll related to water scarcity and waterborne diseases is approximately 12 million [www.worldbank.org/developmentnews/stories/html/051702a.htm]. The statistics on lack of access to improved water become more meaningful when stated in definitional terms. The WHO defines "reasonable access" as the availability of at least 20 liters per person per day from a source within one kilometer of the user's dwelling. Few people in advanced industrial societies, of course, consider such a condition as "reasonable" access.

To make sustainable development efforts work requires development finance. Yet financial flows—both public and private—to developing countries declined significantly following Rio. Official ODA reached an all-time low (0.22 percent of GDP) in 1997 as the world continued to reel from the effects of a global economic crisis. But the "ODA crunch" began long before the global financial crisis of the late-1990s. ODA and other development assistance have declined steadily over the past decade with bilateral assistance flows accounting for most of that decline [*U.N. Development Update*, No. 27, March 1999]. Creating stability for development financing is of particular concern for the LDCs who rely heavily on ODA as the main source of their external resource flows and who are extremely vulnerable to such shifts. As discussed below, significant initiatives have been launched recently to address this concern. However, the need far outstrips potential supply. And ODA for natural resource-oriented projects remains a politically problematic subject.

Looking beyond the immediate context of the Johannesburg summit, two additional development-related issues that loom large for the future are (1) urban capacity building and governance and (2) making new technologies work for development.

As the 1999 *State of the World's Cities Report* concluded, cities across the world are undergoing profound, diverse, and rapid changes. Many of those changes result from dramatic growth in the size of the world's urban population. A recent report by the Cities Alliance pointed out, for example, that only 14 percent of the world's population lived in cities at the beginning of the twentieth century, a mere 233 million people. By the century's end, just under half (47.6 percent) of the world's population lived in urban areas. Moreover, the trend toward urbanization appears likely to continue unabated into the near future. By 2020, it is estimated that nearly 60 percent of the world's population—about 4.4 billion people—will be urbanites [*Cities Alliance*, June 2000, p. 7].

The largest share of this growth is occurring in the developing nations that include much of Asia, Africa, and Latin America. The World Bank's recent analysis makes the point sharply.

> Within a generation the majority of the developing world's population
> will live in urban areas and the number of urban residents in developing

countries will increase by 2.5 billion—the current urban population of the entire world. The scale of this urbanization—and its implications for the ability of countries to meet the needs of their people at relatively low levels of national income—are unprecedented. [World Bank, *A Strategic View of Urban and Local Government Issues: Implications for the Bank*, 1999]

Population growth is not, however, the only force affecting the future of urban regions. Throughout the world, the responsibility for financing and providing public services to urban citizens is being decentralized. As Robert Ebel recently noted, "Of the 75 developing and transition countries with populations greater than 5 million, all but 12 claim to be embarked on some form of transfer of fiscal power from central to subnational (e.g., local) governments" [Robert Ebel, Logic of Decentralization and Worldwide Overview, a paper presented at the Mediterranean Development Forum at Marrakesh, Morocco, 1998]. Of equal importance, globalization of the world's economy is creating what one U.S. observer has termed "city-states" that are forcing a rethinking of a traditional, structural (federal, state, local) view of government. These "city-states" are better understood as networks of interrelated functions that span global, regional, and neighborhood interests [Neil R. Peirce, *City-States: How Urban America Can Prosper in a Competitive World*, Seven Locks Press, 1993]. Thus, cities have become important players in the world economy, sometimes assuming roles previously played by state, provincial, or even national governments. As cities have moved into the competitive process of economic development, those with market advantage have done well, while others have not. This is a pattern that is likely to continue into the future.

Interacting with one another, rapid population growth, decentralization of responsibility to local authorities, and globalization have produced a "crisis of urban governance" that may loom large in attempts to deal with energy, water, sanitation, and other important sustainable development issues [*State of the World's Cities Report*, 1999]. Local leaders have the responsibility to provide public services and to lead the future development of their communities. Unfortunately, many of the cities that are growing most rapidly lack the human resource capacity to meet the demands imposed by the dynamic environment in which they must function. Again, the World Bank's analysis makes the point:

> In many rapidly growing cities in the poorest countries, weak local governments have been unable to perform even minimal functions, so that households and informal institutions have become the main providers of infrastructure, housing, and social services. While this solution meets some essential needs, it has also resulted in fragmented urban economies. In these cities the poorest often pay most dearly for low-quality services; poorly integrated land, housing, and transport markets impose high costs on firms and households; and congestion

and haphazard waste disposal degrade the environment. [World Bank, *A Strategic View*, p. 6]

The urbanization that is being experienced throughout the world offers the prospect of an improved quality of life for many. Cities have the potential to be powerful economic engines, providing jobs, housing, and education for many of the world's poor. However, "whether this potential is realized depends critically on the quality of urban management and on the national and local policies affecting it," or in other words, on good governance [World Bank, *A Strategic View*, p. 1]. It will also require transnational cooperation, as demonstrated by the recently established *Megacities Network*, a network of 11 of the world's largest cities formed to share information, identify shared priorities, develop models and strategies, and promote universal access to medicines and treatments needed to respond effectively to HIV/AIDS [U.N. Wire, February 21, 2002].

(It is ironic that conditions in the host city of the World Summit on Sustainable Development have led Johannesburg city officials to act in opposition to the policies advocated by South African President Thabo Mbeki and promote the distribution of condoms and "correct" information dissemination about HIV/AIDS.) Johannesburg has one of the highest incidences of HIV/AIDS of any megacity in the world [ibid.].

A second rising issue, making new technologies work for development, was the focus of the UNDP's *Human Development Report 2001*. How does one harness the information and communications revolution and biotechnology and direct it in the service of human development? The Internet, wireless telephones, and other information and communications technologies have the potential of increasing popular participation in governance at all levels and promoting sustainable human development. At the same time, however, the very same technologies may also become forces that increase marginalization, social fragmentation, and exclusion—widening the gap between the rich and the poor and breeding increased poverty. Biotechnologies have the potential of substantially improving health and medical conditions. While effective governance at local and national levels will be required to make new technologies work for development, it is unlikely that policies in most developing countries, especially LDCs, can do much to determine decisively the direction things will go in this regard. International cooperation and transnational partnerships will be required.

A prototype of such cooperation is the Global Digital Opportunity Initiative (GDOI) launched in February 2002 by the UNDP, in partnership with the Markle Foundation and in cooperation with other international partners. (Sun Microsystems, Hewlet-Packard, Cisco Systems, AOL Time Warner, the Harvard Center for International Development,

Grameen Bank, other private corporations, NGOs, international organizations, and foundations are part of what is termed the GDOI's International Partners Group.) The mission of the initiative is to provide developing countries with expertise and resources to create e-strategies and solutions to advance their development goals. It will concentrate its initial efforts in 12 developing countries to assist them in building the technological capacities required to improve healthcare, education, and economic opportunities and to reduce poverty.

Enhancing Organizational and Institutional Capacity

As the GDOI example illustrates, making sustainable development work requires building effective organizational and institutional capacity. At the national or local level, this means creating and sustaining enabling environments for domestic resource mobilization. "Without efficient domestic resource mobilization, sustained growth and sustainable development are not achievable" [U.N. Doc. A/AC.257/12, December 18, 2000]. Sound national policies supportive of development strategies are essential both for obtaining and using effectively domestic resources and mobilizing external resources [ibid.]. In turn, creating and sustaining enabling environments requires good governance at both domestic and international levels—that is, it requires participatory, transparent, and accountable governance—an environment in which the institutions of governance are responsive to the people and their needs and operate according to the rule of law.

Stakeholders and Partnerships

A consensus has emerged that new forms of cooperation and partnerships are needed among states, markets, the private sector, voluntary and civic organizations, local communities, and other "stakeholders." As argued in the UNDP *Poverty Report 2000,* "if poverty reduction programmes are to succeed, local government must be strengthened" as must popular participation and the role of civil society in governance processes [UNDP, *Overcoming Human Poverty: UNDP Poverty Report 2000* (New York: United Nations, 2000), chapter 5]. The UNDP has placed special emphasis on governance and has dubbed good governance as the "missing link" between antipoverty efforts and poverty reduction. "Poverty eradication and good governance are inseparable. Good governance brings about a proper balance among state action, the private sector, civil society, and the communities themselves" [UNDP, *UNDP Today: Fighting Poverty,* 1999]. Well-functioning, effective, and accountable public and private institutions that are viewed as legitimate in the eyes of those being governed are required in order to mobilize the social capital required for sustaining development [*Overcoming Human Poverty,* op. cit.].

The UNDP lies at the center of U.N. development work, and at the center of the UNDP's work is a commitment to build stable and open political institutions as described above. "[W]e must . . . ensure that development cooperation supports the polity and not just the economy. . . . The challenges of growing poverty and widening inequity will not be met without democratization and good governance" [*Non-Benign Neglect: America and the Developing World in the Era of Globalization*, National Press Club, Washington, D.C., October 14, 1998]. Priority has been placed on democratization and political empowerment of the poor through participation and strengthening of civil society organizations; strengthening of judicial, electoral, and parliamentary systems; human rights and the rule of law, with special emphasis on women's legal rights; decentralization and strengthening of local governance; policies and frameworks for market-based economic transitions, private sector development, and globalization challenges; public administration reforms for accountable governance; and crisis management and rebuilding government capacities in post-conflict situations, including for reconstruction and rehabilitation [ibid.].

The UNDP in recent years has reprioritized its functions around four themes: advocacy, advice, pilot projects, and partnerships. The partnership function is a wide-ranging one. It begins with the U.N. system and Bretton Woods agencies and expands almost endlessly. It entails building and expanding constructive partnerships with civil society, the private sector, and local authorities. Underpinning this strategy is the belief that "people should guide both the state and the market, which need to work together in tandem, with people sufficiently empowered to exert a more effective influence over both" [UNDP, *Human Development Report 1993*]. Critical to this endeavor is creating the identity of being "stakeholders" in these varied constituencies.

Within the developing world this initiative to forge new partnerships has taken a variety of forms and complexions. In general, there has been a move to strengthen U.N. agencies' direct involvement with diverse elements of society, including NGOs, the private sector, and civil society organizations. Similar efforts have also been made in the Bretton Woods institutions. While active engagement with NGOs has been widely recognized for some time, cooperation with private sector entities at the country level has been less widely publicized.

The Global Compact

These partnership activities with nonstate actors—most especially the Secretary-General's "Global Compact" with business—have brought with them another dimension of the challenge to sovereignty debate. This initiative brings together the Executive Office of the Secretary-General in collaboration with the International Labour Organisation (ILO), the Office of the High Commissioner for Human Rights (UNHCHR), UNEP, UNDP, and the Fund for International Partnerships (UNFIP) and seeks to engage the private sector constructively in helping to make globalization work for all the world's peoples. Partners to the compact are asked to embrace nine principles drawn from the Universal Declaration of Human Rights (UDHR), the ILO's Fundamental Principles on Rights at Work, and the Rio Principles on Environment and Development. It engages a wide diversity of partners, including international intersectoral business associations; international, sectoral business associations; national business associations; workers' organizations; and NGOs.

The main assumption underlying the Global Compact is that development, especially for the LDCs, cannot occur through governmental or intergovernmental means alone, even with the kind assistance of the multitude of nongovernmental development assistance organizations. Neither can it occur through unbridled market forces alone. Creating local, national, and international enabling environments is essential, and a broad-based partnership involving all relevant "stakeholders" is required.

However, bringing the private sector into the United Nations has brought with it some concerns and opposition. Many governments, for example, still hang tenaciously to the tenets of sovereignty and resent actions by multilateral agencies that do not respect the sanctity of that legal norm. On the other hand, various NGOs and civil society groups have expressed concern about U.N. agencies becoming too closely involved with private sector entities, especially large global corporate enterprises and international banks. The response from U.N. agencies has been clear. In order to promote sustainable human development in an effective way, they need to find new mechanisms to generate the needed resources and, perhaps more importantly, to get those resources into the hands of those who most need them, especially the poor at the local level.

Microfinance

One strategy for getting resources into the hands of the poor is microfinance mechanisms. In a major initiative beginning in 1997, the UNDP and UNCDF established the Special Unit for Microfinance (SUM). It has grown to become the leading U.N. agency on all matters dealing with microfinance—that is, providing financial services to the poor at the local level. The chief aim is to support the growth and build the capacity of microfinance institutions. The focus is on start-up institutions, organizations in rural areas in the poorest countries, and established institutions that seek to expand their markets with new products and services. SUM seeks to increase the effectiveness of such institutions in reaching and servicing the poor, especially women, on a sustainable basis.

One of SUM's most important microfinance ventures has been *MicroStart*. The primary goal of this program is to assist young start-up institutions in addressing the problem the UNDP refers to as the "missing middle." "The program is predicated on the concept that most donor support has been so far directed towards large and successful organizations, and that small amounts of capital (up to $150,000) invested primarily in recipient organizations displaying vision, commitment and competence, can help widen tomorrow's market of successful microfinance institutions" [www.uncdf.org/sum/index.html].

The U.N. microfinance activities illustrate one of the most important dimensions of the new development framework at the United Nations: getting the product to the poor. The African Project Development Facility, for example, provides entrepreneurs in 29 African countries with investment funds. The Africa 2000 Network provides small grants up to $50,000 to villages so that they may engage in community-based sustainable human development activities. The Sub-Regional South Asia Poverty Alleviation Programme provides assistance to help train community organization leaders and organize villagers into community-based organizations in Bangladesh, India, Nepal, Maldives, and Sri Lanka.

Other examples of specific microfinance pilot projects include Pride Africa Malawi (PAM) and XAC ("Golden Fund for Development"). Operating on a $3 million UNCDF grant, PAM works with poor borrowers in rural Malawi to form groups, which guarantee each other's very small-scale loans. So far, the repayment rate has been near 100 percent. By the end of its fourth year, PAM expects to have 19,000 clients, show an operating profit, and have accumulated a portfolio of $2.4 million [www.undp.org/dpa/index.html]. In a far distant part of globe, XAC provides the poor in Mongolia with small-scale investment capital. In its two-and-a-half years of operation, it has grown to 13 branches that serve over 3,600 clients and has created a loan portfolio of $854,000 [ibid.].

U.N. Systemwide Cooperation

Since assuming office, Secretary-General Annan has focused on improving U.N. systemwide coordination, including cooperation with the Bretton Woods institutions. To this end, a significant attempt has been made to revitalize the coordinating role of the Administrative Committee for Coordination (ACC) and make it more effective. A special Assistant Secretary-General for policy coordination and interagency affairs has been appointed and given the responsibility to identify ways to strengthen support for the Economic and Social Council (ECOSOC) and its coordinating role and to unify the work of the various autonomous U.N.-related agencies. Furthermore, the Secretary-General took personal charge soon after coming into office and, in August 1998, invited the World Bank president to a retreat. Since that time, working relations with the Bretton Woods institutions have improved dramatically.

Beginning in 1999, joint high-level meetings have been held at U.N. Headquarters between ECOSOC and officials of the Bretton Woods institutions. These meetings have been noteworthy in that they represent a spirit of cooperation between the United Nations and the Bretton Woods *agencies* that has most often been lacking in the past. The World Bank and IMF Executive Boards have also hosted both the ECOSOC Ambassadors and the Bureau of the Financing for Development Conference Preparatory Committee in Washington, D.C. Beyond fostering much greater cooperation among these respective international institutions, these meetings have brought together diplomats representing quite diverse ministries—economic, finance, development, foreign affairs, and others.

A wide variety of collaborative partnership arrangements now exists among U.N agencies and programs, specialized agencies, and the financial institutions in Washington, D.C. The UNDP and World Bank, for example, have initiated a pilot program at the country level to explore the interface between the U.N. Development Assistance Framework (UNDAF) and the World Bank's Country Assistance Strategy. Another collaborative effort has been the Money Matters: Private Finance for Development initiative. It is aimed at assisting emerging market economies in mobilizing and attracting private finance for sustainable human development. It gave rise to the creation in 1995 of the Money Matters Institute (MMI), a forum for exchange of experience and ideas among leaders in financial services, international organizations, and policy-makers in developing countries about the role of private capital in financing sustainable human development. In addition to the UNDP and the World Bank, members of MMI have included the private companies Arthur Andersen, Concord International Investments, Fidelity Investments, LIA Worldwide, MFS Investment Management, Prudential Securities, State Street Corporation, and United Gulf Management [www.worldpartner.com/MMI.html].

In 1996, the World Bank and IMF launched a plan to provide debt relief for the world's poorest, most heavily indebted countries. Under this "Heavily Indebted Poor Countries" (HIPC) Initiative, creditors collectively move to provide exceptional assistance aimed at bringing the debtor country into a position of debt sustainability. As originally envisioned, creditors were to share the cost of HIPC assistance on the basis of equitable burden sharing and provide relief on a basis that is proportional to their share of the debt after the full application of traditional forms of debt relief. Debtor countries must agree to undertake sustained implementation of integrated poverty reduction and economic reform programs.

Over the last several years, the Group of Eight and others have taken additional initiatives to enhance HIPC. Thus far, 24 countries (Benin, Bolivia, Burkina Faso, Cameroon, Chad, Ethiopia, The Gambia, Guinea, Guinea-Bissau, Guyana, Honduras, Madagascar, Malawi, Mali, Mauritania, Mozambique, Nicaragua, Niger, Rwanda, São Tomé and Príncipe, Senegal, Tanzania, Uganda, and Zambia) have reached their decision point under the enhanced HIPC Initiative and 4 countries (Bolivia, Mozambique, Tanzania, and Uganda) reached its completion point under the original HIPC Initiative. These 24 countries are now receiving relief that will amount to some $36 billion over time.

Over the past three years, the IMF and World Bank have moved to further alter their lending approaches to integrate poverty reduction with macroeconomic policies. Since 1999, for example, the IMF and the International Development Association of the World Bank Group support strategies and programs that emerge directly from the borrowing country's Poverty Reduction Strategy Paper (PRSP). These PRSPs reflect each country's own strategy, which is to be prepared in consultation with the poor and other elements of civil society as well as other development partners. A new facility, the Poverty Reduction Growth Facility (PRGF), was created to replace the Enhanced Structural Adjustment Facility. The main difference between the old facility and the new one is the integration of poverty reduction into macroeconomic policy-making and an additional emphasis on good governance [www.imf.org/external/np/exr/facts/prgf.htm].

Strengthening Commitment?

Over the past year or so, a number of important events and activities have occurred that point to an increasing verbal commitment by the international community to invigorate efforts to reduce poverty and move toward attaining the Millennium Development Goals. Simultaneously, however, there are clear indications that good deeds are often slow to follow good words. Two brief examples will serve to highlight this dualism: efforts to enhance the fight against HIV/AIDS and the movement to significantly increase official development assistance.

The decade-and-a-half global response to HIV/AIDS moved forward in June 2001 when the U.N. General Assembly held a special session establishing a framework for national and international accountability in the struggle against the epidemic. According to the framework strategy, each government "pledged to pursue a series of many benchmark targets relating to prevention, care, support and treatment, impact alleviation, and children orphaned and made vulnerable by HIV/AIDS, as part of a comprehensive AIDS response" [UNAIDS, *AIDS Epidemic Update*, December 2001, UNAIDS/01.74E—WHO/CDS/CSR/NCS/2001.2, p. 2–3]. The targets agreed upon are:

- By 2005, to reduce HIV infection among 15- to 24-year-olds by 25 percent in the most affected countries, and globally by 2010;

- By 2005, to reduce the proportion of infants infected with HIV by 20 percent, and by 5 percent by 2010;
- By 2003, to develop national strategies to strengthen health-care systems and address factors affecting the provision of HIV-related drugs, including affordability and pricing; also, to urgently make every effort to provide the highest attainable standard of treatment for HIV/AIDS, including antiretroviral therapy in a careful and monitored manner to reduce the risk of developing resistance;
- By 2003, to develop and, by 2005 implement, national strategies to provide a supportive environment for orphans and children infected and affected by HIV/AIDS;
- By 2003, to have in place strategies that begin to address the factors that make individuals particularly vulnerable to HIV infection, including underdevelopment, economic insecurity, poverty, lack of empowerment of women, lack of education, social exclusion, illiteracy, discrimination, lack of information and/or commodities for self-protection, and all types of sexual exploitation of women, girls, and boys;
- By 2003, to develop multisectoral strategies to address the impact of the HIV/AIDS epidemic at the individual, family, community, and national levels.

Meeting such rigorous targets, of course, will require substantial sustained increases in financial and other resources. UNAIDS has estimated that $7–10 billion per year is needed in low- and middle-income countries, and the U.N. Secretary-General had proposed creating a $7–10 billion initial fund. This proposal has been endorsed by the World Bank, the IMF, and the Group of Seven. However, as of February 2002, the global fund had attracted only about $1.9 billion in pledges.

Real commitment has been slow to follow signs of good intentions. At current funding levels, donor countries would need to increase HIV/AIDS spending by 50 percent annually over the next four years in order to close a growing gap between needs and resources. Speaking before the U.S. Senate Foreign Relations Committee in February 2002, Peter Piot, Executive Director of the Joint U.N. Program on HIV/AIDS, lamented that at current funding levels there will be a $7 billion worldwide funding gap by 2005. Although the UNAIDS Global Fund accounts for about one-third of all resources to fight HIV/AIDS, the current financing in the fund represents only 11 percent of what is needed [U.N. Wire, February 14, 2002]. Despite the fact that the World Bank has recently doubled its financial support for its multicountry HIV/AIDS program for Africa from $500 million to $1 billion, the international community's response to AIDS pales in the face of the pandemic onslaught.

The outcomes of the Ministerial Conference of the World Trade Organization held in Doha, Qatar, in September 2001 and the summit-level U.N.-sponsored International Conference on Financing for Development held in Monterrey, Mexico, in March 2002 both pointed to increased verbal commitment on behalf of the international community to fight against poverty. The "Monterrey Consensus," as the summit-meeting outcome document is called, recognized that a significant increase in official development assistance is required in order to meet Millennium Development Goals. However, the consensus document, which was actually finalized several months prior to the conference, does not set any firm goals for increasing ODA. Nor does the Monterrey Consensus yield support for the U.N. Secretary-General's call to increase ODA from $50 billion to $100 billion per year. Nor does it offer any concrete mechanisms to mobilize the needed financial resources.

Signals regarding real shared commitment coming out of the Monterrey parley were mixed. In preparation for the conference, the U.S. President announced an increase in U.S. ODA of $5 billion over the subsequent three years, and President Bush did attend the conference. However, discord reigned behind the scenes as the U.S., E.U., and other donor-state delegates found insufficient common ground for meaningful consensual action. Yet, at the same time, the event demonstrated a new—what Secretary-General Kofi Annan referred to as "extraordinary"—level of partnership between the United Nations and the Bretton Woods institutions. The two old foes were now committing themselves to a unique partnership whereby "development," traditionally a U.N. preserve, was integrated with "financial instruments," the traditional turf of the international financial institutions.

The U.N. development agenda is an evolving symphony. Many of the bars and notes are already sounding. However, most of the symphony is yet to be composed. The next major movement will be in Johannesburg in September 2002, as the heads of government once again assemble for the World Summit on Sustainable Development. The summit's preparatory work seems to indicate that the earlier signs of increased commitment are real. One can perceive a new unity of purpose as most world leaders acknowledge that security in the 21st century means human security. AIDS, poverty, terrorism, and other social maladies that are inherently linked and cannot be solved alone or in isolation of each other. Will the symphony emerging from Johannesburg and beyond end in a waltz of the flowers or in a dance of the macabre?

3. Environment and Sustainable Development
By Gail Karlsson

Sustainable Development Ten Years After Rio

Preparations for the August 2002 World Summit on Sustainable Development in Johannesburg, South Africa, stimulated numerous evaluations of progress made over the past ten years, promises that remain unfulfilled, and challenges that lie ahead. Addressing the London School of Economics in February 2002, Secretary-General Annan articulated the main question to be considered at the Summit in this way: "Can the people now living on this planet improve their lives, not at the expense of future generations, but in a way from which their children and grandchildren will benefit?"

The Secretary-General acknowledged that much was achieved at the 1992 U.N. Conference on Environment and Development (the "Earth Summit") held in Rio de Janeiro, especially the adoption of a visionary plan of action, Agenda 21, that has influenced communities in almost every part of the world. In addition, several legally binding international conventions—on climate change, biological diversity, and desertification—have entered into force since 1992, and additional plans of action were formulated at various related U.N. conferences through the 1990s. More recently, at the beginning of the new century, heads of state adopted a set of Millennium Development Goals that invoked a new ethic of conservation and stewardship. Yet nevertheless the Secretary-General said he felt a loss of momentum:

> As our attention has been focused on conflict, on globalization, or most recently on terrorism, we have often failed to see how these are connected to the issue of sustainability. . . . Prevailing approaches to development remain fragmented and piecemeal; funding is woefully inadequate; and production and consumption patterns continue to overburden the world's natural life support systems. Sustainable development may be the new conventional wisdom, but many people have not grasped its meaning. One important task in Johannesburg is to show that it is far from being as abstract as it sounds. It is a life-or-death issue for millions upon millions of people, and potentially the whole human race. [Speech of Secretary-General, February 2002, London School of Economics]

The focus of Johannesburg was meant to be on positive actions to get things done, rather than on creating new plans of action or renegotiating existing ones. In order to move the sustainable agenda forward, the Secretary-General issued a report with specific suggestions for realistic actions that could be taken. These include allowing developing countries greater access to markets of industrialized countries, particularly for agricultural products and textiles; removing trade-distorting subsidies; reducing poverty through reform of laws covering land tenure and access to credit; increasing energy efficiency four-fold over the next several decades and promoting use of renewable energy technologies; improving health through safe and affordable access to freshwater; and managing ecosystems on a sustainable basis by eliminating overfishing, irresponsible forest depletion, and water pollution.

Besides producing a political agreement intended to reinvigorate global commitments to sustainable development, as well as a negotiated document containing international, national, and local implementation initiatives, the Summit also encouraged the creation of regional or bilateral partnerships among participants, including governments, international institutions, businesses, and civil society organizations. These so-called Type 2 outcomes do not require consensus among all of the countries represented at the Summit, but ensure that there will be concrete follow-up undertakings to help achieve the goals of the Summit.

Moving Forward on a Binding Climate Change Agreement

At the Seventh Conference of the Parties to the Climate Change Convention, held in Marrakech, Morocco, in November 2001, the Kyoto Protocol was saved from the death sentence pronounced for it last year by U.S. President George Bush. Rallied by the European Union and environmentalists around the world, 160 countries agreed on the terms of a binding agreement to reduce emissions of carbon dioxide and other heat-trapping greenhouse gases by an average of approximately 5 percent below 1990 levels by the year 2012. Last-minute concessions to Russia, Japan, Australia, and Canada added flexibility to the rules for compliance with the emission reduction targets and allowed the Kyoto Protocol to survive politically even without U.S. support. The agreement included rules for a trading program that allows trading of carbon emission "credits" and sets penalties for countries that fail to meet their reduction targets.

The environmental impacts of implementing the Kyoto Protocol may be small, since its goals are quite modest compared to the significant emission reductions said by climate scientists to be needed in order to stabilize greenhouse gas levels in the atmosphere. Nevertheless, the determination of the international community to move forward with it demonstrates the seriousness of the threat and the need to at least begin to introduce worldwide emission reduction and mitigation measures. There was considerable resentment expressed toward the United States for its abandonment of the treaty, especially since it is the largest producer of greenhouse gases (over 20 percent of total emissions), and in general for its unilateralist posture. At the Marrakech meeting, the Dutch Environment Minister, Jan Pronk, remarked that "after the events of September 11, if there is any reason for the United States to call for international global approaches, [it should also] join a global approach to the existing global problem of climate change" [*Washington Post*, November 11, 2001, p. A2].

Last year, President Bush rejected the Kyoto Protocol, saying that it would harm the U.S. economy and was unfair because it did not require binding reduction targets for large developing countries, like India and

China, that have fast-growing emissions levels. In February 2002, he announced a climate change plan based only on voluntary efforts. The 1992 Climate Change Convention called for voluntary actions by industrialized countries to reduce their greenhouse gas emissions to 1990 levels by the year 2000, but few countries met that goal, and U.S. emissions increased by more than 12 percent during that period.

Supporters of the binding emissions control agreement represented by the Kyoto Protocol sought to obtain enough ratifications to allow it to enter into force at the World Summit on Sustainable Development in August 2002. In order to become effective, the protocol must be ratified by at least 55 parties to the Climate Change Convention, including industrialized countries responsible for at least 55 percent of total carbon dioxide emissions in 1990. At the time of the Marrakech meeting, when the guidelines for implementing the provisions of the protocol were finalized, only 40 countries had ratified the protocol and only 1 industrialized country.

In March 2002, a comprehensive report was released that compiled the results of over 100 research studies from around the world documenting the effects of climate change on plants and animals. Significant impacts were reported on the timing of animal migrations and breeding and on plant flowerings. There have been changes in the dominance of species within specific ecosystems as some are thriving and others are devastated by altered climate conditions. Eric Post, a member of the international team of researchers, said they were surprised to see the extent of the disruptions already being observed. "All the major biomes on Earth have been affected by a temperature increase of just a little more than half a degree Celsius—most of which occurred in the last two decades. That such a small change has had such an extensive effect is alarming when you consider that even conservative estimates predict the climate will heat up at least two or three degrees more" [*Science Daily*, April 17, 2002]. The research was sponsored by the Swiss National Science Foundation, the Swiss Federal Institute of Technology, the U.S. National Science Foundation, the European Union Project POSITIVE, and the French National Center for Scientific Research.

Preserving Biological Resources

In April 2002, parties to the Convention on Biological Diversity met in The Hague to discuss progress on the goals of the treaty, which was adopted at the 1992 Earth Summit and entered into force in December 1993, and to discuss long-term strategic planning.

One of the major accomplishments under the Convention was the adoption of the Cartagena Protocol on Biosafety in January 2000. This protocol addresses the safe handling, use, and international shipment of living organisms that have been genetically modified. Although genetic engineering offers significant promise for advances in medicine and greater productivity and pest resistance in food crops, it also raises concerns about unintended harm to naturally growing plant and animals species, as well as damage to human health and to local cultures and agricultural traditions. Before the protocol enters into force, probably before the end of 2002, a number of issues needed to be worked out regarding the handling, transportation, packaging, and identification of living organisms that could possibly replicate or transfer scientifically modified genetic material.

Many developing countries do not have the capability to assess the risks of importing products promoted by modern biotechnology industries. According to Ambassador Philemon Yang of Cameroon, chairman of the intergovernmental planning committee for the protocol: "Information sharing and capacity building, especially for developing countries, are some of the critical priority requirements for the successful implementation of the protocol. We need to empower countries to make informed decisions" [UNEP Press Release, April 2002]. Work has already begun on a pilot phase of the Biosafety Clearing-House, which will facilitate international exchange of information about potential risks posed by specific organisms or products containing genetically modified material.

Other threats to ecosystems and natural resources are caused by invasions of alien species. U.N. Environmental Programme's (UNEP's) Executive Director, Klaus Toepfer, warned that "From tree-killing diseases to rats and other alien predators, invasives have traveled with traders, emigrants, and now tourists to new lands where the native species have not had time to evolve adequate protections against these sudden threats. As globalization continues to accelerate, the risks can only grow" [UNEP Press Release, March 2002]. Border controls and quarantine requirements can help prevent entry of alien species, but raise concerns about the imposition of trade restrictions. Where invaders are already established and spreading, effective containment and control measures need to be applied.

Improved protection for forest ecosystems was another focus of discussion at the meeting in The Hague. Forests represent the world's most important areas of biological diversity, but are rapidly being lost due to logging and land clearing for agriculture. Global concerns about preserving forests tend to conflict with the economic priorities of countries with extensive forest resources that can be exploited. In many cases, subsidies and economic incentives promote unsustainable forest removal practices rather than sustainable forest management. To reverse the current high rates of deforestation, higher market value should be placed on the non-timber value of healthy forests.

The Executive Secretary for the Convention on Biological Diversity, Hamdallah Zedan, argued that "The latent demand for carbon storage, tourism, forest foods and other forest values needs to be recognized, priced and encouraged" [UNEP Press Release, March 2002]. He also emphasized the need for increased collaboration with other international environmental treaties, especially those covering climate change and desertification, as well as the U.N. Forum on Forests.

U.N. Forum on Forests

The March 2002 meeting of the new U.N. Forum on Forests focused on combating deforestation and forest degradation. The Forum was established in 2000 by the Economic and Social Council (ECOSOC) as a subsidiary body to promote the implementation of actions for sustainable forest management and to enhance international cooperation in this area.

Although a set of nonbinding Forest Principles was adopted at the 1992 Earth Summit, there is no formal treaty covering the critical global problem of deforestation. After the Forum was established, the executive heads of various international organizations related to forests were asked by ECOSOC to form a Collaborative Partnership on Forests to assist in its work, including representatives from the Convention on Biological Diversity, the Food and Agriculture Organization, the International Tropical Timber Organization, the Convention to Combat Deforestation, the Global Environment Facility, the U.N. Framework Convention on Climate Change, UNEP, and the World Bank. More recently, the International Centre for Research in Agroforestry and IUCN (The World Conservation Union) were also asked to join the partnership.

The Forum is building on the work of prior U.N. negotiating groups, namely, the Intergovernmental Panel on Forests and the Intergovernmental Forum on Forests. Its primary task is to help countries implement the 270 proposals for action recommended by these prior groups. The Secretary-General's report prepared for the March 2002 meeting found that many countries are experiencing difficulties in implementing their forest policies because they lack necessary resources and trained personnel. It also identified other obstacles to halting deforestation, such as weak law enforcement, insecure forest property rights, and perverse subsidies that promote unsustainable timber harvesting and land use practices [E/CN.18/ 2002/2].

One encouraging development is the increase in national policies promoting opportunities for dialogue with citizens affected by forest-related practices and decisions. This is especially important since over 500 million people in more than 70 developing countries live in or near forests and depend on them for their food and livelihoods.

At the opening of the March 2002 meeting, the representative from Brazil emphasized the importance of financial resources and technology transfer to developing countries to assist them in implementing sustainable forest management practices on a permanent basis [U.N. Press Release, March 5, 2002]. The representative from Indonesia reinforced that request for support from the industrialized countries and pointed out that, despite positive trends, there was no evidence of an end to the decline in total forest area [ibid.]. In the 1990s, over nine million hectares, or 2 percent, of the world's forests were lost, representing an area the size of Venezuela [U.N. Press Release, March 19, 2002].

A ministerial declaration from the Forum expressed concern about the continuing high rate of worldwide deforestation and urged delegates to the World Summit on Sustainable Development to call for immediate action on domestic forest law enforcement and illegal trade in forest products, including biological resources. Substantive resolutions adopted by the U.N. Forum on Forests dealt with the need for protection of unique types of forests and fragile ecosystems, conservation and rehabilitation strategies for countries with low forest cover, reforestation through plantings, and restoration of degraded lands [UNFF News, No. 3, March 28, 2002].

Combating Desertification

Desertification is not caused by the expansion of existing deserts, but by overexploitation of dry lands in arid and semi-arid areas. Deforestation and overgrazing that undermine dry land productivity are often both causes and consequences of poverty and political instability. Global warming is likely to make dry lands even less productive, reducing yields by as much as one-third in tropical and subtropical regions.

In October 2001, parties to the 1994 Convention to Combat Desertification met in Geneva to boost the effectiveness of action to implement this important treaty. Unlike the climate change, biodiversity, and ozone protection conventions, the desertification convention has not had an established multilateral funding mechanism, which has slowed progress in its implementation. Now there is the possibility of adding land degradation due to deforestation and desertification as a new category for funding under the Global Environmental Facility, which would give affected countries a reliable source of international assistance.

Hama Arba Diallo, the Executive Secretary for the convention, emphasized the urgent need for action:

> Desertification affects the poorest of the poor by destroying the natural resources upon which their livelihoods depend, leading to hunger and the migration of millions of people. Recent crises in Mongolia, Afghanistan, and other drought-prone countries demonstrate just how vulner-

able people in dryland countries are to political and social instability. The pay-off for investing in efforts to combat desertification today will be fewer refugees and victims of conflict tomorrow. [U.N. Press Release, October 2001]

National reports have been prepared by 175 countries that are parties to the convention. These reports describe a variety of approaches to desertification, focusing on policies regarding soil management, water conservation, sustainable energy alternatives, improved land use practices for agriculture and livestock grazing, population and health services, and disaster management plans.

Desertification is likely to affect 100 countries, in varying degrees, threatening the livelihoods of more than one billion people. More than 135 million people are at risk of being displaced due to severe desertification [ibid.]. The reports will form the basis for national action programs as well as global strategies and international partnerships.

The U.N. Development Programme (UNDP) has opened a new Drylands Development Center in Nairobi, Kenya, which will focus on activities in Africa, the continent most affected by desertification. In Kenya, desertification affects 80 percent of the country. Forests, which currently cover only 2 percent of the country, are being further reduced by poor land use practices [Nairobi *Daily Nation,* January 18, 2002].

Information called for by the desertification convention, as well as by other international environmental conventions, will be provided by a four-year Millennium Ecosystem Assessment being undertaken by UNDP, UNEP, the World Bank, the World Resources Institute, and other research institutions. The secretariat for the Assessment was opened in Malaysia in January 2002, at the World Fish Center. Scientists and researchers around the world will gather information on the state of various ecosystems, the consequences of ongoing change, and options for response [International Institute for Sustainable Development, *Linkages Journal,* Vol. 7, No. 2, February 2002].

Conserving Fish Stocks

In December 2001, a U.N. agreement entered into force concerning responsible management of fishing on the high seas. It is formally called the U.N. Agreement for the Implementation of the Provisions of the U.N. Convention on the Law of the Sea Relating to the Conservation and Management of Straddling Fish Stocks and Highly Migratory Fish Stocks. While the Law of the Sea gives coastal states jurisdiction over fishing in areas within 200 miles from their shores, until now fishing further out on the high seas was largely unregulated. Increased fishing fleets, unrestrained commercial operations, and wasteful fishing methods have led to significant depletion of important fish species.

The objective of the new agreement is to establish dispute resolution procedures and cooperative arrangements for the conservation and management of fish stocks. Regional fishing organizations will be responsible for enforcing sustainable fishing practices in their areas. Even though the agreement has entered into force, nearly three-quarters of the key fishing nations, representing nearly 80 percent of the world's catch, have not yet ratified the agreement. Until they become parties, the treaty will not be fully effective. The U.N. Food and Agricultural Organization estimated that top fishing countries caught close to eight million tons of fish in 1999 [NGLS, Go Between, No. 89, December 2001–January 2002].

Recent studies conducted in Argentina and Senegal by UNEP's Economics and Trade Branch indicated that when developing countries open up their coastal waters to foreign fishing fleets, the eventual costs (in terms of lost income for local fishermen, environmental damage, and depletion of fish stocks) far outweigh the short-term financial gains. Overexploitation of important fish species leads to sharp declines in their numbers, together with associated environmental damage and threats to food security. Stronger policing measures are needed to protect local fishermen, fine vessels for overfishing, and restrict the types of fishing gear that are allowed to be used. The study of Argentina suggested that a better-managed fishing industry could benefit the country's economy by as much as $5 billion [ibid.].

Protecting the Ozone Layer

The Secretary-General's report prepared for the 2000 Millennium Summit praised the 1987 Montreal Protocol, under which governments agreed to phase out the use of ozone-depleting substances, as "perhaps the most successful environmental agreement to date" [We the Peoples: The Role of the United Nations in the 21st Century]. The agreement was negotiated after scientists realized that certain man-made chemicals were drifting up into the stratosphere and destroying the ozone layer that protects the earth from harmful ultraviolet rays. The chemicals were being used in common products such as refrigerators, air conditioners, aerosol cans, packaging materials, and cleaning solvents. Increased exposure to ultraviolet radiation can cause skin cancer and cataracts in humans, suppress immune system responses, and fundamentally alter terrestrial and marine ecosystems.

The 13th meeting of the parties to the Montreal Protocol, held in Sri Lanka in October 2001, focused on implementation of existing commitments and ways to accelerate the recovery of the ozone layer. It was originally thought that the ozone layer would recover by the middle of this century, but it now seems that the effects of global warming may slow that progress. Warmer ground-level temperatures lead to lower temperatures in the stratosphere, which speeds up the destruction of ozone molecules, especially during spring in Antarctica.

UNEP's Executive Director, Klaus Toepfer, warns that

> Despite the enormous cuts in ozone-depleting chemicals achieved under the Montreal Protocol, the stratospheric ozone layer remains in poor health as a result of past emissions. To minimize the damage to humans and the environment caused by increased ultraviolet (UV-B) radiation reaching the surface, we need to tackle simultaneously all the remaining sources of these chemicals. [NGLS, Go Between, No. 89, December 2001–January 2002]

Although since the adoption of the Montreal Protocol industrialized countries have stopped using most of the ozone-depleting chemicals, developing countries are only now being required to come into compliance. Phasing out the use of ozone-depleting substances and introducing environmentally friendly substitutes is a complex undertaking that requires conversions of equipment and processing procedures in large manufacturing plants as well as a multitude of small dispersed enterprises. The protocol has established a Multilateral Fund to assist developing countries in meeting the deadlines.

Chemical Management

Backers of two important treaties for controlling dangerous chemicals hope they will gain enough ratifications to become effective in 2002 at the World Summit for Sustainable Development. The treaties are last year's Stockholm Convention on Persistent Organic Pollutants (POPs) and the 1998 Rotterdam Convention on the Prior Informed Consent Procedure for Certain Hazardous Chemicals and Pesticides in International Trade.

The POPs convention addresses the risks posed by a group of chemicals, including dioxin, PCBs, DDT, and other pesticides, that remain in the environment over long periods of time and are spread through the air and water to all parts of the world, accumulating even in the most remote areas. These chemicals also accumulate in the fatty tissues of animals and people, interfering with normal hormone functions, decreasing fertility, and compromising immune systems. The POPs convention is designed to eliminate or severely restrict the use of these chemicals and ensure that other chemicals with similar characteristics do not come into use.

The Rotterdam Prior Informed Consent (PIC) convention places controls on trade in toxic chemicals, enabling countries to review basic health and environmental information on specific chemicals before determining whether or not to accept shipments of those substances. If countries cannot manage particular chemicals safely, they can be excluded. When shipments are permitted, sufficient information must be supplied with the potentially hazardous substances to allow them to be handled safely. The original list of chemicals included a number of pesticides and industrial chemicals. Governments have agreed to follow the prior informed consent procedures voluntarily until the convention enters into force.

In February 2002, the convention's Interim Chemical Review Committee recommended the addition of another three pesticides to the PIC list, as well as asbestos. Pesticides are particularly dangerous to developing country farmworkers who do not have access to protective clothing or equipment. In some cases, pesticides that have been banned in industrialized countries continue to be marketed and used in developing countries. Asbestos is still used in some countries for gaskets, brakes, and other applications. It was once widely used for insulation, but was eliminated in many countries after people learned that its tiny fibers can lodge in the lungs, causing cancer and other illnesses.

Also in February 2002, UNEP's Governing Council decided to develop a strategic approach to international chemicals management, in collaboration with the Food and Agriculture Organization of the United Nations (FAO), U.N. Habitat, and the Intergovernmental Forum on Chemical Safety, that would link chemicals management to development assistance. Another international partnership initiative is being organized to clean up stockpiles of obsolete pesticides in Africa.

Globalization, Trade, and the Environment

The November 2001 meeting of the World Trade Organization (WTO), held in Doha, Qatar, produced an agreement among the group's 142 member countries on launching a new round of global trade talks. Poorer countries had complained that they obtained few benefits from the previous Uruguay round of trade talks and were successful in obtaining commitments by industrialized countries to negotiate some reductions in import barriers affecting farm products and textiles, which are by far the largest exports from developing countries.

The European Union pushed for the agenda to include discussions about the relationship between the WTO's trade provisions and the international environmental agreements, some of which include trade sanctions. Developing countries have feared that the industrialized countries will use environmental standards as tools for protectionism.

Improved access to global markets would improve economic opportunities for many developing countries. The World Bank estimated that actions in accordance with the new agreement could help lift millions of people out of poverty and add $2.8 trillion to global economic activity by 2015 [*New York Times*, November 15, 2001]. Critics of the current trade regime complain, however, that globalization of trade and investment has done little to raise the incomes of people in the poorest countries. A World

Bank survey released in March 2002 revealed that annual private capital flows to developing countries fell from $300 billion in 1997 to just about half that amount in 2001 [*New York Times*, March 21, 2002]. Most people living in Africa, Latin America, central Asia, and the Middle East are no better off than they were in 1989, when capitalism began to spread rapidly throughout the world [ibid.].

The U.N. Population Fund's 2001 annual report indicated that the world's population is expected to reach 9.3 billion by 2050, with all the growth occurring in developing countries, and that by then 4.2 million people will be living in countries where their basic needs cannot be met. The Fund's Executive Director, Thoraya Obaid, observed that "Poor people depend more directly on natural resources such as available land, wood and water, and yet they suffer the most from environmental degradation" [*New York Times*, November 7, 2001].

Even leaders of some of the industrialized countries have come to acknowledge that globalization is not the key to development for many poor countries. President Jacques Chirac of France rejected the slogan "trade not aid," which he said characterized the 1990s view of development. According to Chirac, industrialized countries should spend more on "aid for trade" and on building the infrastructure necessary for the creation of wealth in developing countries [*New York Times*, March 21, 2002].

Debt Relief and Financing for Development

The annual World Economic Forum was held in New York in 2002, rather than in Davos, Switzerland, in order to show support for the city in the wake of the September 11 terrorist attacks. The Secretary-General warned the gathered business and political leaders that without greater efforts to alleviate poverty and ill-health in the world, they risked provoking additional resentment and terrorism:

> I think we all have a sense today of having come to a turning point in history. . . . last September we found ourselves entering the new millennium through a gate of fire. . . . You all know that you are sharing this planet with well over a billion people who are denied the very minimum requirements of human dignity, and with four or five billion whose choices in life are narrow compared to yours. . . . Left alone in their poverty, these countries are all too likely to collapse, or relapse, into anarchy, a menace to their neighbors and potentially—as the events of September 11 so brutally reminded us—a threat to global security. [*The Earth Times*, February 5, 2002]

In March 2002, world leaders met in Monterrey, Mexico, for an International Conference on Financing for Development. Responding to criticisms about levels of U.S. foreign aid, especially as compared to military spending, President Bush announced a 50 percent increase in development assistance over three years, which would eventually mean an additional $5 billion per year. The United States has spent about $10 billion per year in foreign aid over the last decade, which currently represents about 0.1 percent of the overall economy. The commitment to increase aid was linked to the initiation of political, legal, and economic reforms in recipient countries: "These new funds will go into a new Millennium Challenge Account, devoted to projects that govern justly, invest in their people and encourage economic freedom. We will promote development from the bottom up, helping citizens to find the tools and training and technologies to seize the opportunities of the global economy" [Speech delivered in Monterrey, March 22, 2002].

James Wolfensohn, President of the World Bank, asked for a doubling of foreign aid by all rich countries, which he said was necessary to meet the Millennium Development Goals adopted by the U.N. General Assembly in 2000—including commitments regarding poverty, child mortality, education, and environmental sustainability. U.S. Treasury Secretary Paul O'Neill criticized the World Bank, saying that lending money to poor countries, rather than giving them grants, has driven them "into a ditch" [*The Economist*, March 16, 2002]. He suggested that the World Bank should instead give more grants to the poorest countries. Representatives of the World Bank, and of many European countries, say that providing loans instead of grants imposes discipline on recipient countries. They are also concerned that without the receipts from loan repayments, there will be a reduction in overall funding assistance available [ibid.].

Many of the poorest countries spend many times more on servicing external debt than on basic social services for their people. A 1996 initiative to provide relief for Heavily Indebted Poor Countries has helped only a few countries so far, and in the meantime, more countries have encountered rising debt levels. Jan Vandemoortele from UNDP's Social Development Group has argued that debt relief is essential if the Millennium Goal of halving poverty by 2015 is to be met [UNDP, *Choices* Magazine, September 2001].

Persistent poverty is not only a cause of widespread human suffering, but is also linked with degradation and overexploitation of the natural environment. Changes in trade, aid, investment, and debt relief policies are critical for implementation of the sustainable development agenda—and are primary topics for the World Summit on Sustainable Development. As explained by the Secretary-General: "Agenda 21 and all that flowed from it can be said to have given us the 'what'—'what' the problem is, what principles must guide our response. Johannesburg must give us the 'how'—how to bring about the necessary changes in State policy; how to use policy and tax signals to send the right signals to business and industry; how to offer better choices to individual consumers and producers; how, in the end, to get things done" [Speech at London School of Economics, February 26, 2002].

4. Food and Population
By Christopher Reardon

An old Mexican proverb admonishes those who fail to plan for the future. "He who doesn't look ahead," the saying goes, "remains behind." Similar reasoning drew more than 1,000 business leaders, civic activists, and public officials—including 48 heads of state—to Monterrey, Mexico, in March 2002 for the International Conference on Financing for Development. The formal purpose of the talks was to consider global macroeconomic reforms that might ease poverty, slow population growth, and safeguard the environment. But one speaker reminded delegates of their urgent, overarching mission.

"We are gathered in Monterrey to try to resolve a paradox," said Thoraya Obaid, the Saudi scholar who succeeded Nafis Sadik as Executive Director of the United Nations Population Fund (UNFPA) on January 1, 2001. "The paradox of a world where wealth is being created faster than ever before, but inequalities are widening faster than ever before; where the ten richest individuals are richer than the ten poorest countries; where education and health care are universally valued, but where illiteracy and ill-health are still the norm for half the world" [UNFPA, statement by Thoraya Obaid, "Invest in Women, Invest in Change," March 18, 2002, www.unfpa.org/about/ed/2002/monterrey.htm]. Looking ahead, Obaid said the first step toward remedying these disparities is for U.N. member states to honor the financial commitments they have made over the last decade. Time, she said, is wasting.

Population: A Time of Scarcity and Abundance

The earth's population now exceeds 6.1 billion and is likely to reach 9.3 billion by midcentury, according to the Fund's latest yearbook [UNFPA, *The State of World Population 2001*, www.unfpa.org/swp/swpmain.htm]. This growth, while less than demographers once anticipated, poses some unresolved challenges. The 49 least developed countries will nearly triple in size, from 668 million to 1.86 billion people. Half of the increase will be concentrated in six countries: India, China, Pakistan, Nigeria, Bangladesh, and Indonesia. And, with populations falling in 39 more affluent nations, today's developing countries will be home to 85 percent of the world's people in 2050.

Population growth certainly complicates development, but its effect on the planet is not uniform. The Fund pointedly focused its 2001 report, titled "Footprints and Milestones: Population and Environmental Change," on the disparate impacts that people in different nations have on the world's ecology [ibid.]. "A child born today in an industrialized country," it said, "will add more to consumption and pollution over his or her lifetime than 30 to 50 children born in developing countries." Now that the United States has backed away from the Kyoto Protocol to the 1992 U.N. Framework Convention on Climate Change, which sought to reduce carbon dioxide emissions that contribute to global warming [*New York Times*, April 1, 2001], the Fund is again urging policy-makers to take a hard look at this consumption gap.

Meeting the challenge of population has been one of the United Nations' success stories. Around the globe, birth rates are falling faster than expected and without the use of coercive methods, like forced sterilization, that used to be the mainstay of population policies. Today the focus on reproductive health care and family planning services that enable individuals to make informed and voluntary choices about the number and spacing of their children. Look at Mexico, Obaid told delegates at Monterrey. When the Fund began its work in 1969, the average Mexican woman gave birth to nearly seven children. Now she has fewer than three, and the country is starting to reap the benefits of this demographic transition. Mexicans are staying in school longer, getting healthier, and generating faster economic growth [UNFPA, statement by Thoraya Obaid, Invest in Women, Invest in Change, March 18, 2002]. Many other developing countries are achieving comparable results.

The shift from population control to reproductive health picked up steam at the International Conference on Population and Development, held in Cairo in 1994. The meeting, which tackled some of the most divisive issues on the U.N. agenda, has been widely hailed as a triumph of consensus building. Yet some countries, including many predominately Catholic and Muslim ones, still object to its candor about sexuality and argue that it promotes abortion. And supporters fault it for lacking teeth.

Delegates in Cairo agreed to mobilize $17 billion for family planning, reproductive health care, HIV/AIDS prevention, and related activities in 2000. Developing countries came up with 80 percent of their $11.3 billion share that year. But industrialized countries failed to provide even half of their $5.7 billion pledge [ibid.]. The United States, in particular, has repeatedly balked at paying its share, both in overseas development assistance and in direct funding for UNFPA. Although Congress authorized a $34 million contribution to the Fund for 2002, the Bush administration vowed to withhold the money because of allegations that the Fund "condones forced abortions in China" [*New York Times*, April 7, 2002].

The shortfall in development assistance has dire consequences, particularly among the 350 million couples who still lack access to safe, modern contraceptives. One result is that 40 million unwanted pregnancies end in abortion each year [UNFPA, *The State of World Population 2001*]. What's more, life expectancy at birth has actually fallen in the least developed countries, in part because HIV/AIDS is spreading faster than expected. In Cairo, and again at the 1999 follow-up meeting in The Hague, delegates vowed to reduce infant mortality to 35 deaths per 1,000 live births by 2015. But since 1996 the number has only fallen from 57 to 55. Insufficient resources have also stymied efforts to curb maternal mortality, which remains 20 to 50 times more prevalent in the developing world than in industrialized countries.

"Now it is time for developed countries to act," Obaid told delegates in Monterrey. "Failure to meet agreed financial targets is derailing the achievement of international development goals, especially in the poorest countries."

Food: Empty Promises, a Tragic Irony

Each night on earth, in small hamlets and in sprawling cities, 815 million people go to bed hungry, according to the latest figures from the Food and Agriculture Organization of the United Nations (FAO) [FAO Press Release, October 15, 2001; FAO, *The State of Food Insecurity 2001*]. The vast majority—777 million individuals—live in the developing world, and most of these are women and children in rural areas. Food scarcity may be the immediate cause of their suffering, but invariably it points to deeper social and political failings. The world produces enough food to feed everyone on the planet, but food does not always get to the people who need it most.

The World Food Programme (WFP), the U.N.'s frontline agency in the fight against global hunger, eased some of the pain by delivering food to 73 million people in 84 different countries in 2001 [WFP Press Release, April 9, 2001]. Some recipients had lost their livelihoods to natural disasters, including earthquakes in El Salvador and flooding in Indonesia. Others had fled their homes to escape armed conflicts, as in Afghanistan and Angola. Genuine food security, however, requires longer-term investments in agriculture and rural development. To that end, the International Fund for Agricultural Development (IFAD) continued making grants and loans aimed at overcoming poverty and distribution problems that exacerbate hunger. In 2001 it approved funding for 25 new projects that serve women and other vulnerable groups in places like Bangladesh, Nigeria, and Panama [IFAD Press Releases, April 26, September 12, and December 6, 2001]. With technical assistance from the FAO's Special Programme for Food Security, farmers in 68 countries adopted low-cost technologies that can quickly increase crop yields [see www.fao.org/spfs].

Even so, 2 billion people—a third of the world's population—still lack food security. Lately the FAO, IFAD, and WFP (all based in Rome) have teamed up in calling for increased and wiser financing for food, agriculture, and rural development. "Hunger in a world of food abundance is principally a result of negligence," they wrote in a joint paper presented in Monterrey, "as it lies within mankind's capacity to put in place the policies, institutions, technologies, and logistics both to prevent and eradicate hunger" [FAO/IFAD/WFP joint paper, *Reducing Poverty and Hunger: The Critical Role of Financing for Food, Agriculture, and Rural Development*, February 2002, www.fao.org/docrep/003/y6265e/y6265e00.htm]. The stakes are staggeringly high. The agencies warned that global stability is at risk if the international community does not do more to eradicate world hunger and poverty. "Eradicating hunger is an investment with high payoff in terms of peace and political stability, overall development, and prosperity," they said [ibid.].

Delegates from 185 countries endorsed this argument at the 1996 World Food Summit and set a goal of reducing hunger by half by 2015. They reaffirmed that goal four years later at the Millennium Summit. Yet, despite these repeated pledges, many countries have not followed through. In their joint paper, the three Rome-based agencies noted "a visible and worrisome downward trend" in public and private funding for both food aid and agricultural development. Much of the needed investment will have to come from the private sector, including farmers themselves, and from governments in developing countries. But bilateral and multilateral funders have not done their part to prime the pump. Food aid, for instance, fell 44 percent between 1990 and 2000, despite increasing need. World Bank lending for agriculture dropped from $3.66 billion to $1.34 billion over the same period. Consequently, the number of hungry people worldwide is declining at a rate of 6 million per year. To reach the goal set for 2015, it now must go down by 22 million per year [ibid.].

Hoping to remedy these shortfalls, the FAO called for a meeting in Rome to regain the momentum lost since the 1996 World Food Summit. The gathering, officially titled "World Food Summit: five years later," was postponed from November 2001 to June 2002 because of the September 11 terrorist attacks. As of this writing, the agenda included proposals to ensure adherence to agreements at past conferences and to find more reliable financial mechanisms to end hunger.

The FAO estimates that freer trade in agriculture could pump an additional $160 billion into developing countries each year, an amount that dwarfs current aid flows [ibid.]. The agency said it was imperative that agricultural trade negotiations lead to greater opportunities for poor nations. It specifically called for lifting trade barriers for sugar, fruits, and vegetables and reducing tariffs on processed tropical commodities like coffee and cocoa. "If left alone," the three Rome-based agencies said, "trade liberalization is unlikely to bring about a massive reduction in poverty and the benefits, if any, could remain in the hands of the few" [ibid.].

Another great global challenge for the coming years will be how to produce more food with less water, said Louise Fresco, the FAO's Assistant Director-General [FAO Press Release, March 22, 2002]. To meet growing needs, the agency estimates that the world's irrigated fields will need to produce

80 percent more crops by 2030 with only 12 percent more water. Public investment in the development and adoption of innovative water technologies will be essential in meeting this goal, Fresco said. But she added that policy-makers must also reform national water policies and secure water rights and access for all users.

In recent years, the developing world has seen a startling new form of malnutrition. Obesity, generally associated with affluent societies, is rapidly emerging as a counterpart to hunger in countries like Colombia, Zimbabwe, and China. People moving from rural areas to urban settings often adopt more sedentary lifestyles as they gain upward mobility. Their diets change, too, as grains and vegetables give way to foods high in fat and sugar. Pressed for time and drawn to new choices, many people fill their stomachs with cheap food that lacks the essential nutrients for a healthy life.

This surge in obesity came to light in a March 2000 report by the World Watch Institute, a Washington think tank [*Underfed and Overfed: The Global Epidemic of Malnutrition*, by Gary Gardner and Brian Halweil]. In January 2002, the FAO followed up with its own publication, calling obesity "a tragic irony" that imperils individuals and impairs development [FAO, *The Developing World's New Burden: Obesity*, www.fao.org/focus/e/obesity/obes1.htm]. The agency found that in Colombia 41 percent of the population is overweight; in Brazil, 36 percent. In Namibia and Zimbabwe, respectively, 21 percent and 23 percent of the women are overweight. In China, which achieved stunning economic and agricultural growth in the 1990s, the number of overweight adults jumped from 10 percent to 15 percent in just three years. "For the first time in history," the FAO said, "the number of overweight people rivals the number of underweight worldwide" [FAO, *The Spectrum of Malnutrition*, www.fao.org/worldfoodsummit/fsheets/malnutrition.pdf].

The prognosis is serious, both for individual health and for public policy. Obesity puts people at greater risk of diabetes, heart disease, hypertension, stroke, and some forms of cancer. At the same time, it creates a new economic burden for developing countries. FAO officials said hunger remains their first priority. But they said they cannot ignore obesity, which diminishes people's capacity to work and diverts precious resources to health care. "For nations whose economic and social resources are already stretched to the limit," the FAO said, "the result could be disastrous" [FAO, *The Developing World's New Burden: Obesity*].

As final preparations were being made for June's Food Summit, many activists questioned the prevailing model of agriculture, which relies on the heavy use of chemicals, water, and mechanization and emphasizes the production of cash crops for export. Instead they called for greater support for family farms that endorse sustainable practices and address local needs. Genetically modified plants and animals are unlikely to prevent hunger and malnutrition, critics said, because these are problems of distribution, not availability [see www.oneworld.net/guides/agriculture].

The FAO maintains that there may be a role for genetically modified plants and animals. But it agreed that the commodity in shortest supply is not food, but rather the political will to see that it gets to those who need it most. As the world becomes increasingly interconnected, the three Rome-based agencies said, extreme poverty and widespread deprivation are "bound to generate social and political tensions which cannot be tamed easily and have destabilizing effects with global dimensions. It is, therefore, in everyone's self-interest—rich and poor alike—to see faster progress in the fight against hunger and poverty" [FAO/IFAD/WFP joint paper].

V
Society

1. Drug Control and Crime Prevention
By Nick Rosen

Through the Lens of International Security

In 1999, the nation of Afghanistan was the largest supplier of heroin in the world. In July of the following year, ruling Taliban authorities imposed a ban on opium poppy cultivation that resulted in a 98 percent reduction in the production of Afghan opium—an achievement hailed as one of the most successful counterdrug eradication campaigns ever. But after the September 11 terrorist attacks in New York and Washington, the U.S.-led war in Afghanistan ensued and toppled the Taliban regime, along with its drug eradication program. International drug authorities announced that in the wake of the war, Afghanistan's drug business had been reborn; the looming poppy harvest of 2002 was expected to put Afghanistan back at the top of world heroin production [Associated Press, February 28, 2002].

The shifting fortunes in Afghanistan—which has become a crucible in the global war against illicit drugs—illustrates the way in which the U.N. drug control and crime prevention efforts have been shaped by the tumultuous events of the past year. Today, more than ever, the drug trade and transnational crime are entwined with broader concerns of violent conflict and terrorism. This was equally evident in Colombia, the fountainhead of world cocaine supply. Escalating civil war and the collapse of the flagging peace process cast uncertainty on the future of U.N. efforts in Colombia to reduce coca production and provide viable alternatives to the cocaine economy.

Illegal narcotics are now perceived as not merely a threat to addicts and vulnerable youth, but also the lifeblood of terrorists. International security has become the lens through which policy-makers have begun looking at the concomitant scourges of drugs, organized crime, and money laundering. The importance of these problems is both enhanced by and subordinated to the fulfillment of larger goals. The U.N. Security Council expressed this clearly in its landmark antiterrorist Resolution

1373. This resolution states that the Council "Notes with concern the close connection between international terrorism and transnational organized crime, illicit drugs, money-laundering, illegal arms-trafficking . . . and in this regard emphasizes the need to enhance coordination of efforts on national, sub-regional, regional and international levels" [S/Res/1373, Section 4].

The U.N. Office for Drug Control and Crime Prevention (ODCCP)

The **U.N. Office for Drug Control and Crime Prevention (ODCCP)** finds itself at the center of this new, complex global scenario. The Vienna-based ODCCP has seen its own share of internal turbulence and change, including the organizational merger of the U.N. International Drug Control Programme (UNDCP) and the Center for International Crime Prevention (CICP) into the single umbrella entity of the ODCCP. Pino Arlacchi, the first Executive Director of this new office, aggressively raised the profile and operational level of the ODCCP. But Arlacchi stepped down in January 2002 after an investigation by the U.N. Office of Internal Oversight Services (OIOS) found the Executive Director responsible for poor management practices. Antonio Maria Costa, an Italian economist, was appointed the ODCCP's new Executive Director in March [Agence France Presse, March 7, 2002].

Before leaving, Arlacchi authored a lengthy introduction to the ODCCP's **World Drug Report 2000 (WDR)**, in which he called for an end to the "the psychology of despair" and defeatism in the war against drugs. He asserted that the international community would likely achieve the objectives set forth in 1998 by the General Assembly in its landmark Special Session on the World Drug Problem. Specifically, the session called for "eliminating or significantly reducing" the illegal drug business by 2008 [Draft Resolution A/S-20/4, chapter V, section A].

Many of the findings of the WDR 2000, particularly long-term trends, seemed to support the former Executive Director's optimism. A surge in coca leaf production of the 1980s reversed, and in 1999 coca cultivation had fallen 20 percent from seven years earlier, thanks to successful counternarcotics efforts in the Andean nations of Peru and Bolivia. Global opium poppy cultivation was also down 17 percent over the decade. In addition, Pakistan and Thailand dramatically curtailed heroin production. Finally, the overall number of producer countries was significantly reduced. On the demand side, the ODCCP celebrated the decline or plateau of drug addiction levels in the Western industrialized countries (exemplified by a 70 percent drop in cocaine use in the United States between 1985 and 1999) and credited the success of prevention and treatment programs. "This good news belies the perception that the drugs problem can only get worse," noted Arlacchi [WDR, 2000].

But despite Arlacchi's sanguine view, great obstacles remain. In Afghanistan, pre-assessment surveys taken by the UNDCP in early 2002 revealed a marked resurgence of opium poppy cultivation back to 1998 levels. The overthrow of the Taliban regime and the war's aftermath left Afghanistan bereft of law enforcement or other institutions in many parts of the country. Much of its infrastructure lay crippled, and economic turmoil, displacement, and drought combined to make legitimate farming alternatives increasingly unviable. With heroin prices in the Western markets still held stable by existing stockpiles of the drug, it seemed inevitable that Afghans would exploit the opportunity afforded by renewed conflict and instability to replant their deleterious crop.

Hamid Karzai, Chairman of post-conflict Afghanistan's Interim Administration, issued a decree upholding the opium ban, but only after the seeds were in the ground. Given the still-embryonic state of the Afghan public security forces, enforcement of the ban remained uncertain. The ODCCP proposed a drug control assistance package—including the creation of a country-level drug commission, the bolstering of law enforcement, and the creation of sustainable alternatives—as part of the broader reconstruction of the war-devastated country. The Office has noted that the issue of drug control in Afghanistan is inextricably linked with the need for viable livelihoods among struggling Afghan farmers and must be considered a "cross-cutting" issue in U.N. development initiatives [ODCCP Update, March 2002]. "Things need to be done very, very soon in order for farmers not to plant opium next year," remarked Bernard Frahi, head of the U.N. Drug Control Program for the region. In the short term, however, authorities admitted there was little that could be done to diminish the looming harvest, which was expected to generate up to 2,000 tons of opium [*New York Times*, April 4, 2002].

In **Colombia**, which became the leading coca producer after drug crops were squeezed out of Bolivia and Peru, coca cultivation has proven stubborn to eradicate. Despite more than two years of scaled up eradication efforts under the billion-dollar Plan Colombia—including the delivery of helicopters and training of special counterdrug brigades of the Colombian army—U.S. officials recently announced disappointing results. Coca production in Colombia increased from 136,200 hectares in 2000 to 169,800 hectares in 2001 (contradictory Colombian government statistics showed a modest decline) [*Miami Herald*, February 8, 2002].

Also alarming is the dramatic spike in the production of opium poppies in Colombia, which rose from producing virtually nothing in the mid-1990s to becoming a major supplier to the United States, serving roughly 70 percent of the U.S. market. Colombian heroin is of renowned purity, allowing for easy, non-intravenous consumption of the drug.

Poppy eradication efforts, made difficult by the steep, mist-enshrouded Andean hillsides on which the drug is grown, have had little impact in Colombia [Associated Press, November 28, 2001].

Meanwhile, UNDCP surveillance has shown signs of an incipient rebound of coca production, and possibly even opium poppies, in the Huallaga Valley of Peru. This shows signs that one of the most important victories for counternarcotics in the 1990s may be unraveling and prompted the Peruvian drug czar to glumly concede, "I really don't like to say we are losing the war. It sounds better if we simply say we are not winning it" [Associated Press, March 13, 2002].

Drug Control Treaties and Policies

In its 2001 Annual Report, the **International Narcotics Control Board (INCB)** warned of the dangerous side effects of globalization and technological progress. The report states that growth in international trade and financial networks have enhanced the ability of drug traffickers to transfer illicit drugs, precursor chemicals, and drug proceeds while avoiding detection. Drugs are sold freely over the Internet, while traffickers communicate with each other in private chat rooms and encrypted messages. INCB President Hamid Ghodse dubbed these modern transgressors *"criminals sans frontières"* and asserted that governments "must address the challenges that new technologies pose to law enforcement in an era of increasing globalization" [INCB Annual Report, Press Release No. 2]. The INCB is charged with monitoring compliance with the three principal U.N. drug control treaties, namely, the 1961 Single Convention on Narcotic Drugs, the 1971 Convention on Psychotropic Substances, and the 1988 U.N. Convention Against Illicit Traffic in Narcotic Drugs and Psychotropic Substances.

Last March, the **U.N. Commission on Narcotic Drugs**, the chief drug policy-making body in the United Nations, held its 45th session, where a range of current narcotics-related issues were reviewed. High on the agenda was the rising trend of recreational drug use, particularly amphetamine-based stimulants, or "club drugs," by young people. The Commission had identified this as a paramount concern during its previous session and had adopted a resolution (44/5) calling on governments to develop programs to prevent such recreational abuse. Based on biennial reporting, the Commission found that few countries had adopted specific programs to prevent experimentation with amphetamines, which is becoming an increasingly regularized aspect of youth culture in the Western industrialized countries [E/CN.7/2002/3].

In a novel action, the Commission also chose to address the spread of **HIV/AIDS** and its link to intravenous drug use (IDU). IDU continues to fuel the epidemic, the Secretariat reported, and there may be as many as three million intravenous drug users with HIV worldwide, a number that continues to increase [E/CN.7/2002/2]. Speaking to the Commission, Kathleen Cravero, Deputy Director of the Joint U.N. Programme on HIV/AIDS, pointed to new, effective initiatives that respond to the HIV problem among drug users in eastern Europe and central Asia, where more than 150 outreach and needle exchange programs have been established [U.N. Information Service, March 15, 2002].

The Commission also held a thematic debate on the implementation of the *Action Plan on International Cooperation on the Eradication of Illicit Drug Crops and on Alternative Development*, as adopted by the General Assembly at its 20th Special Session in 1998. Member states were told that evidence supported the notion of alternative development as a key to eliminating farmers' dependence on drug crops, although certain conditions—such as technical expertise, political climate, and financial resources—must also be in place for successful alternative substitution to take hold [ibid.]. ODCCP Officer-in-Charge Steinar B. Bjornsson told the Committee that because alternative development funds are very limited, "mainstreaming the drug control element in development programmes is essential" [Bjornsson speech, U.N. Information Service, March 11, 2002]. Bjornsson also stressed the need to restore donor governments' confidence in the ODCCP, which was harmed following the management problems identified in the OIOS report. The Commission decided that in its 46th Session in 2003, the ministerial segment would evaluate the progress toward meeting the targets for drug control set out in the 1998 General Assembly special session, namely, eliminating or significantly reducing the illegal drug trade by 2008.

Transnational Crime Prevention Post-September 11

The tragic attacks of September 11 presented a daunting challenge to the U.N. crime prevention bodies, but also an opportunity for unprecedented international cooperation. The U.N. role in combating international crime and terrorism was elevated to a new level of priority, as the situation demanded coordinated global defense against a truly global menace. The CICP's **Terrorism Prevention Branch (TPB)**, established by the General Assembly in 1999, is a natural locus of operations for such a response. The TPB is charged with researching the phenomenon of terrorism, helping countries enhance their investigative capacities, assisting member-states in ratifying U.N. antiterrorism treaties, and implementing relevant Security Council resolutions.

However, it remains uncertain whether the resource-poor terrorism office is up to the task. In October 2001, CICP Director Eduardo Vetere lamented that the TPB, despite the new urgency to address terrorism, remained terribly understaffed and underfunded. In response, the General Assembly passed a resolution [A/Res/56/23] requesting the Secretary-

General to make proposals to strengthen the TPB [U.N. Information Service, October 18, 2001].

The post-September 11 environment has also brought heightened importance to the entry into force of the U.N. Convention against Transnational Organized Crime, known commonly as the *Palermo Convention*. In December 2000, more than 120 countries signed this treaty, which aims to strengthen the power of governments to combat crime, build cooperation on issues such as extradition and witness protection, and harmonize national laws. The Palermo Convention also bore three protocols against illegal firearms, the smuggling of migrants, and the trafficking in women and children.

The trafficking in women and children for the purposes of forced labor and prostitution earns criminals up to $7 billion annually. This practice has been called by Secretary-General Annan "one of the most egregious violations of human rights which the United Nations now confronts" [Inter-Press Services, December 15, 2000]. Aside from the Palermo Convention's Protocol to Prevent, Suppress and Punish the Trafficking in Persons, Especially Women and Children, the United Nations addresses this issue through its Global Programme against Human Trafficking. Launched by the CICP in 1999, the U.N. Global Programme against Human Trafficking supports countries' crackdowns on the trafficking of persons through data collection, assessment, and technical cooperation.

To address the widespread problem of corruption, a new ad hoc committee is charged with the drafting of a *Convention against Corruption*. This committee negotiated through the political brambles at its first meeting in February 2002 and emerged with a draft of the first 39 articles. The committee has until 2003 to complete negotiations.

Many of the issues mentioned above were raised at the June 2002 meeting of the 40-member **U.N. Commission on Crime Prevention and Criminal Justice** held in Vienna. Delegates focused in particular on the reform of the criminal justice system and the fight against terrorism while stressing the importance and the increasing urgency of international cooperation on all crime matters. Thailand was chosen as the host country for a **2005 U.N. Congress on Crime Prevention and Criminal Justice**, where the proposed theme is "Synergies and responses: strategic alliances in crime prevention and criminal justice."

During a world-transforming year, the United Nations is uniquely poised to construct such "strategic alliances" against drug trafficking, organized crime, and the growing linkages of terrorism and criminal enterprise—the emerging "dark side" of global integration. In an increasingly uncertain and complex geopolitical landscape, the Organization's challenge is not just to overcome this awesome threat, but to foster the political will and cooperation among member states that will be vital for the preservation of law, order, and security in the days ahead.

2. Health

By V. Kate Somvongsiri

Portrait of a Global Crisis: HIV/AIDS

In the course of the past few years, one pressing health concern has dominated the U.N. agenda and permeated beyond the boundaries of health issues. The disease is HIV/AIDS: a health concern, a human development obstacle, and a threat to international peace and security. Not only is the issue addressed by the different U.N. agencies in their own programming, but a coordinated effort under the umbrella of the **Joint U.N. Programme on HIV/AIDS (UNAIDS)** has been underway since 1996. This program, spearheaded by Peter Piot, brings together the resources and expertise of the U.N. Children's Fund (UNICEF), U.N. Development Programme (UNDP), U.N. Drug Control Programme (UNDCP), U.N. Educational, Scientific and Cultural Organization (UNESCO), U.N. Population Fund (UNFPA), the World Bank, and the World Health Organization (WHO).

An annual report released by UNAIDS and WHO estimated that in 2001, three million people died of AIDS and approximately five million became infected with the virus. AIDS is now the number four killer worldwide and has "become the most devastating disease human kind has ever faced" claiming more than 20 million lives, so far [*AIDS Epidemic Update*, December 2001, www.unaids.org/epidemic_update/report_dec01, April 14, 2002]. The urgency and magnitude of this situation prompted the General Assembly to convene the 26th Special Session from June 25–27, 2001, to review and address the problem of HIV/AIDS. This historic event drew representatives from the highest levels of government and resulted in the **Declaration of Commitment on HIV/AIDS**, which calls for a "global commitment to enhancing coordination and intensification of national, regional and international efforts to combat [HIV/AIDS] in a comprehensive manner" [www.unaids.org/whatnew/others/un_special/Declaration020801_en.htm, April 21, 2002].

The Declaration identified Africa as the worst affected region "where HIV/AIDS is considered a state of emergency" and recognized the growing threat of HIV/AIDS in the Caribbean region, Asia-Pacific, Latin America, and central and eastern Europe [www.unaids.org/whatnew/others/un_special/Declaration020801_en.htm, April 21, 2002].

In order to deal effectively with the crisis, the Declaration focused on the need for strong leadership; prevention; care, support, and treatment; reduced vulnerability; and additional sustained resources. The Declaration also links HIV/AIDS to human rights, emphasizing access to medicine as the right of infected persons and the obligation of governments to facilitate. Perhaps most importantly, the outcome of the session was a set of agreed upon goals in the global fight against HIV/AIDS [www.unaids.org/

ungass/index.html, April 19, 2002]. The goals are to establish and strengthen mechanisms that involve public–private partnerships, as well as AIDS victims and vulnerable groups; by 2005, reduce HIV prevalence among young men and women aged 15–24 in most affected countries by 25 percent and to do the same worldwide by 2010; by 2005, ensure that 90 percent of the aforementioned age group have access to information and education needed to reduce vulnerability; by 2003, ensure that national strategies are developed to meet international targets; and by 2005, reach an overall annual expenditure of between $7 million and $10 million U.S. on the epidemic in low- and middle-income countries.

The effort to fight HIV/AIDS has extended beyond the realm of government resulting in innovative public–private partnerships as well. **The Global Fund to Fight AIDS/Tuberculosis and Malaria** is one such example of an effort to draw on resources across many sectors. Since its creation following the Secretary-General's call to action in April 2001 and the endorsement at the G8 Summit in July 2001, governments and private contributions have pledged almost $2 billion dollars to the fund [www.global fundatm.org]. The first round of grants, announced in April 2002, commits over $616 million dollars to support prevention and treatment projects worldwide [www.globalfundatm.org].

HIV/AIDS was also on the agenda at the World Conference against Racism in Durban, South Africa, where Peter Piot emphasized the role of discrimination and stigma in spreading the disease. The final declaration from the conference noted that "people infected or affected by HIV/AIDS, as well as those presumed to be infected, belong to groups vulnerable to racism, racial discrimination, xenophobia and related intolerance, which has a negative impact and impedes their access to health care and medication" [Associated Press, September 5, 2001].

December 1 marked World AIDS Day, another U.N. initiative to raise awareness and address the AIDS pandemic. In his message on the day, Secretary-General Annan remarked, "Indeed [HIV/AIDS] is one of the biggest obstacles to development itself. It affects regional and global stability and risks slowing democratic development. In this way, AIDS not only takes away the present. It takes away the future. That is the toll of AIDS" [www.unaids.org/worldaidsday/2001/index.html]. He also praised the efforts of the global community over the past year, noting that this past year "has seen a turning point in the fight against HIV/AIDS" [www.unaids.org/worldaidsday/2001/index.html].

Overall, the past year has seen a surge in the ongoing battle against HIV/AIDS. Not only has the Secretary-General made the issue one of his priorities, but a sense of collective responsibility has been instilled among most of the world's nations. Another notable trend in dealing with HIV/AIDS this year is linking HIV/AIDS with human rights. This has resulted, foremost, in an emphasis on combating discrimination, with

"Stigma and Discrimination," the two-year theme of the World AIDS Campaign 2002–2003. This link has also led to a focus on access to HIV/AIDS medicine, as part of the right to "highest attainable standard of" health. Considerable debate has centered around the responsibility of developed countries to facilitate access to affordable medicine. (In a controversial move that could help bring down the price of HIV/AIDS medicine for poor countries, the WHO has released its first list of manufacturers of safe AIDS drugs [*New York Times,* March 21, 2002].) The most enduring trend regarding HIV/AIDS, however, is that it is no longer seen as a health issue confined to certain populations in particular regions. It is now recognized as a worldwide crisis, a threat to international peace and security, and a global problem that demands the attention and resources of all. HIV/AIDS is a pressing issue that is likely to remain high on the U.N. agenda for years to come.

Other Health Issues

While the specter of HIV/AIDS looms over the health agenda of the United Nations, various U.N. agencies continue to hammer away at other health issues that may not be as high profile, but are just as life-threatening. Health issues before the United Nations are customarily addressed by the World Health Organization (WHO), though other U.N. agencies simultaneously tackle a host of health problems that most directly affect their respective mandates. Working in conjunction with WHO, UNICEF, for example, has focused on diseases most threatening to children. In the past year, one of the areas that has emerged as a cause of concern is **child mental health**. A report released in March 2002 by WHO and UNICEF cites up to one in five of the world's children as "suffering from mental or behavioral problems" and highlights "big increases in depression and suicide among children and adolescents" [BBC News Online, news.bbc.co.uk/hi/english/health/newsid_1867000/1867410.stm, March 12, 2002]. WHO and UNICEF addressed this issue at the U.N. General Assembly Special Session on Children in May 2002.

Elimination of **polio** is also high on UNICEF's priority list. The global immunization campaign, "Race to Reach the Last Child," has brought the world "close to eliminating polio," though a funding gap jeopardizes the goal [*Wall Street Journal Europe,* April 17, 2002]. According to the WHO, the number of polio cases is at its lowest in history: only 537 cases were reported worldwide in 2001. Other issues targeted by UNICEF include malnutrition, environmental hazards, and vaccination [WHO Press Release, March 12, 2002].

UNFPA, which aims to find solutions to population problems worldwide, focuses much of its efforts on reproductive health, family planning, and sexual health. According to its "State of the World Population 2001" report, access to education and health care for women is essential to prevent the world's population from skyrocketing to 10.9 billion people by 2050 [www.unfpa.org/swp/swpmain.htm]. Refugee health continues to be a central concern for U.N. High Commissioner for Refugees; malnutrition is a focus for Food and Agriculture Organization (FAO); and even institutions such as the World Bank have linked health, nutrition, and population to poverty eradication.

WHO Initiatives

WHO's daunting mandate is to directly confront the myriad health concerns that face people globally. To meet this hefty challenge, WHO carries out promotion, research, technical assistance, and coordinated campaigns. Among the major initiatives undertaken this year by WHO under the leadership of Director-General Dr. Gro Harlem Bruntdland are:

- *World Health Day.* The theme for this year's World Health Day, commemorated on April 7, 2002, was "Move for Health." WHO studies indicate that two million people die from diseases linked to inactivity (such as diabetes, obesity, cardiovascular ailments) each year [Associated Press, April 4, 2002]. The "Move for Health" theme was designed to raise awareness and lead people toward a less sedentary lifestyle.
- *AntiTobacco Campaign.* An ongoing WHO initiative toward a global antitobacco treaty continued to make progress over the past year; the fourth round of negotiations for the treaty took place in March 2002. The aim of the treaty is to reduce smoking and tobacco-related diseases, which kill four million people a year. Some of the more sensitive provisions deal with bans on advertising, antismuggling measures, and tobacco industry liability and compensation for smokers [*New York Times*, March 21, 2002]. This effort to curb tobacco use was launched two years ago with hopes that the treaty will be ready for signature by 2003.
- *Global Alliance for Vaccines and Immunizations (GAVI).* According to the Secretary-General's *Report on the Work of the Organization* [A/56/1], the global immunization coverage (of measles, DPT, and TB) is currently at 74 percent, with GAVI "playing a critical role in improving coverage." Formed in 1999, the mission of the alliance is to attempt to protect every child in the world from vaccine-preventable diseases. GAVI is the coordinating mechanism for partner groups, which include the WHO, UNICEF, the World Bank Group, the Rockefeller Foundation, the Bill and Melinda Gates Children's Vaccine Program, various other public health and research institutions, and national governments [www.vaccinealliance.com, May 14, 2002].

- *Commission on Macroeconomics and Health.* The Commission on Macroeconomics and Health was set up in January 2000 by WHO to examine the links between health and economic development. The report of the Commission, released in December 2001, focuses on the importance of health in global economic development. It "concludes that policy-makers have not adequately recognized the importance of investing in health as a means to promote peoples' welfare and reduce poverty. Furthermore, extending the coverage of crucial health services, including a relatively small number of specific health interventions, to the world's poor could save millions of lives each year, reduce poverty, improve peoples' lives, and promote global security" [World Bank News Release, 2002/164/HD].
- *Recent Conferences and other initiatives.* U.N. conferences recently convened that address health issues include the *Second World Conference on Ageing* held from April 8–12, 2002, and *WHO Conference on Health and Disability* held from April 17–20, 2002. Other ongoing initiatives include the *Global Plan to Stop Tuberculosis* and the *Roll Back Malaria* campaigns.
- *Post-September 11 Health Issues.* Following the September 11 terrorist attacks, the anthrax infections in the United States prompted grave concerns and numerous inquiries regarding health aspects of biological weapons. The U.N. response provided information and guidance on anthrax, small pox, and other biological and chemical agents [WHO/44 Press Release, October 18, 2001]. The eradication of small pox, certified in 1979, was one of the greatest achievements of the WHO; the threat of a smallpox attack would pose a serious challenge to the system.

Looking Ahead: An Integrated Approach to Health

Though these issues will undoubtedly confront the 57th General Assembly, it remains unknown what additional health concerns may surface in the coming years. Despite this uncertainty, the United Nations is devoting increasing attention to the intersection between health and other issues such as development, human rights, and international peace and security. Looking ahead, an integrated approach that cuts across different traditional fields and emphasizes cooperation among various sectors may prove most effective in dealing with health and related problems.

3. Women
By Iara Duarte Peng and Khaita Sylla

International Commitment to Achieving Gender Equality and Eliminating Gender Discrimination

Over the last decade, gender issues have become a primary focus of the United Nations. Increasingly, the advancement of women is linked to solving diverse international challenges such as globalization, poverty, HIV/ AIDS, and environmental protection [Ms. Angela E. V. King, Special Adviser on Gender Issues and Advancement of Women Introductory Statement to the Commission on the Status of Women, 46th Session, March 4–15, 2002]. The main U.N. legislative bodies—the General Assembly, the Security Council, the Economic and Social Council (ECOSOC), and its subsidiary body, the Commission on the Status of Women—have all committed to the advancement and empowerment of women and the implementation of the principle that men and women shall enjoy equal rights [www.un.org/womenwatch/daw/csw/].

Women's Rights, Equality, and Nondiscrimination

The Convention on the Elimination of All Forms of Discrimination against Women (CEDAW), often described as an international bill of rights for women, was adopted in 1979 by the General Assembly. CEDAW defines discrimination against women as "any distinction, exclusion or restriction made on the basis of sex which has the effect or purpose of impairing or nullifying the recognition, enjoyment or exercise by women, irrespective of their marital status, on a basis of equality of men and women, of human rights and fundamental freedoms in the political, economic, social, cultural, civil or any other field" [www.un.org/womenwatch/ daw/cedaw/index.html]. The Convention provides the basis for realizing gender equality through "ensuring women's equal access to, and equal opportunities in, political and public life—including the right to vote and to stand for election—as well as education, health and employment" [www.un.org/ womenwatch/daw/cedaw/index.html]. CEDAW is the only human rights treaty that affirms the reproductive rights of women and targets culture and tradition as influential forces shaping gender roles and family relations. The Convention, which entered into force on September 3, 1981, has 169 states parties. As of May 22, 2002, 40 of these states have signed the Optional Protocol to CEDAW, which gives individuals the right to bring their concerns to the Convention's monitoring body [www.un.org/womenwatch/daw/cedaw/ index.html].

At the **1995 Fourth World Conference on Women** held in Beijing, world leaders formally demonstrated their commitment to women's equal rights through the development of the Beijing Platform for Action (PFA) [A/CONF.177/20, Report of the Fourth World Conference on Women, Beijing, China, September 1995 www.un.org/esa/gopher-data/conf/fwcw/off/a-20.en]. Considered a "blueprint" for women's equality, the PFA aimed to empower women by "removing all the obstacles to women's active participation in all spheres of public and private life through a full and equal share in economic, social, cultural and political decision-making" [A/55/293]. It also sought "to promote and protect the full enjoyment of all universal human rights and the fundamental freedoms of all women throughout their life cycle" [ibid.].

After the 1995 World Conference, the Commission on the Status of Women (CSW) was given the mandate to regularly review progress made on the Platform for Action and to help ensure the implementation of its 12 critical areas of concern [ibid]. In 2000, a comprehensive review and appraisal of progress achieved in the implementation of the Platform for Action was undertaken by the 23rd Special Session of the General Assembly entitled *Women 2000: gender equality, development, and peace for the twenty-first century*. The Assembly adopted the outcome document of the Special Session, "Further Actions and Initiatives to Implement the Beijing Declaration and Platform for Action" [A/Res/S-23/2, www.un.org/women watch/daw/followup/ress232e.pdf]. The CSW committed to a multiyear plan from 2002–2006 to ensure the effective implementation of both the PFA and the Special Session's outcome document [www.un.org/womenwatch/daw/csw/].

The 46th Session of the Commission on the Status of Women (CSW)

The Commission on the Status of Women (CSW), established in 1946 as a functional body of ECOSOC, is the primary U.N. body that addresses the advancement of women worldwide. The CSW, which began with 15 members, now consists of 45 members elected by ECOSOC for a period of four years. Its 46th annual session was convened from March 4–15, 2002, in New York. During the session, world leaders considered two thematic issues: the gender perspective in environmental management and the eradication of poverty through the empowerment of women [www. un.org/womenwatch/daw/csw/46sess.htm]. The CSW also considered women and girls in Afghanistan, the HIV/AIDS pandemic, Palestinian women, and gender mainstreaming [CSW Press Release, WOM/1321, March 1, 2002]. The recommendations from the session aim "to expand an agenda for action to be taken at both the international and national levels as outlined in the Beijing Platform for Action and the outcome document of the twenty-third special session of the General Assembly" [Report of the Secretary-General assessing the implications of the reforms of mechanisms in the human rights area (1503 procedure) for communications concerning the status of women, E/CN.6/2002/12, January 9, 2002].

The Gender Perspective in the Mitigation of Natural Disasters

Environmental degradation and disasters often impact women more directly than men [A/CONF.177/L.1, Draft Platform for Action, May 1995, www.un.org/esa/ gopher-data/conf/fwcw/off/al-1.en]. Women also play a vital role in disaster reduction, response, and recovery and in natural resources management [CSW Press Release, March 15, 2002, WOM/1333]. Despite these facts, women are still not fully involved in planning and decision-making processes in this area. To change this imbalance, the CSW invited governments, the U.N. system, civil society, and the private sector to take action on a wide range of issues. Gender equality and gender-sensitive environmental management and disaster reduction, response, and recovery are essential for sustainable development [CSW Press Release, WOM/1333, March 15, 2002; and Ms. Angela E. V. King, Special Adviser on Gender Issues and Advancement of Women, Introductory Statement to the Commission on the Status of Women, 46th Session, March 4–15, 2002]. Global actors were also urged "to develop and implement gender sensitive laws, policies, and programs," including those on land-use, environmental management, and integrated water resources management. Furthermore, global actors were called upon to "provide opportunities to prevent and mitigate damage; and to include, at the design stage of all relevant development programs and projects, gender analysis and methods of mapping hazards and vulnerabilities in order to improve the effectiveness of disaster risk management, involving women and men equally" [CSW Press Release, WOM/1333, March 15, 2002].

Eradicating Poverty Through the Empowerment of Women

The PFA recognized that women and men experience poverty differently and agreed that these differences need to be taken into account if the causes of poverty are to be adequately understood and addressed [CSW 46th Session Provisional Agenda, Thematic Issues before the Commission on the Status of Women, E/CN.6/ 2002/9, January 3, 2002]. Women, who constitute the majority of the 1.2 billion poor in today's world, along with children, often bear the greatest burden of extreme poverty [CSW 46th Session Agreed Conclusions Eradicating Poverty, March 15, 2002]. The CSW, the Fourth World Conference on Women, the 23rd Special Session, and many other intergovernmental processes give significant weight to poverty eradication. The Secretary-General's Millennium Declaration highlights gender equality and the empowerment of women as effective ways to combat poverty, hunger, and disease and to stimulate sustainable development [Carolyn Hannan, Director of the Division for the Advancement of Women, Statement at the CSW, 46th Session, March 4–15, 2002].

At the 46th session of the Commission, world leaders affirmed gender equality and women's empowerment as important strategies to eradicate poverty [CSW Press Release, March 15, 2002]. They further agreed that action must be taken "to address obstacles to the empowerment of women and to the full enjoyment of their human rights and fundamental freedoms throughout their life cycle, with a view to eradicating poverty" [CSW 46th Session Agreed Conclusions Eradicating Poverty, March 15, 2002]. Government and the private sector were urged to support socioeconomic policies that promote sustainable development and support and ensure poverty eradication programs by providing, especially for women, skill training, equal access to control over resources, technologies, credit, and finance. Women should benefit from the pursuit of effective, equitable, development-oriented, and durable solutions to the external debt and debt-servicing problems of developing countries [CSW 46th Session Agreed Conclusions Eradicating Poverty, March 15, 2002].

Women and Girls in Afghanistan

Since 1998, the Commission has dealt with the situation of women and girls in Afghanistan. A recent report of the Secretary-General, Discrimination against women and girls in Afghanistan [E/CN.6/2002/5, January 28, 2002], suggests that special attention be directed to the promotion and protection of the human rights of women and girls in Afghanistan. The CSW revised a resolution that urges the transitional government of Afghanistan to undertake a series of steps aimed at improving the quality of life for Afghan women and girls [CSW Press Release, WOM/1334, March 25, 2002]. Suggested steps are to fully respect the equal human rights and fundamental freedoms of women and girls in accordance with international human rights law; give high priority to the issue of ratification of the CEDAW; and consider signing the CEDAW Optional Protocol [E/CN.6/2002/L.4/Rev.2, *Situation of women and girls in Afghanistan*]. Furthermore, the CSW draft resolution urges the transitional government to repeal all legislative and other measures that discriminate against women and girls; enable the full, equal, and effective participation of women and girls in civil, cultural, economic, political, and social life throughout the country at all levels; and ensure the equal rights of women and girls to education [CSW Press Release, WOM/1334, March 25, 2002].

The HIV/AIDS Pandemic

The CSW draft resolution on **Women, the Girl Child, and HIV/AIDS** called on governments to intensify efforts to challenge gender stereotypes, attitudes, and inequalities in relation to HIV/AIDS [CSW Press Release, WOM/1332, March 15, 2002, and E/CN.6/2002/L.3/Rev.1]. In these efforts, governments should encourage the active participation and involvement of men and boys [ibid.]. By 2005, governments aim to implement measures to increase the capacity of women and adolescent girls to protect themselves from the risk of HIV infection. These measures emphasize the provision of health care and health services (including sexual and reproductive health services), as well as prevention education programs that promote gender equality within a gender-sensitive framework [CSW Press Release, WOM/1332, March 15, 2002]. In addition, governments will work to reduce the proportion of infants infected with HIV by 20 percent by 2005 and by 50 percent by 2010. To achieve these goals, governments seek to expand information, counseling, and other HIV-prevention services available to pregnant women through prenatal care [ibid.].

Palestinian Women

The CSW draft resolution on the situation of Palestinian women specified that the Economic and Security Council would call on the concerned parties, as well as the international community, to ensure the immediate resumption of the peace process [CSW Press Release, WOM/1332, March 15, 2002]. The resolution would also have ECOSOC call for tangible improvements in the difficult situation on the ground and in living conditions faced by Palestinian women and their families. It demands that Israel comply fully with the relevant human rights declarations and treaties, in order to protect the rights of Palestinian women and their families [E/CN.6/2002/3 and CSW Press Release, WOM/1332, March 15, 2002]. The CSW called for Israel to facilitate the return of all refugees and displaced Palestinian women and children to their homes and properties. It also urged member states, financial organizations, nongovernmental organizations, and other relevant institutions to intensify their efforts to provide financial and technical assistance to Palestinian women, especially during the transitional period [CSW Press Release, WOM/1332, March 15, 2002]. 38 countries voted in favor of the resolution; the United States opposed it.

Gender Mainstreaming

According to the ECOSOC, mainstreaming a gender perspective

> is the process of assessing the implications for women and men of any planned action, including legislation, policies or programs, in all areas and at all levels. It is a strategy for making women's as well as men's concerns and experiences an integral dimension of the design, implementation, monitoring and evaluation of policies and programs in all political, economic and societal spheres so that women and men benefit equally and inequality is not perpetuated. The ultimate goal is to achieve gender equality. [A/52/3, Report of the Economic and Social Council, September 18, 1997]

This ECOSOC statement on gender mainstreaming remains a watershed in the struggle for gender equality. Sustained and active attention to progress, constraints, and challenges in gender mainstreaming should be ensured at all levels [Carolyn Hannan, Director of the Division for the Advancement of Women, Statement at the Commission on the Status of Women, 46th Session, March 4–15, 2002]. Gender mainstreaming within the U.N. system has been making progress, principally through policy and strategy development, program and operational activities, as well as coordination and information sharing [E/CN.6/2002/2].

Future Actions Toward the Advancement of Women

In preparation of its multiyear plan from 2002–2006 to ensure the effective implementation of both the Platform for Action and the Outcome

Document, the CSW will address a wide range of issues. Issues on the CSW agenda include the participation and access of women to the media and information and communication technologies; women's human rights and the elimination of all forms of violence against women and girls; the role of men and boys in achieving gender equality; women's equal participation in conflict prevention, management, and resolution; and the equal participation of women and men in decision-making processes at all levels [ECOSOC Resolution 2001/4, Proposals for a multiyear program of work for the Commission on the Status of Women for 2002–2006, July 24, 2001].

4. Children and Youth
By Iara Duarte Peng

International Leadership: From a World Summit to a Special Session

Since the 1990 World Summit on Children in Dakar, Senegal, children and their rights have risen prominently on the world's agenda [www.unicef.org/specialsession/about/index.html]. In part, this prominence is due to the subsequent international commitment to achieve the Summit's precise, time-bound goals "relating to children's survival, health, nutrition, education and protection" [Secretary-General Kofi A. Annan, *We the Children: Meeting the Promises of the World Summit for Children*, September 2001]. Specifically, international leaders pledged their resolve to reduce child mortality rates, cut malnutrition rates in half, ensure safe drinking water and access to sanitation, reverse the spread of HIV/AIDS, deliver basic education to all children, and improve their protection from violence, abuse, and injustice [UNICEF, *The State of the World's Children*, 2002].

To assess the progress made on the goals set in 1990, undertake a renewed commitment to children, and determine what needs to be done next, the General Assembly called an unprecedented **Special Session on Children**, held May 8–10, 2002 [R 54/93]. This marked the first time a Special Session was called specifically to address issues related to children and the first time young people actively participated at a major U.N. conference in such large numbers; more than 300 children were scheduled to serve as delegates [UNICEF Press Release, April 19, 2002]. The Special Session on Children was expected to produce a global agenda with a set of goals and a plan of action devoted to improving the lives of children around the world [www.unicef.org/specialsession/about/index.html]. It was hoped that governments would commit to "specific outcomes for the world's children in the areas of child health and education, in combating HIV/AIDS, and in protecting children from abuse, exploitation and violence" [*The State of the World's Children*, ibid.].

In preparation for the Special Session on Children, a series of high-level meetings with government and private sector leaders took place in every region throughout the world. Each session identified young people's needs and solutions for ensuring their fundamental human rights. And each issued a declaration of commitment to the children of their region [ibid.]. Another series of meetings were called for children and young people. An unprecedented number of children between 11 and 18 years of age from all over East Asia participated in an April 2001 meeting in Jomtien, Thailand. Children from 27 countries across Europe and central Asia met in Budapest. And, in Kathmandu, a group called *The Change Makers* (representing children from the eight South Asian countries) briefed the region's corporate leaders about children's hopes.

Five leading nongovernmental organizations (the Bangladesh Rural Advancement Committee, Netaid.org Foundation, PLAN International, Save the Children, and World Vision) that work with children have joined together with UNICEF to create the **Global Movement for Children**. The Global Movement promotes children's rights and emphasizes participation, action, and accountability. A massive grass-roots campaign by the Global Movement launched between April and June 2001 asks individuals around the world to "Say Yes for Children" [ibid.]. The campaign urges individuals to speak out on ten imperative actions (spanning diverse concerns such as poverty, education, and HIV/AIDS), which the Global Movement believes must be taken in order to improve the lives of children. The results of this initiative were scheduled to be presented at the Special Session in May 2002 [www.gmfc.org/en/about_html].

While the world's commitment to children and their rights has generated significant strides, critical challenges remain. Today, the effects of poverty are most devastating on early childhood. A child born today in the developing world has a 4 out of 19 chance of living in extreme poverty [*The State of the World's Children*, ibid.]. More than 10 million children under the age of five die each year, due to poverty and lack of access to basic social services. 150 million children suffer from malnutrition, and HIV/AIDS is spreading with catastrophic speed. Of the 100 million children who are not in school, 60 percent are girls. In addition, hazardous and exploitative child labor, the sale and trafficking of children, child participation in armed conflict, and other forms of abuse, exploitation, and violence are still prevalent [*A World Fit for Children*, the Preparatory Committee for the Special Session of the General Assembly on Children].

Health and Nutrition

According to UNICEF's most recent statistics, 1 out of 12 children will die before the age of five, almost all from preventable causes [UNICEF Press Release, April 18, 2002]. Despite this discouraging fact, the global average of infant and under-five mortality has declined in the past decade by 11 percent, from 93 to 83 deaths per 1,000 live births. Sixty-three countries achieved the 1990 Summit goal of reducing the death rate of children under five by one-third, while over 100 countries cut such deaths by one-fifth. There are now three million fewer under-five deaths each year than at the beginning of the 1990s. Most children under five die from one or more of five common conditions—diarrheal dehydration, measles, respiratory infections, malaria, or malnutrition—for which treatment is relatively inexpensive [*We the Children*, ibid.]. One-third of children's lives were saved by meeting the Summit goal of reducing child deaths from diarrheal disease by 50 percent [UNICEF Press Release, April 17, 2002].

Malnutrition, implicated in more than half of all child deaths worldwide, lowers children's resistance to infection, making them more likely to die from common childhood ailments like diarrheal diseases and respiratory infections. An estimated 150 million children are malnourished. Poverty, low levels of education, and poor access to health services are major contributors to childhood malnutrition [UNICEF, *Progress since the World Summit for Children: A Statistical Review*, September 2001]. Three-quarters of the children who die from causes related to malnutrition were only mildly or moderately undernourished, showing no outward sign of their vulnerability [www.childinfo.org/eddb/malnutrition/index.htm].

Since the World Summit, significant progress has been made in the reduction of child malnutrition, with underweight prevalence declining from 32 to 28 percent in the developing world. The number of malnourished children in the developing world declined from around 174 million at the beginning of the decade to 150 million at the end of the decade. Half of all malnourished children live in South Asia (specifically India, China, and Bangladesh) [www.childinfo.org/eddb/malnutrition/index.htm]; more than one-fifth live in the sub-Saharan Africa. The actual number of malnourished children in sub-Saharan Africa has actually increased over the decade, partly due to the increase in overall population size.

Immunizations are one of the most important and cost-effective interventions to save children's lives. Every year, nearly three million people die from diseases that could be prevented through immunizations, and most are children under five years old [Global Alliance for Vaccines and Immunization (GAVI), *A Promise to Every Child*, March 2002]. Globally, immunizations currently reach 75 percent of children, short of the 1990 goal of 90 percent. This means that around 30 million of the world's children are still not routinely vaccinated [*We the Children*, ibid.]. The **Global Alliance for Vaccines and Immunization (GAVI)** was created in 1999 as an innovative partnership of governments, international organizations, major philanthropists, research institutions, and the private sector. Through GAVI, these partners work together to encourage renewal of international commitment to equitable access to immunizations that guard all children against major preventable diseases [UNICEF End Decade Databases—Routine Immunization, www.childinfo.org/ eddb/immuni/index.htm]. The Vaccine Fund, developed by GAVI to raise new resources for immunization, provides vaccines and financial support to the 74 poorest countries—those with less than $1,000 GNP per capita—to improve their health systems and introduce newer vaccines such as hepatitis B [GAVI Press Release, February 1, 2002, www.vaccinealliance.org/press/press_release0102a.html and "The Vaccine Fund," www.vaccine alliance.org/reference/vaccinefund.html].

Immunization Plus, one of UNICEF's five strategic priorities for 2002–2005 (to be ratified by the Executive Board), refers to the delivery of a set of essential and cost-effective maternal and child health interventions [www.unicef.org/programme/health/focus/intro. html]. This initiative "aims to ensure routine immunization of children under one year old, at a rate of 90 percent nationally, with at least 80 percent coverage in every district or equivalent administrative unit by 2010" [www.unicef.org/programme/health/focus/ immunization/overview.htm]. By 2005, this initiative seeks to eradicate polio, reduce measles-caused deaths by 50 percent, eliminate maternal and neonatal tetanus, and extend new and improved vaccines to children worldwide [www.unicef.org/programme/health/focus/immunization/overview.htm].

HIV/AIDS

The **HIV/AIDS pandemic** is having a devastating effect on children and those who provide their care. An estimated 8,000 young people become HIV-infected everyday, including approximately 6,000 between the ages of 15 and 24 and 2,000 children under 15 years old [www.unicef.org/aids/people. htm]. A total of 11.7 million children and young people are living with HIV/AIDS [UNAIDS, *Children and Young People in a World of AIDS*, August 2001]. Thus far, 13 million children have been orphaned by AIDS, including nearly 800,000 infants infected each year, 600,000 of whom are infected through mother-to-child transmission [www.gmfc.org//en/fighthiv/learnmore_html and *The State of the World's Children—Official Summary*, April 16, 2002]. Approximately half of all new infections occur among young people.

Sub-Saharan Africa, the hardest hit area, is the epicenter of this disease. Though it is home to only 10 percent of the world's population, it has 70 percent of the world's young people living with HIV/AIDS (8.6 million people), 80 percent of all AIDS deaths, and 90 percent of all AIDS orphans [We the Children, ibid.; www.unicef.org/aids/young.htm]. The disease is spreading rapidly through parts of Asia, eastern Europe, and the Caribbean. The under-five mortality rate (U5MR) due to AIDS in the worst-affected areas is expected to double by 2010 [*Progress since the World Summit*, ibid.].

Given this desperate context, the U.N. Millennium Summit set as an explicit goal the reduction of HIV infection rates in persons 15–24 years old by 25 percent within the most affected countries before the year 2005 and by 25 percent globally by 2010 [UNICEF, *A World Fit for Children*, Draft outcome document of the Special Session, September 10, 2001, p. 18]. More recently, at the **U.N. Special Session on HIV/AIDS** (June 2001), 189 members of the General Assembly approved a **Declaration of Commitment on HIV/AIDS** to achieve several goals by 2005 [GA S-26/2], many of which center on children and youth. Specifically, objectives include reducing HIV prevalence among young people 15–24 by 25 percent in the most affected countries; ensuring that at least 90 percent of young people have access to information, education, and services necessary to reduce their vulnerability to HIV; reducing the proportion of infants infected with HIV by 20 percent (through increased information, counseling, and testing and treatment services available to pregnant women to reduce mother-to-child transmission of HIV) [www.unaids.org/UNGASS/home.html; Progress since the World Summit, ibid.]. Governments have pledged to meet these goals [UNAIDS, "Children and Young People in a world of AIDS," August 2001].

Education

In 1945, the international community approved the constitution of UNESCO, making the commitment to provide "full and equal opportunities for Education for All [EFA]" [ECOSOC High-Level Segment 2002—Issues Note Round Table, New York, February 14, 2002]. More recently, participants at the **World Conference on Education for All** in Jomtien, Thailand, in 1990, pledged to provide primary education for all children. At the **World Education Forum** in Dakar, Senegal, in April 2000, 164 countries adopted the **Dakar Framework for Action**, making a commitment to achieve quality basic education for all by 2015 [www.unesco.org/education/efa/ed_for_all/faq.shtml].

Despite these important commitments to education, nearly 120 million school-age children are still not enrolled in school. One out of every five school-age children in developing countries does not attend school. In sub-Saharan Africa, Southern Asia, and the Arab states, nearly 100 million children, more than 60 percent of them girls, are not in school [UNESCO Press Release, January 28, 2002, embargoed until February 6, 2002]. According to a recent UNESCO report examining the global state of education, an estimated 2 million primary school-age children and 20 million secondary age children in Latin American do not attend school [ibid., www.uis.unesco.org/en/news/news_p/news14.htm]. One-third of all children do not complete five years of schooling, the minimum required for basic literacy [*A World Fit for Children*, the Preparatory Committee for the Special Session of the General Assembly on Children].

An EFA high-level group (comprised of 30 Ministers of Education and of International Cooperation, heads of development agencies, and civil society representatives) was created to help sustain the political momentum created at the World Education Forum [www.unesco.org/ education/efa/ global_co/policy_group/index.shtml]. This group's overriding priority is to help countries achieve the six goals of the Dakar Framework for Action. These are expanding and improving early childhood care and education, ensuring that by 2015 all children have access to and complete free and compulsory primary education of good quality, helping adolescents and youth attain life skills, eliminating gender disparities in education by 2005, achieving gender equality by 2015, and enhancing educational quality [UNESCO Medium-Term Strategy 2002–2007]. To meet the goal of enrolling all children in primary school by 2015, "the world will need to make room for an additional 156 million school-age children" [UNESCO Press Release, October 26, 2001].

Exploitation of Children

Military and economic exploitation of children is rampant worldwide. Some 250 million children between the ages of 5 and 14 work, and the International Labour Organisation (ILO) estimates that 50 to 60 million of them are engaged in intolerable forms of labor [We the Children, ibid.]. Approximately 120 million children work full-time, many for nine or more hours a day. "Almost 80 percent of them earn no money and none of these children attend school. Still another one million children are pulled into the multibillion dollar commercial sex trade" [www.gmfc.org//en/stop/learnmore_html].

There are now 11 million child refugees [We the Children, ibid.]. More than 10,000 children are killed or maimed by landmines every year, and children in at least 68 countries live with the fear of those weapons [ibid.]. Approximately 300,000 children have been recruited in armed conflicts in over 30 countries around the globe [U.S. Senate Foreign Relations Committee, Hearing on U.S. Ratification of the Optional Protocols to the Convention on the Rights of the Child, March 7, 2002]. Children who are among the world's 35 million displaced people are particularly vulnerable to abduction or recruitment as soldiers [We the Children, ibid.]. Worldwide, an estimated 300,000 children are engaged in armed conflict in their countries, with tragic consequences [www.unicef.org/crc/oppro.htm]. These children are often taken from their homes, schools, or refugee camps and forced into combat [UNICEF Joint Press Release, February 12, 2002]. In late February, UNICEF coordinated the demobilization of over 2,500 children between 8 and 18 years of age from the Sudan People's Liberation Army (SPLA) in southern Sudan, airlifting them to transition [www.hrw.org/wr2k2/children.html#Child%20Soldiers]. The process is expected to continue through 2002 until all of the 10,000 SPLA child solders are removed [*Human Rights Watch World Report*, 2002]. UNICEF estimates that more than 2 million children died as a result of war in the last decade, and another 12 million have been left homeless [UNICEF Press Release, July 26, 2000].

International Legal Protection

Violations of children's rights were widespread in 2001. Children were beaten, tortured, and forced to work long hours under hazardous conditions. "Millions crossed international borders in search of safety or were displaced within their own countries. Hundreds of thousands served as soldiers in armed conflicts" [www.hrw.org/wr2k2/children.html#Child%20Soldiers]. The **Convention on the Rights of the Child (CRC)**, adopted in 1989, effectively elevated children's rights to a central place "on the world's agenda by being the most ratified treaty in the world" [www.hrq.org/children/]. The Convention promises children around the world basic rights (including life, liberty, religious freedom, education, and health care) and protection (from discrimination; economic or sexual exploitation; violence in armed conflict; and torture or cruel, inhuman, or degrading treatment or punishment; among other fundamental freedoms) [www.hrq.org/children/].

Other international legal instruments have been adopted to safeguard children in armed conflict, including the 1999 ILO Convention 182, which prohibits the forced recruitment of children for use in armed conflict. Recently, the plight of children affected by armed conflict has been pushed yet higher on the international political agenda: the first **International Conference on War-affected Children** was held in Winnipeg, Canada, in September 2000. On January 18 and February 12, 2002, two Optional Protocols to the Convention entered into force: one on the sale of children, child prostitution, and child pornography and the other on the involvement of children in armed conflict [www.unicef.org/crc/convention.htm].

The **Optional Protocol on the sale of children, child prostitution, and child pornography** obliges governments to take tangible steps to ensure that adults involved in the exploitation of children are punished; prevent the sale of children, child prostitution, and pornography; and protect the rights of child victims. To date, 92 governments have signed and 18 have ratified the protocol. **The Optional Protocol on the involvement of children in armed conflict** is the first international treaty prohibiting the forced recruitment or participation of children under the age of 18 in armed conflict [www.unicef.org/crc/oppro.htm]. According to Mr. Olara Otunnu, the special representative to the Secretary-General on children and armed conflict, "Children have no place in war and deserve the highest level of international protection to keep them from being used as child soldiers" [UNICEF Joint Press Release, February 12, 2002]. The Protocol represents a new global consensus that children should not be used as instruments of war. Since its adoption by the United Nations, it has been signed by 99 governments and ratified by 16 [U.S. Senate Foreign Relations Committee, Hearing on U.S. Ratification of the Optional Protocols to the Convention on the Rights of the Child, March 7, 2002].

Youth

Youth between the ages of 15 and 24 are most vulnerable to the major threats infringing child rights: HIV/AIDS, sexual exploitation, child labor, and abuses in armed conflict [*The State of the World's Children*, ibid.]. Another growing concern for youth is the alarming incidence of suicide: some 4 million adolescents attempt suicide annually, at least 100,000 successfully. The prevalence of suicide and other self-destructive behaviors among youth, such as drug and alcohol abuse, underscores the necessity for programs designed to address adolescents' needs [*We the Children*, ibid.].

The Fourth Session of the **World Youth Forum of the United Nations** (held in Dakar, August 1–10, 2001, and hosted by the Government of Senegal) had as its central purpose the empowerment of youth to participate more effectively in every aspect of society. (The first and second sessions took place in Vienna, Austria, in 1991 and 1996, and the third in Braga, Portugal, in 1998.) Youth delegates from 85 countries gathered together and produced the **Dakar Youth Empowerment Strategy**. This allowed young people to express their intense concern "about the continued deterioration of the status of youth worldwide, who face growing levels of unemployment, poverty, armed conflict, epidemic diseases, functional illiteracy and substance abuse—among other social and economic challenges" [*Dakar Youth Empowerment Strategy*]. Delegates also called for international attention to ten specific areas: education, information, and communications technology; employment; health and population; hunger, poverty, and debt; environment and human settlements; social integration; culture and peace; youth policy, participation, and rights; young women and girls; and youth, sports, and leisure-time activities [Press Release, SOC/4582, August 13, 2001].

Donald Charumbira, Secretary-General of the World Youth Forum and Chairperson of the Forum's fourth session, called it "a landmark meeting with the important task of drafting the Dakar Youth Empowerment Strategy as a set of concrete recommendations for youth empowerment." He said that one of the most important developments during the Forum was the adoption of a special annex on HIV/AIDS, which indicated the commitment and dedication of the world's youth to tackling this major health challenge [Press Release, SOC/4582, August 13, 2001].

5. Ageing
By Eric Wiideman

The Looming Agequake

Few subjects of global concern are as ubiquitous, compelling, and demanding of our attention as the subject of ageing. The raw statistics of ageing are astonishing. The United Nations estimates that there are approximately 629 million people in the world today over the age of 60, or about one out of every ten persons. By 2050, that ratio will become one out of every five persons; by 2150, one out of every three. Human life expectancy has climbed approximately 20 years since 1950. Men who have already reached the age of 60 can expect to live another 17 years; women another 20. The majority of older persons are women, and there are approximately 81 men for every 100 women over the age of 60. Among persons over the age of 80, there are 53 men for every 100 women [www. un.org/esa/socdev/ageing]. The United Nations now faces the staggeringly complex implications of an increasingly older world population that is diminishingly self-sufficient. The looming *agequake* poses imminent challenges on every level, sending tremors across social, cultural, political, and economic systems, policies, and beliefs.

U.N. Response to Ageing

Transcending singular categorization within the U.N. framework, the enormous significance of ageing is a growing focus of U.N. action. The issue of ageing first appeared on the international agenda in 1982, when member states met in Vienna for the World Assembly on Ageing. This gathering produced the **International Plan of Action on Ageing**, which outlines 62 recommendations for action involving health, nutrition, protection, housing and environment, family, social welfare, income security, employment, and education. Nine years later, the General Assembly adopted the **U.N. Principles for Older Persons in 1991**, which addresses independence, participation, care, self-fulfillment, and dignity of older persons.

From April 8 to 12, 2002, Madrid hosted the **Second World Assembly on Ageing** on the 20th anniversary of the first, held in Vienna. Preparatory meetings leading up to the second assembly reviewed and analyzed priority areas for policy action, successes and failures of the 1982 International Plan of Action, and suggestions for the updated International Plan of Action to be derived from the Madrid assembly [www.un.org/esa/socdev/ ageing].

With the support and advice of experts invited by the U.N. secretariat, government, and NGO consultations, the preparatory meetings isolated issues that require special attention within an integrated policy to provide for:

- protection of the rights of elderly persons to contribute to and benefit from society;
- reorientation of the profile of contribution by the elders so as to counter their image as a dependent population;
- development of a nondiscriminatory framework of policy that would root out preconceived biases and prejudices surrounding old age;

- continued growth of interactions and interdependence between generations so as to strike a balance between traditional and new approaches;
- generational opportunities that enable members of the older population to enrich their lives;
- implementation of macro-level decisions by ensuring support not only in family and community environments, but also in social, economic, and cultural institutions.

One noteworthy consultation preceding the Second World Assembly on Ageing was the South Asian Association for Regional Cooperation (SAARC) Consultation hosted by the International Federation on Ageing (IFA) in collaboration with the government of India. In presentations by attendees from India, Bangladesh, Nepal, Sri Lanka, Maldives, and Bhutan, it was poignantly noted that ageing is not a subject that generates wide interest, thereby posing challenges to funding. Also, while older persons may share the commonality of old age itself, their needs and characteristics are far from homogenous, so that efforts to address their disparate requirements must be integrated among governments, NGOs, and communities. Therefore, the challenges remain to generate interest in and attention to the subject of ageing and to ensure that interest and attention is properly integrated among the actors.

International Plan of Action on Ageing 2002

The International Plan of Action on Ageing 2002 is built around a number of central themes that have their roots in previous U.N. declarations, commitments, and programs. As such, it addresses:

- security in ageing;
- empowerment of older persons and participation in society;
- opportunities for individual development, self-fulfillment, and well-being;
- economic, social, and cultural rights;
- gender equality;
- intergenerational interdependence, solidarity, and reciprocity;
- health care;
- partnership between all levels of government, civil society, and the private sector; and
- harnessing scientific research and expertise to focus on the individual, social, and health implications of ageing [www.un.org/esa/socdev/ageing].

In and of itself, the plan is an ambitious step forward in the study and analysis of the subject of ageing and provides a pragmatic guide for further examination and action.

The fundamental goal of the 2002 Plan is to "ensure that persons everywhere are able to age with security and dignity, and to continue to participate in their societies as citizens with full rights" [Advance unedited copy, Madrid, International Plan of Action on Ageing 2002, April 12, 2002]. With this goal in mind, it provides specific recommendations for action to establish a context within which older persons may contribute fully and benefit equally from development. Concretely, the recommendations for action are organized in three priority directions: development, health and well-being, and resource mobilization.

Priority Direction I: Development for an Ageing World

Based on the premise that no individual should be denied the opportunity to benefit from development, Priority Direction I highlights the socioeconomic impact of population ageing. Accordingly, it urges action to ensure the integration and empowerment of older persons in society through active participation in "social, economic, cultural, sporting, recreational and volunteer activities [that] contribute to the growth and maintenance of personal well-being" [International Plan of Action on Ageing, 2002]. Moreover, it outlines specific objectives regarding the (1) recognition of the social, cultural, economic, and political contribution of older persons and (2) participation of older persons in decision-making processes at all levels [ibid.].

Priority Direction II: Advancing Health and Well-Being into Old Age

Recognizing that all persons, regardless of age, are entitled to full access to preventive and curative health care, Priority Direction II outlines fundamental strategies for promoting and ensuring well-being among older persons. Specifically, it focuses on regional health care considerations, early intervention to prevent or delay the onset of disease, proper nutrition, and access to health-care services [ibid.].

Priority Direction III: Ensuring Enabling and Supportive Environments

Focused on the realization of the goals outlined in the International Plan of Action, Priority Direction III iterates the need for the "mobilization of domestic and international resources for social development" to enable all countries to implement the Plan's specific recommendations. As many developing nations are excessively burdened by debt, they would not be able to afford financial support for social development programs, such as those outlined in the International Plan of Action, without additional resources [ibid.].

Social and Economic Participation of Older Persons

In many societies, older persons have been and continue to be marginalized as liabilities, rather than respected as assets to their respective communities. The diminished perception of the social significance of older persons leads to the fallacious and dehumanizing notion that their contribution to society is not substantive and that they therefore deserve to benefit less from its rewards. This misperception is compounded by the erosion of family support systems, frail social security schemes, and cultural influences that idealize and favor youth. The United Nations has noted that older persons represent a resource to society that transcends their economic contribution [ibid.]. Older persons play indispensable roles in family structures, helping to raise children and maintain households. They pass on their tremendous wealth of knowledge, experience, and expertise in volunteering their time and energy to their families and local communities. Furthermore, as the population of older persons increases, their positive and unobstructed contributions to society will become nothing short of imperative, which has inspired and mandated at least a portion of the U.N. recommendations for action relative to ageing. Ensuring that older persons are protected, active in society, and able to receive all of the benefits they deserve are basic preconditions for any successful ageing policy.

Traditional social welfare systems, particularly in Japan, the United States, and western Europe, are already straining under the pressure of an increasing elderly population and a decreasing working-age population needed to support them. Accordingly, the United Nations recommends engaging older persons in active lifestyles to stimulate and enhance their economic contribution, as well as promote their health and well-being. In keeping with the U.N. mission *toward a society for all ages*, greater economic participation among older persons would reinforce their perceived value in communities; ease the burden on already overburdened social welfare schemes; and promote the dignity, independence, and self-fulfillment that older persons most assuredly want and deserve.

Ageing and Gender: The Feminization of Poverty

Unfortunately, the struggle to maintain dignity and independence in old age is more pronounced among older women. Women are far more likely to be marginalized than older men and are often perceived as weak and ineffective. The misguided belief that older women have less to contribute to communities, families, or individuals, overlooks their long experience as domestic caregivers or work force professionals.

Grievous disparities in "economic power-sharing, unequal distribution of unremunerated work between women and men, [and] lack of technological and financial support" [ibid.] have contributed to a so-called **feminization of poverty**. While increasing numbers of older women find themselves without traditional family support structures, many find their poverty exacerbated by cultural norms that resist their economic empowerment. Furthermore, as women tend to live longer than men, older women will increasingly find themselves isolated, particularly in regions where their socioeconomic worth and capacity for self-reliance are actively dismissed.

Recognizing the special requirements of older women, the United Nations addresses the feminization of poverty in its International Plan of Action on Ageing 2002 under the broader pretext of the "eradication of poverty among older persons." The 2002 Plan, however, lacks specific steps to reverse the *feminization of poverty,* protect older women, and reinforce and achieve their positive socioeconomic contribution. The gender dimension of ageing remains a subject that deserves particular, special, and immediate consideration.

An Ongoing Challenge

Unlike some other issues of global concern, ageing is not an issue that can be approached with a single methodology within a single context, nor can it even be perceived as having a beginning or end. With continuing advances in biomedical technology and health care, human beings will quite likely be able to live even longer than our most generous estimates predict. As such, ageing will present an ongoing challenge to future generations. The issues of welfare schemes, socioeconomic participation, self-fulfillment, and education for older persons are just beginning to receive the serious attention called for in the context of the looming agequake. The immense impact of global ageing (and the enormous resources and commitment necessary to respond effectively) is likely to feature prominently on the U.N. agenda over the coming years, as the imperative intensifies for older persons to become active, contributing participants in society.

6. Disabled Persons
By Eric Wiideman

Though often represented and approached as an isolated and homogenous group, disabled persons are far more diverse. Their disabilities include vastly different conditions, such as mental illness, visual and speech impairments, and amputation from landmines. Their particular requirements reflect this broad range of experience and disability. One out of every ten persons in the world, or just over 500 million people, is either physically or mentally disabled. In developing regions, where less resources are available to address their requirements, as many as one out of every five persons is disabled, leaving nearly 50 percent of families affected by disability of one form or another.

The World Health Organization (WHO) defines *disability* as "any restriction or lack (resulting from an impairment) of an ability to perform an activity in the manner or within the range considered normal for a human being" [www.un.org/esa/socdev]. *Impairment* is defined as "any loss or abnormality of psychological, physiological, or anatomical structure or function" [ibid.]. *Handicap* is defined as "a disadvantage for a given individual, resulting from an impairment or disability that limits or prevents the fulfillment of a role that is normal, depending on age, sex, social, and cultural factors, for that individual" [ibid.].

A Growing Movement

Over the last 30 years, the United Nations, its specialized agencies, and nongovernmental organizations have devoted increasing attention to the plight of disabled persons. Through numerous recommendations, reports, declarations, and resolutions, the United Nations has placed the ultimate onus of responsibility for their support and protection on individual governments. It has also formulated a set of clear, actionable steps upon which governments may base policy to ensure an equal and equitable social, economic, and political footing for their disabled populations.

The impetus within the United Nations to address the needs of disabled persons evolved out of a greater concentration on human rights throughout the Organization. The U.N. Educational, Scientific and Cultural Organization (UNESCO), for example, provided special education campaigns; WHO provided technical assistance in health and prevention; the U.N. Children's Fund (UNICEF) developed childhood disability programs [www.un.org/esa/socdev]; and many other organizations soon followed suit. In the 1970s, the U.N. General Assembly adopted the **Declaration on the Rights of Mentally Retarded Persons**, which sought to ensure the rights of the mentally retarded in the medical, educational, and social fields. The ***Declaration on the Rights of Disabled Persons***, adopted by the General Assembly in 1975, proclaimed "the equal civil and political rights of disabled persons and [set] the standard for equal treatment and access to services which help to develop capabilities of persons with disabilities and accelerate their social integration" [www.un.org/esa/socdev].

These declarations, along with many parallel NGO efforts, raised the profile of the issue of disabled persons, leading in part to the proclamation of 1981 as the International Year of Disabled Persons. This commemorative year initiated a flurry of research and campaign projects, culminating in the World Programme of Action (WPA), to address the plight of the world's disabled population. Adopted in December 1982 by the General Assembly, the WPA represented a dramatic step forward in recognition of and reaction to the issue of disabled persons.

The World Programme of Action

Undergoing its fourth fifth-year review in 2002, the WPA's mission is two-fold: (1) to ensure the full and equal participation of disabled persons in society and (2) to present strategies for the prevention, rehabilitation, and equalization of opportunities for this diverse group of individuals. Its strategies for the prevention of disabilities include the avoidance of war; improvement of the educational, economic, and social status of the least privileged groups; identification of types of impairment and their causes; introduction of specific intervention measures through better nutritional practices; improvement of health services, early detection, and diagnosis; prenatal and postnatal care; proper health-care instruction, including patient and physician education; family planning; legislation and regulations; modification of lifestyles; selective placement services; education regarding environmental hazards; and the fostering of better informed and strengthened families and communities.

The WPA's measures for rehabilitation include early detection, diagnosis, and intervention; medical care and treatment; social, psychological, and other types of counseling and assistance; training in self-care activities; provision of technical and mobility aids and other devices; specialized education services; and vocational rehabilitation services, training, and placement in open or sheltered employment.

Following the International Decade of Disabled Persons (1983–1994), which was set up to allow governments and organizations a time frame within which they could implement the WPA recommendations, the General Assembly adopted the Standard Rules of Equalization of Opportunities for Persons with Disabilities. The Standard Rules serve as an ethical and political construct on which governments may elevate the status and lives of disabled persons to "ensure that girls, boys, women and men with disabilities, as members of their societies, may exercise the same rights and obligations as others" [www.un.org/esa/socdev].

Translating Rights into Reality: Toward a Society for All

By and large, U.N. initiatives for the protection, rehabilitation, and equalization of opportunities for disabled persons continue to be focused on human rights. Translating the human rights of disabled persons into "specific measures and programmes," however, is a major challenge and will remain so for quite some time [www.un.org/esa/socdev].

Secretary-General Annan remarked, in his message on the International Day of Disabled Persons, December 3, 2001, that "much has been accomplished, but the world continues its struggle to create societies in which disabled persons enjoy the same opportunities as other members of the human family." In keeping with a growing concentration on the *full participation and equality* of disabled persons, the theme of the 2001 International Day of Disabled Persons, the United Nations and its specialized agencies have begun to focus more on the notion of accessibility—specifically with respect to communications technology. Further, the Organization is promoting the "mainstreaming" of the issue of disabled persons. Adding a "disability dimension" into a wider variety of social and economic concerns may give it more prominence and thereby assist in greater and broader fulfillment of the special needs of the disabled.

One of the guiding themes of the United Nations, *toward a society for all*, resonates throughout its efforts and recommendations relating to disabled persons. Whether working toward the equalization of opportunities, rehabilitation, or protection (as outlined in the array of recommendations put forth in the WPA), the Organization's commitment to enriching and engaging the lives of disabled persons is profound and concrete. Secretary-General Annan pointedly remarked that "people who have to fight daily to overcome not only their disability but also the discrimination they face" possess an uncommon resolve and strength of character. He added that our troubled world needs these people to contribute their skills and ideas; they should enjoy our full respect and support.

Guiding individual governments to protect the human rights of the disabled and to engage and integrate disabled persons into more active and respected roles in societies will require innovative approaches. Ultimately, it will take the commitment of individual governments to ensure fundamental human rights and implement measures for prevention, rehabilitation, and equalization of opportunities for disabled persons. The United Nations has expressed its willingness to provide technical, financial, or other support to assist governments in achieving *a society for all*. Perhaps, as the disability dimension is incorporated into a broader array of social and economic concerns, nations that neglect their disabled populations will become more the anomaly than the norm.

VI

Law and Justice

By Mark A. Drumbl

International law promotes civility among nations, weaves a universal culture of human rights, regulates global public goods, and encourages transparency in international governance. Moreover, international law is a flexible and dynamic field, responding over the past year to new (and diverse) developments such as warlike terrorist attacks by nonstate actors (as in the September 11, 2001, attacks on the United States), electronic commerce, and the possibility of the cloning of humans. In terms of international criminal law, the ad hoc criminal tribunals addressing mass atrocity in Rwanda and the former Yugoslavia continue to issue watershed judgments, and the Rome Statute of the International Criminal Court now has received the requisite number of signatures for it to promptly enter into force. To be sure, as the level of U.N. legal intervention increases, so, too, does the number of U.N.-related legal institutions. In fact, there has been a proliferation of dispute resolution entities within the U.N. system. This creates a palette that includes the ad hoc tribunals, special courts for Sierra Leone, U.N.-assisted courts for Kosovo and East Timor, the nascent International Criminal Court, the International Tribunal for the Law of the Sea, and the International Court of Justice. Although each of these entities has a different mandate, overlap of subject matter may prove to be unavoidable. Accordingly, it will be important for these various entities, which are not hierarchically arranged, to acknowledge each other's activities. This would assist international law in developing in a principled, orderly, and predictable manner, instead of in a destabilized, splintered one.

Activity within international law has not been limited to the highly politicized areas of human rights, terrorism, crimes against humanity, and genocide. Equally steadily, although perhaps somewhat more quietly, international law is crystallizing obligations and defining responsibilities in diverse areas. Specifically, recent developments in international law address state responsibility for wrongful acts, prevention of harm relating to hazardous activities, boundary delimitations, international environmental governance, the professional responsibility of lawyers appearing before international tribunals, transnational contracts, and rights to consular assistance.

1. The United Nations and International Terrorism

Following the appalling terrorist attacks that took place in the United States on September 11, 2001—in which approximately 3,000 civilians were killed—international terrorism became an important subject for discussion during the 56th session of the U.N. General Assembly and also during Security Council deliberations. Although international terrorism previously had been a central focus for international law and international institutions, this focus developed an increased urgency in the wake of the September 11 attacks. Evidence indicates that the attacks were orchestrated and carried out by members of al-Qaeda, a nonstate actor with links to the Taliban, the government of Afghanistan at the time.

The Security Council generally pushes for international solutions to global scourges such as terrorism. However, the Secretary-General concluded that the U.S. and U.K. military intervention in Afghanistan (which began on October 7, 2001) was set in the context of prior Security Council resolutions that condemned terrorism and referenced the right of nations to individual or collective self-defense [see Secretary-General's statements, available at www.un.org/News/ossg/latestsm.htm]. Moreover, the Security Council also recognized the intertwined nature of the Taliban, al-Qaeda, and the fact that the Taliban permitted al-Qaeda to use the territory of Afghanistan for its own purposes in propagating terrorism [S/Res/1378, November 14, 2001]. Nonetheless, the Security Council never explicitly nor unambiguously authorized the use of force in Afghanistan. At the same time, neither the United States nor the United Kingdom requested Security Council authorization, relying instead on their inherent right of self-defense under Article 51 of the U.N. Charter [S/Res 1368, September 12, 2001; S/Res/1373, September 28, 2001].

Moreover, a large number of nations supported this intervention. Some, in fact, sent troops and equipment. This, too, suggests a growing elasticity in state practice regarding self-defense, such that self-defense could extend to attacks not initiated by a state per se, but by nonstate actors. (In this case, al-Qaeda is a nonstate actor whose conduct the Security Council has attributed to the Taliban and, thereby, to the state of Afghanistan.) It also may suggest a greater breadth to self-defense. Indeed, the U.S. Ambassador to the United Nations, John D. Negroponte, informed the Security Council that the United States, acting in self-defense, could go beyond Afghanistan and take "further actions with respect to other organizations and other states" in combating terrorism [Tim Weiner in *New York Times*, October 10, 2001].

These developments also may reveal an expansion in the legal understanding of "war" or "armed conflict," which traditionally has been limited to interstate conflict, as well as the sanction that can be visited upon a state for its connection to individual perpetrators of terrorism. It may well be that nonstate actors now present as significant a threat to national security interests as do state actors and, as such, international law must be responsive to these changes in the modalities of "warfare" in order to retain legitimacy and relevance. On the other hand, another important function for law is to restrict action by insisting on sober, second thoughts undertaken with a view to the proverbial "big picture."

Classically, the Security Council is to have primary responsibility within the U.N. system for maintaining international peace and security. The Security Council is to determine the existence of threats to international peace, make recommendations or take enforcement measures to address those threats, and establish peacekeeping initiatives. The Security Council has 15 members: 5 of which are permanent, and 10 of which are elected for two-year terms. Although decisions on substantive matters require nine votes, a negative vote by any permanent member is sufficient to defeat any proposed motion. This is what is commonly referred to as the "veto power" of a permanent member. It may be that the "policing" powers of the Security Council are diminishing in light of the expansion of coalition-based military interventions in situations when there are serious breaches or threats to international peace and security.

By way of example, the deployment of force without explicit Security Council authorization arguably occurred in Kosovo in 1999 (albeit for humanitarian purposes) and, as discussed previously, in Afghanistan in 2001 (albeit for self-defense purposes). This may reflect the difficulties traditional international law may have with regulating matters internal to nations (e.g., systemic human rights abuses committed against Kosovo Albanians by the Yugoslav government) or attacks launched by nonstate actors (e.g., al-Qaeda). Moreover, even in cases when the use of force was authorized explicitly, such as the 1991 Gulf War, a new development has occurred. In this case, the Security Council turned to member states to actually take enforcement action under Chapter VII of the U.N. Charter [Christine Gray in *European Journal of International Law*, Vol. 13, No. 1 (2002), p. 1].

At the time of writing, the use of force against Iraq once again appears imminent. However, this time around, it is unclear whether Security Council authorization will be sought prior to any deployment of force. Over the course of the past year, U.S. and U.K. official commentary has suggested that the interests of global security would be promoted were the Saddam Hussein regime to be toppled [Thom Shanker and David E. Sanger in *New York Times*, April 28, 2002]. Any military intervention in Iraq or military support of those Iraqis who may oppose the Hussein government gives rise to a number of important legal questions. Would military involvement flout the principle of sovereignty and non-intervention intrinsic to the U.N. Charter? Would it make a difference if the intervention were unilateral or orchestrated through a broad multilateral coalition? Would the cause motivating the intervention matter? For example, could intervention be justified in response to Hussein's domestic rights abuses, such as arbitrary execution, persecution, torture, and forced relocation [*The Globe and Mail*, October 23, 2001]? Would it be justified to base intervention on self-defense regarding Hussein's alleged possession and development of weapons of mass destruction, including chemical and biological weapons? Could national or coalition use of force be based on Iraq's protracted noncompliance with weapons inspections in the country? If so, this might represent the "nationalization" of U.N. peace enforcement functions, which, theoretically, are to be carried out by U.N.-supervised military intervention.

Iraq has, in fact, refused U.N. weapons inspectors entry into the country since December 1998, in defiance of U.N. Security Council Resolutions [for a general discussion, see *A Global Agenda: Issues/56*, pp. 291–92]. Iran has remained subject to U.N. arms inspections since the 1991 Gulf War, but inspectors left in 1998. Iraq also remains subject to economic sanctions, as well as aerial patrols and occasional bombing from U.K. and U.S. planes in the "no-fly zones" located in the northern and southern parts of the country [*The Globe and Mail*, August 27, 2001; *New York Times* August, 10, 2001]. These, too, rest on pronouncements of implicit, as opposed to explicit, authorization of the use of force by the United Nations. The basis of this authorization has given rise to some controversy within the Security Council. Also in relation to Iraq, the U.N. Compensation Commission (UNCC), which was established in 1991 as a subsidiary organ of the Security Council, continues to pay out funds to successful claimants [Christine Gray in *European Journal of International Law*, Vol. 13, No. 1 (2002), p. 1]. The UNCC determines, supervises, and distributes compensation for losses and damages suffered from August 2, 1990, to March 2, 1991, by individuals, corporations, governments, and international organizations as a direct result of Iraq's unlawful invasion and occupation of Kuwait [S/Res/687/1991; S/Res/692/1991].

Criminal justice responses to terrorism could operate on multiple levels: national courts, military commissions, international courts, specially negotiated courts, or U.N.-assisted tribunals. A specially negotiated court, the Scottish High Court of Justice, sitting at Camp Zeist (a former U.S. military base) in the Netherlands, convicted Abdel Basset Ali al-Megrahi, a former Libyan secret serviceman, in January 2001, for the Lockerbie bombing (Pan Am flight 103) [*Her Majesty's Advocate v. al-Megrahi and Fhimah*, Case No. 1475/99, available at www.scotcourts.gov.uk/html/lockerbie.htm]. That same court then acquitted a co-defendant, al-Amine Khalifa Fhimah. The conviction was upheld on appeal in March 2002 [CNN, March 14, 2002]. After departing London's Heathrow airport, flight 103 exploded over Lockerbie,

Scotland, on December 21, 1988, killing 270 people [*New York Times*, January 31, 2001]. The siting of the court in the Netherlands was deliberate. The two defendants had to be extradited through a delicate procedure, and Libyan leader Ghaddafi felt that a Scottish court sitting extraterritorially was a sufficiently neutral location to provide a fair trial [ibid., January 23, 2002].

Al-Megrahi's appeal was heard at Camp Zeist by a panel of five Scottish judges. Al-Megrahi was unable to discharge his burden of proof that the conviction was a miscarriage of justice or to present significant new evidence that could not have been heard in the initial trial, these being the standards required under Scottish law to quash a conviction. Al-Megrahi remains sentenced to life imprisonment, which he will serve in the Barlinnie prison in Scotland [CNN, March 14, 2002].

At trial, the judges held that it had been "amply proved" that the cause of the Pan Am crash was the explosion of a device from within the aircraft [*Her Majesty's Advocate v. al-Megrahi and Fhimah*, para. 2]. This explosive device, accompanied with a Swiss timer, had been placed in a Toshiba radio cassette player located in a suitcase that had also contained clothing. This suitcase traveled unaccompanied from Malta to London (Heathrow), via Frankfurt, where it was placed as tagged on Pan Am flight 103, destined for New York. The Appeals Court was not persuaded by new evidence raised by al-Megrahi that there was a break-in at London's Heathrow airport on the eve of the explosion. Some new evidence came in the form of depositions by Heathrow security guards [*The Globe and Mail*, February 14, 2002]. Apparently, a padlock had been forced on a secure door near a baggage build-up area where luggage for flight 103 was stored prior to take-off. The defense was unaware of this evidence at the time of trial, and the prosecution did not pursue this information, despite having interviewed a security guard after the bombing [*New York Times*, January 23, 2002]. According to the defense, this could lead to an inference that the bomb was placed on the flight in London, not in Malta, thereby casting reasonable doubt on the prosecutor's theory that al-Megrahi was responsible for placing the bomb on the flight. Ultimately, this argument was rejected.

As mentioned earlier, national courts have also been involved in prosecuting terrorists. U.S. courts have prosecuted some of those responsible for the African Embassy bombings in 1998 and the World Trade Center bombing in 1993. Military commissions may also be invoked to combat terrorism, including those to be established for prosecution of individuals detained by the United States at Guantanamo Bay, Cuba. At the time of writing, it remains unclear when these commissions would begin their work and precisely how they would proceed.

International treaties, many of which have been negotiated under U.N. auspices, also form part of antiterrorism strategies. The International Convention for the Suppression of Terrorist Bombings (entered into force on May 23, 2001) criminalizes and creates jurisdiction for, inter alia, unlawfully and intentionally detonating an explosive in a public place and covers those participating in the acts as accomplices or organizers or directors. The International Convention for the Suppression of the Financing of Terrorism (entered into force on April 10, 2002) makes it an offense for a person willfully to provide or collect, directly or indirectly, funds with the intention that these funds be used, in full or in part, to carry out a terrorist act. Following the September 11 tragedies, both of these Conventions saw a rapid increase in the number and rate of ratifications. Other instruments that could be invoked to combat terrorism over the longer term include the Rome Statute for the International Criminal Court, the Biological Weapons Convention, treaties on nuclear proliferation and testing, the Chemical Weapons Convention, and negotiations restricting trade in handguns and small weapons. In the wake of September 11, it may be opportune to seriously revisit these treaties (whether finalized or in draft), so as to improve their effectiveness and implementation.

It also may be timely to encourage the ongoing efforts of the General Assembly, assisted by the International Law Commission and ad hoc working groups, to develop a comprehensive convention on international terrorism and an international convention for the suppression of acts of nuclear terrorism. One of the hurdles to overcome in advancing international antiterrorism agreements is that *terrorism* has proven difficult to define as a legal term. Although the preponderance of terrorist acts are unequivocally criminal, and some may well constitute crimes against humanity, in certain cases it may prove difficult to distinguish between acts of terrorism and the legitimate struggle of peoples for national liberation from colonial and other forms of foreign occupation.

2. The Sixth Committee (Legal), the International Law Commission (ILC), and the U.N. General Assembly

The Sixth Committee (Legal), comprised of governmental delegates and representatives, advises the U.N. General Assembly on issues of international law [U.N. Doc., A/C.6/54/L.1, September 21, 1999]. The General Assembly, of course, is the main deliberative organ of the United Nations and consists of all member states. The Sixth Committee often presents its recommendations to the General Assembly in the form of draft resolutions. It is assisted in this advisory capacity by the **International Law Commission (ILC)**, a body of independent legal experts established in 1947 by the General Assembly to promote the progressive development of international law and its codification.

In fall 2001, the Sixth Committee considered the ILC's Report of the activities of its 53rd session, held in Geneva in a split session from April 23 to June 1 and from July 2 to August 10, 2001 [Summaries of the Work of the Sixth

Committee, Agenda Item 162; A/Res/56/82, January 18, 2002]. During its most recent session, the ILC made progress on a broad array of issues [Report of the ILC on the work of its fifty-third session, www.un.org/law/ilc/index]. Specifically, the ILC worked on the state responsibility for "internationally wrongful acts," prevention of transboundary harm from hazardous activities, formulation of reservations to treaties and interpretative declarations, diplomatic protection, unilateral acts of state, and international terrorism.

The ILC finalized, with commentaries, 59 draft Articles on the **Responsibility of States for Internationally Wrongful Acts**. The Sixth Committee took note of this tremendous accomplishment, for which work initially had begun nearly 50 years ago [Summaries of the work of the Sixth Committee, Agenda Item 162]. The ILC recommended that the General Assembly consider the possibility of convening an international conference of plenipotentiaries to examine these Articles with a view eventually to adopting a convention on the topic. The Articles are to have general application to all areas of international law. They develop a regulatory framework for the obligations states owe one another. Broadly speaking, state responsibility involves the consequences to states of their internationally wrongful activities. State responsibility flows from two sources: "a breach of an international obligation of the state" and (ostensibly, with more significant consequences) "a serious breach (i.e., a gross or systemic failure) of an obligation under a peremptory norm of general international law" [Articles 2, 40(1)]. The language of this latter category was deliberately chosen over the more controversial term "state crime."

The Articles address circumstances precluding wrongfulness (such as consent, self-defense, or necessity), determination of breach, responsibility of a state in connection with the acts of another state, cessation, assurances of nonrepetition, reparations, compensation, which state may invoke a breach of responsibility, countermeasures, procedure to be followed prior to initiating countermeasures, and whether states that are not individually injured can implement countermeasures. The draft Articles also clarify the law regarding the attribution of wrongful conduct to a state; this, of course, is relevant to ascribing responsibility for terrorism committed by nonstate actors. On another note, the availability of countermeasures must be balanced insofar as too restricted an availability may unduly cramp national sovereignty, whereas too generous an availability may roil order in international affairs. Owing to their breadth and comprehensiveness, the draft Articles sparked an energized debate within the Sixth Committee and will likely continue to do so as they progress through the U.N. process.

The ILC also completed draft Articles on the **Prevention of Transboundary Harm from Hazardous Activities** and recommended that a framework convention be elaborated on the basis of these draft Articles. Although the focus here is on prevention, these Articles touch on the broader legal concept of state liability, particularly liability for acts not prohibited by international law. Liability differs from state responsibility insofar as no illegal or wrongful conduct has occurred, although the conduct has triggered harm. Indeed, sometimes non-illegal behavior can have harsh effects on others. One very relevant example is the transboundary environmental harm that may arise from a nation's pursuit of its economic development. In this vein, one observer has noted that developing nations "welcomed the draft Articles on prevention, but emphasized the need to place the entire effort of managing risks of hazardous activities in the overall context of the right to development" [Pemmaraju Sreenivasu Rao in *Environmental Policy and Law*, Vol. 32, No. 1 (2002), p. 28].

By way of overview, the draft Articles apply to activities not prohibited by international law that involve a risk of causing significant transboundary harm [Article 1]. Central to the Articles is the obligation of due diligence [Article 3]. The content of due diligence is that which is generally considered to be appropriate and proportional to the degree of risk of transboundary harm in the case in question. This necessitates a state's properly informing itself of factual and legal components that relate in a foreseeable manner to the activities contemplated and, moreover, a correlative obligation to take appropriate responsive measures in a timely fashion. A contextual analysis—accounting for a state's economic level—is appropriate in determining whether the obligation of due diligence has been complied with. But, on the other hand, a state's economic level cannot be used to exempt a state from its obligations.

The draft Articles also require states to authorize hazardous activity prior to the initiation of that activity. There is thus an important procedural aspect to the Articles that parallels obligations in domestic law for the undertaking of impact assessments before commencing projects that could have deleterious effects on the environment. The precautionary principle and the polluter-pays principle are noted, although neither is suggested as a strict legal obligation [Article 10]. When this risk assessment is likely to cause significant transboundary harm, the state of origin is to provide notification and information to other states that are likely to be affected [Articles 6 to 13]. Moreover, the obligation to inform extends not only to the state, but also to the populations likely to be exposed to the risk involved (regardless of whether that population is in the state of origin or not) [Article 13]. Foreign nationals are to be provided with access to domestic judicial and quasi-judicial fora in order to pursue remedies [Article 15]. The Articles provide for compulsory fact-finding in any dispute between states, in the event that there is not a mechanism already established by mutual agreement or another obligatory mechanism of dispute resolution.

These Articles were well received by the Sixth Committee, although some concerns were expressed that they did not cover areas beyond national jurisdiction (e.g., the global commons). Going beyond the draft

Articles on prevention, the General Assembly requested the ILC to undertake, at its 54th session, consideration of the liability aspects of transboundary harms, bearing in mind the interrelationships between prevention and liability [A/Res/56/82, January 18, 2002]. For the moment, it remains unclear whether the Articles on prevention will move forward on their own or as part of a broader legal instrument in which liability is also addressed.

The Sixth Committee expressed support for the ILC's draft guidelines regarding the formulation of **reservations to treaties and interpretative declarations**. These are to supplement ambiguities that inhere in preexisting international treaties and customs. The ILC also referred draft guidelines dealing with form and notification of reservations and interpretative declarations to a drafting committee. One contentious issue is the merit of and procedure for "late" reservations. Precisely defining the scope of a reservation is important: although reservations permit states the flexibility to sign onto a treaty even though they may not agree with all of its contents, too broad a reading of reservations will create porousness within conventional international law. Moreover, it is also important to distinguish the rules governing reservations from those governing interpretive declarations. Many important multilateral treaties—for example, the Rome Statute of the International Criminal Court and certain global environmental treaties—forbid reservations. Such treaties do permit declarations. As such, it is essential to clearly distinguish declarations from reservations so that the scope of declarations does not defeat the rationale behind forbidding reservations.

The ILC considered the topic of **diplomatic protection**, which has formed part of its work for a number of years. Here, the ILC is codifying existing customary rules. This past year, the ILC dealt with questions of continuous nationality and the transferability of claims. The General Assembly has called for all governments to submit relevant national legislation, decisions of domestic courts, and state practice relevant to diplomatic protection in order to assist the ILC with its codification project [A/Res/56/82, January 18, 2002]. There is some conceptual overlap between diplomatic protection and the broader legal issue of the nationality of natural persons in relation to the succession of states, in which the ILC is also engaged. The ILC has prepared draft Articles on the nationality question, although these attach to a much longer-term project. Among other things, these Articles strive to avoid citizens' becoming stateless as nation-states dissolve, unify, have a region separate, otherwise alter their boundaries, or simply see themselves ruled by a successor regime. Last year, the Sixth Committee recommended that the General Assembly include this issue in the agenda of its 59th Session [Summaries of the Work of the Sixth Committee, Agenda Item 160, November 16, 2000; see also GA/Res/55/153, December 12, 2000]. The General Assembly approved this recommendation.

The ILC's work in the area of **unilateral acts of states** met with some resistance by the Sixth Committee [Summaries of the work of the Sixth Committee, Agenda Item 162]. The view was expressed that developing a body of rules applicable to all unilateral acts may not be well founded. Therefore, it was argued that no further work should take place on the elaboration of draft articles until a new methodology is adopted [ibid.]. Other members supported the work of the ILC. To be sure, it is a challenge to develop common rules of classification applicable to all unilateral acts given the diversity of unilateral acts. Another complexity is the distinction between the form of a unilateral act and the effect or interpretation thereof. Furthermore, it is unclear what importance is to be ascribed to the silence of a state toward a unilateral act of another in terms of assessing the effect or interpretation of a unilateral act. In the end, the Sixth Committee felt that, before codification regarding unilateral acts (particularly determinations regarding which unilateral acts have legally binding effects) can be made, an adequate analysis of state practice would have to be undertaken. To this end, a questionnaire was circulated to all governments on August 31, 2001 [A/Res/56/82, January 18, 2002]. The purpose of this questionnaire is to define what exactly is a unilateral act of a state as well as survey perspectives regarding what should be the legal effect thereof. This information, in turn, may assist in consolidating greater consensus within the Sixth Committee regarding whether the project should move forward, under what terms, and on what subject matter.

During its 2001 meetings, the Sixth Committee also discussed its support for the establishment of the International Criminal Court, commenting on the "need for globalized justice in the globalized world" [Summaries of the work of the Sixth Committee, Agenda Item 164; see also part 3 of this chapter]. The ILC and Sixth Committee have also been involved in addressing international terrorism. Owing to the events of September 11, 2001, the General Assembly discussed directly in the plenary measures to eliminate international terrorism. These discussions led to a number of resolutions that condemned international terrorism and, ultimately, implicated al-Qaeda and the Taliban. (Part 1 of this chapter details more of the discussion on the U.N. role in combating international terrorism.)

The General Assembly also requested that the ILC begin its work on the topic of the responsibility of international organizations [A/Res/56/82, January 18, 2002]. The ILC is also to begin work on the issue of shared natural resources and expulsion of aliens (although some hesitation was expressed about the inclusion of this latter item in the ILC's agenda). An ad hoc committee established by the General Assembly met for two weeks in 2002 to continue work on a draft convention on jurisdictional immunities of states and their property [for a discussion of the work of the ILC in this area, see *A Global Agenda: Issues/56*, pp. 242–43]. These immunities must be considered in light of the growing participation of states in commercial activities. The 54th session of the ILC is to be held in two split sessions, from April 29 to June 7 and then from July 22 to August 16, 2002, in Geneva [A/Res/56/82, January 18, 2002]. In its 56th session, the General Assembly elected the 34 members of the ILC for a period of five years, beginning on January 2002.

The Sixth Committee established an ad hoc committee to study the elaboration of an international convention against the reproductive **cloning of humans**. The item was included in the agenda of the General Assembly's 56th Session at the request of France and Germany. The impetus for this request was the announcement by certain laboratories of their intention to proceed with the cloning of human beings. Human cloning is feared and perceived by some as a threat to human dignity. Delegates pointed out that the proposed legal instrument would codify the relevant provisions of the Universal Declaration on the Human Genome (adopted by UNESCO in 1997), build upon General Assembly resolution 53/152 (1998), and refer to the Convention on Human Rights and Biomedicine and its Additional Protocol on the Prohibition of the Cloning of Human Beings, developed in the context of the Council of Europe [Summaries of the work of the Sixth Committee, Agenda Item 174].

It was proposed that the Convention consider all of the various purposes of cloning, including therapeutic purposes, and that it should, for example, ban the marketing of services relating to cloning [Summaries of the work of the Sixth Committee, Agenda Item 174]. Some delegates suggested that a more neutral title for the convention be adopted since an outright ban might serve to drive the research underground, making it more difficult to regulate. Other delegates supported extending the scope of the convention to include banning therapeutic cloning, the production of embryos as suppliers of specialized stem cells, and the use of embryos in the treatment of certain illnesses. Needless to say, these are each controversial topics already debated in national politics. The intervention by the United Nations in these hot-button issues demonstrates the ability of international law to adjust to rapid changes in technology and science.

The Sixth Committee also reviewed the Report of the 34th session of the **U.N. Commission on International Trade Law (UNCITRAL)** [Summaries of the Work of the Sixth Committee, Agenda Item 161]. UNCITRAL was established by the General Assembly in 1966 and began its work in 1968. Its mandate is to unify international trade law so as to encourage the globalization of international trade and the free flow of goods [GA/Res/2205(XXI), December 17, 1966]. UNCITRAL's greatest achievements may well be the Vienna Convention on Contracts for the International Sale of Goods (1980) and its Arbitration Rules (1976). UNCITRAL is also involved in providing developing nations with training and assistance in international trade law. At the 56th session of the Sixth Committee, UNCITRAL was congratulated for the successful completion and adoption of its work on the Convention on the Assignment of Receivables in International Trade and the Model Law on Electronic Signatures. A majority of the Sixth Committee called for the adoption of the Receivables Convention by the General Assembly. A majority also invited states to adopt national legislation on the basis of the Model Law: focal points here include the validity of electronic signatures, electronic contracting, on-line dispute settlement, and the dematerialization of title documents and property law instruments. Moreover, the Sixth Committee also encouraged the continuation of UNCITRAL's work in the areas of arbitration, insolvency law, electronic commerce, transport law, security interests, and privately financed infrastructure projects [Summaries of the Work of the Sixth Committee, Agenda Item 161]. The expansion of UNCITRAL's workload has prompted calls to enlarge UNCITRAL membership.

The Sixth Committee considered the scope of legal protection under the Convention on the Safety of United Nations and Associated Personnel [available at www.un.org/law/cod/safety.htm, December 9, 1994]. It urged states to ratify this Convention, particularly given the increase in the numbers of attacks on U.N. personnel in recent years [Summaries of the work of the Sixth Committee, Agenda Item 167]. The Sixth Committee continued its longstanding work relating to the activities of the Special Committee on the Charter of the United Nations and on the Strengthening of the Role of the Organization [Summaries of the Work of the Sixth Committee, Agenda Item 165]. Much of the work of the Special Committee on the Charter involves the topic of economic sanctions. The Sixth Committee urged that sanctions be imposed with great caution and only as an exceptional measure when all other means of peaceful dispute settlement have been exhausted. Another important issue is the question of assistance to third-party states affected by sanctions. Some delegates expressed support for the creation within the U.N. system of a trust fund and permanent mechanism to address the humanitarian, social, and economic problems confronted by third-party states due to sanctions against target states. The Special Committee is also involved in matters other than sanctions. For example, the Russian and Belarus delegations suggested that an advisory opinion from the International Court of Justice be sought on the legality of the use of force without Security Council authorization. This could bear upon the ability of nations to defend themselves outside the parameters of Security Council endorsement. The Sixth Committee also urged the Special Committee to coordinate its work regarding the fundamentals of the legal basis for U.N. peacekeeping operations under Chapter VII of the Charter with the Special Committee on Peacekeeping. Also, Sierra Leone and the United Kingdom presented a working paper on dispute prevention and settlement.

3. Ad Hoc International Criminal Tribunals

The U.N. Security Council has created ad hoc criminal tribunals to punish those responsible for mass atrocity in the former Yugoslavia [the International Criminal Tribunal for the Former Yugoslavia (ICTY)] and in Rwanda [the International Criminal Tribunal for Rwanda (ICTR)]. Although both tribunals operate separate Trial Chambers [the ICTY in The Hague (Netherlands), the ICTR in Arusha (Tanzania)], they share common judges in their Appeals Chambers and a single Chief Prosecutor, Carla Del Ponte of Switzerland. ICTY and ICTR judgments clarify the statutory and general law governing military behavior, human rights, crimes against humanity, and genocide (as well as defenses to these charges). The judgments establish a strong foundation for the incipient International Criminal Court (ICC), a permanent institution established by the Rome Statute of the International Criminal Court. The ICC will have jurisdiction over the most serious crimes of concern to the international community as a whole. However, this jurisdiction will only be prospective. In other words, it will only capture activity that follows the creation of the ICC. Thus, ad hoc approaches will remain necessary until the ICC enters into force.

The International Criminal Tribunal for the Former Yugoslavia (ICTY)

The ICTY was established by Security Council Resolution 827 [May 25, 1993]. Its mandate is to prosecute persons responsible for serious violations of international humanitarian law committed since 1991 on the territory of the former Yugoslavia. As its jurisdiction is open-ended, the ICTY can prosecute offenses occurring after its creation. The ICTY has jurisdiction to prosecute the four clusters of offenses that are set out in its Statute. These include grave breaches of the 1949 Geneva Conventions (Article 2 of the Statute), violations of the laws or customs of war (Article 3), genocide (Article 4), and crimes against humanity (Article 5).

The ICTY has had another busy year, making significant progress in investigations, indictments, detentions, judgments, and appeals. The most newsworthy development at the ICTY is the ongoing trial of **Slobodan Milosevic** (see below), the former Head of State of Yugoslavia, who faces three indictments covering atrocity in Kosovo, Bosnia, and Croatia. Milosevic is widely considered to be the main protagonist behind conflicts among Serbs, Croats, Muslims, and Albanians throughout the 1990s that left approximately 250,000 people dead. The Milosevic trial has been heralded as "Europe's most important war crimes case since the Nuremberg proceedings against Nazi Germany leaders after the Second World War" [*The Globe and Mail*, February 12, 2002]. However, Milosevic is but 1 of 43 accused in custody at the ICTY as of the time of writing; another 8 await trial, but have been provisionally released (akin to parole) [Fact Sheet on ICTY Proceedings, April 2, 2002].

ICTY Judgments of the Trial and Appeals Chambers

Trial Chamber

On August 2, 2001, the Trial Chamber convicted Bosnian Serb General Radislav Krstic of war crimes, crimes against humanity, and genocide for his role in the massacre of 7,000 unarmed Muslim men and boys in Srebrenica, a purported U.N. "safe haven" in eastern Bosnia, in July 1995 [Summary of Krstic Judgment, ICTY Press Release, OF/P/I.S./609-e, August 2, 2001]. This was the first finding of genocide by the ICTY. For the most part, the ICTY has focused on war crimes and crimes against humanity and has characterized "ethnic cleansing" as persecution (a crime against humanity). However, the Srebrenica massacre was seen as particularly egregious and as calling for characterization as genocide, namely an act committed with intent to destroy, in whole or in part, a national, ethnic, racial, or religious group.

In concluding that genocide occurred at Srebrenica, the Trial Chamber had to account for the fact that women, children, and the elderly were transferred and not killed. Only Bosnian men of fighting age were killed. According to Krstic's defense, this fact is one of several militating against a finding of genocide. Nor does it appear that there was a plan to commit genocide in Srebrenica prior to its having fallen under Bosnian Serb control. The Trial Chamber responded to this latter argument as follows: "[A] plan of genocide need not have been formed. Nor is it indispensable that, should such a plan exist, some time must pass between its conception and its implementation" [ibid.]. On the question of whether killing only of men and boys could constitute genocide against a group as a whole, the Trial Chamber concluded:

> At issue is not only the commission of murders for political, racial or religious reasons, which already constitutes a crime of persecution. At issue is not only extermination of the Bosnian Muslim men of fighting age alone. At issue is the deliberate decision to kill the men, a decision taken with complete awareness of the impact the murders would inevitably have on the entire group. By deciding to kill all the men of Srebrenica of fighting age, a decision was taken to make it impossible for the Bosnian Muslim people of Srebrenica to survive. Stated otherwise, what was ethnic cleansing became genocide. [ibid.]

According to the Trial Chamber, the intent to destroy a group means "seeking to destroy a distinct part of the group as opposed to an accumulation of isolated individuals within it. Although the perpetrators of genocide need not seek to destroy the entire group . . . they must view the part of the group they wish to destroy as a distinct entity which must be eliminated as such" [*Krstic Trial Judgment*, para. 590]. This part must have some significance to the survival of the group as a whole: for example, community leaders, intellectuals, or persons with special meaning to the community. The fact that the targeted part of the community in the *Krstic* case were men and boys of military age—and that the crimes, although egregious, were committed on a narrow, regional scale—has prompted one esteemed observer to question whether a genocide conviction is appropriate given that these victims were neither community leaders nor representative figures [William Schabas in *Fordham International Law Journal*, Vol. 25, pp. 45, 47 (2001)].

Krstic was sentenced to 46 years in prison. This is the lengthiest sentence yet issued by the ICTY, demonstrating that genocide indeed may be the "crime of crimes." As of the time of writing, the prosecution and Krstic are appealing the conviction and sentence. This will offer another opportunity for the ICTY Appeals Chamber to pronounce itself on the law of genocide (it has affirmed the Trial Chamber's decision summarily to acquit another indictee, Goran Jelisic, on genocide charges regarding the killing of Muslims in concentration camps in northwest Bosnia). Krstic's conviction will also weigh heavily in the Milosevic genocide prosecution, as well as the eventual prosecution of Bosnian Serb President Radovan Karadzic and Krstic's military commander, Gen. Ratko Mladic, both of whom remain as fugitives from ICTY arrest warrants. The careful historical record built in the *Krstic* judgment of transfers of women, children, and the elderly; of mass executions of men and boys; and of subsequent Serb cover-ups—as well as the forensic evidence thereof—will facilitate subsequent prosecutions regarding the Srebrenica tragedy. On another note, it is important for peacekeeping forces—particularly Dutch forces and the then French U.N. commander for Bosnia—to consider how the Srebrenica safe-haven became overrun by Bosnian Serb forces and why defensive action was not undertaken. Public inquiries in the Netherlands and a parliamentary report in France have been critical of the U.N. forces [*The Globe and Mail*, April 7, 2002]. In fact, the Dutch cabinet, along with the Netherlands' top general, resigned following the publication of a government commissioned report that faulted Dutch peacekeepers for failing to prevent the Srebrenica massacre and for unwittingly engaging in a pattern of conduct that actually facilitated its execution [*The Globe and Mail*, April 16, 2002].

On November 2, 2001, the Trial Chamber issued judgment against Miroslav Kvocka, Mladen Radic, Milojica Kos, Zoran Zigic, and Dragoljub Prcac [ICTY Press Release, CC/P.I.S./631-e, November 2, 2001]. These individuals were accused of crimes against humanity and war crimes committed against Bosnian Muslims and Croats at the Omarska, Trnopolje, and Keraterm concentration camps in the Prijedor municipality in northwest Bosnia. This trial, which had commenced on February 28, 2000, was procedurally complex. In the end, the five accused were sentenced to terms of imprisonment ranging from 5 to 25 years for their participation in what the Trial Chamber called a "hellish orgy of persecution" [ibid.]. All accused have filed notices of appeal. The Trial Chamber concluded that the camps were the result of an intentional policy to impose a system of discrimination against the non-Serb population of Prijedor. Furthermore, it has concluded that the five accused were fully aware of the atrocities committed at the camps (along with the larger persecutorial role that the camps played) and actively participated in that persecution. Zigic, sentenced to 25 years, was singled out as particularly vicious and brutal in his commission of crimes at all three camps.

On March 15, 2002, the Trial Chamber convicted Milorad Krnojelac, the warden of the KP-Dom prison for men in Foca, on two counts of crimes against humanity (persecution) and two counts of violations of the laws and customs of war [ICTY Press Release, JL/P.I.S./663-e, March 15, 2002]. Krnojelac, a Bosnian Serb in the Yugoslav Army reserve, was sentenced to seven-and-a-half years imprisonment. The particulars of the charges against Krnojelac involved beatings, cruel treatment, and inhumane living conditions, all committed in 1992 and 1993 within KP-Dom. The prosecution could not establish that Krnojelac had personally participated in these abuses. Instead, it was submitted that he was part of a joint criminal enterprise to commit the offences charged; he had aided and abetted those who had personally committed the offences; and he was criminally responsible as a superior for the acts of his subordinates [ibid.].

In the end, the Trial Chamber found that he failed to stop guards under his command from abusing hundreds of Muslim detainees and in fact aided and abetted those crimes, but refused to find that he was part of a joint criminal enterprise. As for sentencing, the Trial Chamber found that Krnojelac "expressed no regret for the part he played in the commission of these crimes, and only insubstantial regret that the offences had taken place" [ibid.]. The sentence in this case is intended to make it clear to others who (like the accused) seek to "avoid the responsibilities of command which accompany the position which they have accepted that their failure to carry out those responsibilities will still be punished" [ibid.]. As to mitigating factors, the ICTY took note of the fact that Krnojelac was not well experienced, and perhaps not well suited, for the task that he undertook. The ICTY also noted that his participation in these crimes was limited to aiding and abetting the criminality of others. There was also some evidence presented that he helped individual detainees who had approached him with particular requests, and he attempted to improve the condition of all detainees by securing more food for KP-Dom [ibid.]. Krnojelac and the prosecution have filed a notice of appeal against the judgment on April 12, 2002, and April 15, 2002, respectively.

On November 13, 2001, the ICTY issued its sentencing judgment against Dusko Sikirica, Damir Dosen, and Dragan Kolundzija [ICTY Press Release, CC/P.I.S./635-e, November 13, 2001]. All three previously had pled guilty to one count of persecution, a crime against humanity [ICTY Press Release, SP/P.I.S./620-e, September 19, 2001]. As in the *Kvocka et al.* case, this matter involved command responsibility over the horrors visited upon Bosnian Muslims and Croats near Prijedor in northwest Bosnia in the summer of 1992, specifically at the Keraterm camp. Sikirica was alleged to have been the commander of the Keraterm camp, the other two, shift leaders. Sikirica was sentenced to 15 years imprisonment, Dosen to 5 years, and Kolundzija to 3 years [ICTY Press Release, CC/P.I.S./635-e, November 13, 2001]. All parties have agreed not to appeal these sentences. The convictions and sentences therefore are final. The three convicts admitted responsibility for their crimes in the camp, and also admitted that they had some authority over activities at the camp. In the *Sikirica* case, the Trial Chamber previously had granted a defense motion to dismiss genocide charges after the prosecution's evidence had been heard [ICTY Press Release, XT/P.I.S./615-e, September 6, 2001]. It was following this dismissal that Sikirica agreed to plead guilty to the persecution charge. At the same time, the Trial Chamber had also dismissed the counts charging Dosen with torture, inhumane acts, and cruel treatment [ibid.]. All convicts received credit for time served pending trial; in Kolundzija's case, this means that he has already been released.

The Trial Chamber issued a sentencing judgment in the "Celebici" case [ICTY Press Release, P.I.S./628-e, October 9, 2001]. This case involves events that took place in 1992 in a prison camp near the town of Celebici, in central Bosnia. This part of central Bosnia—predominantly inhabited by Bosnian Serbs—had been taken over by Bosnian Muslim and Bosnian Croat forces. Many of the Bosnian Serb civilian inhabitants were held at the Celebici prison camp. Three defendants (Hazim Delic, Esad Landzo, and Zdravko Mucic) were convicted by the Trial Chamber on October 15, 1998, of grave breaches of the Geneva Conventions (Article 2 of the Statute of the ICTY) and of violation of the laws or customs of war (Article 3 of the Statute of the ICTY). A fourth defendant was acquitted. Appeals were then heard. On February 20, 2001, the Appeals Chamber upheld some of the convictions and suggested some modifications to the sentences [see discussion in *Issues/56*, pp. 252–55]. In particular, the Appeals Chamber dismissed for cumulative convictions all counts charging Mucic, Delic, and Landzo with violations of the laws or customs of war (Article 3 of the ICTY Statute). The question here was whether conduct simultaneously can violate both Article 2 of the ICTY Statute (grave breaches of the Geneva Convention) as well as Article 3 (violation of the laws or customs of war). The Appeals Chamber "held that reasons of fairness to the accused, and the consideration that only distinct crimes justify cumulative convictions, require that cumulative convictions are permissible only if each statutory provision involved has a materially distinct element not contained in the other" [ICTY Press Release, JL/P.I.S. 564-e, February 20, 2001]. If this material distinctiveness is not established, then a judicial decision must be made regarding the offence for which a conviction will be entered. The conviction must be for the offense containing the more specific provision. In a situation such as that faced by some of the Celebici defendants, namely when the evidence establishes guilt based upon the same conduct under both Articles 2 and 3, the conviction must be entered for the offense under Article 2. Accordingly, the Appeals Chamber dismissed the convictions of all counts on violations of the laws or customs of war (Article 3).

In light of this dismissal, the Appeals Chamber remitted the case back to the Trial Chamber for possible adjustment to the original sentences. On October 9, 2001, the Trial Chamber sentenced Delic to 18 years imprisonment, Landzo to 15 years, and Mucic to 9 years. This meant an increase in Mucic's initial sentence (7 years), a reduction in Delic's initial sentence (20 years), and no change in Landzo's initial sentence. The increase in the Mucic sentence arose from a specific suggestion by the Appeals Chamber to this effect. In the end, the Trial Chamber found that the reduction of the accuseds' number of convictions based on the Appeals Chamber decision did not reduce the "totality of their criminal conduct" [ICTY Press Release, P.I.S./628-e, October 9, 2001]. Once again, all three defendants have filed notices of appeal, this time only regarding sentence.

Appeals Chamber
Pursuant to Article 25 of the Statute of the ICTY, the role of the Appeals Chamber is limited to correcting errors of law that invalidate a decision and errors of fact that trigger a miscarriage of justice. Appellants bear the burden of argument in terms of errors of law, although the Appeals Chamber may step in and formulate its own arguments.

The prosecutor's appeal in the matter of Goran Jelisic was issued on July 5, 2001. Jelisic, who called himself the "Serb Adolf," held a position of authority at the Luka Camp, located in Brcko in northeastern Bosnia. From early May until early July 1992, Bosnian Serb forces confined hundreds of Muslims and Croats under inhumane conditions at this camp. Jelisic was indicted on 31 charges of crimes against humanity and violations of the laws and customs of war, along with 1 count of genocide [*Prosecutor v. Jelisic*, IT-95-10-A, *Appeals Judgement*, para. 2 (ICTY App. Chamber, July 5, 2001)]. Allegations were made that Jelisic murdered, tortured, and beat detainees at Luka. He pleaded guilty to the 31 charges, resisting only the genocide charge. On October 19, 1999, the ICTY Trial Chamber acquitted Jelisic on the genocide charge and sentenced him to 40 years imprisonment on the charges to which he had pled guilty [*Jelisic Appeals Judgement*, para. 5]. The lengthy sentence was based on the Trial Chamber's observation of Jelisic's "scornful attitude towards victims, his enthusiasm for committing the crimes, his dangerous nature, and also the inhumanity of the crimes" [ICTY Press Release, JL/P.I.S./454-e, December 14, 1999]. The *Jelisic* trial was the first genocide proceeding undertaken by the ICTY.

The prosecutor appealed the genocide acquittal, and Jelisic appealed the sentence. The ICTY Appeals Chamber affirmed the sentence. The

ICTY Rules provide that a convicted person may be sentenced to imprisonment for a term up to and including the remainder of that person's life. Accordingly, the Trial Chamber has the discretion to impose life imprisonment. The Appeals Chamber held that the ICTY Trial Chamber "has broad discretion as to which factors it may consider in sentencing and the weight to attribute to them" [*Jelisic Appeals Judgement*, para. 100]. The Appeals Chamber found that the Trial Chamber had not exercised this discretion in an erroneous fashion.

As for the prosecutor's appeal, although the Appeals Chamber found some error in the Trial Chamber's treatment of the law, it declined to reverse the genocide acquittal. The Appeals Chamber held that the correct test for determining whether prosecution evidence is insufficient to sustain a conviction "is whether there is evidence (if accepted) upon which a reasonable [trier] of fact could be satisfied beyond reasonable doubt of the guilt of the accused on the particular charge in question" [*Jelisic Appeals Judgement*, para. 37]. Although in this case there was sufficient evidence to allow the genocide case to proceed, the Appeals Chamber held that returning the case back to the Trial Chamber for such a purpose would not be in the interests of justice [*Jelisic Appeals Judgement*, paras. 57, 77]. It therefore declined to reverse the acquittal. As for the law on genocide, the Appeals Chamber clarified that the requisite intent is one to destroy, in whole or in part, a national, ethnic, racial, or religious group through one of the acts prohibited by the Statute of the ICTY. The existence of a plan or policy is not a legal ingredient of the crime of genocide, although it may certainly constitute probative evidence [*Jelisic Appeals Judgement*, para. 48]. This conclusion was relied upon to secure a conviction—notwithstanding absence of a plan—in the *Krstic* Trial Chamber decision discussed previously. However, in practice, it may be difficult to conceive of genocide that is not planned by the state or not part of a state policy or, in the least, not an official plan or policy of an entity or organization tied to a state or seeking control over the state.

On October 23, 2001, in *Prosecutor v. Kupreskic*, the Appeals Chamber restated and, to some extent, reshaped the law concerning standards of review on appeal, especially with regard to errors of fact and admission of new evidence on appeal [IT-95-16-A, *Kupreskic Appeal Judgement* (ICTY App. Chamber, October 23, 2001)]. This is an important clarification given that most Trial Chamber decisions are appealed, often by both prosecution and defendants. As the jurisprudence of the ad hoc tribunals becomes settled, an increasing number of appeals involve the factual bases underpinning Trial Chamber judgments. In the *Kupreskic* case, the Appeals Chamber reversed the convictions of Zoran and Mirjan Kupreskic, two brothers, along with that of their cousin, Vlatko Kupreskic. All three previously had been found guilty by the Trial Chamber of either committing or aiding and abetting persecution as a crime against humanity (and had been sentenced to 10, 8, and 6 years imprisonment, respectively) [for a discussion of the Trial Chamber decision, see *Issues/55*, pp. 233–35]. The Appeals Chamber also reduced the sentences of the remaining two defendants, Drago Josipovic and Vladimir Santic, from 15 to 12 and 25 to 18 years, respectively. All in all, the Appeals Chamber called the trial "critically flawed" [*The Globe and Mail*, October 23, 2001].

The nub of this case involved atrocities committed in 1993 against Bosnian Muslims by Bosnian Croat forces. The crimes were perpetrated particularly in the small village of Ahmici, which was "shelled from a distance . . . then groups of . . . soldiers went from house-to-house attacking Bosnian Muslim civilians and burning their houses, barns and livestock" [ICTY Trial Information Sheet, Kupreskic & Others Case (IT-95-16-T), February 2, 2000]. In total, 116 Bosnian Muslim inhabitants of the village were massacred, 24 other villagers were wounded, and 169 houses (along with two mosques) were destroyed [ICTY Press Release, JL/PIS/462-e, January 14, 2000].

The Appeals Chamber began its analysis by emphasizing that its function is not to carry out a new trial. Instead, it is to consider specific errors of law or fact. Traditionally, errors of law may be more freely reviewed than errors of fact. Claiming an error of law requires identifying the alleged error and advancing some arguments in support of the existence of error. As for errors of fact, the basic standard for review gives deference to the Trial Chamber. However, when the evidence relied on by the Trial Chamber could not reasonably have been accepted by any reasonable person or when the evaluation of evidence at trial was wholly erroneous, the Appeals Chamber "will overturn the conviction since, under such circumstances, no reasonable tribunal of fact could be satisfied beyond reasonable doubt that the accused had participated in the criminal conduct" [*Kupreskic Appeals Judgement*, para. 41]. The Appeals Chamber in *Kupreskic* also pointed out that "what constitutes a 'wholly erroneous' evaluation of the evidence must . . . be determined on a case-by-case basis" [*Kupreskic Appeals Judgement*, para. 225]. The Appeals Chamber may engage in an in-depth reevaluation of evidence in order to make this determination. In the *Kupreskic* case, the Appeals Chamber engaged in such reevaluation because the convictions of some of the accused (e.g., the Kupreskics) rested primarily upon the testimony of a single eyewitness, identified as "Witness H." Without reversing the rule that uncorroborated eyewitness testimony may support a finding of guilt beyond a reasonable doubt, the Appeals Chamber discussed at length cases from both civil and common law countries recognizing problems raised by eyewitness testimony [*Kupreskic Appeals Judgement*, paras. 33–40]. It then undertook an examination of factors that affected the credibility of Witness H. Based on this evaluation, the Appeals Chamber rejected the decision of the Trial Chamber to accept the testimony of Witness H as evidence that could prove the participation of the accused beyond reasonable doubt [*Kupreskic Appeals Judgement*, paras. 222–27].

The Appeals Chamber was convinced that, had the Trial Chamber properly considered all the factors, "it would not have accepted the identification evidence of this single witness as the basis upon which to convict [some of] the Defendants" [*Kupreskic Appeals Judgement*, para. 225].

The Appeals Chamber can also allow new evidence on appeal. Although this is a regular feature of appellate courts in many civil law systems, this practice is often disfavored in the common law. This is a particularly timely issue for the ICTY given that, over the past few years, the changing political climate in some of the states of the former Yugoslavia has resulted in the opening of war archives and the release of documents hitherto unavailable to the parties at trial. If new evidence is admitted, the entire record can then be reexamined to determine whether there has been a factual error that has occasioned a miscarriage of justice [*Kupreskic Appeals Judgement*, para. 44]. The evidence generally must have been unavailable to a reasonably diligent counsel at trial. Admission of the new evidence must be in the interests of justice. In particular, according to the *Kupreskic* decision, "[the] standard for the admission of additional evidence . . . is whether that evidence 'could' have had an impact on the verdict, rather than whether it 'would probably' have done so" [*Kupreskic Appeals Judgement*, para. 68]. And then, as for quashing a Trial Chamber decision, the relevant standard is whether no reasonable tribunal of fact could reach a conclusion of guilt based on the preexisting evidence together with the additional evidence newly admitted during the appeal proceedings.

When applied to the *Kupreskic* case, these newly minted review standards resulted in the following determinations:

> Zoran and Mirjan Kupreskic: The indictment against them was defective because it failed sufficiently to plead the material facts of the prosecution's case. This infringed their right to prepare their defense and thereby rendered the trial unfair. Also, the evidence relied upon by the Trial Chamber to support their convictions was inadequate. In particular, the identification evidence was from a single, 13-year-old witness (Witness H) who affirmed identification under extremely difficult circumstances. Another potentially relevant witness did not testify for health reasons. These convictions were reversed. The accused were ordered released [ICTY Press Release, P.I.S./629-e, October 23, 2001].
>
> Vlatko Kupreskic: Additional evidence admitted on appeal demonstrated that the circumstantial evidence associating him with planning the attack on Ahmici could not support his conviction. A miscarriage of justice had occurred. The conviction was reversed, and he was ordered released [ibid.].
>
> Drago Josipovic: The indictment against him was partially defective because it failed to plead all of the material facts of the prosecu-

tion's case. Moreover, the trial record did not disclose sufficient evidence for the Trial Chamber's finding that he played a command role during the Ahmici attack. Nonetheless, the conviction was affirmed. However, the sentence was reduced from 15 to 12 years imprisonment [ibid.].

Vladimir Santic: He successfully appealed against the Trial Chamber's finding that he assisted in the strategic planning of the attack on Ahmici. The Appeals Chamber also found that he had partially accepted guilt for his involvement and that he had cooperated with the prosecution since his conviction. Nonetheless, the conviction was affirmed. However, the sentence was reduced from 25 to 18 years imprisonment [ibid.].

The Appeals Chamber has also been involved in matters related to the professional responsibility of lawyers appearing before it. Ante Nobilo is one such lawyer. Nobilo was defense counsel for Tihomir Blaskic, a defendant before the ICTY [*Prosecutor v. Aleksovski (Nobilo Contempt Appeal)*, Appeals Judgment, Case No. IT-95-14/1-AR77 (May 30, 2001), para. 2]. On December 11, 1998, the Trial Chamber found that, in reexamination of a defense witness in the Blaskic trial, Nobilo had disclosed information relating to the identity of a different witness (under protective order and appearing in another trial, that of Zlatko Aleksovski) [*Le Procureur c. Zlatko Aleksovski*, Affaire IT-95-14/1-T (Chambre de première instance, December 11, 1998) (judgment available only in French)]. The Trial Chamber held that this amounted to a "knowing violation" of an order which it had made prohibiting the disclosure of such information regarding the witness. It found Nobilo in contempt and ordered payment into court of 4,000 Dutch guilders. On May 30, 2001, the Appeals Chamber allowed Nobilo's appeal and directed the Registrar to repay the fine. For the Appeals Chamber, a basic question was whether Nobilo's violation of the witness protection order was a "knowing" one [*Nobilo Contempt Appeal*, para. 37].

According to the Appeals Chamber, actual knowledge of the order was not required before it could be knowingly violated. "Willful blindness" could suffice. The Appeals Chamber defined willful blindness as follows: "proof of knowledge of the existence of the relevant fact is accepted in such cases where it is established that the defendant suspected that the fact existed (or was aware that its existence was highly probable) but refrained from finding out whether it did exist because he wanted to be able to deny knowledge of it (or he just did not want to find out that it did exist)" [*Nobilo Contempt Appeal*, para. 43]. As for Nobilo, the Appeals Chamber found no evidence of willful blindness. "There can be no willful blindness to the existence of an order unless there is first of all shown to be a suspicion or a realization that the order exists" [*Nobilo Contempt Appeal*, paras. 51]. On a related note, the Appeals Chamber held that it is not necessary for the prosecution to establish an intention to violate the order and that it is sufficient that the person charged "acted with reckless indifference as to whether his act was in violation of the order" [ibid.].

ICTY Ongoing Trials and Appeals

Trials
Several trials are ongoing before the ICTY Trial Chamber. The trials are of Radoslav Brdjanin and Momir Talic; Stanislav Galic; Milan Simic, Miroslav Tadic, Simo Zaric, and Blagoje Simic; Vinko Martinovic and Mladen Naletilic; and Milomir Stakic. Ongoing, too, is the trial of **Slobodan Milosevic**, which began on February 12, 2002. Milosevic faces a single trial on three indictments of 66 charges involving atrocity in each of Kosovo (in 1999), Bosnia (in 1992–1995), and Croatia (in 1991–1992). The charges run the gamut of the ICTY's jurisdiction, covering genocide, crimes against humanity, and war crimes under Articles 2 and 3 of the Statute of the ICTY. The genocide charges are in connection with the war in Bosnia, including the Srebrenica massacre [ICTY Press Release, X.T./P.I.S./638-e, November 23, 2001]. The Appeals Chamber's decision to allow a "joinder" (in other words, a single trial) overturned a Trial Chamber's decision for there to be two separate trials (one on Kosovo, the other on Bosnia/Croatia) [ICTY Press Release, XT/P.I.S./657-e, February 1, 2002]. This represents a "victory" for the prosecution, insofar as a key prosecutorial strategy is to argue that all three conflicts "were part of a master plan to create an ethnically 'pure' Greater Serbia" [Suzanne Daley in *New York Times*, February 2, 2002].

The first phase of the trial involves Kosovo, where prosecutors contend that Serb forces under Milosevic's command killed hundreds of ethnic Albanians and deported another 740,000. Proceedings on the Croatia and Bosnia indictments are expected to begin in July 2002. Milosevic is defending himself, although the ICTY has appointed a team of experienced international lawyers as friends of the court to assist in protecting the defendant's rights and help ensure a fair trial [ICTY Press Release, CC/P.I.S./617-e, September 6, 2001]. This trial is foreseen to last no less than two years. Hundreds of witnesses will testify. The trial is expected to raise complex factual issues and also questions involving the law of command responsibility, genocide, and immunities from arrest. Milosevic earlier had challenged the legitimacy of his arrest, transfer, and trial by the ICTY, but this challenge was dismissed by a Dutch court [*Milosevic v. The Netherlands*, KG 01/975, August 31, 2001]. A challenge to that dismissal was itself dismissed by the European Court of Human Rights on the basis that Milosevic had not exhausted domestic remedies prior to seeking the intervention of the European Court of Human Rights. Milosevic's transfer was controversial in the Federal Republic of Yugoslavia (FRY). Although arrested on April

1, 2001, by FRY police (after his regime was toppled by a popular revolt in October 2000), Milosevic was transferred to the ICTY only on June 28, 2001 [ICTY Press Release, C.C./P.I.S./597-e, June 29, 2001]. Contrary to his prior statements, Yugoslav President Kostunica did not actively resist the transfer, no doubt influenced by the prospect of losing billions of dollars in Western aid necessary to rebuild the country after Milosevic's rule. The transfer was supported by the Serbian leadership and others in the FRY government.

On another note, Mitar Vasiljevic's trial ended on March 14, 2002. He is currently awaiting the judgment of the Trial Chamber. Many other proceedings find themselves at various points in the pretrial stage.

Appeals

The docket of the Appeals Chamber is crowded. Nearly every Trial Chamber judgment is appealed; so, too, are sentences. Appeals have been initiated by Kvocka, Radic, Kos, Zigic, and Prcac (filed in November 2001); Krstic (filed in August 2001); and Mucic, Delic, and Landzo of the "Celebici" case (filed in October 2001) [see www.un.org/icty/glance/procfact-e.htm]. Appeals also are underway in the Kordic and Cerkez judgment (two Croats sentenced to 25 and 15 years imprisonment, respectively, on February 26, 2001, for their activities in the Lasva Valley of central Bosnia); Blaskic (sentenced to 45 years imprisonment on March 3, 2000, also regarding Croat activity in the Lasva Valley); and Kunarac, Kovac, and Vukovic (sentenced on February 22, 2001, to 28, 20, and 12 years, respectively, for their involvement in "rape camps" in Foca, southeast of Sarajevo). The Kunarac, Kovac, and Vukovic case was the first international judicial decision that characterized sexual violence as enslavement, and the first time an international tribunal ruled that enslavement can constitute a crime against humanity. The case also produced the first ICTY convictions of rape independently as a crime against humanity.

ICTY Indictments

As of April 2, 2002, the ICTY has issued 30 arrest warrants that remain outstanding. Indictees include notorious individuals such as Radovan Karadzic, Ratko Mladic, and Milan Milutinovic, the current President of the Republika Srpska. Capturing these indictees and securing the cooperation of the FRY government or of Serb officials in this process constitute major challenges for the ICTY. The United States and other countries have used withdrawal of aid as a mechanism to encourage compliance [Misha Savic for Associated Press, April 3, 2002]. They also have pressured the government of the Republika Srpska by threatening further international isolation until cooperation becomes effective. These pressures sparked the Milosevic transfer. In a similar vein, in April 2002, the Yugoslav Parliament approved a law to allow the handover of suspects to the ICTY and thereby end a freeze on U.S. aid [*The Globe and Mail*, April 10, 2002]. Hours after this law was passed, one of the indictees, former Serb interior minister Vlajko Stojiljkovic, shot himself on the steps of the legislature in Belgrade. The FRY government also published a list of names of some of the fugitives and urged these individuals to surrender to the ICTY. As of the time of writing, this carrot-and-stick approach is prompting the surrender of a number of fugitives to the ICTY and, it is anticipated, the further surrender of others by fall 2002 [*The Globe and Mail*, April 23, 2002, and April 25, 2002]. Those who do not surrender will be subject to indictments within the FRY issued by an FRY court.

Well before the April 2002 legislation, three senior Bosnian Muslim wartime army officers were arrested and transferred to the ICTY (in August 2001) [ibid., August 3, 2001; ICTY Press Release, GB/P.I.S./610-e, August 3, 2001]. These individuals, who had been indicted for war crimes committed mainly by foreign Islamic *mujahidin* fighters, are Brigadier Amir Kubura and retired Generals Mehmed Alargic and Enver Hadzihasanovic. On April 1, 2002, NATO-led forces arrested Momir Nikolic, accused of involvement in the Srebrenica massacre [ICTY Press Release, RC/P.I.S./664-e, April 2, 2002]. Serbian authorities arrested Nenad Banovic and his twin brother Predrag Banovic, who are Bosnian Serbs accused of crimes at the Keraterm camp [ICTY Press Release, JL/P.I.S/633-e, November 9, 2001].

A number of indictees have also voluntarily surrendered to the ICTY. Among those indictees who have voluntarily surrendered are Gen. Rahim Ademi (a Croatian, at the time of transfer serving as an assistant to the chief inspector of the Croatian defense ministry); Pasko Ljubicic (a Bosnian Croat former military chief); Gen. Pavle Strugar (a former Yugoslav army official); Dusan Fustar (a shift leader at the Keraterm camp); Miodrag Jokic (accused, along with Pavle Strugar, of involvement in the shelling of Dubrovnik, which resulted in civilian deaths and the destruction of cultural monuments); Dragan Jokic (accused in the Srebrenica massacre); and Sefer Hailovic (charged with involvement in killings of Bosnian Croats). Some of these voluntary surrenders were related to indictments that had only been unsealed this past year. There still remain an unknown number of unsealed indictments.

ICTY Sentences

On December 11, 2001, Stevan Todorovic was transferred to Spain to serve his ten-year sentence [ICTY Press Release, JL/P.I.S./684-e, December 11, 2001]. Todorovic, a police chief, had agreed to a plea bargain with the ICTY on December 13, 2000, in which he pled guilty to a single count of persecution (a crime against humanity), and also agreed to drop a complaint he had filed alleging that NATO peacekeepers illegally paid mercenaries to arrest him in 1998 [ICTY Press Release, XT/P.I.S./556-e, January 19, 2001]. Todorovic in fact was kidnapped by bounty hunters and turned over to NATO troops [Marlise Simons in *New York Times*, August 1, 2001]. The Trial Chamber entered a guilty finding on January 19, 2001, and sentenced him on July 31, 2001 [ICTY Press Release, JL/P.I.S./684-e, December 11, 2001]. The accusations against Todorovic involve his conduct directed against Bosnian Croats, Bosnian Muslims, and other non-Serb civilians residing in the Bosanski Samac and Odzak municipalities in Bosnia and Herzegovina. The Trial Chamber was influenced in the sentencing process by Todorovic's remorse, his willingness to cooperate by providing testimony in the future, and his decision to participate in a plea bargain process before his trial had even begun [ICTY Press Release, JL/P.I.S./608-e, July 31, 2001]. His sentence has been characterized as "unusually light," considering that the specifics of the charges involve murder, beatings, expulsion, and the forcing of prisoners to practice sexual violence against each other [Marlise Simons in *New York Times*, August 1, 2001].

Drago Josipovic was transferred to Spain to serve his sentence on April 9, 2002 [ICTY Press Release, JL/P.I.S./665-e, April 9, 2002]. Vladimir Santic was also transferred to Spain to serve the remainder of his sentence on April 11, 2002 [ICTY Press Release, JL/P.I.S./6692, April 12, 2002].

Zlatko Aleksovski, one of the first detainees convicted by the ICTY, was released from prison in Finland on November 14, 2001 [see www.un.org/icty/glance/procfact-e.htm].

ICTY Finances and Administration

On November 23, 2001, Judge Claude Jorda was reelected President of the ICTY by acclamation and Judge Mohamed Shahabuddeen was elected Vice-President [ICTY Press Release, CVO/P.I.S./639-e, November 23, 2001].

The ICTY's workload is growing quickly. Still to be added to this workload are the results of 40 remaining investigations involving 150 suspects [ICTY Press Release, GR/P.I.S./642-e, November 27, 2001]. Some of these may lead to trials. This number includes two investigations regarding violence in Macedonia: one into crimes allegedly committed by Macedonian soldiers against ethnic Albanian civilians, the other into crimes allegedly committed by ethnic Albanian militants [*The Globe and Mail*, November 25, 2001]. All in all, the prosecutor has estimated that the work of the ICTY may stretch into 2008 [ICTY Press Release, GR/P.I.S./642-e, November 27, 2001; ICTY Press Release, JdH/P.I.S./671-e, April 24, 2002].

The ICTY requires institutional reform in order for it realistically to dispatch all actual and potential cases by the projected deadline of 2008. These reforms must equip it to judiciously process these cases while respecting tenets of due process. In this vein, ICTY judges have approved a number of reforms and amendments to the Rules of Procedure and Evidence. These include improving the operations of the Appeals Chamber; providing the ICTY with a defense lawyers' organization; reforming the code of professional conduct; creating a pool of *ad litem* judges who would be called upon to rule in specific cases; and shoring up judges' control over the proceedings to expedite trials and the presentation of evidence [ICTY Press Release, JD/P.I.S./641-e, November 27, 2001]. The addition of *ad litem* judges has proved particularly valuable, permitting the Trial Chamber to double its capacity [ICTY Press Release, CC/P.I.S./618-e, September 7, 2001]. Initially, the Security Council by resolution established a pool of 27 *ad litem* judges [S/Res/1329 (2000), November 30, 2000]. These 27 judges were elected by the U.N. General Assembly on June 12, 2001, for a term of four years [U.N. Press Release, A/9878, June 12, 2001]. From this pool, six judges were appointed to the ICTY in July 2001 and began to hear trials in September 2001 [ICTY Press Release, SB/P.I.S./607-e, July 31, 2001]. Three other *ad litem* judges were assigned to trials in April 2002 [ICTY Press Release, JL/P.I.S./666-e, April 10, 2002]. In addition, at a plenary session held from December 12–13, 2001, the ICTY judges amended the Rules of Procedure and Evidence to address issues such as contempt, the giving of false testimony, notices of appeal, and interlocutory appeals. Moreover, in order to promote transparency, public proceedings at the ICTY—including the Milosevic trial—now can be followed on video on the Internet [ICTY Press Release, CC/P.I.S./659-e, February 15, 2002].

The ICTY is endeavoring to better integrate itself with domestic initiatives. For example, the ICTY has expressed a willingness—albeit reserved—to be complemented by the Yugoslav Truth and Reconciliation Commission, established on March 29, 2001 [Jelena Pejic in *Fordham International Law Journal*, Vol. 25, p. 8; ICTY Press Release, JL/P.I.S./591-e, May 17, 2001]. The ICTY also is warming to the idea of "relocating" some trials and investigations to national courts throughout the Balkans [ICTY Press Release, JD/P.I.S./641-e, November 27, 2001; ICTY Press Release, GR/P.I.S./642-e, November 27, 2001; ICTY Press Release, JdH/P.I.S./671-e, April 24, 2002]. However, for the moment, both President Judge Jorda and Prosecutor Del Ponte are reluctant to do so and certainly not until national courts are "reconstructed on democratic foundations" [ICTY Press Release, JD/P.I.S./641-e, November 27, 2001; ICTY Press Release, GR/P.I.S./642-e, November 27, 2001]. To be sure, some proceedings are taking place in Serbian and Croatian courts. These trials are few in number and have resulted in lenient sentences. For example, in January 2002, a Croatian court found three former Croatian military policemen guilty of torture and killings of ethnic Serbs but then sentenced all three to the minimum term of one year in prison, describing the three accused as "Homeland War defenders" [Deutsche Presse Agenthur, January 25, 2002].

The International Criminal Tribunal for Rwanda (ICTR)

In late 1994, the ICTR was established and mandated to prosecute those responsible for the massacre of approximately 800,000 Rwandans (overwhelmingly from the Tutsi ethnic group) [S/Res/955, November 8, 1994]. The Tutsi were subject to genocidal attacks by the majority Hutu ethnic group between April and July 1994. The ICTR Trial Chamber is based in Arusha (Tanzania); the Appeals Chamber is in The Hague, although it sometimes sits in Arusha as well.

Over the past year, the number of detainees awaiting trial by the ICTR has increased substantially. Many new arrests have been made, although over 20 indictees still remain at large [ICTY Press Release, GR/P.I.S./642-e, November 27, 2001]. Moreover, very important trials have begun recently. As of March 28, 2002, there are, in total, 59 detainees at the ICTR. This includes six individuals serving sentences, two individuals awaiting transfer, one individual appealing his conviction, and Ignace Bagilishema, who was acquitted of his charges on June 7, 2001, but who remains conditionally released in France pending a prosecutorial appeal [see *ICTR Detainees—Status*, available at www.ictr.org]. Moreover, the prosecutor has indicated that 136 investigations, involving 136 potential accused, remain to be completed [ICTY Press Release, GR/P.I.S./642-e, November 27, 2001]. The prosecutor has also evinced an interest in investigating allegations of crimes committed by Tutsi armed forces (the RPA). Any such investigation will be to a large extent contingent upon the support of the Rwandan government (led by the RPF, whose armed forces are the RPA). As is the case with the ICTY, the prosecutor anticipates that the work of the ICTR will draw to a close by the end of 2008 [ibid.].

ICTR Judgments of the Trial and Appeals Chambers

Trial Chamber
The Trial Chamber issued its first ever acquittal in the matter of Ignace Bagilishema [ICTR/INFO-9-2-271.EN, June 7, 2001]. Bagilishema, the *bourgmestre* (mayor) of Mabanza *commune*, was accused of seven counts of genocide, crimes against humanity, and war crimes related to the murder of thousands of Tutsi in Kibuye *préfecture* [ICTR/INFO 9-2-202EN, September 18, 1999]. ICTR Judge Mose held in a lengthy judgment that the prosecution failed to prove beyond a reasonable doubt that Bagilishema had committed the alleged atrocities. The ICTR ruled that the testimony of prosecution witnesses was "riddled with inconsistencies and contradictions" [ICTR/INFO-9-2-271.EN, June 7, 2001]. Whereas the prosecutor alleged that Bagilishema held meetings in which he encouraged the local population to kill Tutsi, the defense contended that Bagilishema actually held "pacification" meetings during the genocide in an attempt to restore security. The Trial Chamber found that the evidence supported Bagilishema's contention that he acted to prevent killings of Tutsi and reestablish law and order [ibid.]. The prosecutor also alleged that Bagilishema personally attacked and killed Tutsi men, women, and children; ordered *Interahamwe* militia to dig a mass grave; and directed massacres of Tutsi refugees in various areas of Kibuye *préfecture*. Bagilishema was also accused of meeting with Clément Kayis-

hema, another local political official (as discussed below, the ICTR has convicted Kayishema of genocide and sentenced him to life imprisonment). However, at trial several witnesses failed to recall Bagilishema's presence at the massacre sites and in fact gave conflicting accounts. Moreover, witnesses could not prove that a meeting occurred between Kayishema and Bagilishema.

In the end, the majority held that Bagilishema's individual criminal responsibility for the crimes simply could not be established. However, in a dissenting opinion, Judge Güney held that he was "thoroughly convinced" that Bagilishema was guilty of complicity in genocide and crimes against humanity [ICTR/INFO-9-2-271.EN, June 7, 2001]. The prosecution has advised of its intent to appeal the judgment. Following the acquittal, Bagilishema was conditionally released on June 8, 2001, and allowed to reside in France while the prosecutor's appeal is pending [ICTR/INFO-9-2-284.EN, September 21, 2001].

Appeals Chamber

The appeal judgment in the matter of Jean-Paul Akayesu, a local mayor, was pronounced on June 1, 2001 [*Le Procureur c. Akayesu*, ICTR-96-4-A, *Arrêt (Judgement)* (ICTR App. Chamber, June 1, 2001)]. Akayesu's appeal had been heard on November 1 and 2, 2000. The charges relate to Akayesu's failure to prevent the killing of Tutsi or otherwise respond with assistance to quell the violence in his *commune*, notwithstanding that he had authority and responsibility to do so. The Trial Chamber's groundbreaking 1998 judgment in the *Akayesu* matter provided judicial notice that the Rwandan violence was organized, planned, ethnically motivated, and undertaken with the intent to wipe out the Tutsi (this latter element, of course, being required to constitute genocide). Akayesu was the first person convicted of genocide by an international court. In addition, the initial *Akayesu* judgment marked the first time that an international tribunal ruled that rape and other forms of systematic sexual violence could constitute genocide. It was also the first conviction of an individual for rape as a crime against humanity. Akayesu was sentenced to life in prison.

The Appeals Chamber rejected Akayesu's appeal against his conviction and sentence. In so doing, it dealt with a broad array of issues, some of which were not raised by counsel on appeal. Of significance is the Appeals Chamber's finding that the right of an indigent person to be represented by a lawyer free of charge did not imply the right to select the assigned lawyer [*Akayesu*, Appeal Judgment, para. 61]. In other words, the right to free assistance from a lawyer does not confer the right to choose one's counsel. According to the Appeals Chamber, the right to choose counsel is only guaranteed for those who can assume the financial burden of a lawyer's fees. Nonetheless, indigent defendants can choose from a list of counsel kept by the ICTR Registrar who, in turn, will take that choice into account when assigning counsel. But the Registrar is not necessarily bound by the wishes of the indigent accused person and has wide powers of discretion that can be exercised in the interests of justice. The Appeals Chamber also held that there were insufficient grounds to find that the lawyers representing Akayesu were incompetent, as alleged by Akayesu [*Akayesu*, Appeal Judgment, paras. 80–84]. Also rejected were Akayesu's arguments that the ICTR was pursuing selective justice, was biased, and was lacking in impartiality and that the examination of witnesses was irregular and that Akayesu's detention was illegal [*Akayesu*, Appeal Judgment, paras. 92, 97, 101, 319, 326, 376]. The Appeals Chamber also rejected a motion by Akayesu that it reconsider an earlier decision that had rejected additional grounds for appeal. In fact, the Appeals Chamber held that a motion of an abuse of process as reconsideration of final decisions must remain absolutely exceptional. Akayesu's lawyers were sanctioned under the Rules of the ICTR, and the Appeals Chamber ordered the ICTR Registrar to withhold payment to these lawyers for the preparation of the impugned motion.

On May 21, 1999, the Trial Chamber had convicted Clément Kayishema, a former local governmental official, and Obed Ruzindana, a businessman, jointly of genocide and crimes against humanity and sentenced them to life imprisonment and 25 years imprisonment, respectively. On June 1, 2001, the Appeals Chamber dismissed both defense and prosecution appeals from this judgment and thereby confirmed the convictions and sentences [*Le Procureur c/ Kayishema*, ICTR-95-1-A, *Motifs de L'Arrêt (Reasons for Judgement)* (ICTR App. Chamber June 1, 2001)]. The appellants had unsuccessfully alleged lack of equality of arms (*égalité des armes* in French), defective indictment, and inadequate proof. *Equality of arms* means that the prosecutor and defense must have access to identical resources and means. The Appeals Chamber held that, although the right to a fair trial implicitly includes "equality of arms," this does not mean that the prosecution and defense must have equal resources and personnel at their disposal [*Kayishema*, Appeal Judgment, paras. 67, 69]. Rather, there must be sufficient resources made available to allow a good defense to be put forward [*Kayishema*, Appeal Judgment, para. 72]. This judgment clarifies the law regarding the mental element for genocide and the type of circumstantial evidence that could establish that mental element. It also addresses the defense of command authority by affirming the approach taken by the ICTY in the "Celebici" case [discussed in *Issues/56*, pp. 252–55]. Kayishema and Ruzindana, along with Akayesu, now are serving their sentences in prison in Bamako, Mali [ICTR/INFO-9-2-296.EN, December 11, 2001]. There they join Jean Kambanda, the former Prime Minister of Rwanda, and Omar Serushago, a former *Interahamwe* militia leader.

Alfred Musema's appeal was judged on November 16, 2001. Musema, the director of a tea factory at Gisovu (in Kibuye *préfecture* in western

Rwanda), had been convicted on January 27, 2000, of one count of genocide and two counts of crimes against humanity (extermination and rape) [ICTR/INFO 9-2-218EN, November 27, 2000]. The three counts for which he had been convicted relate to his participation in anti-Tutsi attacks in Kibuye at the end of April and early May 1994. In one such attack, Musema was found to have ordered that a cave in which 300 to 400 Tutsi had sought refuge be sealed and then set on fire. All but one of these Tutsi perished. He was also held liable for the acts carried out by the employees of his tea factory over whom he was found to have *de jure* control. This is an important extension of the doctrine of superior responsibility outside the military context and into the context of a civilian workplace [*Prosecutor v. Musema*, judgment, January 27, 2000, paras. 141–48]. The Appeals Chamber confirmed the genocide and crimes against humanity (extermination) convictions, but quashed the crimes against humanity (rape) conviction on the basis of new evidence. Regardless, Musema's sentence of life imprisonment was upheld. The Appeals Chamber held that the quashing of the rape conviction "could not affect the exceptional gravity of the crimes for which he had been convicted" [ICTR/INFO-9-2-294.EN, November 16, 2001]. Musema argued that the Trial Chamber erred in law by convicting him of both genocide and extermination on the basis of the same facts. The Appeals Chamber noted that the requisite test was whether each alleged crime included "a significantly distinct constituent element" [ibid.]. "A constitutive element was to be considered significantly distinct from another if it required the proof of a fact which was not required in the case of the other crime" [ibid.]. According to the Statute of the ICTR (which largely tracks conventional and customary international law), genocide requires evidence of "the intent to destroy, in whole or in part, a national, ethnic, racial or religious group." Extermination as a crime against humanity requires proof that the crime "had been committed as part of a widespread or systematic attack against any civilian population." Consequently, according to the Appeals Chamber, the criterion for a double conviction for the crimes of genocide and extermination as a crime against humanity was satisfied in this case and both convictions were confirmed [ibid]. The ICTY has also extensively discussed the differences between genocide and extermination (as a crime against humanity). Musema joins other convicts in prison in Mali. He is serving a life sentence.

ICTR Ongoing Trials and Appeals

Trials

A number of important joint proceedings are being heard by the ICTR. Joint proceedings involve multiple defendants among whom there is a nexus justifying their being tried together. The ICTR has organized important proceedings based on the occupational role the defendants played in the genocide. These roles are as follows: (1) political, governmental, and administrative leaders of the genocidal Hutu regime (often organized geographically in the area where they committed atrocities); (2) military leaders; and (3) key figures of the Rwandan media who disseminated genocidal propaganda.

The "media" case, which began on October 23, 2000, "is recognized as breaking new legal ground" insofar as it explores the role, responsibility, and liability of the media in exhorting genocide [ICTY Press Release, JL/P.I.S./ 542-e, November 24, 2000]. This is the first time since Julius Streicher, the Nazi publisher of the anti-Semitic weekly *Der Stürmer*, appeared before the Nuremberg Tribunal that a group of journalists stands similarly charged (though Streicher did not face genocide charges) [Marlise Simons in *New York Times*, March 3, 2002]. Accused of inciting genocide through the media are Jean-Bosco Barayagwiza (former director of political affairs in the Rwandan Ministry of Foreign Affairs), Hassan Ngeze (editor of the extremist *Kangura* newspaper), and Ferdinand Nahimana (former director of Radio-Télévision Libre des Mille Collines, the national radio station). This has been a controversial trial, replete with obstructionist behavior by the defendants, management problems, strong invective by some defense counsel, and concern over harmonizing different national approaches to the breadth of freedom of expression [ibid.].

On June 12, 2001, the joint trial of the "Butare" group began [ICTR/ INFO-9-2-273.EN, June 12, 2001]. The "Butare" group consists of six accused, including Pauline Nyiramasuhuko, the former Minister for Family and Women's Affairs and the first woman to be indicted by an international criminal tribunal (she also is the only woman to be indicted thus far by the ICTR). All accused have pleaded not guilty. Butare is a city in southern Rwanda and the seat of the national university.

In another very important matter, the "Military" trial began on April 2, 2002, but was adjourned shortly thereafter for several months, due to the prosecution's lack of translation of certain documents that are to be distributed to the defense [ICTR/INFO-9-2-312.EN, April 2, 2002; Associated Press, April 3, 2002]. This trial involves Col. Théoneste Bagosora, the Director of Cabinet in the Ministry of Defense, and a number of senior military officials (four defendants in total). It will deal with how the genocide allegedly was planned, masterminded, and implemented at the highest levels of the Rwandan army.

Other ongoing trials include André Ntagerura, Emmanuel Bagambiki, and Samuel Imanishimwe (mixed trial of political, military, and administrative leaders focusing on violence in Cyangugu *préfecture*); Laurent Semanza (a local politician in Bicumbi *commune*); and Jean de Dieu Kamuhanda (the former Minister of Higher Education, Research, and Culture in the genocidal government, whose trial recommenced in

September 2001). The trial of Elizaphan Ntakirutimana (a pastor with the Seventh Day Adventist Church in Rwanda) and his son Gérard began on September 18, 2001 [ICTR/INFO-9-2-281.EN, September 18, 2001]. They are accused of numerous counts of genocide related to widespread killing of Tutsi in Kibuye. One accusation is that the accused lured several hundred Tutsi to a church complex in the initial days of the genocide and then led Hutu militia forces to the church, resulting in the massacre of those Tutsi who had sought shelter. The prosecution maintains that seven Tutsi pastors wrote a letter to Elizaphan Ntakirutimana pleading for his intervention. "We wish to inform you that we have heard that tomorrow we will be killed with our families. We therefore request you to intervene on our behalf and talk to the Mayor," read the letter (which has since been popularized as the title of Philip Gourevitch's broadly read account of the Rwandan genocide) [ICTR/INFO-9-2-281.EN, September 18, 2001]. Ntakirutimana's response, according to the prosecution, was contained in a "brief, heartless letter," which stated "there is nothing I can do for you. All you can do is prepare to die for your time has come" [ibid.]. In order to stand trial at the ICTR, Elizaphan Ntakirutimana had to be transferred from the United States, where he had been arrested pursuant to an ICTR indictment. Ntakirutimana vigorously used the U.S. courts to contest his extradition to the ICTR. He was initially successful before a magistrate, whose decision was then reversed by a U.S. District Court judge. The District Court decision was affirmed by the Fifth Circuit Court of Appeals, which held that Ntakirutimana could be surrendered to the ICTR, notwithstanding the fact that the U.S. government has not executed a formal extradition treaty with the ICTR [see *Ntakirutimana v. Reno*, 1999 WL 587963 (5th Cir. 1999), cert. denied January 24, 2000]. Former Secretary of State Madeleine Albright then authorized Ntakirutimana's transfer, and he entered the custody of the ICTR on March 24, 2000.

Also ongoing is the trial of Juvénal Kajelijeli (the former mayor of Mukingo and an *Interahamwe* militia leader), which had begun on March 13, 2001 [ICTR/INFO-9-2-259.EN, March 13, 2001]. Kajelijeli is accused of 11 counts of genocide, crimes against humanity, and violations of the Geneva Convention [ICTR/INFO-9-2-256.EN, January 26, 2001].

Many more cases remain pending at the pretrial stage.

Appeals
Georges Rutaganda's appeal is currently pending. Rutaganda had been sentenced to life imprisonment by the Trial Chamber on December 6, 1999, following conviction on one count of genocide and two counts of crimes against humanity [ICTR/INFO 9-2-216.EN, December 6, 1999]. When the genocide broke out, Rutaganda was a leading member of the governing Hutu Power party (the MRND) as well as second Vice-President of the national committee of the *Interahamwe* militia. The *Interahamwe* are no-

torious for having been a major force in the anti-Tutsi pogroms. The Trial Chamber held that Rutaganda incurred individual criminal responsibility for having ordered, incited, and carried out murders and for causing serious bodily or mental harm to members of the Tutsi ethnic group.

ICTR Indictments

A large number of important indictees were brought to the ICTR for initial appearances in 2001 and 2002. The fact that these individuals were arrested in a variety of African and European countries demonstrates the respect and support foreign national governments exhibit toward the ICTR. Trial dates have not yet been fixed for these individuals. These include Emmanuel Ndindabahizi, arrested in Verviers, Belgium, on July 12, 2001, and appearing before the ICTR on October 19, 2001 [ICTR/INFO-9-2-277.EN, July 12, 2001]. Ndindabahizi was Minister of Finance in the genocidal Hutu regime. Sylvestre Gacumbitsi, a mayor, was arrested on June 20, 2001, in a refugee camp in Tanzania and brought into custody at the ICTR shortly thereafter. He made his first appearance on June 26, 2001, when he pleaded not guilty to five counts of genocide and crimes against humanity including extermination, murder, and rape [ICTR/INFO-9-2-274.EN, June 26, 2001]. While traveling along Nyarubuye road, Gacumbitsi is said to have announced with a megaphone: "Search in the bushes, do not save a single snake. Hutu that save Tutsi would be killed. Tutsi girls that have always refused to sleep with Hutu should be raped and sticks placed in their genitals" [ICTR/INFO-9-2-274.EN, June 26, 2001]. François Karera, another local political official, was arrested in Nairobi, Kenya, on October 20, 2001, and appeared on October 26, 2001 [ICTR/INFO-9-2-293.EN, October 26, 2001]. Jean Mpambara, also a local political official, was arrested in Tanzania and pleaded not guilty to one count of genocide [ICTR/INFO-9-2-279.EN, July 27, 2001].

Emmanuel Rukondo, a military chaplain, was arrested in Geneva, Switzerland, and appeared before the ICTR on September 26, 2001, when he pleaded not guilty [ICTR/INFO-9-2-285.EN, September 26, 2001]. Rukondo is one of a number of clergy whose trials are pending before the ICTR. Among the accusations against Rukondo are charges that he organized and participated in hunts for Tutsi priests and nuns in various seminaries and convents and identified many individuals to soldiers so that they would be killed [ICTR/INFO-9-2-277.EN, July 12, 2001]. Hormisdas Nsengimana, a priest, was arrested in Cameroon in March 2002 and pleaded not guilty before the ICTR [ICTR/INFO-9-2-315.EN, April 16, 2002].

Protais Zigiranyirazo, a businessman, was arrested in Brussels on July 26, 2001, and appeared before the ICTR on October 10, 2001, on charges that he planned, ordered, and facilitated the genocide [ICTR/INFO-9-2-289.EN, October 10, 2001]. Zigiranyirazo, a brother of former President Habyarimana's wife, was a member of the *akazu* (inner circle) of Habyari-mana [ICTR/INFO-9-2-278.EN, July 27, 2001]. Vincent Rutaganira, a politician from Kibuye *préfecture*, was arrested in Tanzania and transferred to the ICTR, where he faces several charges to which he pleaded not guilty [ICTR/INFO-9-2-304.EN, March 4, 2002; ICTR/INFO-9-2-309.EN, March 26, 2002].

Siméon Nshamihigo, a deputy prosecutor, was arrested in Tanzania on May 19, 2001, and transferred to the ICTR, where he pleaded not guilty to three counts of genocide, crimes against humanity, and war crimes [ICTR/INFO-9-2-275.EN, June 27, 2001]. Nshamihigo was arrested while traveling under an assumed name on a Congolese passport and while working for the ICTR as a defense team investigator [ICTR/INFO-9-2-266.EN, May 21, 2001]. Defense investigators are not staff members of the ICTR, but, rather, independent contractors recruited by defense counsel. Their fees are paid as part of the legal aid package funded by the ICTR for indigent accused persons. Joseph Nzabirinda, a youth organizer (and another for-mer defense investigator), was arrested on December 21, 2001, in Brussels and transferred to the ICTR, where he entered a plea of not guilty to four counts of genocide [ICTR/INFO-9-2-310.EN, March 27, 2002].

Simon Bikindi, a musician accused inter alia of fomenting anti-Tutsi hatred through his popular songs, was arrested in the Netherlands on July 12, 2001, and arrived at the ICTR on March 27, 2002 [ICTR/INFO-9-2-277.EN, July 12, 2001; ICTR/INFO-9-2-311.EN, March 28, 2002]. Bikindi's accusation raises is-sues similar to those in the "media" trial—namely the extent to which expression can be criminalized if that expression incites genocide. Aloys Simba, a Lieutenant Colonel and former member of Parliament arrested in Senegal on November 27, 2001, appeared before the ICTR on March 18, 2002, together with Paul Bisengimana, a former mayor, arrested on December 4, 2001, in Mali [ICTR/INFO-9-2-307.EN, March 18, 2002].

Finally, Athanase Seromba, a priest, was arrested on February 6, 2002, in Arusha, Tanzania, and transferred shortly thereafter to the ICTR. The Seromba warrant, issued on July 4, 2001, alleges that he ordered a bulldozer to raze a Catholic church in western Rwanda, killing about 2,000 Tutsi who were sheltered inside [Reuters, February 7, 2002]. Seromba volun-teered himself into ICTR custody after reports of his involvement circu-lated in Italy, where he had been living since 1997. Catholic officials in Italy had been criticized for housing Seromba. Seromba vigorously denies any wrongdoing [ICTR/INFO-9-2-301.EN, February 8, 2002].

ICTR Personnel and Administration

Judge Laïty Kama of Senegal, ICTR President from 1995 to 1999, passed away on May 6, 2001 [ICTR/INFO-9-2-265.EN, May 7, 2001]. At the time of his death, Judge Kama was presiding judge of one of the ICTR Trial Cham-bers. He had a distinguished career as a jurist, lecturer, and prosecutor.

Judge Kama was succeeded in his capacity as ICTR judge by Andrésia Vaz, also of Senegal [ICTR/INFO-9-2-270.EN, June 4, 2001; ICTR/INFO-9-2-276.EN, July 9, 2001].

Judge Navanethem Pillay of South Africa was reelected President of the ICTR for a second and final two-year term on May 31, 2001 [ICTR/INFO-9-2-268.EN, June 1, 2001]. Judge Mose of Norway was reelected as Vice-President [ibid.].

Lovemore Green Munlo of Malawi was sworn in as ICTR Deputy Registrar on October 4, 2001 [ICTR/INFO-9-2-287.EN, October 4, 2001].

The ICTR has been dogged by scandals involving defense work. In addition to the embarrassing fact that three suspects, Siméon Nshamihigo, Thaddée Kwitonda, and Joseph Nzabirinda, were on the ICTR legal aid payroll as investigators for defense teams, there are reports that some paid defense investigators had never visited Rwanda during the course of their work [ICTR/INFO-9-2-266.EN, May 21, 2001]. In summer 2001, evidence also surfaced that a number of defense investigators were on the list of most serious genocide suspects wanted by the government of Rwanda for its national prosecutions. Needless to say, the employment contracts of these individuals with the ICTR consequently were not renewed or were suspended [ICTR/INFO-9-3-03.EN, July 16, 2001]. This negative publicity prompted the ICTR to increase the rigor with which defense investigators are screened.

Moreover, there are also allegations of improprieties on the part of defense counsel, such as fee-splitting. Andrew McCartan, a defense counsel from the United Kingdom, was discharged as lead counsel for Joseph Nzirorera after evidence was unearthed of his inflation of legal bills and other financial irregularities [ICTR/INFO-9-2-299.EN, February 6, 2002]. Nzirorera had earlier applied for the withdrawal of McCartan and his Belgian co-counsel Martin Bauwens on the ground of loss of confidence. The Trial Chamber denied the application and the Appeals Chamber affirmed that denial on February 1, 2002. However, as part of its judgment, the Trial Chamber had directed the Registry to further examine financial improprieties, and it was this investigation that ultimately led to McCartan's discharge (along with that of Bauwens). In addition, the ICTR is also subject to allegations of mistreatment of witnesses, in particular witnesses called from Rwanda to testify for the prosecution [ICTR/INFO-9-3-09.EN, March 28, 2002]. Although these allegations remain under investigation, because of an inability of the ICTR and the government of Rwanda to agree on the terms of reference, a proposed joint commission of inquiry was not pursued [ICTR/INFO-9-3-10.EN, April 17, 2002; ICTR/INFO-9-3-11.EN, April 23, 2002].

The Rwandan Courts, Other National Courts, and Genocide Prosecutions

Courts in Rwanda continue to issue verdicts in genocide prosecutions conducted under domestic Rwandan law (called the *Organic Law*). However, given the present rate at which these judgments are issued, it would take literally hundreds of years to adjudicate everyone awaiting trial (over 100,000 individuals). This reality has prompted the Rwandan government to consider community-based dispute resolution, called *gacaca* in Kinyarwanda, as an alternative method to promote accountability for lower-level participants in the genocide. *Gacaca* legislation was passed in Rwanda in October 2000. *Gacaca* is to take effect throughout Rwanda by the second half of 2002 (a delayed start-date from what initially had been planned). *Gacaca* has been used as a method of dispute resolution historically in Rwanda. Although its principal focus has been property crimes, *gacaca* has also been used to mediate more serious crimes, though its implementation to genocide remains unprecedented.

The *gacaca* tribunals will be composed of elders and "people of integrity" (*Inyangamugayo*) elected from local communities throughout Rwanda. Two-hundred-and-sixty thousand such individuals were chosen in October 2001. Suspects will be brought to the villages where they are said to have committed their crimes, and there will be adjudged by *gacaca* panels also composed of individuals from that area. Given that in many cases the accused will also be from the same village, *gacaca* truly is an exercise in community-based justice. *Gacaca* will not have jurisdiction over the planners, organizers, instigators, supervisors, and leaders of the genocide, all of whom are more formally to be prosecuted in court. *Gacaca* will have to straddle the difficult position of operating as part of the legal response to genocide (but still differentiating itself from the criminal justice response), but retaining sufficient formalities and regularities such that it does not become a legitimizing whitewash for vigilantism and revenge or, in a different vein, trivialize the crimes that were committed.

On another front, in June 2001, a court in Belgium tried, convicted, and sentenced (to terms of 12 to 20 years) four Rwandans (two nuns, a professor, and a factory owner) residing in Belgium since they had fled Rwanda following the genocide [*The Globe and Mail*, June 8, 2001]. These four Rwandans were charged with violations of international humanitarian law. A jury of 12 Belgians convicted them of homicide. This trial took place under an amended Belgian law that provides for universal jurisdiction for certain international crimes. This was the same law used to issue an arrest warrant against the sitting Congolese Minister of Foreign Affairs. Subsequently, this was deemed by the International Court of Justice to infringe international law owing to the Minister's immunity from prosecution (the immunity would not apply to non-Ministers or non-Heads of State) (see discussion *infra* in Part 7). Belgium has been involved in investigating more than 20 suspects of crimes committed in Rwanda, including a number of situations when there was no connection at all with Belgium. Extraterritorial prosecutions also occur elsewhere. For example, in *Niyonteze v. Public Prosecutor*, a Swiss decision issued on April 27,

2001, a Rwandan national was convicted for war crimes committed in an internal armed conflict. The Rwandan government fully supported the Swiss proceedings after Switzerland refused to accede to the Rwandan government's request for the defendant to be extradited to Rwanda. The Niyonteze trial parallels that of Akayesu, insofar as the indictment and factual allegations are very similar.

4. U.N. Legal Involvement in Other Post-Conflict Situations

When it comes into effect, the International Criminal Court will only be able to address crimes prospectively. As a result, accountability for mass atrocity preceding the ICC's entry into force will have to be pursued on an independent basis. In addition to the ad hoc tribunals for the former Yugoslavia and Rwanda, the United Nations recently has been encouraging other mechanisms to promote justice and accountability following systematic conflict. Such mechanisms include hybrid (i.e., mixed national/international) tribunals, courts negotiated between the United Nations and the post-conflict state, and alternative institutions to courts/tribunals. These initiatives have met with varying degrees of success—from disappointment in Cambodia to promise in Sierra Leone. Lessons learned from these myriad experiences could prove helpful in constructing civil society and promoting accountability in post-Taliban Afghanistan.

Cambodia

The United Nations abruptly withdrew its efforts in **East Timor** in February 2002. "Worn down by the stubbornness of the Cambodian government," U.N. legal counsel Hans Corell ended nearly five years of negotiations regarding the creation of an international tribunal in Cambodia. The tribunal was intended to prosecute human rights abuses and mass atrocity that took place under Khmer Rouge rule [Seth Mydans in *New York Times*, February 10, 2002; BBC News, February 8, 2002]. From 1975 to 1979, the Khmer Rouge massacred approximately 1.7 million Cambodians.

These five years of negotiations have at times been acrimonious, at other times ossified. Basically, the position of the Cambodian government has been that Cambodia should be allowed to organize its own tribunal, with the United Nations limited to playing a supporting role. Cambodian Prime Minister Hun Sen has voiced concerns that the U.N. tribunal would not help the reconciliation process that Cambodia is undertaking and could, in fact, reignite civil war in the country (civil conflict only ended in 1998). The United Nations has responded with concerns that Cambodia trials might not conform to international due process standards or might be pursued to shield certain Khmer leaders from liability in order to avoid domestic political conflict. Many current members of the Cambodian government and legislature are former Khmer members who defected prior to 1979. The United Nations has also suggested that Cambodia lacks the infrastructure to launch trials and has raised concerns related to corruption in the Cambodian judiciary.

In late April 2000, these negotiation positions were synthesized into a compromise agreement, largely brokered by U.S. Senator John Kerry [Seth Mydans in *New York Times*, June 25, 2000]. Under this agreement, responsibilities would be shared between the United Nations and Cambodia. Indictments against suspects would be drawn up by two prosecutors—one appointed by the United Nations, the other by the Cambodian government. In the event of a disagreement between the two prosecutors, a separate panel of three Cambodian and two international judges could prevent an indictment from being issued, but only if four of the five judges vote to do so [BBC News, April 29, 2000]. The Cambodian government therefore would not have a veto over who is selected for prosecution. Cambodia would also retain a one-judge majority at each level of the proposed tribunal, but at least one international judge must side with these judges in order for any judgment to be binding. The tribunal would be located in Phnom Penh, the Cambodian capital. The working language was to be Khmer, with translations into English and French. Unlike the ICTY or ICTR, this tribunal would be composed of three tiers: a trial court, an appeals court, and a supreme court.

In July 2001, drawing from the brokered compromise, Cambodia's upper and lower Houses of Parliament passed legislation to set up a tribunal [Reuters, July 23, 2001]. This was the second time such approval was required: the first time the legislation had been approved, the Cambodian Constitutional Council expressed concerned about an indirect reference to the death penalty (which no longer exists in Cambodian law). The second time around, the legislation was approved by the Cambodian Constitutional Council in August 2001 and signed by King Norodom Sihanouk shortly thereafter [Reuters, August 7, 2001; Associated Press, August 10, 2001]. However, the process stalled owing to discrepancies between the law and the brokered draft tribunal statute, discrepancies between the law as passed and international criminal law, and alterations in the role accorded to the United Nations. Moreover, U.N. legal counsel Hans Corell concluded that the independence, impartiality, and objectivity of the court proposed by the domestic legislation could not be guaranteed [BBC News, February 8, 2002]. The United Nations felt that the law as passed did not conform to international standards of justice and "left too many loopholes" [Seth Mydans in *New York Times*, February 10, 2002]. Moreover, disagreement persisted on many issues, including the time frame for the tribunal, procedures, financing, staffing, and the number of individuals who should be prosecuted (Cambodia wants to restrict prosecution to about ten selected

Khmer Rouge leaders) [BBC News, February 13, 2001]. The Cambodian government's insistence that national law would take precedence over the agreement concluded with the United Nations was also reported to be a sticking-point [BBC News, February 8, 2002]. As such, the United Nations did not approve the law, and, thus, the required memorandum of understanding between the Organization and the Cambodian government permitting the establishment of the tribunal was not enacted. For its part, the Cambodian government has stated that it will make no further concessions to the United Nations regarding the tribunal [BBC News, February 3, 2002].

To be sure, it is unclear whether the U.N. pull-out is irrevocable. In fact, the European Union, United States, United Kingdom, and Australia each have suggested that the United Nations return to the discussion table. Even Cambodia has urged the United Nations to reconsider its withdrawal of support, although Prime Minister Sen has set a deadline of mid-June for the United Nations to reenter negotiations [BBC News, February 11, 2002; BBC News, March 20, 2002]. As such, the negotiation drama may continue. If, however, the pull-out is permanent, then this leaves the composition, structure, and even existence of trials in the hands of the Cambodian government (unless bilateral or multilateral involvement with foreign countries outside of the U.N. framework is achieved). This has prompted skepticism within the Cambodian human rights community, which fears that most major abusers from the Khmer Rouge period would thereby be spared judicial accountability. So far, only two prominent Khmer leaders are in custody: Kang Kek Ieu (head of the Khmer Rouge secret police and commandant of the infamous Tuol Sleng prison) and Ta Mok (a notorious military commander) [Seth Mydans in *New York Times*, August 20, 2001]. As yet, not one member of the Khmer regime has stood trial for offenses.

East Timor

In September 1999, militia forces supported by the Indonesian army massacred thousands of East Timorese and engaged in a widespread campaign of property destruction, rape, and sexual enslavement [BBC News, April 25, 2001; Seth Mydans in *New York Times*, March 1, 2001; Barbara Crossette in *New York Times*, March 4, 2001]. This violence was triggered by a plebiscite in East Timor that lopsidedly supported the region's independence from Indonesia. Following the massacres, the Indonesian administration of East Timor collapsed. Voters in East Timor voted in the country's first free elections for a constituent assembly on August 30, 2001. The first presidential election was held in April 2002, and the country's independence from U.N. administration is imminent as of this writing [*New York Times*, August 30, 2001; *The Globe and Mail*, April 14, 2002; BBC News, April 17, 2002]. However, difficulties persist. These include poverty, unemployment, and lack of infrastructure [BBC News, April 17, 2002]. Moreover, over 100,000 East Timorese refugees remain in squalid camps in Indonesian West Timor, the other half of the island of Timor [*The Globe and Mail*, May 4, 2001].

International lawyers, as well as domestic officials, have called for those responsible for the September 1999 violence to be held accountable. The United Nations has played an important role in this process. First, the Security Council established the **U.N. Transitional Administration in East Timor (UNTAET)**. Under the aegis of UNTAET, a number of regulations relating to the administration of justice have been promulgated. These established four district courts and one appeals court for East Timor. The Dili District Court is vested with exclusive jurisdiction over the entire territory of East Timor with respect to the six most serious offenses. These are genocide, war crimes, crimes against humanity, torture, murder, and sexual offenses (the latter two crimes are prosecuted under the Indonesian Criminal Code, the former crimes under universal jurisdiction) [UNTAET Regulation 2000/15, June 6, 2000]. Special panels of three judges of mixed national and international provenance have been established to prosecute these serious offenses in the Dili District Court. Indonesia, the former governing state, plays no role in these proceedings. A number of indictments alleging serious international crimes have been filed; the first trial to include charges of crimes against humanity resulted in a guilty verdict against ten defendants on December 11, 2001 [*American Journal of International Law*, Vol. 95 (2001), p. 945].

In addition to assisting with trials, the United Nations has been involved in creating a truth commission for East Timor. On July 13, 2001, UNTAET established as an independent authority the Commission for Reception, Truth and Reconciliation in East Timor [UNTAET Regulation 2001/10, July 13, 2001]. The Commission is to have 5 to 7 national commissioners, along with up to 30 regional commissioners, nominated by special selection panels composed of international, national, and civil society representatives [ibid.]. The goals of the Commission are to promote national reconciliation and healing, facilitate reintegration of lesser offenders, and weave together a broadly accepted narrative of violence in East Timor and Indonesia's role therein. The Commission is to complement the criminal proceedings in Dili District Court. Serious criminal offenses are exempted from the reconciliation process [ibid.]. The creation of the Commission is a first for the United Nations and an important acknowledgment of the fact that post-conflict justice can best be secured through a variety of co-incident mechanisms.

Many potential top-level accused reside in Indonesia [Seth Mydans in *New York Times*, March 4, 2001]. In fact, it is estimated that Indonesia harbors thousands of anti-East Timorese independence militiamen [*New York Times*, August 30, 2001]. It is not at all apparent that such individuals will ever be transferred to East Timor to face trial. One important trial is underway in Indonesia itself, where 18 senior government officials and members of the security forces face charges of crimes against humanity for their role in the East Timorese violence [BBC News, April 12, 2002].

To be sure, political instability in Indonesia does not facilitate the justice process. In July 2001, former Indonesian President Wahid was ousted by a unanimous Parliament and replaced by Megawati Sukarnoputri [Seth Mydans in *New York Times*, July 27, 2001]. This proved to be a peaceful process, although tensions did run quite high. Furthermore, violence in East Timor is but one example of interethnic and separatist violence occurring throughout the Indonesian archipelago. In recent years, thousands of ethnic Madurese have been massacred by Dayak fighters in the Kalimantan provinces on Borneo Island. Sectarian violence is occurring in eastern Maluku province and Sulawesi Island, separatist violence in Aceh and West Papua. In September 2000, three U.N. aid workers were killed by pro-Indonesian militia in West Timor. And in May 2001, an Indonesian court sentenced the six convicted of these murders to jail terms of 10 to 20 months, prompting an angry response from the U.N. High Commissioner for Refugees [*The Globe and Mail*, September 28, 2000, and May 4, 2001]. One final indication of ongoing instability in Indonesia (along with the vulnerability of the judicial system) is the assassination of an Indonesian judge who had sentenced the youngest son of former Indonesian dictator Suharto to 18 months in jail for corruption [ibid., July 26, 2001].

Sierra Leone

In June 2000, the government of **Sierra Leone** requested U.N. assistance to establish a Special Court to prosecute those responsible for atrocities committed during that country's civil war [BBC News, June 20, 2000]. Tens of thousands of people were killed and maimed during this conflict. Although the violence was anarchic and chaotic, the conflict essentially pitted the Sierra Leonean government against the rebel Revolutionary United Front, led by Foday Sankoh (who was captured in May 2000). The atrocious practice of cutting off limbs of civilians was widely undertaken by the rebels in order to spread terror, erode governmental authority, and assume control over the diamond mines that were an important source of financing. However, gross human rights abuses were also committed by government forces, pro-government militias, and foreign (e.g., Nigerian) soldiers supporting the government [BBC News, January 17, 2002]. Over the course of 2001, some measure of peace returned to Sierra Leone and decommissioning of weapons began under the auspices of a U.N. peacekeeping force [ibid.].

The Special Court was negotiated between the U.N. Secretary-General and the Sierra Leonean government [Sierra Leone Special Court Agreement, pursuant to S.C. Res 1315 (2000), August 14, 2000]. It will have jurisdiction to prosecute crimes against humanity, war crimes, other serious violations of international humanitarian law, and certain crimes under Sierra Leonean law (abuse of girls and wanton destruction of property) [Statute of the Special Court for Sierra Leone, arts. 2, 3, 4, 5, available at www.sierra-leone.org/specialcourtstatute.htm]. The jurisdiction of the Special Court would be over persons "who bear the greatest responsibility" for "serious violations" committed in Sierra Leone as of November 30, 1996, the date of Sierra Leone's first comprehensive—and unsuccessful—peace agreement [ibid., art. 1]. Accused persons are afforded full due process rights as specified by international human rights law [ibid., art. 17]. The Rules of Procedure and Evidence will be those found in the ICTR, supplemented in cases of ambiguity by the contents of the 1965 Sierra Leonean Criminal Procedure Act [ibid., art. 14]. As for sentences following conviction, the Special Court may impose imprisonment and forfeiture of proceeds, property, and assets unlawfully obtained [ibid., art. 19]. Consistency among sentences—and with preexisting international and domestic criminal law—is ensured by virtue of the fact that the Special Court is to have recourse to ICTR and Sierra Leonean sentencing practices [ibid., art. 19(1)]. Imprisonment shall be effected in Sierra Leone [ibid., art. 22(1)].

The creation of the Special Court is very different than that of the ad hoc tribunals for Rwanda and the former Yugoslavia, insofar as the Special Court is the product of an international agreement between the United Nations and the government of Sierra Leone, rather than a Security Council resolution. The Special Court combines Sierra Leonean and international law. In this regard, too, it differs from the ad hoc tribunals. Moreover, whereas the ICTR and ICTY are staffed by international lawyers and judges elected by U.N. entities, the Special Court would avail itself of both international as well as Sierra Leonean judges and prosecutors (although the lead prosecutor would be appointed by the U.N. Secretary-General) [ibid., art. 15]. Both the United Nations and Sierra Leone will be able to appoint judges [ibid., art. 12]. The Special Court will sit in Sierra Leone. Its official language will be English. The Special Court shall have primacy over the national courts of Sierra Leone. Moreover, no person shall be tried before a Sierra Leonean national court for anything for which that person previously had been tried by the Special Court [ibid., arts. 8(2), 9]. It will begin to operate on the day after both the United Nations and Sierra Leone have notified each other that the legal instruments for entry into force have been complied with [ibid., art. 20]. In practical terms, this is when the United Nations has been able to secure adequate financing and Sierra Leone has enacted the necessary domestic implementation legislation and has made any required amendments to preexisting Sierra Leonean domestic criminal (or other) law. In January 2002, protocols were signed in Sierra Leone's capital, Freetown, to set up the Special Court [BBC News, January 17, 2002]. It is anticipated that one of the first trials undertaken by the Special Court will be of rebel leader Foday Sankoh, currently in captivity and charged in domestic Sierra Leonean court with murder [BBC News, March 4, 2002].

Much of the violence in Sierra Leone—including conduct of incredible barbarity—was committed by children, defined by international law as individuals under the age of 18. There are estimated to have been 5,400 child fighters in Sierra Leone, many of whom may themselves have been the victims of abusive commanders who abducted them, drugged them, and forced them to kill or maim [Nicole Winfield in *Arkansas Democrat-Gazette*, October 6, 2000]. Accordingly, the Special Court squarely faces the difficult question of whether children can be prosecuted in trials for serious violations of international humanitarian law. In the end, it was determined that the Special Court has no jurisdiction over any person under the age of 15 at the time of the alleged commission of the crime [Statute of the Special Court for Sierra Leone, art. 7(1)]. The Special Court will have jurisdiction over persons over the age of 15 at the time the crime was allegedly committed, but defendants younger than 18 will be treated "with dignity and a sense of worth, taking into account . . . young age and the desirability of promoting . . . rehabilitation, reintegration into and assumption of a constructive role in society, and in accordance with international human rights standards, in particular the rights of the child" [ibid., art. 7(1)]. For example, in the disposition of a case against such a defendant, the Special Court shall order "any of the following: care guidance and supervision orders, community service orders, counselling, foster care, correctional, educational and vocational training programmes, approved schools and, as appropriate, any programmes of disarmament, demobilization and reintegration or programmes of child protection agencies" [ibid., art. 7(2)]. Juvenile offenders are excluded from the general penalty provision that requires imprisonment for a specified number of years [ibid., art. 19(1)]. Moreover, many of the victims of the Sierra Leonean violence were also children. As such, the Special Court will have to develop a sophisticated awareness of and methodology for juvenile justice issues generally.

At the national level, a truth and reconciliation commission has been proposed [Sierra Leone Truth and Reconciliation Commission Act of 2000, available at www.sierra-leone.org/trc.html]. This commission is vested with far-reaching subpoena, search, and seizure powers [ibid., para. 8(1)(g)]. It also actively incorporates community-based mechanisms and traditional and religious leaders, in order to promote reconciliation [ibid., para. 7(2)].

Kosovo

The U.N. Interim Administration Mission in Kosovo (UNMIK) has been active in rebuilding the judiciary in Kosovo [S.C. Res. 1244, June 10, 1999]. Regulations have been promulgated relating to legal institutions, appointment of international judges and prosecutors, the law applicable to Kosovo, procedural and sentencing matters, and the creation of new criminal offenses. In Kosovo, regular domestic courts hear all cases involving war crimes and other prosecutions. However, international judges and prosecutors can be appointed to panels within these courts [UNMIK Regulation 2001/ 2, January 12, 2001]. The maximum sentence under the UNMIK regulations is imprisonment for a term not to exceed 40 years [UNMIK Regulation 2000/59, October 27, 2000]. A number of indictments covering genocide, war crimes, and other ethnically motivated crimes in Kosovo have been tried and many are pending. For example, in June 2001 a Serb was sentenced to 20 years for his role in the killing of more than 90 ethnic Albanians in Kosovo [*New York Times*, June 14, 2001]. All in all, these are successful examples of hybrid domestic/international proceedings. It is important to recall that the ICTY also has jurisdiction over crimes in Kosovo.

5. The Preparatory Commission for the International Criminal Court

On July 17, 1998, 120 nations participated in the U.N. Diplomatic Conference of Plenipotentiaries, held in Rome, which culminated in the adoption of the **Rome Statute for the International Criminal Court** (ICC) [U.N. Doc. A/CONF.183/9, July 17, 1998]. Since then, the number of countries that have signed the Rome Statute has increased significantly and, at the time of writing, stands at 139. Whereas the ad hoc tribunals and other examples of U.N. post-conflict legal initiatives are specifically targeted and temporary, the ICC is general and permanent. The ICC has jurisdiction over genocide, crimes against humanity, war crimes, and aggression. The ICC will be able to try individuals for these crimes when national courts are unwilling or unable to do so [for an overview of the provisions of the Rome Statute, see *Issues/54*, pp. 245–60]. In very general terms, there are three ways a case can be referred: by a country that has ratified the Rome Statute, by the U.N. Security Council, or by the ICC prosecutor after approval by judges.

While a signature, which is generally made by the executive branch, demonstrates a state's general agreement with a treaty, *ratification* indicates that a state has agreed to adhere to that treaty and that such adherence has passed through the domestic legislative channels of that state. By and large, it is following ratification that a state becomes a "party" to a treaty. The ICC is heading steadily toward its entry into force. The ICC officially enters into force after the deposit of the 60th instrument of ratification [Rome Statute, Doc. A/CONF.183/9, art. 126]. The 60th instrument was deposited on April 11, 2002 (ten countries simultaneously submitted their instruments of ratification) [*New York Times*, April 11, 2002]. In fact, at the time of writing, 66 nations have become parties to the ICC. It appears that the Rome Statute will enter into force on July 1, 2002 [see www.un.org/law/icc/index.html]. As of that date, the ICC will have permanent jurisdiction over the most serious breaches of international humanitarian and human rights law.

The United States is not a party to the Rome Statute, nor does it appear likely that it will become a party, at least not in the foreseeable future. The Rome Statute must be ratified by the U.S. Senate in order for it to become operative for the United States. Thus far, the Bush Administration refuses to send the Rome Statute to the Senate for ratification. Although President Clinton had signed the Rome Statute on December 31, 2000, President Bush informed the treaty depository on May 6, 2002, that the United States recognizes no obligations toward the Statute and would like its intention not to become a party reflected in the U.N. depository status list. Additionally, as a peremptory measure, in December 2001, the Senate voted in favor of an amendment to defense appropriations that restricted the use of U.S. funds to support or negotiate with the ICC during the 2002 fiscal year. In so doing, the Senate altered a vote it had taken two weeks earlier in favor of significantly more restrictive amendments. These legislative debates demonstrate the extent to which adherence to the Rome Statute is a hot-button issue in the United States, as it is in many countries. Additional debates are expected to arise in spring 2002, when it seems that amendments barring U.S. participation in the ICC once again will be tabled before Congress [*New York Times*, April 11, 2002]. The primary U.S. concern relates to perceived infringements of national sovereignty triggered by the ICC (e.g., the possibility of American citizens being subjected to politically motivated prosecutions judged by non-Americans).

Participants to the Rome Conference felt it was best to leave many of the details of the implementation and structure of the ICC to ongoing development [see *Issues/54*, pp. 260–62]. In this vein, delegates to the Rome Conference established a Preparatory Commission for the International Criminal Court, whose membership is composed of state delegates [Final Act, Annex I.F, s. 1, A/CONF.183/10]. The Preparatory Commission is charged with enhancing the effectiveness and acceptance of the ICC. It met in its eighth session from September 24 to October 5, 2001, and its ninth session from April 8 to 19, 2002. It is to also meet for a final session in July 2002, after which point the management and administration of the ICC will devolve to the Assembly of States Parties. The Assembly of States Parties will be composed of one representative from each state that has ratified the Rome Statute; those states that have signed but not ratified will be granted observer status.

The Preparatory Commission, aided by working groups that report to it, has been busy over the past year drafting agreements regarding several critical areas. These five areas are (1) the relationship between the ICC and the United Nations; (2) a headquarters agreement between the ICC and the Netherlands (the host state); (3) financial regulations, rules, and the ICC's budget for its first financial year; (4) the ICC's privileges and immunities; and (5) the rules of procedure and other preparatory documents for the Assembly of States Parties [Proceedings of the Preparatory Commission, PCNICC/2001/L.3/Rev.1, October 11, 2001]. By and large many of these issues represent the final stages preceding the entry into force of the ICC. For example, the working group regarding the Assembly of States Parties is drafting documents regarding the nomination and election of the 18 ICC judges, the prosecutor and deputy prosecutors, and the registrar. In a similar vein: also at the eighth session, a road map was introduced to identify issues that remained to be addressed in order to "facilitate the speedy and effective establishment" of the ICC [ibid., PCNICC/2001/L.2, September 26, 2001]. These include not only the elections and nominations discussed previously, but also "internal rules and regulations" regarding human resources, administration, staff job descriptions, remuneration, codes of conduct, and security (to name just a few). It is anticipated that the Assembly of States Parties will finalize much of these details and, subsequently, oversee nominations and elections early in 2003.

In its earlier sessions, the Preparatory Commission drafted complex documents such as the Rules of Procedure and Evidence, as well as the Elements of the Crimes that fall within the jurisdiction of the ICC. The Preparatory Commission has been working to develop a definition of the crime of aggression and the situations in which the ICC might exercise jurisdiction regarding this crime (the definition of this crime being left open in the Rome Statute itself) [Proceedings of the Preparatory Commission, PCNICC/2001/L.3/Rev.1, October 11, 2001]. This has proven to be a daunting task. The crime of aggression basically involves the use of armed force by an individual, who controls the political or military action of a state, against another state in violation of the U.N. Charter. Because this crime bears upon the ability of a state to wage war against another (as opposed to simply regulating the methods with which war can be waged), it is a particularly controversial part of the ICC's jurisdiction. One specific controversy within the Preparatory Commission sessions is whether the ICC definition of the crime of aggression should codify existing customary international law or establish new law.

Discussion of all these issues continued at the ninth session of the Preparatory Commission. It was during this session that the 60th instruments of ratification were deposited, and a special ceremony was held to this effect at the United Nations. Given the imminence of the ICC's entry into force, these are exciting times for those who have worked for many years toward the establishment of a permanent international criminal court. Upon the deposit of the 60th instrument of ratification, U.N. legal counsel Hans Corell stated: "A page in the history of humankind is being turned" [*New York Times*, April 11, 2002]. The progress of the Preparatory Commission and the speed of ratifications have far exceeded initial expectations. When the Rome Statute was signed in 1998, many anticipated it would take between 10 and 20 years for the ICC to enter into force [ibid.]. Instead, entry into force will have been attained in four years.

6. National Courts and International Crimes

National courts can complement the work of international tribunals in enforcing international law, punishing transnational crime, and holding responsible those who commit human rights abuses. In so doing, they, too, contribute to a global culture of human rights, promote justice, educate the public, and encourage individual accountability. International law was once influenced nearly exclusively by the principle of national sovereignty that asserts nations should not interfere in each other's affairs. This view is now giving way to the principled belief that, in certain situations, human rights trump national sovereignty and that courts (even at the national level) constitute an appropriate forum to punish those who systematically violate human rights. When national courts become involved in prosecuting crimes committed in other jurisdictions by citizens of other jurisdictions, this may threaten international comity, challenge traditional notions of foreign policy, and unduly politicize the judicial system.

One highly publicized example of national courts addressing international crimes is the attempted foreign prosecution of **General Augusto Pinochet Ugarte**, President of Chile from 1973 to 1990 [for more information, see *A Global Agenda: Issues/56*, pp. 281–82; *A Global Agenda: Issues/55*, pp. 257–60]. Although ultimately unsuccessful, and now sputtering out even within the domestic Chilean courts purportedly due to Pinochet's age and infirmities, prosecutions commenced extraterritorially effectively dislodged much information about abuses in Chile and prompted considerable public discussion about the violence committed during the Pinochet regime [BBC News, July 10, 2001]. Another example is Hissène Habré of Chad, for whom the possibility of eventual extraterritorial prosecution still exists [BBC News, September 27, 2001].

National courts have also been involved in overseeing compensatory payments to victims of war crimes and other abuses. These payments may engender reparative justice and offer symbolic vindication. Examples of these kinds of payments include the funds created by governments, banks, and corporations in Germany, Switzerland, France, and Austria to compensate victims of abuse, slave labor, and theft perpetrated during World War II. In the case of Germany, payouts from the fund began in June 2001. The creation of these funds was to some degree sparked by class action lawsuits (and the threat of many future lawsuits) in U.S. federal court and elsewhere. However, not all lawsuits related to World War II are prompting extrajudicial settlements or litigation success. For example, a suit against the French National Railroad asserting violations of customary international law filed in U.S. federal court in New York was dismissed recently on the ground that the defendant was immune from suit given its status as a part of a foreign government. This lawsuit alleges that the railroad delivered thousands of people to their deaths in Nazi camps. National courts have also been called upon to hear forced labor claims against Japan. These claims largely have been dismissed by the courts. As far as U.S.-initiated proceedings, reasons for dismissal include their being waived by the Treaty of Peace with Japan (1951) and barred by the statute of limitations. Another reason cited is that a California statute, which actually authorized some claims, was unconstitutional because (as a matter of domestic constitutional law) it infringed upon the U.S. federal government's exclusive power over foreign affairs [*American Journal of International Law*, Vol. 96 (2002), pp. 261–62]. A lawsuit filed in the United States by mostly Korean former "comfort women" was also dismissed. In the end, lawsuits in national court have not done much to influence the official policy of the Japanese government, although some settlement and compensation initiatives have been implemented [Fareed Zakaria in *Newsweek*, August 27, 2001; *International Herald Tribune*, July 15, 2001].

National lawsuits for financial damages may also play a small part in the war on terrorism. Moreover, given that an official Libyan connection was found in the Lockerbie trial, Libya may face civil lawsuits and, as a designated terrorist state, it may have lost its immunity from suit in U.S. court.

7. The International Court of Justice (ICJ)

The International Court of Justice (ICJ) is the principal judicial organ of the United Nations. Located in The Hague, the ICJ settles legal disputes submitted to it by those states that have accepted its jurisdiction. It can also render advisory opinions on legal questions referred to it by authorized international agencies. The ICJ decides all questions before it in accordance with international treaties and conventions, international custom, and the general principles of law. It supplements its analysis by reference to decisions of other courts as well as the writings of very well known jurists. There are 15 judges on the ICJ, elected to nine-year terms by the U.N. General Assembly and Security Council. Special judges may be appointed on an ad hoc basis in any given case. The ICJ's docket is increasingly "congested," prompting calls by its President, Judge Gilbert Guillaume, that the United Nations reaffirm its support to its principal judicial organ [ICJ Press Release, 2001/31, October 31, 2001]. As part of the process of alleviating this congestion, the ICJ has promulgated new practice directions that streamline certain procedures [ibid.]. In April 2002, the ICJ took further measures to expedite its caseload [ibid., April 4, 2002]. It is important to recall that, whereas in the 1970s the ICJ had only one or two cases on its docket at any one time, it presently has 23 cases [ibid.].

ICJ Judgments and Orders

On June 27, 2001, the ICJ ruled, by 14 votes to 1, that the United States breached its obligations to Germany and to Karl and Walter LaGrand (two brothers) as individuals, by failing to notify them promptly of their right to consular assistance following their 1982 arrest in Arizona [*Germany v. U.S.*, ICJ Press Release, 2001/16, June 27, 2001]. Eventually, U.S. officials tried the LaGrand brothers for capital murder; both were executed in 1999. The right to consular assistance arises from article 36(1) of the Vienna Convention on Consular Relations (1963), of which subsection (b) specifically provides that, if requested:

> the competent authorities of the receiving State shall, without delay, inform the consular post of the sending State if, within its consular district, a national of that State is arrested or committed to prison or to custody pending trial or is detained in any other manner. . . . The said authorities shall inform the person concerned without delay of his rights.

Other subsections of article 36 accord consular officers the freedom to communicate with and have access to their nationals, including rights to visit nationals in custody and to arrange for their legal representation. Both the United States and Germany are parties to this treaty. In *Germany v. U.S.*, the ICJ held that article 36(1) creates individual rights that may be invoked by the state of which the detained individuals are nationals [Judgment, paras. 65–78].

The ICJ further held (by a vote of 13 to 2) that the United States was in violation of a provisional order issued by the ICJ on March 3, 1999. The ICJ had ordered the United States to "take all measures at its disposal" to ensure that Arizona did not execute Walter LaGrand before the ICJ proceedings were concluded, which the United States failed to do [Order, General List No. 104, March 3, 1999]. In fact, Walter LaGrand was executed the same day on which the ICJ issued its provisional order. This is a very important judgment insofar as it represents the first time that the ICJ held that its provisional orders and the measures contained therein create international legal obligations that have binding effect on the concerned parties. In addition, the ICJ ruled that, in the event that other German nationals deprived of Vienna Consular Convention rights are sentenced by U.S. courts to severe penalties, the United States must, through means of its own choosing, "allow the review and reconsideration of the conviction and sentence by taking account of the violation of the rights" [Judgment, paras. 117–27].

Although the facts are limited to Germany, this dispute reflects a somewhat pervasive practice by the U.S. law enforcement system not to abide by the terms of Vienna Consular Convention article 36. This had previously prompted a claim—discontinued in 1998—by Paraguay in the ICJ, in which similar Vienna Consular Convention violations were alleged regarding the conviction of a Paraguayan national, Angel Breard, who subsequently was executed in Virginia. During the LaGrand proceedings, the United States did undertake to commit itself to ensure implementation of article 36. However it remains unclear whether U.S. courts will view the ICJ decision as compelling strict adherence to the Vienna Consular Convention in all future cases (or whether some courts will enforce the right to consular assistance while others choose not to). In this vein, the judgment raises important issues regarding national responsibilities for failures by subnational authorities to adhere to the international obligations consented to by national authorities. It also raises related questions: in the event that a future ICJ provisional order is not complied with, what kinds of enforcement mechanisms can be undertaken? Can the Security Council enforce such an order?

The ICJ issued another important decision in the criminal law and human rights areas on February 14, 2002 [*Case Concerning the Arrest Warrant of 11 April 2000 (Democratic Republic of the Congo v. Belgium)*, General List, No. 121, February 14, 2002]. Here, it found in favor of the Democratic Republic of Congo (DRC) in a dispute with Belgium. The DRC had initiated proceedings against Belgium regarding an international arrest warrant issued on April 11, 2000, by Judge Damien Vandermeersch of the Brussels court of first instance against Abdulaye Yerodia Ndombasi. At the time the warrant was issued, Yerodia was the DRC's acting Minister of Foreign Affairs [ICJ Press Release, 2000/32, October 17, 2000]. The arrest warrant sought Yerodia's detention and extradition to Belgium for alleged "crimes of international law," including war crimes and crimes against humanity, triggered by accusations he incited the Congolese population to kill Tutsis at the beginning of the rebellion against now deceased Congolese President Laurent Kabila in August 1998. This arrest warrant represents another attempt by national courts extraterritorially to enforce international human rights law through what is called "universal jurisdiction." Universal jurisdiction entitles a state to initiate proceedings in respect of certain serious crimes, irrespective of the location of the crime and irrespective of the nationality of the perpetrator(s) or the victim(s). This jurisdiction can be established by treaty (e.g., as is the case with the Convention Against Torture) or, more controversially, may exist as a customary principle of international law for certain very serious international crimes. In the Yerodia case, the extraterritorial reach is particularly long, insofar as Yerodia had no connection to Belgium nor did the victims, nor was Yerodia physically present in Belgium at the time process was issued. The relevant Belgian statute permitted a Belgian court to exercise jurisdiction even when the suspect is not present on Belgian territory.

By a vote of 13 to 3, the ICJ found the arrest warrant to be unlawful. It did so on the basis of Yerodia's immunity from prosecution in his capacity as Minister of Foreign Affairs. The ICJ held that the issuance and circulation of the arrest warrant contravened international law by derogating from the ministerial immunity in national courts from prosecution for war crimes and crimes against humanity under customary international law. The purpose of this immunity is to promote comity among nations and to allow sitting ministers to perform their work, which includes foreign travel, without fear of facing prosecution for acts they perform while in office. Although this was not an issue in Yerodia's case, heads of state can also have immunity under customary international law from certain criminal charges. Head of state immunity recently was confirmed in the case of terrorism by the French *Cour de Cassation*'s dismissal of terrorism charges brought against Mouammar Ghaddafi of Libya [Salvatore Zappala in *European Journal of International Law*, 12:3, 2001, pp. 595–612].

As the majority itself recognized (and some separate opinions strongly emphasized), the ICJ's logic is somewhat inverted, as immunities can only arise after the issue of jurisdiction has been determined [Judgment, para. 46; Separate opinion of Judges Higgins, Kooijmans, and Buergenthal, paras. 3, 71; Dissenting opinion of Judge Van den Wyngaert, para. 4]. The ICJ did not invalidate the warrant on the basis of an absence of an underlying universal jurisdiction to prosecute. As such, the ICJ decision does not impugn the Belgian law nor assess the extent to which states may adopt "long-arm" statutes empowering their courts to prosecute through universal jurisdiction. The ICJ was careful to point out that it is only the immunity from criminal jurisdiction and the inviolability of an incumbent Minister for Foreign Affairs that it had to consider [Judgment, para. 51]. The ICJ accorded considerable breadth to this immunity, which it described as "full" [Judgment, para. 54]. "[N]o distinction can be drawn between acts performed by a Minister for Foreign Affairs in an 'official' capacity, and those claimed to have been performed in a 'private capacity,' or, for that matter, between acts performed before the person concerned assumed office as Minister for Foreign Affairs and acts committed during the period of office" [Judgment, para. 55]. Thus, the ICJ decision appears to leave as operative the Belgian statute insofar as it would relate to persons other than ministers (in particular, Ministers of Foreign Affairs) or heads of state.

The question whether an arrest warrant for crimes against humanity for an individual with no connection to the prosecuting state can repose in universal jurisdiction was addressed by some separate and dissenting opinions. The results were splintered. Judge Guillaume wrote that "neither treaty law nor international customary law provide a State with the possibility of conferring universal jurisdiction on its courts where the author of the offence is not present on its territory" [Separate opinion of Judge Guillaume, para. 13]. He also concluded that "international law does not accept universal jurisdiction; still less does it accept universal jurisdiction *in absentia*" [ibid., para. 16]. On the other hand, Judges Higgins, Kooijmans, and Buergenthal wrote that "[t]here are . . . certain indications that a universal criminal jurisdiction for certain international crimes is clearly not regarded as unlawful" [Separate opinion of Judges Higgins, Kooijmans, and Buergenthal, para. 46]. "[W]e believe to be the case [that] a State may choose to exercise a universal criminal jurisdiction *in absentia*" [ibid., paras. 59, 65]. In the end, the ICJ leaves open many important questions of international criminal and human rights law. This raises implications for pending Belgian proceedings against other senior ministers and heads of state, including those involving Cuba, Israel, Chile, Iran, and Chad. But even within this narrow area, the ICJ judgment gives rise to new, and opaque, questions. For example, the judgment did not specify the standards by which an individual can be declared by a state to be a Minister of Foreign Affairs, thereby making it difficult to determine when such a declaration is made for the purpose of shielding potential foreign prosecution. Nor does the decision fully appreciate how conventional international law—for example, the statutes of the ad hoc tribunals and the ICC, which eliminate the types of immunities advanced by the DRC—may affect the content of customary international law. As such, an individual may benefit from immunity before foreign national courts, but not before international tribunals, even should that individual be charged with the same offense. It also is unclear whether these immunities can be extended to civil claims.

On October 23, 2001, the ICJ denied a Philippine request to intervene in a preexisting dispute between Indonesia and Malaysia (initiated on November 2, 1998) concerning sovereignty over the islands of Pulau Ligitan and Pulau Sipadan, located in the Celebes Sea [ICJ Press Release, 2001/28bis, October 23, 2001]. The Philippines alleged that its intervention would preserve its own long-standing claims to dominion and sovereignty over the territory of North Borneo, given that these claims might become affected by any decision of the ICJ on the merits in the Indonesia/Malaysia dispute. In order to intervene as a nonparty to a dispute, the country that seeks to intervene must demonstrate the existence of an "interest of a legal nature" in the preexisting dispute [Judgment on Philippines Application to Intervene, October 23, 2001, paras. 37–83]. The fact that the Philippines does not have a territorial dispute regarding the islands, but, rather, regarding another territory, North Borneo, is an important consideration. Moreover, the ICJ pointed out that the principal document relied upon by the Philippines to assert a claim to North Borneo is not even at issue in the Indonesia/Malaysia dispute. As such, the Philippines were found not to have discharged the burden of demonstrating an interest of a legal nature specific to it that may be affected by the reasoning or interpretations of the ICJ in the principal proceedings. In the past, the full ICJ had once granted a third state permission to intervene as a nonparty (Equatorial Guinea's intervention in a land and maritime boundary dispute between Cameroon and Nigeria) [discussed in *Issues/54*, pp. 289–90; *Issues/55*, pp. 265–70]. Public hearings in the dispute between Indonesia and Malaysia are scheduled for June 3 to 12, 2002 [ICJ Press Release, 2002/09, March 13, 2002].

Newly Initiated Proceedings of the ICJ

Liechtenstein instituted proceedings against Germany on June 1, 2001 [ICJ Press Release, 2001/14, June 1, 2001]. Liechtenstein alleges that property purportedly belonging to its nationals is being improperly treated as German assets, for the purpose of German World War II reparation payments. This dispute originates with a 1945 decision by Czechoslovakia to seize German property located on its territory. At the time, Czechoslovakia treated the nationals of Liechtenstein as German nationals. The seized property of Liechtenstein nationals has never been returned nor has compensation been offered or paid. Since the dissolution of Czechoslovakia, accounting for this Liechtenstein property has remained an unresolved issue between Liechtenstein and the Czech Republic, where most of this property is located. After World War II, Germany agreed that it would raise no objections against the seizure of external German assets. Liechtenstein maintains (and allegedly Germany at the time had pledged and understood) that this agreement only covered German assets and thus did not cover Liechtenstein assets. Nor should it, according to the Liechtenstein complaint, given "Liechtenstein's neutrality and the absence of whatsoever links between Liechtenstein and the conduct of the war by Germany" [ibid., June 1, 2001].

However, Liechtenstein alleges that this understanding changed in 1998, when the Federal Constitutional Court of the Federal Republic of Germany ruled that a painting that was among the Liechtenstein property seized in 1945 by Czechoslovakia should be treated as German property. This painting was consequently released back to the Czech Republic. Liechtenstein alleges that this decision is unappealable and as a matter of international law is binding upon Germany. Liechtenstein claims that Germany is ignoring and undermining the rights of its nationals in respect of Liechtenstein property and, moreover, is failing to provide any compensation for losses suffered. The treatment of the painting, Liechtenstein alleges, represents a German change of position demonstrating a new understanding that Liechtenstein assets generally were seized for the purpose of reparation or restitution as a result of World War II. The ICJ set March 28, 2002, and December 27, 2002, as time limits for the filing of written memorials by Liechtenstein and Germany, respectively [ibid., 2001/19, June 29, 2001]. It has been suggested that Germany is likely to challenge the ICJ's jurisdiction to entertain this complaint. One point that Germany might raise is the "necessary third party" rule. This stipulates that the ICJ can dismiss the proceedings if its decision necessarily would affect the rights and obligations of the Czech Republic, an absent third state that has not consented to these proceedings and that any determination of these rights and obligations would form the very subject matter of the ICJ's decision on the merits of the case [Pieter H. F. Bekker in *American Society of International Law Insights*, June 5, 2001].

Nicaragua initiated suit against Colombia on December 6, 2001 [ICJ Press Release, 2001/34, December 6, 2001]. This complaint involves a sovereignty dispute over certain islands in the western Caribbean and delimitation of the maritime area between the two states. Nicaragua alleges that Colombian assertions of title to the islands are suspect. As such, Nicaragua requests the ICJ to declare that Nicaragua has sovereignty over these islands and to fix a single maritime boundary between the areas of both states' continental shelf. Nicaragua has reserved the right to claim compensation for Colombia's alleged unjust enrichment flowing from its ongoing possession of the disputed islands and for its interference with Nicaraguan fishing vessels. The ICJ has set April 28, 2003, as the time limit for the filing of pleadings by Nicaragua and June 28, 2004, as the filing of response documents by Colombia [ibid., 2002/27, March 1, 2002].

Ongoing Proceedings of the ICJ

The ICJ remains seized of a number of other matters. These include the Diallo unlawful imprisonment/expropriation case (*Republic of Guinea v. D. R. Congo*); Nicaragua's suit against Honduras on an issue of maritime delimitation in the Caribbean Sea; and a land and maritime boundary dispute between Cameroon and Nigeria in which Equatorial Guinea has been granted leave to intervene (the ICJ is ready to consider its judgment in this latter dispute, for which public hearings concluded on March 21, 2002).

The DRC has also maintained its complaint against Uganda regarding armed activities on the territory of the DRC, in which the ICJ deemed two of Uganda's counterclaims to be admissible and fixed the time for further pleadings to be filed [ibid., 2001/24, October 10, 2001, and 2001/36, December 13, 2001]. The DRC alleges that Uganda has violated rules of conventional and customary international law by way of military and paramilitary actions against DRC, illegal exploitation of Congolese resources and acts of oppression against Congolese nationals. It seeks the immediate cessation of "any internationally wrongful act," reparation for damage, and guarantees for the future. Uganda's counterclaims involve alleged acts of aggression against it by the DRC and attacks on Ugandan diplomatic premises and personnel in Kinshasa and on Ugandan nationals. This is a complicated proceeding involving the extensive military conflict in East Africa. Other cases comprising the ICJ's docket include the Oil Platforms case (*Iran v. United States of America*), the Gabcíkovo-Nagymaros Project (*Hungary v. Slovakia*), and the Lockerbie case (*Libya v. United Kingdom/United States*).

The Federal Republic of Yugoslavia (FRY) remains involved as defendant in proceedings before the ICJ that relate to alleged genocide in Bosnia and Herzegovina and alleged genocide in Croatia. The FRY is a complainant in a case involving the 1999 NATO military intervention (in which the FRY is suing eight NATO members for breaching international law regarding the use of force). All complaints are affected by procedural complexities and challenges [ibid., 2002/10, March 22, 2002]. For example, the complaint by Bosnia and Herzegovina initially was filed on March 20, 1993, and has therefore been in the docket of the ICJ for a very long time [ibid., 2001/22, September 13, 2001]. In a 1996 judgment, the ICJ found it had jurisdiction to deal with the claim by Bosnia and Herzegovina. On April 24, 2001, the FRY requested a revision of this 1996 judgment on grounds that, inter alia, the FRY did not continue the international legal and political personality of the Socialist Federal Republic of Yugoslavia [ibid., 2001/12, April 24, 2001]. It will be interesting to see how the ICJ eventually pronounces upon questions of whether genocide was committed in Bosnia in light of the past jurisprudence and pending cases of the ICTY. As discussed earlier, the ICTY Trial Chamber has found that the Srebrenica massacre, which took place against Bosnian Muslims, formed a basis to convict General Krstic of genocide. It is unclear what precise weight the ICJ is to give to the jurisprudence of the ICTY. However, if Slobodan Milosevic is convicted of genocide in Bosnia while the ICJ still remains seized of this matter, then it may be difficult for the ICJ to remain unaffected by the ICTY conviction.

In terms of personnel, Nabil Elaraby of Egypt was elected Member of the ICJ, succeeding Judge Mohammed Bedjaoui of Algeria, who had resigned on September 30, 2001 [ibid., 2001/25, October 12, 2001].

Eritrea–Ethiopia Boundary Commission

In April 2002, the **Eritrea–Ethiopia Boundary Commission** issued a ruling that defined a new border between Eritrea and Ethiopia [see www.un.org/ NewLinks/eebcarbitration/]. The determination of this border is part of the process of terminating a bloody conflict between the two nations that has resulted in tens of thousands of deaths and the displacement of hundreds of thousands of individuals. Fighting began in 1998 when Eritrea, which became independent from Ethiopia in the early 1990s, invaded territory Ethiopia viewed as its own. Ethiopia, a much larger country, then captured important Eritrean agricultural land, before Eritrea agreed to a cessation of hostilities in June 2000. The Commission was established in December 2000 as part of a frequently strained peace deal between Ethiopia and Eritrea that flowed from this cessation of hostilities.

This ruling was presented at the Permanent Court of Arbitration in The Hague. Arbitrators consisted of five distinguished jurists: Sir Elihu Lauterpacht, Prince Bola Adesumbo Ajibola, Professor Michael Reisman, Judge Stephen Schwebel, and Sir Arthur Watts. Both countries have pledged to respect the decision, which both described as a victory for them individually. According to a news report: "The ruling gives Eritrea large territorial awards in the border's western sector but hands Ethiopia symbolically important towns that Ethiopians have long claimed as theirs" [Reuters, April 16, 2002]. The new border demarcates a disputed region that covers large areas of fertile farmland. The Commission used colonial treaties, deals struck between Italy and Britain, and applicable international law in arriving at its decision. The task of actually demarcating the new boundary will be difficult; it will prompt some displacement. Moreover, much of the area is intensively mined, making the placement of actual boundary markers a dangerous exercise.

8. International Tribunal for the Law of the Sea (ITLOS)

The International Tribunal for the Law of the Sea (ITLOS) is an independent judicial body established by the **U.N. Convention on the Law of the Sea (UNCLOS)**. UNCLOS lays down a comprehensive legal regime for the world's oceans and seas by establishing rules governing all uses of the oceans and their resources. ITLOS has jurisdiction over any dispute concerning the interpretation or application of UNCLOS. It has created special chambers for disputes regarding fisheries, the seabed, and marine environment. At the suggestion of disputants, ITLOS can also proceed through arbitration.

ITLOS is a relatively young institution and recently celebrated its fifth year of operation. ITLOS is composed of 21 independent judges, elected to nine-year terms from among experts in the law of the sea. Seven judges were elected or reelected on April 19, 2002 [ITLOS Press Release, 65, April 22, 2002]. The President of ITLOS is Judge P. Chandrasekhara Rao. Its new Registrar, elected on September 21, 2001, is Philippe Gautier of Belgium [ibid., 56, September 21, 2001]. In November 2000, ITLOS moved into an impressive new headquarters complex in Hamburg, Germany [ibid., 58, October 18, 2001].

ITLOS's docket is comprised of a broad array of disputes on a variety of issues, including the prompt release of vessels and crews, the prescription of legally binding provisional measures, procedural and substantive issues regarding vessel registration, hot pursuit, and use of force [ibid., 58, October 18, 2001]. This past year, ITLOS was summoned in two new disputes.

The first dispute was between Panama and Yemen. On July 3, 2001, Panama made application against Yemen for the prompt release of the vessel *Chaisiri Reefer 2*, its crew, and cargo [ibid., 51, July 5, 2001]. Shortly following the filing of the application, however, the case was removed from the ITLOS docket by virtue of an agreement between the two parties [ibid., 52, July 16, 2001]. Yemen agreed to release the vessel, its cargo, and crew; Panama agreed to discontinue the proceedings [ibid., 52, July 16, 2001].

Ireland filed suit against the United Kingdom regarding the opening of a new plant, the MOX plant, to process nuclear materials at Sellafield, in Cumbria on the United Kingdom's west coast. The MOX plant is to reprocess spent nuclear fuel into a new fuel, known as mixed oxide fuel (MOX) [ibid., 62, December 3, 2001]. Ireland is concerned that pollution from the plant could affect the Irish Sea. It also is concerned about the potential risks involved in the transportation of radioactive material to and from the plant [ibid., 59, November 13, 2001]. A third concern is that the plant, sited across the Irish Sea from Dublin, may be a potential target for terrorist attacks [Brian Lavery in *New York Times*, November 24, 2001]. On October 25, 2001, Ireland requested that this dispute be submitted to an arbitral tribunal to be established under UNCLOS. Then, on November 9, 2001, Ireland requested that ITLOS adopt provisional measures pending the constitution of the arbitral tribunal. In particular, Ireland requested that the United Kingdom suspend the authorization of the MOX plant (or otherwise prevent the operation of the plant). It also requested that the United Kingdom ensure that there is no dumping of nuclear wastes and no movements of radioactive substances through the Irish Sea related to the plant [ITLOS Press Release, 59, November 13, 2001]. Essentially this amounts to a request for an injunction pending the establishment of the arbitral tribunal. ITLOS may prescribe provisional measures if, among other criteria, it considers such measures appropriate to "preserve the respective rights of the parties to the dispute or to prevent serious harm to the marine environment" [ibid., 62, December 3, 2001]. Also, it may prescribe provisional measures if it considers that the urgency of the situation so requires.

On December 3, 2001, ITLOS unanimously denied Ireland's request for provisional measures. It "found that the urgency of the situation did not require the prescription of the provisional measures as requested by Ireland, in the short period before the constitution of the . . . arbitral tribunal" [ibid.]. ITLOS also took note of and placed on record the assurances given by the United Kingdom that there will be no additional marine transports of radioactive material either to or from Sellafield as a result of the MOX plant until summer 2002. ITLOS also "considered that the duty to cooperate is a fundamental principle in the prevention of pollution of the marine environment [under UNCLOS] and general international law" and that "rights arise therefrom" [ibid.]. As such, "prudence and caution require that Ireland and the United Kingdom cooperate in exchanging information concerning risks or effects of the operation of the MOX plant and in devising ways to deal with them, as appropriate" [ibid.].

As the MOX dispute moves forward, it will air important legal issues related to national sovereignty, procedural rights involving cooperation and the provision of information, the duty to avoid environmental harm, the international movement of radioactive materials, and the protection of the marine environment.

VII

Finance and Administration

By Anthony Mango

In accordance with the Fifth Committee's biennial program of work, the focus at the 57th Session will be on personnel-related issues. Under the agenda item "U.N. common system," the Committee will consider a report by the International Civil Service Commission containing the results of its review of the U.N. pay and benefit system and of how to strengthen the international civil service. On human resources management, the Committee will receive from the Secretary-General a progress report on young professionals, as well as several additional reports covering a range of issues. In particular, these reports address the delegation of authority, consultants and individual contractors, the mandatory age of separation, the employment of retirees, the composition of the Secretariat, and the placement of staff members serving in the Executive Office of the Secretary-General. Some of these questions have been deferred from the 56th Session.

The Committee's agenda will also include items on financial reports, audited financial statements, and the related reports of the Board of Auditors; the financial situation of the Organization; the scale of assessments; the first performance report on the program budget for 2002–2003; administrative and budgetary coordination of the United Nations with the specialized agencies and the International Atomic Energy Agency (IAEA); the annual report of the Office of Internal Oversight Services (OIOS); reports by the Joint Inspection Unit (JIU); the financing of peacekeeping operations; and appointments to fill vacancies in subsidiary bodies.

1. The Financial Situation of the United Nations

On October 10, 2001, the Under-Secretary-General for Management, Joseph E. Connor, told the Fifth Committee that the financial situation of the United Nations had improved considerably during the year. He further reported that the Organization had already received, or expected to receive by the end of 2001, some $4.72 billion in assessed contributions, in contrast to $2.89 billion collected in 2000. The United States was expected to pay a total of $1.67 billion and the remaining member states $3.05 billion. Aggregate unpaid assessments at year-end were projected at some $1.8 billion. He estimated aggregate assessment levels for year 2001 at some $4.25 billion, of which $3 billion related to peacekeeping operations [U.N. Press Release, GA/AB/3456, October 10, 2001].

By December 31, 2001, unpaid assessed contributions amounted to a total of $2,102.6 million (more than $300 million higher than projected by Mr. Connor). Of this amount, $239.6 million related to the regular program budget, $1,819.2 million related to peacekeeping operations, and $43.8 million to the international war crimes tribunals for the former Yugoslavia and Rwanda. The corresponding total on December 31, 2000, had been $2,259 million [*A Global Agenda: Issues/56*, p. 297]. The improvement was mainly attributable to the fact that the United States paid in November 2001 the amount of $582 million promised in the context of the consensus reached at the end of 2000. According to this agreement, the U.S. rate of assessment for the regular budget had been reduced from 25 percent to 22 percent.

Unpaid assessed contributions to the **regular program budget** increased by $17.6 million (they had stood at $222 million on December 31, 2000). At the same time, the number of countries that had paid all of their regular-budget assessments by the end of 2001 had declined (135 at the end of 2001, compared to 141 at the end of 2000). Ten countries owed more than $1 million each, as follows:

Table VII-1

Member state	Unpaid assessments $000,000	% of total unpaid assessments
United States	165.4	69.0
Brazil	20.7	8.7
Argentina	17.7	7.4
Iraq	9.8	4.1
Turkey	4.4	1.8
Israel	4.0	1.7
Venezuela	3.7	1.5
Georgia	2.5	1.0
Peru	1.4	0.6
Uruguay	1.1	0.5
All other member states	8.9	3.7
	239.6	100.0

There was virtually no change in the amount of assessed contributions to the regular budget owed by the United States (it had been $165 million on December 31, 2000).

The total of $1,819.2 million in unpaid assessments for **peacekeeping operations** as of December 31, 2001, included $262.4 million for assessment periods extending into 2002. The amount outstanding on December 31, 2000, had been $1,989 million. The United States owed $690 million (including $98 million for assessment periods extending beyond January 1, 2002), as opposed to $1,144 million on December 31, 2000—a reduction of $454 million. The Russian Federation, which owed $47 million at the end of 2000, was fully paid up at the end of 2001. But the fact that the overall reduction amounted to only $169.8 million indicates that other countries' unpaid assessments for peacekeeping operations had increased by some $330 million.

The unpaid assessments for the two international **war crimes tribunals** declined from $47 million on December 31, 2000, to $43.8 million, of which almost $14.7 million was owed by the United States, almost $14 million by the Russian Federation, and almost $6.9 million by Brazil.

Overall, therefore, while the financial situation of the United Nations at the end of 2001 was better than it had been at the end of 2000, the underlying financial problems persisted. Several speakers in the Fifth Committee emphasized this point during the debate on this question on October 17, 2001 [U.N. Press Release, GA/AB/3463, October 17, 2001].

Regular program budget assessments for 2002, which became due in January, totaled $1,149.2 million. By the end of January, the United Nations had collected $272.2 million, that is, almost a quarter of the total. Forty-two member states had paid their 2002 assessments in full, and others made partial payments; on the other hand, 107 member states made no payments in January 2002.

On March 13, 2002, when he next reported to the Fifth Committee on the financial situation of the Organization, Mr. Connor characterized the situation as "overall better" [U.N. Press Release, GA/AB/3500, March 13, 2001]. In 2001, member states had paid some $4.44 billion in assessed contributions, more than in any previous year. The 2001 year-end aggregate cash balances amounted to some $1.33 billion, the bulk of it in the peacekeeping accounts, while the amount due to member states for troops and contingent-owned equipment had been reduced to $748 million (18 percent less than at the end of 2000). But the chronic regular budget deficit remained unresolved. It was expected that the regular budget would experience a cash deficit at various times during the second half of 2002, before ending the year with a zero cash balance; thus there would still be need to cross-borrow from peacekeeping accounts. To resolve this "very fragile" regular budget situation, member states must not only pay on time, but they must also pay in full. The need for cross-borrowing would also arise for the international tribunals. A potential problem was that the Secretary-General's ability to cross-borrow was now limited to borrowings from closed peacekeeping operations, whose combined cash balances amounted to some $400 million as of March 2002. Final reports on several of the closed peacekeeping operations would be submitted in 2002, and thereafter the amounts available for cross-borrowing would be greatly reduced [ibid.].

While all member states that are late in paying their assessed contributions share the blame for the ongoing financial difficulties of the United Nations, the attitude of the United States continues to be a major contributing factor to its chronic financial stress. For the past 20 years, the United States has been funding its assessed contributions to the United Nations for a given calendar year from the appropriations for the following Financial Year (FY) beginning on October 1. Thus, the FY 2002 appropriations bill approved by U.S. Congress in November 2001 included funds for the payment of U.S. assessed contributions for the U.N. financial year 2001. But the bill did not include an initiative contained in the U.S. Senate version of the bill that allowed a double appropriation of the U.S. assessed contribution to the U.N. regular budget. That would have enabled the United States to pay its assessed contributions for 2002 early in the year, when they were due, instead of after October 1. As a result, the United Nations will continue to experience cash-flow difficulties in the third quarter of the year. The congressional bill also contained language that excluded funds for cooperation with, or assistance to, the International Criminal Court (ICC) in FY 2002 (the Statute of the ICC enters into force on July 1, 2002). The FY 2002 appropriation bill provided $266.2 million for the U.N. regular budget for 2001, $32 million for the two international war crimes tribunals, and $844 million for peacekeeping operations. The U.S. State Department appropriations bill was signed into law on November 28, 2001 [*Washington Report*, November 20, 2001, and January 9, 2002].

On February 4, 2002, the White House released the FY 2003 budget request. It includes $279 million for U.S. assessed contribution to the U.N. regular budget for 2002, $27.2 million for the two international war crimes tribunals, and $725.9 million for peacekeeping operations. The request for peacekeeping operations is lower than in FY 2002, in the expectation that the operation in Bosnia will be terminated at the end of 2002 and that the operations in Sierra Leone and East Timor will be scaled back. In a statement to the U.S. Senate Foreign Relations Committee on February 4, 2002, Secretary of State Colin Powell urged the Senate to complete action on the FY 2002–2003 State Department authorization bill. He also referred to the need to lift the 25-percent cap on U.S. contributions to U.N. peacekeeping operations that had been in place since 1995. The failure of Congress to lift this cap prevented the United States from meeting its revised assessment rate for peacekeeping operations approved by the General Assembly in December 2000 [*Issues/56*, pp. 308–9]. The result has been that U.S. arrears of unpaid contributions increased by $77 million in just one year [*Washington Report*, February 13, 2002].

2. Scales of Assessments

The scales of assessments for 2001–2003 for the regular budget were approved by the General Assembly in its A/Res/55/5B of December 23, 2000 [*Issues/56*, pp. 306 ff.]. At its 56th Session, the Assembly considered the response of the **Committee on Contributions** to the requests for suggestions of measures to encourage the timely, full, and unconditional payment of assessed contributions [A/Res/55/5A, October 26, 2000]. On December 24, 2001, the Assembly saw merit in multiyear payment plans, subject to careful formulation, and requested the Secretary-General to propose guidelines for such plans through the Committee on Contributions [A/Res/56/243].

In November 1995, the government of the Russian Federation decided to pay off the arrears to the U.N. regular budget and to peacekeeping operations within seven years; in fact, all of these arrears were paid off in six years. On the other hand, a few member states failed to pay off their debt in installments, as they had undertaken to do when faced with the prospect of losing their vote in the General Assembly pursuant to Article 19 of the U.N. Charter.

The Group of 77 and China opposed the idea of biannual calculations (on January 1 and July 1, instead of only on January 1) of assessed contributions in arrears for the purpose of the application of Article 19 of the U.N. Charter. This opposition was asserted on the grounds that (1) it might result in the earlier loss of voting rights than under the current procedure and (2) the countries most likely to be affected would be developing countries. The ideas that arrears might be subject to indexation or interest charges or that discounts should be granted for payments earlier in the year were also criticized—as they already had been on previous occasions. The same fate befell the suggestion that member states in arrears be barred from election to governing bodies. The question of how to alleviate the problem of unpaid assessed contributions remains on the agenda of the Committee on Contributions.

The Committee was also requested to report to the General Assembly at its 57th Session on the question of arrears of contributions, amounting to some $16.2 million, owed by former Yugoslavia (the Socialist Federal Republic of Yugoslavia). The former Yugoslavia's membership was automatically terminated upon the admission of the Federal Republic of Yugoslavia to membership in the United Nations. The alternatives facing the General Assembly are either to write off the amount due or to seek payment from the five successor states (Bosnia and Herzegovina,

Croatia, the Federal Republic of Yugoslavia, the Former Yugoslav Republic of Macedonia, and Slovenia).

3. Program Budget for the Biennium 2002–2003

The consideration and approval of the U.N. program budget for 2002–2003 was the main item on the Fifth Committee's agenda at the 56th Session in 2001. Secretary-General Annan's initial estimates for the biennium amounted to $2,648.7 million. The Secretary-General indicated that, in real terms, those estimates reflected a reduction of 0.5 percent and that, for the first time, the budget document included indicators of expected achievements, reflecting the concept of results-based budgeting [*Issues/56*, p. 313]. The initial estimates included $93.7 million (before re-costing) for special political missions to be carried out pursuant to decisions to be taken by the Security Council. But they excluded the estimated cost of decisions taken by the Economic and Social Council (ECOSOC) and other U.N. organs. Estimates also excluded additional requirements attributable to a recalculation, based on more up-to-date data, of the impact of currency fluctuations and inflation at various duty stations. Requirements after re-costing were later estimated by the Secretary-General at $2,681 million.

Introducing the report of the **Advisory Committee on Administrative and Budgetary Questions (ACABQ)** on the initial estimates, the Committee's Chairman, C.S.M. Mselle, recalled that the General Assembly had frozen regular budget expenditures since the 1996–1997 biennium, but without a corresponding freeze on demands for more activities. Despite the redeployment of staff and other resources, the consequence, in some cases, had been an overload past the capacity to absorb; it did not appear possible any longer to accomplish more with less. The political decision on the level of the regular budget was often arbitrary, in spite of the agreed budgetary process.

Thirty-eight delegations participated in the general debate on the initial estimates. The introduction of indicators of expected achievements received general support. At the same time, several speakers, mostly from developing countries, voiced reservations on the ground that the new approach was still at the exploratory stage. Developing countries believed that resources approved by the Assembly should be commensurate with mandated programs and activities; they were concerned that insufficient resources were earmarked for programs in the area of economic and social development. Predictably, the delegations of the major contributors and other developed countries stressed the need to accommodate additional requirements within available resources, through new savings, redeployment, and the elimination of activities that had outlived their usefulness.

Several delegations voiced concern over the Organization's great dependence on extra-budgetary resources—which often came with donor-mandated conditions attached to them—in financing what ought to be regular-budget activities. In this context, the representative of Norway pointed out that priority activities should not depend on voluntary contributions.

Unlike past practice, there was no discussion of individual budget sections in open meetings: all such discussions took place in informal meetings, of which no official records are kept. The representative of Algeria criticized the practice of closed consultations within small groups of countries on the ground that it violated the principle of transparency.

The Fifth Committee did discuss in open meetings the Secretary-General's requests for additional resources for certain activities. Specific activities needing additional resources included enhanced safety and security arrangements for U.N. personnel; the measures to be taken to implement recommendations of the U.N. Panel on Peacekeeping Operations (the so-called *Brahimi* report); the World Assembly on Ageing; a special session of the General Assembly on children; a meeting on small arms; secretariat arrangements for the U.N. Forum on Forests; a subregional center for human rights and democracy in Central Africa; and the expansion of U.N. international radio broadcasting. The costs associated with these activities were not included in the Secretary-General's initial estimates. The Assembly decided that some of them would be charged to the Contingency Fund or would be reflected in the program budget performance reports to be considered by the General Assembly at its 57th and 58th Sessions. The informal consultations led to the decision to reduce the program budget by $75 million in real terms. All the upward reclassifications requested by the Secretary-General were disallowed (many delegations, in their statements in the general debate, had expressed concern over the top-heavy nature of the Secretariat). Cuts totaling $49.5 million were made in several areas, as follows:

- travel of staff: by $2.8 million;
- contractual services: by $6.4 million;
- general operating expenses: by $19.7 million;
- supplies and materials: by $1.4 million;
- furniture and equipment: by $7.2 million;
- consultants and experts: by $2 million;
- information technology: by $10 million.

The General Assembly appropriated $2,625.2 million for the biennium 2002–2003 [A/Res/56/254A, December 24, 2001]. The final budget appropriations for the biennium 2000–2001 in the amount of $2,561.2 million were approved on March 27, 2002; the corresponding final income estimates amounted to $383.4 million [A/Res/56/240C]. Consequently, the net budget for 2000–2001 was $2,177.8 million. A section-by-section comparison between the final appropriations for 2000–2001, the Secretary-General's initial estimates for 2002–2003, and the appropriations for 2002–2003 is given in *Table VII-2*.

The General Assembly also adopted a resolution on "Questions relating to the proposed program budget for the biennium 2002–2003" [A/Res/56/253, December 24, 2001]. An extensive annex reproduces changes to the program narratives in the Secretary-General's proposed program budget, as recommended by the Committee on Program and Coordination. A second annex to the same resolution contains the staffing table for 2002–2003, as approved by the Assembly. The approved staffing table totals 8,919 regular-budget posts (3,814 in the Professional category and above, 2,922 in the General Service category, and 2,183 in other categories—most of them being local-level posts). The breakdown by grade of the posts in the Professional category and above is as follows: Deputy Secretary-General (1); Under-Secretary-General (26); Assistant Secretary-General (19); D-2 (80); D-1 (244); P-5 (687); P-4/3 (2,300); P-2/1 (457).

Faced with the Assembly's decision to reduce the program budget by $75 million in real terms, the Secretary-General issued a *note verbale* on February 28, 2002, and information circular [ST/IC/2002/13] stating that the Organization did not have sufficient financial resources to maintain meetings and other services at existing levels. Accordingly, there would be no servicing of weekend or evening meetings, except for the Security Council and plenary meetings of the General Assembly, and cuts would be made in Internet services to the permanent missions, in elevator service, and in services provided by sound engineers and other contract personnel. The Fifth Committee criticized the economy measures outlined by the Secretary-General, and on March 27 the Assembly adopted a resolution noting concern that the reductions directly affect services provided to member states [A/Res/56/240D]. The resolution further requested the Secretary-General to immediately restore Internet services to permanent missions by utilizing resources released as a result of the Assembly's decision to discontinue the payment of honoraria to members of several organs [*see below*]. The implementation of economy measures that would not adversely affect services provided to member states is to be considered further in the context of the program budget performance report at the Assembly's 57th Session.

The performance report is likely to reflect additional requirements, including those related to the follow-up of the World Conference against Racism, Racial Discrimination, Xenophobia and Related Intolerance. The financial implications of the follow-up activities were estimated by the Secretary-General at somewhat over $1 million, but the Fifth Committee reduced them by deleting the requirements for regional meetings.

Table VII-2

Part/Section	2001–2002 final appropriations $ million	2002–2003	
		Secretary-General's estimates $ million	Appropriations $ million
PART I: Overall policy-making Direction and coordination	492.5	495.1	499.1
1. Overall policy-making, direction, and coordination	45.7	50.1	49.3
2. General Assembly affairs and conference services	446.8	445.0	449.8
PART II: Political affairs	245.6	251.7	248.1
3. Political affairs	158.5	156.3	155.0
4. Disarmament	13.8	15.3	15.4
5. Peacekeeping operations	69.9	76.3	73.6
6. Peaceful uses of outer space	3.4	3.8	4.1
PART III: International justice and law	55.5	59.2	59.1
7. International Court of Justice	22.2	23.1	23.8
8. Legal affairs	33.3	36.1	35.3
PART IV: International cooperation for development	260.8	267.8	273.1
9. Economic and social affairs	114.3	121.0	121.0
9A. Office of the High Representative for the Least Developed Countries	—	—	3.1
10. Africa: New Agenda for Development	5.1	6.9	5.9
11A. Trade and development	82.4	82.8	84.9
11B. International Trade Centre UNCTAD/WTO	16.8	16.9	18.0
12. Environment	8.5	7.8	7.7
13. Human settlements	14.8	12.3	11.5
14. Crime prevention and criminal justice	4.8	5.4	5.7
15. International drug control	14.0	14.7	15.3
PART V: Regional cooperation for development	328.2	353.3	335.2
16. Economic and social development in Africa	72.0	84.5	80.8
17. Economic and social development in Asia and the Pacific	53.4	56.0	52.8
18. Economic development in Europe	39.2	38.3	40.6

Table VII-2 (continued)

19.	Economic and social development in Latin America and the Caribbean	76.8	81.1	69.2
20.	Economic and social development in Western Asia	45.7	50.7	49.1
21.	Regular program of technical cooperation	41.1	42.7	42.7
PART VI: Human rights and humanitarian affairs		120.8	128.4	132.5
22.	Human rights	38.0	42.1	44.7
23.	Protection of and assistance to refugees	40.4	41.2	42.9
24.	Palestine refugees	24.0	24.8	24.8
25.	Humanitarian assistance	18.4	20.3	20.0
PART VII: Public information		141.1	147.0	144.7
26.	Public information	141.1	147.0	144.7
PART VIII: Common support services		439.6	453.8	428.5
27.	Management and central support services	439.6	453.8	428.5
PART IX: Internal oversight		18.5	20.7	20.3
28.	Internal oversight	18.5	20.7	20.3
PART X: Jointly financed administrative activities and special expenses		61.8	69.2	77.8
29.	Jointly financed administrative activities	7.5	8.2	8.4
30.	Special expenses	54.3	61.0	69.4
PART XI: Capital expenditures		47.9	45.7	45.4
31.	Construction, alteration, improvement, and major maintenance	47.9	45.7	45.4
PART XII: Staff assessment		335.8	343.6	348.3
32.	Staff assessment	335.8	343.6	348.3
PART XIII: Development account		13.1	13.1	13.1
33.	Development account	13.1	13.1	13.1
GRAND TOTAL		2,561.2	2,648.7	2,625.2

[Sources: A/56/6, Introduction, Table 4; A/Res/56/240C; A/Res/56/254A]

4. Budgets of Peacekeeping Operations and International War Crimes Tribunals

The financial year of peacekeeping operations runs from July 1 to June 30. The number and scale of these operations depend on decisions of the Security Council that may be taken at any time in response to the emergence or abatement of situations likely to endanger international peace and security. For this reason, the costs of peacekeeping operations are subject to considerable fluctuations from year to year. They are assessed on member states on the basis of a special peacekeeping scale, which entered into force on July 1, 2001 [*Issues/56,* p. 308]. The budgets of peacekeeping operations for the period July 1, 2001, to June 30, 2002 (including voluntary contributions and after application of unencumbered balances from previous financial period), as approved by the General Assembly through its resumed 56th Session in March 2002, are given in Table VII-3. The total, at $2,774.4 million, is approximately 10 percent higher than for the financial year July 1, 2000, to June 30, 2001.

Table VII-3

Mission	*$ million*
U.N. Observer Mission in Georgia (UNOMIG)	27.0
U.N. Mission in Bosnia and Herzegovina (UNMIBH)	140.0
U.N. Interim Administration Mission in Kosovo (UNMIK)	400.0
U.N. Peacekeeping Force in Cyprus (UNFICYP)	41.0
U.N. Disengagement Observer Force (UNDOF)	34.5
U.N. Interim Force in Lebanon (UNIFIL)	136.6
U.N. Iraq–Kuwait Observation Mission (UNIKOM)	51.1
U.N. Transitional Administration in East Timor (UNTAET)	455.0
U.N. Mission for the Referendum in Western Sahara (MINURSO)	48.9
U.N. Mission in Sierra Leone (UNAMSIL)	692.0
U.N. Organization Mission in the Democratic Republic of Congo (MONUC)	450.0
U.N. Mission in Ethiopia and Eritrea (UNMEE)	198.4
Subtotal	2,674.5
Costs to be charged on a pro-rata basis to the budgets of individual missions:	
Support account	92.0
U.N. Logistics Base at Brindisi	7.9
Total	2,774.4

[Source: document A/C.5/56/36/Rev.1]

Revised gross appropriations for the biennium 2002–2003 for the two **international war crimes tribunals** were approved by the General Assembly on March 27, 2002, in the following amounts:

- International Tribunal for the prosecution of persons responsible for serious violations of international humanitarian law committed in the territory of the former Yugoslavia since 1991 [A/Res/56/247B] $248.9 million

• International Criminal Tribunal for the prosecution of persons responsible for genocide and other serious violations of international humanitarian law committed in the territory of Rwanda and Rwandan citizens responsible for genocide and other such violations committed in the territory of neighboring states between January 1 and December 31, 1994 [A/Res/56/248B] $197.1 million

The corresponding net appropriations are $223.2 million and $177.7 million, respectively. The costs of the tribunals are assessed on member states on the basis of a composite scale—half based on the regular-budget scale and half on the peacekeeping operations scale.

5. Personnel and Administration

Although personnel questions are considered as a rule at General Assembly sessions that begin in an even-numbered year, several personnel-related items were on the agenda of the 56th Session. One of them was the report of the **International Civil Service Commission (ICSC)**, which was considered under the agenda item "U.N. common system." Endorsing ICSC recommendations, the General Assembly increased the base/floor salary scale for the Professional and higher categories, effective March 1, 2002, by 3.87 percent, through the consolidation of a portion of post adjustment, thus ensuring that take-home pay would be neither increased nor decreased. The Assembly also decided that emoluments payable in the 12 euro-zone countries would be converted from national currencies into euros as of January 1, 2002 [A/Res/56/244].

The Fifth Committee also considered a number of reports by the Secretary-General on personnel-related issues, including delegation of authority, the employment of consultants and individual contractors, the employment of retirees, the mandatory age of separation, young professionals, and the contractual status of staff.

Delegation of authority was discussed in the context of human resources management and in the light of a report by the **Joint Inspection Unit (JIU)** [A/55/857]. The JIU concluded that no significant progress had been made, authority must be clearly defined, and formal responsibility should attach to individual staff members to whom authority had been delegated. The ACABQ also pointed out that there existed no effective machinery to monitor the delegation of authority and that what was being delegated should be clearly spelled out in writing. The General Assembly will revisit this question at the 57th Session, when the Secretary-General, in response to A/Res/55/258, will submit a report on responsibility in the reform of human resources management and on the monitoring and control mechanisms and procedures.

On *consultants and individual contractors*, the Secretary-General submitted two reports with statistical data for 1999 and 2000. In the latter year, 3,054 persons (including 51 retirees) were engaged as consultants, and 1,314 persons (including 33 retirees) were employed as individual contractors. The cost of employing consultants and individual contractors in 2000 amounted to some $41.9 million. The corresponding numbers for 1999 had been lower. The geographical distribution of consultants has been of interest to the Fifth Committee for years. In 2000, consultants were employed from 152 different countries, but 45.5 percent of them came from only 11 countries (Argentina, Australia, Canada, Chile, Ethiopia, France, Germany, India, the Netherlands, the United Kingdom, and the United States). The need for so many consultants and individual contractors was questioned in the debate. In this context, the Committee was informed that the preparation of an inventory of skills available in the Secretariat was underway [U.N. Press Release, GA/AB/3496, March 7, 2001]. This question will be discussed further at the Assembly's 57th Session.

In his report on the employment of retirees [A/55/451], another question of considerable interest to the Fifth Committee, the Secretary-General stated that 342 retirees had been employed in the biennium 1998–1999. Two-thirds of the related expenditure ($10.3 million) had been incurred by the language services.

As regards the mandatory age of separation, the question before the Fifth Committee was whether to accept the Secretary-General's proposal that the mandatory age of separation be raised from 60 to 62 for staff engaged before 1990, to bring them into line with their colleagues engaged since 1990. Several delegations were opposed to the proposal on the ground that it was inconsistent with the objective of rejuvenating the Secretariat. In this context, the representative of China recalled at the Committee's 21st meeting on October 31, 2001, that the average age of staff in the Professional category was 46; insufficient young candidates were being appointed to the junior Professional levels P-1 and P-2. To remedy this situation, recruitment of candidates who had passed the national competitive examinations should be accelerated, and the upper age limit for candidates taking these examinations should be lowered. In the absence of a consensus, the question of the mandatory age of separation was deferred to the 57th Session of the General Assembly.

The presidents of the two staff organizations in the U.N. system (FICSA and CCISUA) addressed the question of the contractual status of staff. At the 25th meeting of the Fifth Committee on November 7, 2001, they pointed out that permanent contracts guaranteed the independence of the Secretariat, which is the bedrock of the Organization. By contrast, the representative of the Russian Federation said at the Committee's 27th meeting, on November 9, that permanent contracts should be gradually phased out. (Opposition to permanent contracts had been a hallmark of the attitude of the USSR toward the U.N. Secretariat.)

Preliminary comments were made on a review, being carried out by the ICSC, of the U.N. staff pay and benefits system with a view to modernizing that system and providing for flexible compensation policies that rewarded staff for individual and team contributions. In this connection, the representative of the Russian Federation struck a cautionary note, saying that he was not sure that payment systems borrowed from the private sector or certain national civil services could be applied in the United Nations. The president of CCISUA pointed out that the nature of the United Nations differed from corporate culture, because the Organization did not sell anything and its work was based on the objectives of the U.N. Charter, which were not quantifiable. In the same vein, the president of FICSA said that flexibility and accountability went hand in hand and that innovations in civil service pay should not result in higher salaries for just a select few. The ICSC's report on this question will be submitted to the General Assembly at its 57th Session.

Preliminary comments were also made on the Secretary-General's annual report regarding the composition of the Secretariat [A/56/512] for the period July 1, 2000, to June 30, 2001. As of the end of this period, the total number of staff holding appointments of one year or more was 35,441, of whom 14,874 served in the Secretariat and 20,567 were assigned to other entities of the United Nations. The number of staff in posts subject to geographical distribution was 2,445 (staff with specialized qualifications, such as language skills, are not covered by strict geographical distribution requirements, though every effort is made to recruit them on as wide a geographic basis as possible). At the end of the reporting period, 18 member states were not represented (10 of them were very small, including 6 small island states in the Pacific), 10 member states were underrepresented, and 17 were overrepresented. Most of the speakers in the debate on the composition of the Secretariat tended to argue that the number of their nationals in posts subject to geographical distribution should be increased. At the Fifth Committee's 46th meeting on March 8, 2002, the representative of Japan pointed out that the number of Japanese nationals in such posts was less than half the low point of the desirable range for his country. The representative of India argued for more weight to be given to the population factor in the calculation of desirable ranges for individual member states. Further consideration of the composition of the Secretariat was deferred to the 57th Session.

Also deferred to the 57th Session was a report by the Secretary-General on the placement of staff members serving in his Executive Office [A/56/816]. In this report, the Secretary-General seeks discretionary power for transferring staff from his Executive Office (who are no longer required in that Office) to suitable posts in the Secretariat. (He already has discretionary power to appoint and promote staff in his Executive Office outside the established procedures.) The questions of gratis personnel and the administration of justice in the United Nations were also deferred to the 57th Session.

Another question on the Fifth Committee's agenda concerned the regulations governing the status, basic rights, and duties of **officials other than Secretariat officials and of experts on mission**. This item had been on the Assembly's agenda since 1998, and the documentation before the Assembly included comments drafted at meetings of special rapporteurs, special representatives, independent experts, and chairpersons of working groups of the Commission on Human Rights. On March 27, 2002, the General Assembly adopted a resolution that specified regulations and accompanying commentary [A/Res/56/280]. The regulations applicable to officials other than Secretariat officials and to experts on mission are patterned, mutatis mutandis, on the Staff Regulations while at the same time taking into account the independence required of such officials and experts. The regulations specify, inter alia, that their responsibilities "are not national but exclusively international" [regulation 1(a)]. They further specify that the privileges and immunities enjoyed by the United Nations by virtue of Article 105 of its Charter are conferred on them in the interests of the Organization and do not furnish an excuse for nonperformance of private obligations [regulation 1(e)] [ibid.]. Regulation 2 provides that officials and experts on mission shall uphold the highest standards of efficiency, competence, and integrity and that, in the performance of their duties, they shall neither seek nor accept instructions from any government or from any other source external to the Organization [ibid.]. Loyalty to the aims, principles, and purposes of the United Nations is a fundamental obligation; personal views and convictions must not adversely affect their official duties or the interests of the United Nations. Regulation 2(e) prohibits their using their office or knowledge from their official functions for private gain, financial or otherwise, or for the gain of their family or other third party [ibid.]. Regulation 2(i) mandates the filing of financial disclosure statements, if they are requested to do so by the Secretary-General, and Regulation 3 provides that "officials and experts on mission are accountable to the United Nations for the proper discharge of their functions" [ibid.].

On March 27, 2002, the General Assembly decided that, as of April 6, 2002, the **honoraria** currently payable on an exceptional basis to the members of certain U.N. bodies be set at $1 (one dollar) a year [A/Res/56/272]. These bodies include the International Law Commission (ILC), the International Narcotics Control Board (INCB), the U.N. Administrative Tribunal, the Human Rights Committee, the Committee on the Elimination of Discrimination against Women, and the Committee on the Rights of the Child. The members of these bodies had been receiving honoraria of $2,500–5,000 a year, and the Secretary-General had proposed that they be increased to take account of inflation since they were set.

The General Assembly also welcomed the initiatives of the United Nations Association of the USA, the prospective donor, to mobilize resources in order to provide new facilities for the **visitors' experience** [A/Res/56/236]. The initiative would be a donation in kind to the United Nations; the Assembly authorized the Secretary-General to invite the Association to proceed with the preparation of a schematic design. The Assembly noted the desirability of expanding the number of potential contributors to the project by including the U.N. Associations of other countries. A decision on this question will be taken after it had considered a comprehensive report by the Secretary-General, in the light of any further decision on the capital master plan [*Issues/56*, p. 324].

A reorganized advisory appointment and promotion machinery for the U.N. Secretariat was introduced on May 1, 2002, which is comprised of several components: Central Review Boards, Committees, and Panels. Central Review Boards in New York, Geneva, Vienna, and Nairobi advise the Secretary-General on the appointment and promotion of staff in the Professional category to the P-5 and D-1 levels. Central Review Committees in New York, Geneva, Vienna, Nairobi, Addis Ababa, Bangkok, Beirut, and Santiago advise on the appointment and promotion of staff in the Professional category up to the P-4 level. (These review committees do not advise on the appointment of candidates who successfully passed a competitive examination; in these cases, the Board of Examiners provides advice.) Central Review Panels at the same duty stations as the Committees advise on the promotion to the senior levels in the General Service and related categories.

Each review body consists of three members and at least three alternates selected by the Secretary-General; three members and at least three alternates selected by the staff representative body at the duty station concerned; and a chairperson who is selected jointly by these two groups of members. The members and alternates are appointed for two years and may serve for a maximum of four years. In selecting members and alternates, every effort is made to ensure a balanced representation with respect to geography, gender, and departmental or office affiliation. Each body also has a nonvoting ex officio member (the Assistant Secretary-General for Human Resources Management or his/her authorized representative). Together with the introduction of the new advisory appointment and promotion machinery, the Secretary-General also promulgated a new staff selection system, one of whose objectives is to promote greater mobility among functions, departments, and duty stations. One of its features is the establishment of occupational networks and generic job profiles.

Index

Join the Nationwide Movement for a More Effective United Nations

As the United Nations enters its second half-century, nations must work together to prevent conflict, promote economic and social development, and preserve the environment. The United States and other countries must cooperate in making the United Nations work even better.

The United Nations Association of the USA (UNA-USA) is the nation's largest foreign policy organization, building public support for constructive U.S. leadership in a more effective United Nations.

UNA-USA is an incubator of new ideas on such issues as conflict resolution, nuclear non-proliferation, and sustainable development.

UNA-USA is a constructive critic of the U.N. and of U.S. policy at the U.N. We believe that the U.N. is so important that we must point out problems and offer alternative solutions.

UNA-USA is a force for change. Through the work of its 175 community-based Chapters, its 145 affiliated national organizations, and its vigorous Washington/ New York-based staff, UNA-USA is creating a powerful national constituency for an even better U.N.

UNA-USA is building for tomorrow. The Association's programs, including the renowned Model United Nations program for high school and college students, are preparing new members of all ages for active participation in a world of global change and challenge.

The bottom line is this: one country alone cannot solve the world's problems. The organization best suited to affect global problem-solving is the United Nations, and no other group is doing more to make the U.N. stronger than is UNA-USA.

M E M B E R S H I P   A P P L I C A T I O N

❏ $1,000 . . . . . . Lifetime (One-time dues payment)
❏ $500 . . . . Patron
❏ $100 . . . . Sponsor
❏ $40 . . . . Member: Individual ❏   Household ❏
❏ $25 . . . . Introductory (first year only) / Fixed income
❏ $10 . . . . Student: ❏ Please send me information on UNA-Student Alliances

Status: ❏ New   ❏ Renewal

Membership type:
❏ Personal ❏ Local Organization/School/Business

In addition to my membership dues, I would like to make a contribution to:

❏ UNA-USA National Programs. . . . . $_____
❏ My Local Chapter . . . . $_____
(Contributions are tax deductible to the extent provided by law.)

❏ Please send me information on making a Planned Gift through the Eleanor Roosevelt Society.

❏ My check is enclosed in the amount of . . .$_____
❏ If using a credit card:

NAME (please print)

NAME ON CREDIT CARD

ADDRESS

BIILLING ADDRESS

CITY   STATE   ZIP

Charge my credit card the amount of ....$_____

HOME PHONE

Check one: ❏ AMEX   ❏ MasterCard   ❏ Visa

BUSINESS PHONE

Credit Card Number: _____

Please return this form, along with your payment to UNA-USA, to:

Expiration Date: _____

UNA-USA Membership Services
801 Second Avenue, New York, NY 10017-4706

Signature: **X**_____

www.unausa.org